WHO KNEW?

10,001 HOUSEHOLD SOLUTIONS

Money–Saving Tips, DIY Cleaners,
Kitchen Secrets, and Other Easy Answers
to Everyday Problems

BRUCE + JEANNE LUBIN

Castle Point Books
New York

WHO KNEW? 10,001 HOUSEHOLD SOLUTIONS © 2018 Castle Point Publishing, LLC.
All rights reserved. Printed in the United States of America. For information, address
St. Martin's Press, 175 Fifth Avenue, New York, N.Y. 10010.

www.stmartins.com
www.castlepointbooks.com

The Castle Point Books trademark is owned by Castle Point Publishing, LLC.
Castle Point books are published and distributed by St. Martin's Press.

Please note: While this compilation of hints and tips will solve many of your household
problems, total success cannot be guaranteed. The authors have compiled the information
contained herein from a variety of sources, and neither the authors, publisher, manufacturer,
nor distributor can assume responsibility for the effectiveness of the suggestions. Caution is
urged when using any of the solutions, recipes, or tips in this book. At press time, all internet
addresses contained herein were valid and in working order; however, Castle Point Publishing
is not responsible for the content of these sites, and no warranty or representation is made by
Castle Point Publishing in regard to them or the outcome of any of the solicitations, solutions,
recipes, or tips herein. Castle Point Publishing shall have no liability for damages (whether
direct, indirect, consequential, or otherwise) arising from the use, attempted use, misuse,
or application of any of the solutions, recipes, or tips described in this book.

ISBN 978-1-250-10885-2 (trade hardcover)

Cover design by Katie Jennings Campbell
Interior design by Tara Long

Images used under license from Shutterstock.com.

Our books may be purchased in bulk for promotional, educational, or business use. Please
contact your local bookseller or the Macmillan Corporate and Premium Sales Department
at 1-800-221-7945, extension 5442, or by email at MacmillanSpecialMarkets@macmillan.com.

First Edition: August 2018

10 9 8 7 6 5 4 3 2 1

TO JACK, TERRENCE, AND AIDAN,
as always

CONTENTS

SAVE TIME, MONEY & HASSLE

WITH BRUCE + JEANNE

When we began compiling household tips around our kitchen table almost 25 years ago, we never dreamed we could turn our hints into a book series and help so many folks save time and money. What started with, "Hey, did you know that eggs last longer when they're stored upside down?" turned into thousands of tips, hints, and advice to help solve problems the second they spring up—and make life just a little bit easier.

In the pages that follow, we share our time-tested household tips and life hacks to help you live better, solve everyday problems, and save money. Our hope is that as you read through our book, you'll gain the practical wisdom you need to make the most of every day and every dollar. We've always said saving money doesn't have to be difficult, and we hope this book proves it. With a total of 48 chapters, 400 pages, and thousands upon thousands of tips, our most authoritative book of money-saving wisdom is guaranteed to save you time and money in every room in your home—and beyond.

While it's true that Bruce will never get sick of showing off his latest DIY concoction to repel bugs at our barbecues, what we really love is knowing money-saving secrets like how to get the most juice out of a lemon (page 177), get rid of wood damage with water (page 76), or even relieve a cough with a sweet cure (page 305). We've spent years gathering and testing thousands of such tips, and we hope you find them as useful as we do. In these pages, you'll also find ideas that inspire you to "DIY," finally tackle that home repair project or pest problem, and maybe even have a homemade spa day when you're done. (And if you don't get that far, at least you'll learn how to get that mystery stain out of your rug!)

The easiest way to use our book is to refer to the index at the back. There you'll find tips on everything from Acne (how to eliminate) to Zipper (use pencil if stuck) and all sorts of useful solutions in between. Find our favorite tips in the "Jeanne Says" and "Bruce Says" sidebars throughout, along with our "Readers' Favorite" tips and those that we consider so simple they're brilliant, which are noted with a light bulb, naturally. Of course, you can always refer to the table of contents and simply enjoy reading all our practical solutions to life's little problems in the order we've presented them.

After the amazing success of our last book, we heard from readers across the country who inspired us to find new answers to all kinds of household problems. We'd love to hear from you, too—whether to ask questions or share your own hints and tips! **Don't forget to visit us at WhoKnewTips.com or Facebook.com/WhoKnewTips.**

With gratitude,
Bruce + Jeanne

WHO KNEW?

PART 1

HEROES

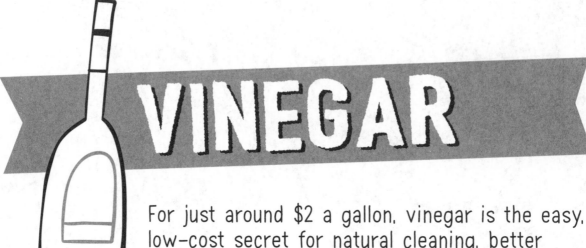

VINEGAR

For just around $2 a gallon, vinegar is the easy, low-cost secret for natural cleaning, better cooking, and health and beauty needs.

SIMPLY NATURAL CLEANING

Try a Mirror Miracle

Make your mirrors shine with a solution of equal parts vinegar and water. Use old newspapers to wipe mirrors with the mix, then add extra shine by rubbing with a clean dry-erase or blackboard eraser.

Stop Windshield Wiper Streaks

Dampen a cloth with vinegar and run it down each blade. The acetic acid cleans away any dirt and residue but also coats the wipers to keep them frost-free.

Make Chrome Gleam

Need a chrome polish? It's as simple as vinegar. Apply directly on chrome with a rag for a quick and easy shine.

Keep Ceramic Sparkling

For ceramic tile that always looks new, wipe it regularly with a sponge dampened with water and a splash of vinegar. Avoid soapy or oily cleaners, and never use abrasives, which will dull the finish and make glazed tiles more prone to dirt.

Whiten Grout—Without Bleach

You can dissolve nasty buildup without harsh bleach. Simply create a paste from baking soda and water and apply it to the grout. Spray the area with a 1:1 mixture of vinegar and water. Let it sit for a few minutes before scrubbing with a brush. Then rinse with warm water and admire the results!

Power Your Shower Spray—Naturally

Stay on top of mold and mildew by keeping this daily shower spray within easy reach of all family members. Mix 1 part vinegar with 10 parts water in an empty spray bottle and you're ready to go. Bonus: You don't have to worry about a toxic cleaner hitting the baby's bath toys.

Clean Your Toilet While You Sleep

To remove hard-water deposits in your toilet bowl, pour 1 cup white vinegar into the bowl and allow it to sit for several hours or overnight before scrubbing.

Clogged Showerhead? A Solution Is in the Bag

It's easy to remove mineral deposits from a showerhead without using harsh chemicals. Just unscrew it and submerge it in white vinegar overnight, and the clogs will disappear. If you can't unscrew it, fill a small, sturdy bag with vinegar and attach it to the showerhead with duct tape, or use an old toothbrush and vinegar. To clean the screen in your showerhead, wash it with water mixed with a dash of dishwashing liquid.

Brighten Cloudy Glass

Embarrassed by your cloudy glasses when company comes to visit? It's not uncommon for glassware to begin to develop a fine film after so many trips through the dishwasher. Before you run out to buy new ones, try this inexpensive little trick. Treat your glasses to a soak in a bath of warm vinegar for an hour. They'll emerge sparkling clean!

Get a Dishwasher Like New

Soap film coating your dishwasher? Run it on an empty cycle using vinegar instead of detergent. It will be sparkling clean, and your next load of dishes will be sparkling, too.

Freshen Up the Garbage Disposal

Keep your garbage disposal running properly and odor-free with this simple once-a-month trick: Fill an ice-cube tray with white vinegar, and when frozen, grind about a dozen cubes. The ice sharpens the blades while the vinegar deodorizes the drain.

BRUCE SAYS

Wipe Away Decals

As a dad to three boys, I found a solution for when the kids outgrow Thomas or adopt a new favorite team. Sponge a solution of equal parts lukewarm water and white vinegar on the decal thoroughly; let sit a few minutes. Stubborn sticker? Saturate it with straight vinegar and let sit for 15 minutes.

Mop Away Dirt and Grime

For mopping vinyl or ceramic floors, use ½ cup white vinegar added to 1 gallon warm water. It's cheap, effective, and completely nontoxic.

Vanquish Smells with Vinegar

Vinegar absorbs and neutralizes odors—from smelly pets and paint to smoke. Place a cup of vinegar in any room the odor reaches. In the kitchen, try boiling 1 cup vinegar in 2 cups water. In 15 minutes, the smell should be gone. To remove odors from washable items, add 1 cup white vinegar during the wash cycle.

Make Oven Cleaning Safer

To reduce fumes after you've used a powerful oven cleaner, wipe down the inside of the oven with white vinegar. It will remove any remaining residue and help neutralize the cleaner. Your lungs will thank you.

JEANNE SAYS

Get Fresh-Car Smell

A bowl of vinegar set in the car overnight will remove odors left by pets, kid athletes, takeout food, and more!

Use a Virtually Free Freshener

Vinegar is so perfect for neutralizing odors and cutting back on dust. Keep a little in a small jar near heating vents. Our favorite Who Knew? hero will leave your room smelling cleaner than it ever did with an air freshener. Just be sure to replace it once a week.

Deodorize Your Cutting Board

Do you have a cutting board with a lingering odor that just won't quit? Remove the smell by rubbing the board with white vinegar.

Help Black Appliances Shine

Vinegar can help remove streaks on black appliances. After cleaning them with warm, sudsy water and a sponge, rub them with a rag dampened with straight white vinegar. The vinegar will remove soap residue and make your appliances shine.

Try a Spot-On Stainless Steel Cleaner

You've scrubbed it twice, but you can't seem to get those water spots out of your stainless steel sink! The solution? A little white vinegar. Just rub into the spots and they'll disappear.

Clean That Ice Dispenser

It's so convenient to have a refrigerator with built-in ice and water dispensers, but you may have noticed how gross the dispenser tray can look after a while. That whitish mineral buildup seems impossible to wash off with soapy water, but vinegar will do the trick. Soak the tray in straight vinegar for a few minutes, then scrub the stains with an old toothbrush. Rinse with warm water, and your dispenser will look like new again!

Steam Away Microwave Mess

Microwave walls can take a beating from food and drink explosions. But cleanup and deodorizing are simple when you use vinegar. In a microwavable bowl, combine ½ cup vinegar and 1 cup water. (You can also add a few drops of lemon juice, if you like.) Microwave for 3 to 5 minutes, then let sit for a few minutes while the steam goes to work. You should be able to easily wipe away any formerly caked-on mess.

Boost Your Dish Soap

Did you know that the acetic acid in vinegar dramatically increases the cleaning power of soap? Boost your dishwashing liquid's effectiveness by adding a couple of teaspoons of white vinegar to the bottle (agitate gently to combine). You'll need less to get your dishes clean, saving you money!

Clear Coffee Stains

Blot the stain with a solution of 1 part vinegar and 1 part water, then let sit for 10 minutes. If it's a tablecloth or piece of clothing, wash in the washing machine as usual. If it's a carpet, then dab with a clean paper towel and repeat with the vinegar mixture until the stain is lifted.

Never Buy Fabric Softener Again!

Instead, simply use white vinegar. Use the same proportions as you would for a liquid fabric softener—you'll never notice the difference.

Make Sweat Stains Disappear

Is your laundry nemesis a perfectly good white tee yellowed by pit stains? Vinegar to the rescue! Just pour a small amount of white vinegar directly onto the stain and gently rub it into the fabric before washing.

MAKE YOUR OWN FABRIC REFRESHER!

In a spray bottle, add a 1:3 mixture of vinegar and water plus a few drops of an essential oil. Mist onto clothing and let dry.

YOUR SECRET INGREDIENT IN THE KITCHEN

Stop Pasta from Sticking

Skip the oil, which can chase away your pasta sauce; turn to vinegar instead. Adding a bit of white vinegar to the cooking water will lower the pH level and stop starch from getting pulled into the water, creating a sticky situation.

Moist, Spreadable Icing Every Time

To keep icing from hardening, just add a very small amount of vinegar after it's whipped. This addition will help the icing retain some moisture so it won't dry out as fast.

WANT TO GUARANTEE A FLAKY PIE CRUST? Add a teaspoon of vinegar to your recipe when you add the water.

Out of Eggs? Vinegar to the Rescue!

Already started a baking recipe and realized you don't have eggs? Just mix 1 teaspoon vinegar with 1 tablespoon baking soda for every egg needed. The combination will cause dough to leaven, much like eggs do.

One Simple Step for Fluffier Meringue

When making a meringue, add ¼ teaspoon white vinegar for every three egg whites and watch it really fluff up.

DIY Fruit and Veggie Wash

Don't bother with those expensive produce washes! You can make your own that's just as effective by simply spraying a bit of vinegar on your fruits and vegetables and rinsing. Natural, easy, smart.

A Solution Your Hands Will Love

Working with berries, beets, or other stain-producing foods? Keep vinegar close by—it will remove any stains from your hands. Rub it on after washing your hands with soap to finish off stubborn stains.

WHO KNEW?

READERS' FAVORITE

Buttermilk Anytime You Need It

Most of us don't regularly keep buttermilk stocked in the fridge. And there's no need to—you can transform regular milk with a bit of vinegar. Mix 1 cup milk (whole or 2 percent works best) with 1 tablespoon white vinegar. Then let it set for about 10 minutes at room temperature. *Voilà!*

HEALTH AND BEAUTY

Get Rid of Greasy Hair

Vinegar is not just for the kitchen; it gets grease out of oily hair, too! Simply shampoo your hair as usual, rinse, then pour ¼ cup vinegar over it and rinse again.

Hair Color That Lasts and Lasts

To preserve that amazing color you got at the salon, rinse your hair regularly with white vinegar to seal the hair cuticle.

Make Your Own Dry Shampoo

Between washes, vinegar can help revive hair. Add 1 teaspoon vinegar to 2 cups water in a spray bottle, and spritz onto your roots.

COOL SUNBURNED SKIN To ease sunburn pain, rub vinegar on the affected area with a cotton ball or soft cloth.

Bring Back Beautiful Nails

If you have an unsightly nail fungus that makes you want to hide your hands or feet from view, you'll love this tip. Soak your nails in a mixture of 1 cup vinegar and 2 cups warm water every day for 15 minutes. The acid in the vinegar will attack the fungus, leaving you with lovelier nails.

Fight Foot Fungus and Odor

Before you head to the doctor, give this simple home remedy a try. Soak your feet in white vinegar once a day for a few days. If it doesn't clear up, it's time to seek professional help. A vinegar bath will also help tackle foot odor.

Take the Sting Out of Jellyfish

The acid in vinegar can soothe the stinging and pain caused by jellyfish venom. Some research has found that it can actually prevent the release of more venom as well. Be prepared by keeping a small container in your beach bag.

Cheap and Easy Denture Cleanser

Here's an effective method for cleaning dentures that works just as well as the expensive tablets: Soak them overnight in a solution of one part white vinegar and one part water. The acidity of the vinegar fights tartar buildup and removes stains.

Stop a Nosebleed Fast!

Just dampen a cotton ball with vinegar and plug the nostril. The acetic acid in the vinegar cauterizes the wound.

Soften Cuticles

Prep for manicures and pedicures by soaking your fingers and toes in a bowl of white vinegar for just 5 minutes. Bonus: If you plan on applying nail polish, prepping with vinegar may help the polish last longer.

Banish Bruises

You can speed healing of simple bruises with vinegar! It helps dissolve the pooled blood that causes the bruise by enhancing blood flow. Simply soak a cotton ball in vinegar to create a compress and apply to your skin for up to 30 minutes. Gently massage the area as you apply, if it feels comfortable. Use twice a day and rinse after each application.

Cure Hiccups in Seconds

Just drink a teaspoon of any kind of vinegar (though some say apple cider vinegar is more palatable). You can mix it in a bit of water, as needed. Exactly why it works hasn't been discovered, but it's suspected that it somehow calms the spasms that bring on hiccups.

Soothe Insect Bites

Is the itch driving you crazy? Dab the area with a cotton ball soaked in vinegar. (Skip this remedy if you've already scratched the area raw. Remember, scratching will only make the itch worse and slow healing.)

Enlist to Help Fight Lice

While it won't get rid of lice on its own, white vinegar can make it much easier to remove those sticky eggs, called nits. Vinegar works by dissolving the sticky solution that secures the lice eggs to your hair. Then you can use a special nit comb to remove nits from the hair. Mix equal parts white vinegar and water, then dip the nit comb into the mixture. Repeat dipping the comb as needed, and be careful not to get vinegar near the eyes.

WHO KNEW?
READERS' FAVORITE

Prevent Swimmer's Ear

If you or your children are prone to swimmer's ear, a bacterial infection of the ear canal, take this precaution when enjoying time in the pool, ocean, or lake: Dab a solution of 1 part vinegar and 5 parts warm water into each ear three times a day. The vinegar will ward off bacteria and keep ears pain-free.

BAKING SODA

A simple box that you likely have in your kitchen right now can freshen up your home inside and out, bring solutions to your kitchen, and even help with common health concerns.

SMART CLEANING ANSWERS

A Gentle Swap for Scouring Powder

The best thing about scouring powder is its abrasive action. The worst is the harsh chemical smell. To get all the benefits without the caustic chemicals, use baking soda instead. In most instances, baking soda will work just as well as scouring powder.

Simply Clean Tiles

For an easy, natural tile cleaner, mix together ¼ cup baking soda and 1 gallon warm water. Scrub with a sponge or mop, then rinse. For tough stains, wait 10 to 15 minutes before rinsing.

Love Your Grout Again

Is there anything more satisfying than nice, clean grout? A simple paste of 3 parts baking soda and 1 part water is all you need. Make a new batch each time you plan to attack the space between your tiles.

Get Rid of Mildew

Looking for an easy mildew remover? Simply scrub the affected area with an old, damp toothbrush sprinkled with baking soda. This natural cleaner works great for shower curtains—if small spots of mildew appear, dab with baking soda on a damp cloth.

Remove Scuffs

To get rid of scuff marks left on vinyl flooring by dark-soled shoes, rub some baking soda into the spot with a wet rag. The marks will disappear.

Show Off Crystal-Clean Crystal

To clean your cut crystal, mix a teaspoon of baking soda with warm water, then dab it onto the crystal with a soft rag. Rinse with water, and buff with a dry, soft cloth.

Supercharge Your Detergent

To boost the power of your dishwasher detergent, sprinkle a little baking soda in the dishwasher every time you run it. It will also help fight foul odors before they start.

Know This Skillet Saver

The teriyaki chicken you made for dinner was delicious, but the sweet sauce left terrible black burns on the bottom of your frying pan. To clean it, first sprinkle the pan with ¼ to ½ cup baking soda, and fill the pan halfway with water. Bring the water to a boil, and the burned pieces should start to release. As the water boils, you may want to use a spatula to help the process along. When most of the pieces are removed, turn off the heat, dump the water, and wash as usual.

BRUCE SAYS

Refresh Water Bottles and Thermoses

I can't even count how many times our boys have left something to fester in a container! Simply fill the container with hot water and ½ cup baking soda, then let it sit overnight. In the morning, rinse well and it should be as good as new.

Perk Up Your Plastic

Have plastic storage containers with lingering odors? Wash them with hot water plus 2 tablespoons baking soda.

Get Better-Tasting Coffee

The secret many of us miss: Make sure you clean your coffee maker regularly. Just add several tablespoons of baking soda to your pot, fill it with water, and run it as usual. Then repeat using only water.

Tackle Tough Appliances

If you haven't had time to clean up and now there's dried-on food stuck in the blades of your blender or food processor, bring baking soda to the rescue. Add 1 tablespoon baking soda along with 1 cup warm water to the bowl, put the lid on, and let it blend for 10 to 15 seconds. Wash as usual.

The Brightest White Cabinets

White kitchen cabinets can be beautiful, but they can also show grease, dust, and dirt more than their darker counterparts. To keep them looking their best, add water to a small amount of baking soda until it's a runny paste. Scrub the mixture on the cabinets, and then rinse with warm water.

Simple Step to a Shiny Sink

For a spectacularly shiny finish on a stainless steel or aluminum sink, rub a liberal amount of baking soda in a circular motion all over its surface with a damp sponge.

Disposal Smarts

Instead of throwing away baking soda when it's finished its 30-day stint in your fridge, dump it down the garbage disposal with running water. It will keep your disposal fresh, too!

VACUUM CLEANER TREAT

Sprinkle some baking soda into the bag of your vacuum cleaner to keep it smelling fresh.

Freshen Rugs and Upholstery

Sprinkle rugs, couches, and upholstered chairs with baking soda and let it sit an hour before you vacuum. It will keep them cleaner and fresher over the long haul.

Save Money on Delicate Detergents

Use this homemade solution: Dissolve 1 cup baking soda in 1 cup warm water. Add the solution directly to your standard washing machine, or add it to the soap dispenser of a front loader. The baking soda will clean your clothes without harming their delicate fibers.

Erase Wall Marks

What's the easiest way to remove crayon, pencil, ink, and furniture scuffs from painted surfaces? Sprinkle baking soda on a damp sponge, rub clean, and rinse.

WHO KNEW?

READERS' FAVORITE

Less-Yuck Cleanup

If you have kids, you've had to clean up vomit. Baking soda can make the job a little less gross if you sprinkle some on top as soon as possible. It will soak up some of the mess and make the smell easier to deal with when you have to go at it with the paper towels.

Vinyl Siding Super-Cleaner

While brand-name cleaners will no doubt get the job done, they tend to be costly and loaded with toxic chemicals. Instead, combine baking soda with enough water to form a paste, then scrub into your siding with a damp rag until the stains lift. Rinse off with a hose and, if necessary, repeat on stubborn stains.

Lift Oil Stains

Cleaning oil spots off the driveway is difficult, and the cleaners can be quite expensive. Instead, sprinkle baking soda over the stains, then rub with a wet scrub brush soaked with hot water. The baking soda breaks apart oil particles, so with a little elbow grease, you can have your driveway looking new in no time.

Clean Battery Leaks

If battery acid leaks inside the compartments of your appliances, there's no need to throw them away. Simply take a few spoonfuls of baking soda and add water until it's the consistency of toothpaste. Spread it on your battery terminals, let it sit for 15 minutes, and wipe clean. The acid should come off easily.

Must-Try for Musty Books

Place the books in a paper grocery bag with an open box of baking soda. Fold over the bag, staple it shut, and let it sit for a week or two. Your books should smell considerably better when you take them out.

Refresh Suitcases

Is your suitcase a bit musty? The night before packing, pour a cup of baking soda in it, close it, and shake. In the morning, vacuum up the baking soda and the smell should be gone.

Get Gloves on More Easily

Sprinkle a little baking soda into each of your latex gloves, and they'll stick less when you're putting them on and taking them off.

KITCHEN CURES

Enjoy Beans with Less Gas

You don't have to avoid baked beans because you fear they'll make you gassy. Instead, just add a dash or two of baking soda to the beans when they're cooking, and their gas-producing properties will be dramatically reduced.

ALL-NATURAL FABRIC SOFTENER

Just add ¼ to ½ cup baking soda to the wash cycle.

Extend Your Milk

Adding a teaspoon of baking soda or a pinch of salt to a carton of milk will keep it fresh for a week or so past its expiration date.

Make Coffee More Drinkable

If you're sensitive to acidity in coffee but love the pick-me-up in the morning, here's a way to reduce the acid level: Just add a pinch of baking soda to the cup! You can also use this tip to decrease the acidity in other high-acid drinks and foods.

Clean Greens

To wash spinach, Swiss chard, or any other leafy vegetable, fill a large bowl with cold water and add a teaspoon of baking soda. Move the vegetables around in the water, soaking them for 3 minutes, then rinse. All the dirt will fall to the bottom of the bowl and you'll have clean greens.

Prevent Curdling

To keep milk from curdling, simply stir in a pinch of baking soda before you heat it.

Save Your Cream

If your cream has begun to develop an "off" odor, but you desperately need it for your coffee, try mixing in ⅛ teaspoon baking soda, which will neutralize the lactic acid that is causing the cream to sour. Before you use the cream, however, taste it to make sure the flavor is still acceptable.

FOR A SUPER-FLUFFY OMELET Add ½ teaspoon baking soda for every three eggs.

Try This Tenderizing Trick

To tenderize tough meat without store-bought tenderizer, use baking soda. Just rub baking soda all over the meat, refrigerate for a few hours, and rinse well before cooking.

Knock Out Fishy Smells

We know fresh fish should always smell clean like the sea. However, every once in a while, you do end up with fillets that are a bit, well, fishy smelling. To neutralize this odor, soak the raw fillets in a pan with 2 cups water and 1 tablespoon baking soda. Wait 10 minutes, rinse, and pat dry. The smell will be virtually gone!

Kill a Kitchen Fire

Baking soda is one of the best fire extinguishers. Because it creates carbon dioxide, it will prevent oxygen from feeding the flames. Always keep an open box next to the stove to dump onto grease fires—and never use water.

HEALTH AND BEAUTY

Don't Buy a New Brush!

To make hairbrushes and combs fresh again, soak them in a mixture of 1 quart hot water and 2 tablespoons baking soda for an hour. Rinse and enjoy your like-new styling tools!

JEANNE SAYS

Secret to a Great Hair Day

The next time you wash your hair, add a teaspoon of baking soda to your hand along with the shampoo. Wash as usual, and get ready for super bouncy hair. Even Bruce noticed when I used it!

Professional Hair Color at Home

Ingredients in at-home hair color can soak in faster in lighter sections of your hair, creating an uneven look. The fix: baking soda. Dissolve 2 tablespoons baking soda in 2 cups water, and rinse your hair with the solution before coloring. The baking soda will lift the cuticle, which will allow the color to penetrate evenly.

Goodbye, Gummy Hair

Your child has gum in her hair—now what? Before you get out the scissors, try this technique. Make a paste by slowly adding water to baking soda, then add a bit more water so the consistency is more of a slurry. Rub the mixture into the hair and begin to work out the gum, adding more slurry if necessary. Once the graininess of the baking soda has helped you get out the sticky gum, shampoo the hair.

Great Breath Fast

You don't need expensive mouthwashes to get better breath. Simply gargle with a mixture of 1 cup water, ½ teaspoon baking soda, and ½ teaspoon salt. This combo will knock out any germs that are causing your bad breath.

Keep Feet Fresh

You know that baking soda is great for absorbing odors in your refrigerator, but did you know that you can also use it to keep your feet smelling sweet? Try this odor-busting foot powder: Mix ¼ cup baking soda and 5 drops of your favorite essential oil, breaking up any lumps. Dust your feet with the powder to reduce perspiration and odor. You can also sprinkle a little into stinky shoes.

A Treat to Fight Odor

When hot weather arrives, we can all feel a little not-so-fresh. Enjoy a bath with ½ cup baking soda a few times a week. It helps eliminate the bacteria that cause odor all over your body, not just under your arms.

Supercharge Your Deodorant

To kick your deodorant's effectiveness up a notch, particularly on a very hot day, dust your armpits with baking soda after you've applied your usual brand. The baking soda will absorb excess moisture and fight odor.

Stop Grease Stains in Their Tracks

If you're cooking over the stove and grease splatters onto your clothes, think fast. Grab some baking soda from the cupboard and rub it into the spot to absorb as much grease as possible. This will make the stain harder to set, and will soak up most of the grease before it works its way into the fibers of your clothes.

WHITE SHOES SUFFERING FROM SCUFFS?
Rub a little baking soda on the marks to make them disappear.

Sanitize Your Toothbrush

A great way to keep your toothbrush clean is to soak it overnight, every few weeks, in a solution of equal parts water and baking soda. Rinse well before using.

A Cheap Cure for Cold Sores

You can spend a lot of money on expensive cold sore remedies, or try this DIY version that will cost you mere pennies. Mix a small amount of baking soda with enough water to make a paste, and apply the paste to the cold sore. Allow it to dry, then rinse and pat dry. Repeat every day until the cold sore disappears, usually about a week.

Soothe Diaper Rash

An effective and natural way to calm diaper rash (and your baby!): Just add a cup of baking soda to your baby's bathwater.

Ease Sunburn

Simply add ½ cup baking soda to lukewarm bathwater, then slide in. You can also create a paste with baking soda and water and apply it as a compress.

Tame Indigestion

Just ½ teaspoon baking soda dissolved in 1 cup water will provide comfort to your tender tummy in less than half an hour.

Loosen Splinters

Splinters are painful when stuck in your finger, and they can be excruciating to remove. Our most important tip: Don't squeeze. Instead, try this homemade splinter solution: Combine baking soda and water until you have a thick paste-like mixture. Apply to the affected area, and wait several hours until the splinter works its way out of the skin.

Stop Your Sweet Tooth

Mix about a teaspoon of baking soda into a glass of warm water, then rinse your mouth out and spit (don't swallow). The baking soda tends to stimulate the production of saliva, which eliminates your sweet craving.

LEMON

A little lemon is one mighty tool—around the house, in the kitchen, even as part of your health and beauty routine. And it smells amazing as it works!

FRESH HOUSEHOLD SOLUTIONS

Perfect Porcelain

Steel wool and scouring powders give you cleaning power but will scratch porcelain. If your sink or tub is made of this fragile material, rub a freshly cut lemon around the surface to cut through grease and grime. Then rinse with running water.

Fight Shower Scum

To attack that stubborn scum on your glass shower door, slice one lemon in half and dip it in a bowl of kosher salt, which adds an abrasive scrub to the already-powerful juices. Scrub the shower door and leave for a few minutes while the lemon gets to work. Rinse off with water, and say goodbye to scum!

Whiten Toilet Bowls

Forget the nasty chemicals and overpowering scents! You can use ½ cup lemon juice in your toilet bowl to deodorize and remove stains naturally. Let it sit for several minutes before scrubbing clean.

Make Mineral Deposits Disappear

If mineral deposits have built up in your faucet, cut a lemon into quarters, then push one piece up into the faucet until it sticks. Leave for about 10 minutes, then twist the wedge out. Repeat with the remaining lemon quarters until the deposits are gone. That was easy.

Shower Curtain Saver

If mildew has made your shower curtain more disgusting than you'd like to admit, first wash it in hot, soapy water. Then rub a wedge of lemon on the stains and leave the curtain out in the sun. By the time it dries, the stains will be gone.

Clean Cutting Boards

To quickly disinfect a plastic cutting board, wash it thoroughly, rub half a cut lemon over it, and microwave it for a minute. Stubborn stains? Pour some lemon juice on the stain and let it sit for 20 minutes, then rinse with water.

Renew Aluminum Pots

To remove stains from aluminum pots, fill the pot halfway with water and add ¼ cup lemon juice. Bring to a boil and simmer for several minutes before washing as usual.

JEANNE SAYS

Quick Fix for a Stinky Microwave

Microwave odors? They plague every busy household. Simply cut a lemon into quarters and put it in a bowl of water, then place in the microwave on high for 2 minutes. Wipe the inside with a soft cloth and any stains will lift easily.

Shine Copper

One of the best cleaners for copper is a simple lemon! Cut it in half, sprinkle the cut side with salt, and rub over the surface you're cleaning. Rinse with cold water and watch it shine.

Remove Silver Spots

If your silver develops spots, dissolve a little salt in lemon juice, then dip a soft cloth into the mixture and rub it onto the piece. Rinse in warm water and finish by buffing to a shine with a chamois.

Green Cleaning for the Grill

Grill cleaners often contain harsh chemicals. But if you want to remove rust and sanitize your grill, you can use a simple lemon. Just cut in half and rub on the grill grate.

Super-Shiny Glass

Lemon juice makes an excellent glass cleaner, and will even add an extra shine. Spray it directly onto glass and rub with a soft cloth to dry. Rub newspaper over the area to get rid of any streaks.

Beat Tough Fridge Odors

No matter how often you try to clean out the fridge, odor happens. The solution: Soak a sponge in lemon juice and let it sit in your fridge for a few hours. Ahh, better!

Whip Up Your Own Wood Cleaner

It's simple: Just combine the juice from one lemon with 2 cups vegetable or olive oil. Use it just like you would use a store-bought cleaner, and fill your room with the fresh scent!

Deodorize the Disposal

A quick and easy way to deodorize your in-sink garbage disposal is to grind a lemon peel inside it every so often. It will get rid of grease—and smell wonderful!

Tackle Garbage Cans Naturally

You don't need chemical scents, just common sense and some lemon help. Wash and deodorize trash cans with a solution of 1 teaspoon lemon juice mixed with 1 quart water.

A Lemony-Fresh Kitchen

To give your kitchen a fresh scent, you don't need to buy expensive air fresheners. Just use a real lemon! Slice it and boil in some water on the stovetop for 10 to 15 minutes.

Freshen Your Humidifier

Humidifier smelling musty? Add 2 tablespoons lemon juice, and it will never smell fresher!

Enjoy the Scent

Vacuuming? Put a few drops of lemon juice in the dust bag to multitask and freshen as you clean. It will make the chore more enjoyable!

Skip the Bleach

You can bring your lackluster whites back to sparkling with ¼ to ½ cup lemon juice added to the wash cycle. Need a stronger concentration? Boil discolored whites in a pot of water with a few slices of lemon.

Get a Brighter Shoeshine

Place a few drops of lemon juice on your shoes when you are polishing them. This simple step makes all the difference.

> **BRUCE SAYS**
>
> **Use This Surprise for Kindling**
>
> The best kindling for your fire isn't newspaper (or old to-do lists). It's lemon peels! Lemon (and orange) peels contain oils that not only make them burn longer but also help ignite the wood around them. Plus, they smell delicious and produce less creosote than paper, which will help keep your chimney clean.

Keep Insects Out

Many little buggers—including ants, silverfish, roaches, and fleas—hate the smell of lemon. Squirt some lemon juice around cracks and openings where they may be tempted to enter. For extra defense, mop your floors with a solution of the juice of four lemons and ½ gallon water.

SUPER FOOD TIPS

Protect Those Shells

Surprise! You can prevent boiled eggs from cracking with lemon. Just cut a lemon in half, then rub the cut side on the shells before cooking them.

Keep Guacamole Looking Fresh

To keep the avocados from oxidizing (which causes the brown color), sprinkle lemon juice on the surface of the dip, and cover tightly with plastic wrap until you're ready to eat.

CLEAN A MESSY GRATER

Rub the pulp-side of a cut lemon across it to remove any stuck-on food. Easy!

Unstick Your Rice

If your pasta or rice sticks together when you cook it, next time add a teaspoon of lemon juice to the water when boiling. Your sticky problem will be gone! The lemon juice will also help naturally fluff up the rice.

Quick Fish Trick

If you're grilling or broiling thick fish steaks, marinate them for 15 minutes in lemon juice before cooking. The acid from the juice "cooks" the fish a bit, cutting down on the time it needs to stay on the heat—so your steaks are less likely to dry out.

Master That Marinade

Make a simple marinade for meats by combining lemon juice with your favorite oils and herbs. The acid in the lemon juice breaks down the meat to tenderize it and allow flavor in.

WHO KNEW?

READERS' FAVORITE

Keep Your Jack-o'-Lantern Smiling

To keep your jack-o'-lanterns fresh this Halloween, rub the insides with lemon juice before you put the lights inside. The lemon juice will prevent your pumpkin from rotting.

Lemon Aid for Grilling

Grilling fish is always a drag because the skin inevitably gets stuck to the grate—particularly when cooking salmon. Avoid this by placing a few thin slices of lemon on the grill, with the fish on top. Not only will your cleanup be easier, but also the citrus flavor will taste great with the seafood.

Give New Life to Lettuce

You've left the lettuce in the crisper for a few days, and now it's wilted. Perk up any greens (including herbs such as cilantro) by submerging them in a bowl of ice-cold water with 1 tablespoon lemon juice. Let sit for 5 to 10 minutes, and it will be as good as fresh.

Cut Down on Cabbage Odor

Whether you're braising or boiling cabbage, the kitchen tends to get a bit odoriferous. To reduce those unpleasant sulfur aromas, add half a lemon to the pot.

Looks as Good as It Tastes

Love the taste of cauliflower and potatoes but don't like that "off" color they sometime get when you boil them? Just add a small amount of lemon juice to the water to keep them white during cooking.

Mushroom Magic

To make cleaning mushrooms easier, rub them lightly with a paper towel dipped in lemon juice. The acid in the lemon juice will lift off grit without taking the rest of the delicate mushroom top with it. As a bonus, the lemon juice will keep the mushroom from turning brown.

Bright Idea for Sweet Potatoes

You may have noticed that when you boil sweet potatoes, some of their vibrant orange color fades. To keep them looking bright, add the juice of half a lemon to the boiling water. The citric acid will preserve the color.

Quick-Rising Solution

It's not always a good idea to artificially cut the amount of time it takes your bread dough to rise (the flavor of the bread may not be as full). But if you're in a time crunch, it's nice to have a backup plan. To speed whole wheat bread dough's rising time, add 1 tablespoon lemon juice to the dough as you are mixing it.

WHIPPING UP SOME CREAM?
Heavy cream will set up faster if you add 7 drops of lemon juice to each pint of cream.

Weightless Cakes

We all know homemade cakes should not double as free weights, but what's the secret to keeping them light? A dash or two of lemon juice added to the butter-and-sugar mixture. That's it!

Refresh Your Hands

Left with food odors (think: fish or onion) on your hands after kitchen prep? Rub them with a freshly cut lemon half.

HEALTH AND BEAUTY

Fight Flakes

Did you know that bacteria clogging up your hair follicles cause dandruff? Fight back with lemon juice! Squeeze the juice from one lemon and add ½ cup warm water, then pour over your scalp and let sit for 5 minutes before shampooing.

Simple At-Home Highlights

If you have brown or dark blond hair, you can add highlights without chemicals and with hardly any cost. First, cut a lemon into quarters or eighths, then make a slit in the middle, as if you were going to put the wedge on the rim of a glass. Wash your hair as usual, and while it's still wet, place a strand of your hair in the slit, beginning at your scalp, and run the wedge down to the tips. Sit outside in direct sunlight until your hair dries, and you'll have lovely blonde streaks. Repeat in 1 week to make the highlights even brighter.

Love Your Skin

There's no need to spend money on facial toners and astringents. Just dab lemon juice on your face with a cotton ball to tighten your pores and prevent blemishes. Use it in the morning and the scent will also help wake you up.

Beat Brown Spots

Brown spots on your skin are usually caused by dead skin cells. Slough off this skin and brighten what's underneath by rubbing lemon juice on the spot. Let it dry, then rub vigorously with a washcloth.

Quick Foot Freshener

Smelly feet? To freshen them easily, simply rub a few slices of lemon over them. This trick will also help prevent athlete's foot.

Whiten Nails

Take advantage of the natural acid in lemons to lighten and brighten nails. Dip your fingers in a mixture of lemon juice and warm water for about 5 minutes. When you're in a hurry, you can just rub a lemon wedge right over your nails.

Boost Your Bath

You've finally found a few secret minutes to have a relaxing bath. Supercharge it by adding some lemon juice. Lemon is a natural exfoliant that will help get rid of dry skin. It also makes the water smell wonderful!

Treat Your Feet

Walking all day? You'll love this invigorating foot soak. Fill a basin with cold water, then slice up a lemon and add the slices along with several sprigs of mint. The oils in the lemon and mint will help revive your skin while leaving it smelling fresh.

KEEP AWAY MOSQUITOES!
Rub any exposed skin with lemon peels. Mosquitoes hate the smell.

Get Rid of Garlic Breath

Mix together a tablespoon or two of lemon juice with a pinch of sugar. Swirl it around your mouth and then swallow it. It will neutralize the smell so you can breathe out without fear!

Ease a Scratchy Throat

Sore throat? Here's a great lemon remedy: Gargle with 1 part lemon juice and 1 part warm water. Lemon helps fight bacteria and soothes your throat.

Natural Remedy for Motion Sickness

If you get nauseated every time you ride in a car, boat, or train, take some lemon wedges with you. Suck on them as you ride to relieve nausea.

Drink to Better Digestion

Add lemon slices or squeeze fresh lemon juice into your water glass. The healthy acids in lemon help your stomach break down food and improve overall digestion. Experts say warming the water provides the greatest belly benefits.

Soothe Stings

If you're stung by a wasp, hornet, or bee, reach for a lemon. Make sure the stinger is gone, and quickly rub the area with some lemon juice. It will neutralize the venom.

Get Rid of Warts

Warts can be stubborn, and many remedies seem less than gentle. Start with a simple cure: lemon juice. Squeeze the juice of a lemon onto a cotton ball, then dab on two to three times a day until you see the wart disappear. The acidity of lemon juice breaks down warts gradually—and naturally.

Soften Corns

Soak your feet in warm water, then apply a lemon juice compress made with a washcloth or cotton ball. You can repeat up to three times a day. The acid in the lemon juice will soften corns and help them fall off.

SALT

There are so many ways to use this common, inexpensive ingredient—all over your house, in your cooking and food storage, even for healthy hair and glowing skin!

HOUSEHOLD HELPER

Drip-Free Candles

To keep candles from dripping, soak them in a strong saltwater solution after purchasing. To make sure your salt water is as strong as possible, heat up some water and add salt until it won't dissolve anymore—then you'll know the water is completely saturated. Leave your candles in this solution for 2 hours, then remove and dry.

Arrange Flowers with Ease

Make a holding place for artificial flowers using salt. Fill your vase with salt and add just enough cold water to get the salt wet but not submerge it. Then stick the stems of your artificial flowers inside. The salt-and-water mixture will turn hard, keeping your flowers exactly where you want them. When you're ready to take the flowers out, fill the vase with warm water until the salt starts to dissolve.

Homemade Glitter

If your kids need glitter in an emergency (and who hasn't had a glitter emergency?), you can make your own at home. Just take a cup of salt, add 10 to 15 drops of your favorite food coloring, and mix it thoroughly. Microwave on high for 2 to 3 minutes, then spread it out on a sheet of foil or wax paper to dry. If you don't use it all right away, store it in an airtight container.

SAVE THE SPONGES

Just soak stinky old sponges in cold salt water and rinse, and they're good to use again.

Put Out a Fire

You're ready to go to bed, but the fire you started a few hours ago is still awake, glowing with its last few embers. Instead of making a mess with water, throw some salt over anything that's still burning. It will snuff out the flames and you'll end up with less soot than if you let it smolder.

Clean Basting Brushes

That gooey, smelly basting brush is not a lost cause. After your usual washing routine with hot water and soap, dry it off a bit by shaking it, then pour some salt into a cup and place the brush inside. Any remaining wetness will be absorbed by the salt, leaving the bristles as clean as can be!

Wipe Away Sticky Dough

When you're done with an afternoon of baking, there's an easy way to clean the stuck-on dough from your counter. Just sprinkle your messy countertop with salt, and you'll be able to use a damp sponge to easily wipe away the doughy, floury mess you've left behind.

No More Burned Milk

If you've ever scorched milk in a pan, you know it's almost impossible to remove the stain. However, salt can help. Dampen the pan, then sprinkle salt all over the bottom. Wait 10 minutes and scrub away the stain. The odor will be gone, too!

Hassle-Free Spill Solution

Oops, that pot in your oven boiled over, and there's a sticky mess on the bottom of your oven! To easily clean any oven spill, sprinkle salt on top as soon as possible. After a little while in a hot oven, the spill will turn to ash and you can easily clean it.

Natural Fridge Cleaner

When cleaning your refrigerator, don't use chemicals, which can linger on your foods. After emptying the fridge, simply dissolve 1 cup salt in 1 gallon hot water and wipe down the surfaces. Squeeze in the juice of a lemon for a nice scent.

A Sparkling Coffee Pot

To remove coffee stains from inside a glass coffee pot, add 1 tablespoon water, 4 teaspoons salt, and 1 cup crushed ice. Gently swirl until it's clean, then rinse thoroughly. Make sure the coffee pot is at room temperature before cleaning.

Lipstick Disappears from Glass

Who knew salt was the best way to remove lipstick from a glass? Rub a little over the stain to remove an imprint on the side of the glass, then wash as usual. Sticking lipstick-marked glasses in the dishwasher hardly ever works, because lipstick is made to resist water.

Polish Your Silver

Line a pan with aluminum foil, add a tablespoon of salt, and fill with cold water. Then add your silverware to the mix and let it sit for a few minutes before removing and rinsing. The aluminum acts as a catalyst for ion exchange, a process that will make the tarnish transfer from your silver to the salt bath.

Salt Those Suds

If there are a bunch of soap suds in your sink that refuse to go away, throw a bit of salt on top of them. The salt will break their bonds and the bubbles will disappear down the drain instantly.

No More Sink Clogs

Pour ½ cup salt down the drain of your kitchen sink with warm running water. This simple step will freshen your drain and keep it from getting bogged down with grease.

Make Mops Like New

You can revive porous cleaning materials, like the head of your mop, with a little salt. Fill a bucket with a mixture of ¼ cup salt and 1 quart warm water. Soak your mops and sponges for 8 to 10 hours, and the grunge will be gone!

Help That Iron Glide

If your iron is beginning to stick to fabrics, sprinkle some salt on a piece of wax paper and iron it. The salt will absorb the stickiness.

Dust a Wreath

Go outside in the backyard with a large paper grocery bag and ½ cup salt. Pour the salt into the bag, place the wreath inside, and fold the bag closed. Then shake gently for 20 seconds and your wreath will look as good as new. This trick works for artificial flowers, too.

MAKE CUTTING BOARDS LOOK LIKE NEW
Vigorously rub some salt into them.

29

The Cleanest Carpet

For a cleaner, brighter carpet, sprinkle with a small amount of salt before you vacuum. The salt provides a mild abrasive cleaning action that will scrub the carpet without hurting the fibers.

Solution for Stains

If you spill any liquid on your carpet, pour salt on the area as soon as possible and watch it absorb the liquid almost instantly. Wait until it dries, then vacuum it up. Salt tends to provide a special capillary attraction that will work for most liquids. There are a few stains that salt will actually help set, however—never sprinkle it on red wine, coffee, tea, or cola!

Make Colors Last

Brighten faded rugs by rubbing them down with a rag that has been soaked in salt water, then wrung out. You can also submerge throw rugs and drapes in a solution of salt water, then wash as usual.

Wicker That Won't Age

To keep wicker from yellowing in the sun, bathe it in salt water with a wet rag when it's new.

Fresh Flower Scent

Who hasn't wanted to make a beautiful bouquet of flowers last longer? Give your flower petals a second life by layering them with noniodized salt in a small jar. This technique works best with flowers that have pulpy petals and woody stems, like roses, lavender, and honeysuckle. The salt will bring out their natural scent and help freshen your entire room. Keep a lid on the jar when you're not around to make the scent last even longer.

Frost Fix

If your windows are frosting over, dissolve 1 tablespoon salt in 1 gallon hot water and rub on the panes with a soft cloth. Then wipe away with a dry cloth to keep your windows frost-free to a lower temperature.

Say Goodbye to Ants

If you can figure out where ants are entering your house, you can keep them out. Simply sprinkle salt on their path of entry, and they'll turn around and go elsewhere.

Get Rid of Fleas

You can remove pesky fleas from your pet's coat without having to pay for expensive flea collars or medications. Simply bathe your pet in salt water and the fleas will stay away.

SUPER FOOD TIPS

Juiciest Corn on the Cob

Nothing says summer like freshly picked sweet corn. When it's grilled, it takes on a smoky-sweet flavor that's irresistible. Try this simple trick to keep those kernels juicy. First, husk the corn, removing any silk. Then soak the ears in salted water for 10 to 15 minutes. Not only will you season the corn, but the water will also help the corn stay moist on the grill.

Sweet, Sour, and Salty!

It's surprising, but true: A small amount of salt will make a grapefruit taste sweeter.

Protection from Grease Splatters

Add salt to the pan when you're cooking greasy foods like bacon, and the grease will be less likely to pop out of the pan and burn your hand.

Easy Walnut Cracking

Need to crack a lot of walnuts? Soak them overnight in salted water and they'll open more easily.

Prep Garlic Quickly

Mince garlic more quickly and efficiently by adding a pinch of salt. The salt helps break down the garlic into a paste and absorbs some of the juices so that the garlic doesn't stick to your knife.

JEANNE SAYS

Perk Up Your Coffee

Make stale coffee taste like it's just been brewed by adding a pinch of salt and a dollop of fresh water to your cup. Heat it up in the microwave, and you're ready to power through the rest of your workday. Works for me every time!

WHO KNEW?

READERS' FAVORITE

Save a Tomato

If your tomatoes have started to shrivel, don't despair! Simply dip them in cold water, then sprinkle a bit of salt over them and leave them for several hours or overnight. They'll be firm to the touch the next day.

Fix a Cracked Egg

If an egg cracks while it's boiling, it's easy to fix. Just remove it from the water and, while it is still wet, pour a generous amount of salt over the crack. Let the egg stand for 20 seconds, then put it back into the boiling water.

Crispy Chicken Secret

The secret to crispy chicken skin: salt! The next time you buy a whole chicken, sprinkle it with about a tablespoon of coarse salt and place it uncovered in the refrigerator overnight. The salt and the dry air in the refrigerator will draw out moisture—the enemy of crispiness—and you'll roast up a super-tasty bird.

Simple Steak Tenderizer

To tenderize a tough steak, salt it generously for an hour before cooking, which will break up tough proteins. Then just wipe off the salt before cooking.

Delicious Frozen Shrimp

Frozen shrimp often turn out mushy when you cook them—unless you know this tip. Before you cook them, toss with a generous amount of salt, then cover with cool water in a bowl and let sit in the fridge for 20 minutes. You can cook them the same way as always, but you won't believe how much better they taste!

KEEP FISH FROM STICKING

Toss a handful of salt in the skillet before the fish.

Prevent Soggy Coleslaw

Place a head of cabbage in a large bowl or pot, fill it with ice-cold water, then add 1 tablespoon salt for every 2 quarts water. Let soak for 10 minutes. The salt absorbs water, helping the cabbage stay hydrated and crisp even once it's shredded and mixed into a salad.

Banish Bugs from Cauliflower

Eliminate the bugs that sometimes make their home in cauliflower by soaking the head upside down in salt water for half an hour. Then simply lift the head straight up out of the water. The little bugs will stay behind in the bowl, and you can use the cauliflower as usual.

Clean Vegetables More Easily

If you're having a hard time getting the last pieces of grit off of leafy vegetables or herbs, add a pinch or two of salt to the water.

HEALTH AND BEAUTY

Fix Puffy Eyes

Soak cotton pads in a solution of ½ teaspoon salt and 1 cup hot water, then apply them to your eyes and relax. Your eyes will be less swollen in 15 minutes or less.

Boost Your Shampoo

Don't spend extra money on a fancy shampoo that boasts sea salt as a volume- and shine-booster. Just mix a teaspoon or so into your regular shampoo bottle!

Get Beachy, Wavy Hair

For that just-off-the-beach look, try this simple DIY salt spray that will cost you virtually nothing. In a spray bottle, combine a teaspoon or so of salt with warm water and shake until fully dissolved. Then spray all over damp hair and style as usual. The salt acts as a natural volumizer, resulting in perfectly tousled waves without a trip to the ocean—or an expensive styling product.

ENJOY A SIMPLE SPA

Just add 2 tablespoons sea salt and a few drops of essential oil to any bath for a special treat.

Deal with Dandruff Naturally

Try this homegrown fix: Rub 2 tablespoons salt into your scalp before shampooing and watch those flakes become a thing of the past.

Make Hands and Feet Glow

You can pay a lot of money for a fancy sea salt scrub, or you can make your very own version in just a few minutes. Sea salt contains natural minerals not present in regular table salt. It also helps remove dead cells and toxins from the skin. In a small bowl, add 1 cup sea salt and just enough olive oil to make a slightly runny mixture—you don't want it to be too loose. Rub into dry hands and feet for several minutes before rinsing off.

Repel Pantyhose Runs

If your nylons seem prone to getting runs, try soaking them in salty water before you wash and wear them. Use ½ cup salt for each 1 quart water, let them soak for 30 minutes, then launder as usual.

Freshen Shoes

Get rid of nasty shoe odors by sprinkling salt in them and leaving overnight. The salt will absorb moisture and odors.

Bathe Away Itch

A soak in hot salt water works wonders when you're suffering from poison ivy. Try a basinful if it's just in one area. If you fell into a patch of the itchy stuff, treat yourself to a nice hot, salty bath.

Ease into Sleep

If you're having trouble sleeping, try this salty tip: At bedtime, drink a glass of water, then let a pinch of salt dissolve on your tongue, making sure it doesn't touch the roof of your mouth. Studies have shown that the combination of salt and water can induce a deep sleep.

OLIVE OIL

You know that olive oil is amazing in the kitchen. Now discover all the smart ways you can use this natural wonder throughout your home and for health and beauty remedies.

HOUSEHOLD SOLUTIONS

Furniture Polish from the Pantry

Olive oil (and vegetable oil, too) works wonderfully on wood furniture. A very light coat will nourish the wood and help protect the finish, but be sure to rub it in well so it doesn't leave a residue. You can put it in a spritz bottle, or just pour a bit on. Add a little lemon juice for a great scent.

Condition a Baseball Glove

With a soft cloth, work a bit of olive oil over the dry areas. Leave on for 30 minutes, then wipe off any excess. Baby oil works, too.

STOP THAT SQUEAK!
Squeaky hinge on a door? Rub on a little olive oil to silence it.

Keep Candleholders Clean

To prevent wax from sticking to a candleholder, rub a thin coat of olive oil inside the base of the holder before lighting the candle. If your holder already has some wax buildup, mix olive oil with dish soap to clean it out.

Remove Sticky Residue

To get rid of duct tape residue, simply rub with olive oil or vegetable oil. Let it sit for 5 to 10 minutes, then wipe. The residue should be much easier to scrape off— try the rough side of a kitchen sponge and some warm water. Olive oil also works to loosen stuck-on gum.

Reveal Shiny Leaves

Using a cotton ball or rag, rub a little olive oil on each side of houseplants' leaves. It will repel dust and keep the foliage gleaming!

Clear Paint from Hands and Hair

It's hard not to get paint all over yourself when painting a room. An old household trick is to wipe turpentine on your hands to get latex paint off, but there's a much less smelly (and less toxic) way. Simply rub your hands with olive oil, let it sit for a couple of seconds, then rub off with a damp, soapy sponge. Not only will the olive oil remove all kinds of paint, but it's great for your skin, too! For stubborn paint, add a little salt or sugar.

If your kids love to paint, they'll inevitably get some paint in their hair—or in the dog's fur! Don't fret, though—you can easily remove it by using a cotton ball soaked in olive oil. The amazing oil also works on car grease.

Protect Your Tools

Olive oil makes an easy lubricant for metal. Use it on kitchen and gardening tools to lubricate and protect. Just start with a clean surface by removing any dirt or rust.

No More Hairball Cleanup

Add up to ¼ teaspoon olive oil to your cat's moist food once a week to stave off hairballs. Bonus: It will also make his coat extra-shiny.

Save a Trip to the Vet

Skin irritation is a common complaint in pets—and a common source of vet bills! Olive oil can soothe irritation caused by fleas or dry skin. It also helps heal sore, cracked paws that can bother your four-legged buddies in summer heat or icy, snowy winter conditions.

Keep the Hummingbirds, Not the Ants

Are ants overrunning your hummingbird feeder? Rub a bit of olive oil at the tip of the feeding tube, and they'll stay away. The ants can't get through the oil, but hummingbirds can.

BRUCE SAYS

Make Your Own Leveling Tool

You're hanging a new shelf, but you don't have a level in your toolbox. Luckily, a quick substitute is a bottle of olive oil! Place the bottle on its side and hang the shelf when the liquid looks like it's parallel to the floor.

Say Goodbye to Moles

Moles are pretty cute, until they're wreaking havoc in your yard. Use this all-natural solution to get rid of them: Just soak some old rags in olive oil, then stuff them in all the holes you can find. Moles hate the smell and will stay away.

KITCHEN MAGIC

No-Stick Grilling Trick

Before grilling, place veggies or meat in a zip-tight plastic bag. Add a small amount of olive oil to the bag, seal it up, and rub the oil onto the surface of the food through the plastic. The light oil rub will ensure that your food is juicy and ultra-tasty, and it won't stick to your grill!

Healthier Eggs with No Taste Sacrifice

If your recipe requires eggs but you don't want the calories of egg yolk, use the egg white mixed with a teaspoon of olive oil instead. This combo gives a better consistency than using the whites on their own, plus you'll reap extra health benefits.

A Fix for Sticky Pasta

If your pasta came out too sticky, let it cool, then sauté it with enough olive oil to lightly coat each noodle. Be sure to stir or toss it while reheating.

Mincing Magic

Solve the sticky mess of mincing garlic by drizzling it with a few drops of olive oil beforehand. The oil will prevent the garlic from sticking to your hands or the knife.

HEALTH AND BEAUTY

Secret to Silky Locks

To transform dry hair into soft, shiny hair, rub in olive oil, starting at the ends and working at least halfway up. Then blow-dry on the hottest setting and let sit for at least 30 minutes. Wash and condition as usual, and get ready for super-sleekness!

Natural Help for Dryness

Mash a banana and mix with a teaspoon of olive or almond oil. Rub the mixture into your hair and scalp, and let sit for 20 minutes. Rinse off and shampoo and condition as usual. You'll love the results!

Sweet Treat for Hair and Scalp

You can make a simple, organic conditioner from honey and olive oil. Mix equal parts together and warm in the microwave. Then apply the mixture to clean, damp hair and wrap in a warm towel for 20 minutes before washing out. Your hair will be smooth, shiny, and ultra-soft.

Tame the Frizzies

Try this moisturizing treatment: Mix together 1 egg yolk and 2 tablespoons olive oil (double the recipe if you have longer hair). Rub on your hair and cover it with a shower cap; leave in for 15 to 30 minutes before rinsing out. You won't believe how smooth and silky your hair becomes!

Try Dandruff Dressing

We admit it: This rinse sounds like salad dressing, but it works on dandruff! Whisk together 2 tablespoons olive oil and 2 tablespoons cider vinegar, and massage into your scalp for a few minutes before shampooing. The olive oil helps loosen the dandruff (and moisturizes the scalp), and the vinegar removes the flakes. You can also try this tip with cider vinegar alone.

Homemade Super-Smoothing Exfoliant

Mix a handful of Epsom salts with a tablespoon of olive oil and rub over wet skin to cleanse, exfoliate, and soften the rough spots. Rinse off well for a polished finish. This tip also works great when applied to calluses and corns. If you don't have Epsom salts, use the coarsest table salt you can find. You can also combine this with sugar or coffee grounds.

Remove Mascara Naturally

Moisten a cotton ball with some olive oil and apply. Then simply wipe off with a tissue. Coconut oil works in the same way.

Soothe Diaper Rash

Just rub a little on the affected area for immediate relief! The vitamins in olive oil fight inflammation. Coconut oil can serve the same function, providing moisture and creating a barrier to protect baby's skin.

Ease Eczema Flares

Rub olive oil directly on any irritated areas. You can even cover with plastic wrap overnight for severe cases on areas like backs of knees.

Hand-Moisturizing Miracle

Ask any model and she'll tell you that olive oil works better than most antiaging hand creams. Simply keep some in a spray bottle and mist over your hands before bed. Massage into your hands each night and they'll stay supple and soft. Add light gloves for extra moisture lock-in.

Cuticle Cure

Using a cotton swab, simply dab a bit of olive or vegetable oil on your cuticles to keep your nail bed moisturized. You'll also be less likely to get hangnails!

Homemade Cream for Healthy Nails

Try this homemade cuticle cream and you'll give up the store-bought variety forever: Mix 2 tablespoons olive oil and 2 tablespoons petroleum jelly with the zest of half an orange. Store in the refrigerator and apply at bedtime for soft, lovely-smelling nails.

Speed Nail Growth

Because olive oil contains vitamin E, it can help your nails grow. Soak your nails in straight olive oil for about 20 minutes once a week to give them a natural boost.

Super-Smooth Feet

Don't stop at your hands! Rub some olive oil on your feet before bed, then slip on socks to lock in the moisturizing and work magic overnight.

Love Your Lips

The same moisturizing effect that olive oil brings to your hair, hands, and feet also works wonders for your lips. Just a dab is all you need.

Keep Razor Blades Good as New

If your razor gets dull easily, it's probably due to rust that you can't even see. Keep rust away by storing your razor blade-down in a glass of olive oil. As a bonus, any olive oil left on the blades will help moisturize your skin!

HEAD-TO-TOE BENEFITS

Want to enjoy the moisturizing benefits of olive oil all over? It's easy! Just add a bit straight to a bath.

No Need for Shoe Polish!

Shining your leather shoes? Simply dampen a cloth and wipe away any dirt, then put a few drops of olive or vegetable oil on a clean, soft cloth and rub into your shoes. The oil will remove the scuff marks, and they'll shine like new. Another way to treat scuffs is by wiping them with the cut edge of a raw potato, then buffing with a soft cloth.

Swap for Shaving Cream

Olive oil not only makes it easier for the blade to glide over your face or legs, but it will moisturize your skin as well. In fact, after trying this, you may swear off shaving cream altogether.

Unstick a Zipper

Zipper won't budge? Try adding a tiny bit of olive or vegetable oil to the stuck teeth with a cotton swab, being careful not to get any on the fabric. This step will lubricate your zipper and allow it to move more easily. Other smart lubricants you can rub on: a beeswax-based candle or lip gloss. You can also try rubbing the zipper with the lead of a pencil.

MAKE YOUR OWN MASSAGE OIL

Certain flavored olive oils (think: lemon and orange) work great as oils for massage and bodywork at a fraction of the cost of store-bought.

Help a Ring Glide Off

If you are unable to remove a ring from your finger, run your hands under very cold water for a few seconds. The cold will make your blood vessels (and, in turn, your finger) a little bit smaller, allowing you to slip off the ring. For a really stubborn situation, go the messier route—rub olive or baby oil over the area for a little lubrication. A stuck ring also can be gently coaxed off by coating the area of the finger around the ring with lip balm.

Eliminate Earwax Buildup

Using a glass dropper, put 5 drops of olive oil into each ear, then place cotton balls in your ears for 5 minutes to allow the oil to soak in. It will nourish the skin and reduce your body's need to produce wax.

Enjoy Healthy Joints

Olive oil is high in healthy (monounsaturated) fats and anti-inflammatory and antioxidant compounds that protect against rheumatoid arthritis (RA). Even if you already have RA, the good stuff in olive oil protects your joints from further damage and slows progression of the disease. So use olive oil in your cooking, and consider buying some gourmet extra virgin olive oil that you can enjoy as a simple accompaniment to pasta.

Natural Medicine for Headaches

As soon as you feel a headache coming on, don't head for the medicine cabinet; instead, try olive oil. Scientific studies have shown that just a few teaspoons of olive oil eaten at the onset of a headache can have an anti-inflammatory effect, reducing pain as well as ibuprofen does.

TEA

Tannins and other key ingredients in tea can power up household cleaning, enhance the taste of your favorite foods, and even become beauty and health remedies.

HOUSEHOLD HELPER

Make Dinner Cleanup a Breeze

Remove cooked-on food from pots and pans effortlessly by filling them with water, adding a tea bag, and simmering. The tea's acid will break up food, so no harsh scrubbing is needed.

POLISH WOOD FURNITURE

Steep two tea bags in 1 cup hot water for at least 10 minutes. Dip a soft cloth in the cooled tea and wipe your way to new shine.

Protect Your Stove

Crazy but true: You can use tea to keep gunk from sticking to your stove. Brew a pot of tea that is four times normal strength, then wipe it on your stove. The tannins in the tea will make it hard for grease and food to stick, giving you the gift of quick and easy cleaning.

Get Gorgeous Wood Floors

Those tannins in black tea also work wonders to shine and enrich the color of hardwood flooring. Simply rub on some brewed tea (keeping moisture to a minimum) and let air-dry.

Shine Glass

Spray weak tea onto windows and mirrors, then wipe with a clean cloth and watch all kinds of smudges and gunk disappear.

Freshen Carpets

Sprinkle dry, used green tea leaves on your carpet; let them sit for 10 minutes. Then vacuum away with any dirt and mustiness.

Clear the Air

Transform a dry, used tea bag into an air freshener by sprinkling on a few drops of a favorite essential oil. You can even hang this DIY freshener by the string attached to most tea bags—perfect for your vehicles! To refresh the scent as needed, simply add a few more drops of oil.

Chase Away Mice

Pesky rodents don't like the smell of tea. So give them a tea party by scattering tea bags in cupboards, pantries, and other problem areas.

Remove Toilet Stains

The tannins in tea can help lift any stubborn stains. Tannins also have antimicrobial properties. To take advantage, just leave some brewed tea in the toilet bowl for several minutes to several hours (depending on the severity of the stains). Then brush the bowl and flush the stains away.

Refresh Your Hands

Prepping food can be a stinky job—from onions to fish. But you can clear away lingering odors on your hands by scrubbing them with used tea bags. Enjoy a cup of tea before prepping your meal and save the bag for cleanup time.

Get Creative with Stains

If you can't get a coffee or tea stain out of a white tablecloth, try one last solution. Soak the tablecloth in a bucket of strong coffee or tea (depending on the type of stain) for 2 hours. You won't get the stain out, but you will dye your linen a lovely earth tone!

Perk Up Plain Paper

Make weak tea with used tea bags, then use it to transform any kind of white paper into antiqued parchment.

JEANNE SAYS

Tea Takes Away Odors

We hate to throw anything away, so we love this way to repurpose used tea bags. Place them in a bowl and put them at the back of your refrigerator, or drop a few dried ones in the bottom of your trash can. They'll remove odors just as well as baking soda!

Fight Fungus on Your Plants

Brew up an extra-strong cup of chamomile tea, and spray the cooled tea all over the leaves. Repeat daily until the fungus is gone.

Treat Your Grass

Did you know that watering your plants with tea every now and then is good for them, because it supplies them with nutrients that help them grow? In fact, using tea bags when planting new grass can be your secret to success. Wet the bags and lay them on the dirt to make an inviting "bed" for the grass seeds. Then sprinkle on the seeds and water frequently.

Feed Those Plants

Place a lining of tea bags along the bottom of a plant container, then pot and water as usual. This simple step will nurture your plants with nutrients and help keep them moist.

Boost Compost

Pour strong tea into your compost bin to encourage more friendly bacteria and speed the process.

DEODORIZE THE CAT BOX

Mix dry green tea leaves with the litter in your cat's box to help absorb odors.

Guard Garden Tools

Toss a handful of tea leaves in whatever container you keep your garden tools in. The leaves will help keep the metal nice, new, and rust-free.

Gentle Ear Cleaner for Pets

Remove wax buildup in your pet's ears with green tea. Using an eyedropper, place several drops of room-temperature tea into each ear, massaging at the base of the ear to loosen the wax. Wipe away any excess. Repeat twice daily until you see an improvement. (You should double-check with your vet to make sure this tip is OK for your particular furry friend.)

YOUR SECRET INGREDIENT IN THE KITCHEN

Natural Meat Tenderizer

The tannins in strong black tea can tenderize meat in a stew, as well as reducing the cooking time. Just add ½ cup strong tea to the stew when you add the other liquid. It will also give your stew rich color.

Great Flavor for Grains

Add tea bags to a pot of water while it comes to a boil, then remove the bags before adding your grain. Some flavors to try: jasmine tea with rice, green tea with pasta or quinoa, orange pekoe with couscous, and chai or cinnamon spice tea with oatmeal.

Something Special for the Smoker

Add tea to a smoker to make tea-infused cheeses and meats. Your guests will wonder where the delicious flavor came from!

HEALTH AND BEAUTY

Pore-Cleansing, Stress-Relieving Facial

This super-effective pore cleanser couldn't be simpler. Place three bags of chamomile tea in a medium-size bowl and add several cups of boiling water. Cover the bowl with a towel and allow the tea to steep for 10 minutes. Then remove the towel, place it over your head, and hold your face over the bowl. The steam will open your pores, and the chamomile will help unclog them. (As a bonus, chamomile is also a great stress reliever!) After 5 to 10 minutes, rinse your face with cold water. Alternatively, you can use chilled chamomile tea as a refreshing facial spritzer.

Simply Natural Toner

For acne-prone skin or dark spots, try this antioxidant-rich toner. Brew a strong cup of chamomile tea, allowing the bag to steep for 5 minutes or more. Allow the tea to cool, and mix in an equal amount of witch hazel, a powerful astringent that can be found at most drugstores. Apply the toner to clean skin with a cotton ball and rinse after 10 minutes. The leftovers can be stored in the refrigerator for several weeks.

Herbal Help for Oily Skin

Here's a great toner for oily skin, and it couldn't be simpler than just brewing up a really strong cup of peppermint tea! Bring 1½ cups water to a boil in a small saucepan. Remove the water from the heat, then place three peppermint tea bags in it to steep for 20 minutes. Remove the bags, and transfer the tea to a bottle. You can store it in the refrigerator to make it last longer. Apply to clean, acne-prone skin.

> **BRUCE SAYS**
>
> **Erase Pen Marks from Skin**
>
> Our kids drive us crazy by writing notes and drawing all over their hands (thankfully, not answers to tests, as far as we know). The fastest way to clean them up? Green or black tea bags. Once you've brewed a cup of tea, use the wet bag to dab at ink stains.

Go Green for Younger Eyes

Reduce puffy or swollen eyes with a green tea compress. Dip a cotton ball into the green tea, drain off excess moisture, and dab gently around the eye area. This natural treatment will help tighten the skin around the eyes.

Calm Puffy Eyes with Chamomile

The same chamomile tea that calms an upset stomach can also ease puffy, irritated eyes. Soak two chamomile tea bags in cold water for a few minutes until they are plump. Squeeze out a bit of excess water and place the bags on closed eyes for several minutes.

TREAT A CUT

Carry a tea bag with you on the go. A wet tea bag placed on a bleeding cut will help coagulate the blood.

Refresh and Nourish Skin

Freshen up your face with an easy green tea mist! Place two green tea bags in a spray bottle filled with water and allow to steep for several hours. Store the bottle in the refrigerator, and mist on your face whenever you need a little refreshment. Not only will the mist feel great, but the green tea will also nourish the skin with essential antioxidants.

Total-Body Treat

Here's an easy way to have a relaxing soak in a bath without having to buy bath salts. Just place one or two green tea bags under the faucet as you fill up your bath. The antioxidants in the tea will leave your skin feeling fresh.

Add Moisturizing Milk to Your Tea

Combine the revitalizing qualities of peppermint with the soothing and exfoliating properties of milk. Heat 2 cups milk until warm, then add four peppermint tea bags. Allow to steep for 20 minutes before removing the bags. Add this mixture to your bath.

Freshen Your Feet

Add tea bags to warm water, then treat your feet to a soak that neutralizes odors, softens calluses, and nourishes your skin.

All-Natural Self-Tanner

Brew 2 cups hot water with 10 tea bags and let cool. Then pour into a spray bottle and spray onto clean, dry skin and let dry. Repeat as often as you'd like for a subtle glow without chemicals or sun damage.

Relieve Razor Burn

Shaving left you with irritation? Black tea to the rescue! Soak a bag in water until it's plump, then squeeze out the excess. Apply directly to irritated skin. The tannins in tea help reduce inflammation.

Soothe Bleeding Gums

So simple! A cold, wet tea bag placed on an area of irritation or where a child has lost a baby tooth can reduce bleeding and soothe pain.

Cool Burns Quickly

If you've burned yourself in the kitchen, help is close by. Researchers at UCLA found that the tannins in tea can soothe burns in as little as 5 minutes. After rinsing and cleaning a minor burn, place a cool, wet tea bag directly on the area for relief.

After-Sun Soother

Lots of people swear by aloe lotion for treating sunburns, but green tea is a cheaper option and just as effective. Use a cooled, tea-soaked washcloth as a compress on your tender skin. (Some people say topically applied green tea may even protect against skin cancer.) This treatment is also a great way to ease a sunburned scalp. After washing and rinsing your hair as usual, pour the cooled tea over your scalp. Your poor skin will thank you!

Bug Bite Remedy

Tame that annoying bug bite with a little tea. Soak a bag of black tea in warm water and then apply it to the bite. The tannins will help reduce swelling and pain.

Beat Bruises

Simply holding a tea bag against a bruise can ease discomfort and help speed healing. Those anti-inflammatories and healing nutrients in tea are pretty amazing!

WHO KNEW?
READERS' FAVORITE

Healthier Hair from Peppermint Tea

Greasy hair? Get rid of excess oil with a weekly treatment of cold peppermint tea. Simply wash your hair as usual, then pour the cooled tea over your hair. It will get rid of grease and make your hair smell fresh and minty all day long!

Chamomile for Canker Sores

The same chamomile tea that soothes a sour stomach can also calm canker sores. Allow the tea to cool, and then swish it around your mouth for a minute. Chamomile contains chamazulene, a natural anti-inflammatory agent, which will accelerate the healing process. You also can hold a damp, cool tea bag over the sore.

Black Tea for a Black (or Pink) Eye

Use a tea bag as a compress for a black eye. Black tea contains an anti-inflammatory ingredient, and the caffeine will help reduce swelling as well. You can also use a warm, wet tea bag as a compress to soothe the pain of pink eye.

Dry Poison Ivy

Strongly brewed tea can work wonders to heal a weepy poison ivy rash. Simply dip a cotton ball into the tea, dab on the affected area, and let it air-dry. Repeat as needed.

GET BETTER BREATH FAST!

Gargling with strong tea can help reduce odors on your breath.

BEER

Beer's not just for drinking! Fresh or left over, it can be put to work in practical ways all over your home and yard—even for gorgeous hair, healthy skin, and better sleep.

HOUSEHOLD SOLUTIONS

Love Your Cast Iron

To clean and season your cast-iron cookware, cover the bottom of your warm pan with fresh beer. Let the liquid sit for 5 to 10 minutes so the carbonation can go to work. Then rinse away any stuck-on food and enjoy the flavor the beer leaves behind.

Clean Gold Jewelry

A light or medium brew makes a great polish for gold jewelry. Pour onto a soft cloth and rub it in, then buff with another clean cloth. The beer's acid will dissolve oil and dirt and get your jewelry sparkling again.

Chase Coffee Stains

Coffee stains can be frustrating, but you can get them out of your carpet by pouring beer on them. Just dribble a couple of sips onto the stain, and it should vanish. Dab up the extra beer with a paper towel, and if the coffee stain doesn't go away completely, repeat the task a few more times.

Remove Rust

Rusty spots on metal lawn furniture or garden tools? Cover the area with a beer-soaked rag and let sit for about an hour. The beer's carbonic acid will dissolve the rust. Try this tip to loosen rusty bolts as well.

SHINE COPPER POTS

Soak copper pots in beer to renew shine and remove stains. Throughout history, breweries have used the last of beer to shine copper vats.

Frost a Window

Need some bathroom privacy, or want to have a little creative fun with the kids? You can create a temporary frost for a window by mixing a solution of 1 cup beer and 4 tablespoons Epsom salts, then paint the mixture onto the window. The frost will wash off easily with water and ammonia when you're ready to go clear again.

Attract Butterflies

Who doesn't love watching butterflies glide around the yard? Invite them to your house with beer! Just mix a little flat beer with mashed overripe bananas. Spread it onto surfaces around your yard—try fences, trees, or rocks. Your neighbors might think you're strange, but the butterflies will love it! Extra add-ins you can try: sugar, fruit juice, molasses, syrup, and rum.

Plants Like Beer, Too

If you host a big party at your house, don't throw away all the beer from those half-empty bottles or cans. Instead, pour it into a bucket, let it sit for a day or two until the beer gets flat, then pour it into your potted plants. The nutrients from the beer will give the plants an extra boost.

Give Grass a Boost

You can revive dead spots on your lawn by pouring on just enough beer to wet the affected grass. The beer's acids kill fungus while its fermented sugars nourish healthy growth.

Offer Pests Their Own Drink

At your next picnic party, give stinging party crashers like bees and wasps a treat of their own—a few open cans of beer around the perimeter of your yard. They'll go for the beer and stay away from your guests. You can also try using sugar-covered grapefruit halves.

Save Flat Beer to Shine Furniture

Stale beer is a great cleanser for wooden furniture. The next time you have flat beer left over, don't dump it out. Instead, use it to dampen a soft, clean cloth, then wipe it onto your wood furniture. Finish with a dry cloth for an amazing shine.

Solve a Snail or Slug Problem

Need to get rid of snails or slugs in your garden? Find the cheapest beer you can, then pour it into several shallow containers (shoeboxes lined with aluminum foil work well). Dig a few shallow holes in your garden and place the containers inside so that they are at ground level. Leave overnight, and the next morning you'll find dozens of dead (or drunk) snails and slugs inside. These critters are attracted to beer, but it has a diuretic effect on them, causing them to lose vital liquids and die.

Trap Mice

Slugs aren't the only pests lured by beer. Set out a bucket, with a ramp leading up to the lip. The mice will smell the beer, hop in to drink, then be unable to climb out.

De-Skunk a Dog

The yeast in beer cuts through the skunk spray's water-resistant oils, then the beer's carbonic acid dissolves them. Rub one or two cans on the pooch, and rinse with water. Finish with your usual dog shampoo.

Put Out a Fire

A can or bottle of beer can work as a fire extinguisher if a real one isn't available. Simply shake and spritz.

YOUR SECRET INGREDIENT IN THE KITCHEN

Tender and Tasty Meat

Beer is a great tenderizer for tough, inexpensive cuts of beef, and it will add great flavor. All you need to do is poke and soak the meat for an hour before cooking, or marinate it overnight in the refrigerator. Try it with your meat for chili, stew, or stir-fry. Bonus: Studies have found that beer marinades reduce levels of cancer-causing compounds that form on grilled meat when fats and juices interact with an open flame. Go with a darker beer for the most health benefit.

Steam Clams

Replace half of the usual water in the steamer pot with beer, and bring to a boil. Steam until the shells open, then enjoy the flavor the beer lends.

BRUCE SAYS

Grill Super-Juicy Steak

If you're grilling a steak on a closed barbecue, here's a neat trick to impress your friends. Open a can of beer and place it on the hottest part of the grill. It will boil and keep the meat moist while adding flavor, too.

Flavorful Chicken

Want juicy chicken from the grill? A beer can is the secret! Just place a half-full can of lager in the cavity of a chicken and barbecue. The beer will evaporate as it cooks, filling the chicken with moisture and flavor. Bonus: The beer can props the chicken up for even cooking with no rotating required. To get the most benefit from the beer, remove the entire top of the can with a can opener.

Spice Up Shrimp

To give shrimp a little something extra, boil flat beer with spices such as Cajun seasoning. Add raw shrimp and cook for 5 minutes. Serve over pasta or rice. Try the same technique for lobster, cooking for 12 to 15 minutes.

Fluffier Pancakes

Beer's carbonation and yeast can help make pancakes airy yet thick. Simply swap in beer for a bit of the milk or water called for in the recipe.

Boozy Watermelon

Cube a watermelon, place in a bowl, then pour beer on top. Let it marinate for an hour or two at room temperature. Then thread onto wooden skewers, cover, and freeze for at least 1 to 2 hours. Enjoy frozen.

HEALTH AND BEAUTY

Get Bounce from Beer

Beer acts as a clarifying agent to remove product buildup, plus it infuses hair with protein and B vitamins. Mix 3 tablespoons of your favorite brew with ½ cup warm water, and rub into your hair after shampooing. Let it sit for a few minutes before rinsing out and reaping the bounce. Bonus: It also helps prevent dandruff.

Set for Shine

After shampooing and towel drying, spray beer from a pump bottle onto your hair as a setting solution, then simply blow-dry or style. The brew will help the style hold and give your hair healthy shine. Don't worry—beer's scent fades quickly on hair!

Bathe in Beer

Beer baths have been popular in Europe for centuries. Yeast, hops, and barley offer antioxidant properties that help prevent cell damage to your skin. Translation: They fight visible signs of aging. Antibacterial and anti-inflammatory benefits can be especially helpful for those with skin conditions such as eczema or acne. Plus, the bubbles are refreshing! Just add one bottle of beer to your bath.

Refresh Tired Feet

If a full bath isn't doable, treat just your feet to a beer bath. While the vitamins and compounds do their work to benefit your skin, you can simply enjoy the soothing carbonation.

Sleep Better

Many people swear by the sleep-inducing power of hops. But it's the scent (not ingestion) that's purported to be a sleep aid. To give the hops remedy a try, wash your pillowcase in beer.

PETROLEUM JELLY

This classic skin protectant has been around since the 1870s. But you're missing out on so many of its uses if you don't bring it out of the medicine cabinet for much more than a simple skin treat!

HOUSEHOLD HELPER

Make Your Fridge More Efficient

If your refrigerator is more than a couple years old, its seal is probably not as tight as it used to be. To save energy and keep your food cooler, first clean the door's gasket (that rubber lining that goes around it), then rub it with petroleum jelly to ensure a tighter seal.

Solution for Sticky Jars

To stop the lids of honey, molasses, and other sweet stuff from sticking, rub a little petroleum jelly on the rim of the jar when you first open it. The petroleum jelly will lubricate the threads of the jar so it won't stick. This tip works great on nail polish bottles, too!

Smoother Sliding

Do the rings on your shower curtain squeak as they run along the rod? The solution is simple: Just rub some petroleum jelly or car wax along the rod and they'll slide right over it.

Another Ring Solution

Ring stuck on your finger? Petroleum jelly can act as a lubricant to help it slide off.

Silence Squeaky Faucets

If the handles of your sink shriek when you turn them, try this easy fix. Unscrew the handles and rub petroleum jelly on all the threads. The jelly will keep them lubricated and (hopefully) squeak-free.

Remove Water Rings

If you have kids, you probably have water marks on your finished wood table. Use a little petroleum jelly to remove the white stains. Just rub the area with the jelly and let it sit for several hours (or even overnight). Then rub again with a soft cloth—the stain should disappear.

Get the Gum Off

Find gum stuck under a table or on other wood furniture? Slather the wad with some petroleum jelly, then rub in until the gum starts to disintegrate.

Cleaner Candlesticks

What a pain it can be to clean candleholders! Try rubbing a little bit of petroleum jelly inside each holder before you burn a candle. Then when the candle burns down, you'll be able to remove the remaining wax with ease.

New Life for Leather

Stain on your leather? Rub a bit of petroleum jelly into the area and let set for 5 minutes. Stains should rub right off. Just lackluster appearance from wear? Use petroleum jelly on leather as a conditioner or polish—works on jackets, purses, shoes, belts, baseball mitts, and more.

Lipstick on Your Collar?

To remove a lipstick stain from fabric, cover it with petroleum jelly for 5 minutes, then wash as usual. The glycerin in the jelly will break down the oils in the lipstick, making it easy to wash away. This tip works for tough tar stains, too.

Ant Problem Solved

Petroleum jelly will keep ants out of a pet food dish. Simply rub a small amount on the rim around the bottom of the bowl.

BRUCE SAYS

Get the Most from Your Plunger

Add a little petroleum jelly to the rim of your rubber plunger. It helps achieve greater suction so the disgusting job ahead is a little bit easier.

Away with Aphids

If aphids are infesting your plants, here's an easy solution. Cover a tennis ball with petroleum jelly and leave it nearby. The bugs will be attracted to its bright color and then get stuck on its surface.

Save Your Trees from Caterpillars

If caterpillars are destroying your trees, the solution can be as easy as keeping them from climbing up. Do this by wrapping the base of the tree in aluminum foil; secure with duct tape. Then wipe petroleum jelly all over the aluminum foil. It might be sort of icky, but imagine how the caterpillars feel! The petroleum jelly will keep them from climbing up the tree's trunk.

Confuse All Kinds of Pests

Sometimes, getting rid of insects is as easy as making it hard for them to get where they're going. Smear petroleum jelly around the base of plant stems, and ants and other crawling insects will slide right off, protecting your plants.

Barricade Your Grub from Bugs

Here's a simple and safe way to defend your picnic from insect invasions. Smear petroleum jelly onto the legs of your table—from the very bottom to about 2 inches up. Little bug legs are no match for the gummy, sticky barricade.

Winterize Deck Furniture

To keep your metal deck furniture free from rust and wear all winter long, reach for the petroleum jelly. Just apply a thin layer (especially in areas where the furniture tends to rust) after cleaning the surface with simple soap and water.

A Bright Idea for Outdoor Lights

Before you screw a new bulb into your outdoor light fixtures, coat the bulb's threads with some petroleum jelly. The jelly will not only prevent rust but will also make the bulb easy to remove when it burns out.

WHO KNEW?
READERS' FAVORITE

Better Than Painter's Tape

Painting doors? Avoid getting paint on the hinges and knobs by coating them lightly with petroleum jelly before you start. It's easier to protect rounded parts than when using painter's tape, and it wipes right off!

AUTO AND TRAVEL

Keep Your Battery Clean

To prevent your car's battery from corroding, wipe down the battery posts with petroleum jelly once every couple of months.

No-Fail Fire Starter

Before a camping trip, smear petroleum jelly on some cotton balls and keep them in a plastic storage bag. Even if you find yourself camping in the middle of a rainstorm, these bits of kindling will definitely get your fire roaring.

Plunge a Car Dent

Believe it or not, there may be a way to remove that dent from the side of your car without spending a penny. Rub petroleum jelly on the edge of a clean toilet plunger, then place it over the dent and pump it out just like you would a toilet clog. Your family will laugh at you—until the dent pops out and you save a $300 trip to the body shop!

HEALTH AND BEAUTY

Tame Unruly Brows

It's happened to the best of us: You look in the mirror and notice that your eyebrows are out of control. When you're in need of a fix, a little dab of petroleum jelly—or even, in a pinch, lip gloss—can help keep curly hairs in a sleek, sophisticated line. Alternatively, a little hair spray on your eyebrow brush will help smooth them into place.

No More Shampoo Tears

Stop the shampoo tears without buying a special formula! Just rub a good amount of petroleum jelly on your child's eyebrows to set up a protective barrier against shampoo.

From Chapped to Luscious Lips

The best remedy for chapped lips? Buy a child's toothbrush with a really soft head, dip it in petroleum jelly, and scrub your lips. It will gently get rid of rough patches while moisturizing.

Make Your Own Lip Gloss

In a bowl, mix a bit of petroleum jelly with a few sprinkles of a pink or red powdered drink mix. Blend well, and keep adding drink mix until you get your desired lip color. Wait several hours until the crystals dissolve, and then transfer to a small tin for use. This DIY makes great party favors or valentines.

Save a Too-Dark Lipstick

Want to turn a too-dark lipstick into a just-right shade? In a small bowl, heat a little petroleum jelly in the microwave until it is warm. (Try 5 to 10 seconds to start.) Then stir in a piece of your lipstick, and combine until well blended. If it's still too dark, add a little more petroleum jelly. Once you're satisfied with the shade, transfer it to a small container or tin for storage.

Whip Up Creamy Eye Shadow or Blush

You can make a simple blush, eye shadow, or lip gloss by adding a bit of food coloring to petroleum jelly. So versatile!

Nail Polish Protection

Painting your nails at home? For a salon-fresh look, before you begin, apply petroleum jelly to your cuticles and the skin around your nails. When the polish is dry, wipe away the jelly, along with any stray polish on your skin.

Give Your Hands a Makeover

Once a month, cover your hands in petroleum jelly or thick hand cream, then slip them into some soft cotton gloves for the night. In the morning, your skin will have absorbed all the cream, leaving you with the smoothest, softest hands you've ever had. You can also soften your feet the same way (using socks rather than gloves, of course).

Get Summer-Ready Soles

Slough the dry, rough patches off your feet with this great, basic foot scrub using two common household ingredients. Simply mix ½ cup Epsom salts with 1 tablespoon petroleum jelly. If you like, add a few drops of your favorite essential oil for a little fragrance. Use to scrub the soles of your feet, and soon they'll be sandal-worthy!

JEANNE SAYS

Remove Ticks with Ease

Oh no, you've got a tick! If you're having trouble prying the little bugger off, apply a large glob of petroleum jelly to the area. Wait about 20 minutes, and you should be able to wipe the tick off with ease.

Cure "Cold Nose"

Nose sore and raw from blowing with tissues? Use a cotton swab to dab on petroleum jelly.

Kick Those Corns

Painful corns can put a cramp in your style. Flatten them with this easy tip. All you need are bandages, petroleum jelly, and an emery board. Every night before you go to sleep, rub a little petroleum jelly on the corns and cover with a bandage. Then, in the morning, file the corns gently with the emery board. Repeat the process until they're gone, usually in 10 to 14 days. (Be sure not to use the emery board for any other purpose.)

Ease Painful Pads on Pets

Many dogs love to play outside in the snow, but their paws can cause them pain if ice starts to build up between their pads. Before heading out for a winter walk, rub some petroleum jelly between each pad. The ice will stay away and your dog can enjoy the outdoors! If your poor pet's pads are already cracked or dry, gently rub a little petroleum jelly into her pads while she's sleeping. Rest assured that petroleum jelly is completely safe if your pet decides she wants to lick it off later.

MAKE SCENTS LAST LONGER!

To make perfume or cologne last longer, rub a small amount of petroleum jelly onto your skin before you dab on your favorite scent.

Prevent a Nosebleed

Moisturize the inside of your nostrils with a bit of petroleum jelly to keep delicate tissue from drying and cracking.

Help a Cut Heal

Keeping wounds moist and covered can speed healing by as much as 50 percent! Use simple petroleum jelly to keep it moist, then cover with a bandage. Wash and repeat each day to minimize scarring.

Relieve Windburn

Petroleum jelly is gentle enough to moisturize delicate areas of your face. So go ahead and enjoy that hike on a cool day!

DUCT TAPE

Do you know where your handy roll of duct tape is at all times? You should! Here are more than 35 reasons to keep duct tape close by— around the house and on the go.

HOUSEHOLD HELPER

Stick It to Gum

It sounds crazy, but it's true: You can get rid of gum with the help of a sticky tool! To remove gum from upholstery, wrap a piece of duct tape around your fingers, with the sticky side facing out. Then, with a quick motion, press onto the gum and lift. Repeat until all of the gum is gone.

Lift Away Lint

You don't need fancy lint-removing tape rollers! Just double over duct tape, sticky-side out, and use it to lift away lint from clothing.

Easy Vacuum Fix

Save yourself the cost of expensive replacement parts. If your vacuum hose has developed a crack and is leaking air, simply cover the crack with duct tape and keep on cleaning.

No More Vacuum Bags? No Problem!

If your disposable vacuum cleaner bag is full and you don't have a replacement on hand, get out the duct tape! Remove the bag and cut a slit straight down the middle. Empty it into the garbage, then pinch the sides together at the slit and fold over. Tape the fold with a liberal amount of duct tape. The bag will hold a little less, but you'll be ready to vacuum again.

JEANNE SAYS

Make Folders That Last Forever

For a pocket folder you know is going to take a beating—like the one we keep near our tool kit that holds instructions— reinforce it on the sides and pockets with duct tape. It will last forever!

Save That Basket

If you have a plastic laundry basket that has cracked or has a handle partially torn off, cover the rip with duct tape on both sides. It may not be pretty, but it works just as well as a new one.

Stop Shower Leaks

If you have a shower that has a detachable showerhead, use duct tape to repair any holes when the connecting arm inevitably begins to leak. That was easy, huh?

Unstick a Stubborn Light Bulb

Got a light bulb stuck in its socket? Avoid breaking both the bulb and the socket by making two "handles" out of duct tape that you can use to twist the broken bulb out. (This tip also works well if you have already accidentally shattered the bulb in the socket.) First, cut a foot-long length of duct tape and stick the ends of the strip together to form a big loop, adhesive side in. Place the loop around the bulb so that the bulb is at its center. Then bring the two sides of the loop together, allowing the tape to stick to itself and form two long ends of tape on either side: these are your handles. Grab them between your thumbs and forefingers, and gently twist counterclockwise to unscrew the bulb.

Clever Drip Catcher

When painting a room directly from the can, it's nearly impossible to keep paint from dripping down the side. So instead of stopping the drips, catch them! The easiest way? Affix a paper or Styrofoam plate to the bottom of the can with some duct tape. That way, it goes with the can wherever you move it, and you can just tear it off when you're done painting.

Close Extra Vents

Close the heating and air-conditioning vents in rooms in your home you don't frequently use, such as a guest room or laundry room. If your vents don't have closures, simply seal them off with duct tape.

Mend a Shingle

If one of your roof's shingles has fallen off, you can make a temporary replacement using duct tape. Cut a ¼-inch-thick piece of plywood to match the size of the missing shingle. Then wrap it in duct tape (you will need several strips), and wedge it in place. Use extra duct tape to keep it there, if necessary.

WINTERIZE YOUR DOOR

Have a sliding glass door that's rarely used during the winter? Seal it with duct tape to keep cold air from coming in.

Patch Damaged Siding

Duct tape can hold small rips in your vinyl siding for a season or two. With so many color choices now, you can match it to your house's hue. Make sure the area is dry before applying, and smooth it out to form a tight seal.

Keep Wood from Splitting

When cutting plywood, first reinforce where you plan on cutting with a strip of duct tape. The tape will keep the wood from splitting as you saw, and then you can peel the tape right off.

Protect Your Grill

Make sure squirrels, mice, and other critters don't chew through the rubber pipeline that connects your propane tank with your grill—reinforce the entire thing with duct tape. This step is a good idea for anything else in your yard made out of rubber, as it's a favorite chew toy of rodents!

Patch Pool Liners

When pool liners tear, it can be very costly to repair them. But duct tape can do the job. Simply cover the tear, and keep an eye on it to make sure it doesn't start to peel off. Believe it or not, a single piece of duct tape can usually last underwater for an entire summer.

Repair Outdoor Furniture

Whether the damage affects an outdoor cushion or chair webbing, use duct tape to engineer an easy fix and save your furniture for more years of enjoyment. It's waterproof and holds strong.

Better Than a Bookmark

You're trying to read from a cookbook or other book hands-free, and it keeps snapping shut! Here's an easy solution: Make a weighted bookmark by lining up two rows of 15 pennies each, then pressing a piece of duct tape on top of them. Turn it over and press another piece of duct tape to the back. Use colored duct tape and some stickers if you want to jazz it up.

Last-Minute Halloween Costume

Transform your little candy seeker into a robot or the Tin Man. Use a box as a mask with cutout eyes and a mouth. Cover the box, as well as a shirt and an old pair of jeans, with duct tape.

ON-THE-GO SOLUTIONS

Secret Key Saver

Duct tape a spare key to the undercarriage of your car or in a wheel well, and you'll never get locked out again. Be sure to place it in a location other than near the driver's door, where thieves may check.

Quick Window Seal

If the seal around your car window is leaking air, making an annoying sound as you drive, patch it up with duct tape until you have the time (and money) to take it to the shop.

Anytime, Anywhere Rope

Duct tape is so sturdy that you can use it as a rope by twisting it around itself. Use as a backup for clotheslines, leashes, tying twine, or anything else for which you would normally use rope.

So Many Camping Uses!

Always, always pack duct tape when you're going camping. It's a must-have to repair rips or holes in tents and air mattresses and can be used to string up food out of bears' reach. You can even use it while you're hiking: Tape your pant legs to your boots with duct tape to avoid bites from ticks, flies, and mosquitoes.

Goodbye, Flies

Flying insects waiting to greet you at a vacation home? Tape five to ten pieces of duct tape to themselves (making a ring with the sticky side out), then hang them near overhead lights. When the bugs get stuck, simply throw out the tape and problem solved!

FAST WARDROBE FIXES

Make Mud Stains Disappear

When kids come home with fresh mud stains on their clothes, don't apply water! Instead, let the mud dry, then use a piece of duct tape (or packing tape) to lift up all of the hardened dirt you can. Then wash as usual.

Peel Away Pollen

Pollen stain on your shirt? Don't rub at it! Carefully shake off the excess pollen and then remove the rest with a piece of masking or duct tape.

PICNIC PEACE

Duct-tape the sides of a tablecloth to a picnic table and you won't have to worry about it blowing away.

Your Warmest Boots

Make your winter boots a little warmer—and make sure they're completely waterproof—by lining the bottom of the insides with duct tape. The tape will create a waterproof seal, and the shiny silver will reflect your body heat back onto your feet.

Big Hat (or Small Head)?

Make your ball cap tighter by cutting a piece of duct tape lengthwise and wrapping a few layers around the sweatband.

Hem in a Hurry

You've bought a great pair of jeans, but they're too long and you don't have time to hem them before you need to wear them. Simply fold them up and tape with duct tape. The hem will last the whole night—and maybe even through a couple of washings. This strategy is also smart if you're not sure exactly where you want to hem your pants. Have a "trial run" using the duct tape.

Make Slippers Even Better

To make your slippers waterproof and therefore safe to wear on a quick trip outdoors, simply cover the bottoms with overlapping layers of duct tape.

HEALTH REMEDIES

Simple Treatment for Warts

It may seem strange, but medical studies have concluded that when patients cover their warts with duct tape every day for a month, 85 percent of them will see a reduction in the wart. That's compared to only a 60 percent reduction in patients who used cryotherapy (having the wart frozen off by a dermatologist). Give it a try!

Easier Splinter Removal

If you get a splinter, a little duct tape does the trick to get it out. Cut off a piece and gently press it to the affected area, then pull it off.

Create a Bandage

Use a tissue or paper towel secured and covered with duct tape as a simple bandage.

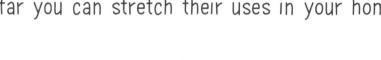

RUBBER BANDS

These inexpensive elastic goodies are known for their flexibility. But you may not realize how far you can stretch their uses in your home!

HOUSEHOLD HELPER

Open a Stuck Jar or Bottle

For a simple but effective grip, wrap a thick rubber band around the rim of a jar lid or bottle top and then twist. Plastic wrap and rubber kitchen gloves work well as grippers, too.

Prevent a Cutting Board from Sliding

A rubber band wrapped around the board will create enough resistance to stop any counter glide. Safer and easier!

Keep Tea Bags in Place

Whether you're brewing a single cup or setting a jar out for sun tea, this trick can keep your tea bag tags from sinking into your beverage. Simply wrap a rubber band around the rim of the drink's container and over the string.

Track Ingredient Levels

Have canisters or other kitchen containers that are difficult to see inside? Keep track of how much is left by securing a rubber band around the outside to mark the level of whatever's inside. This little trick works well for paint containers, too.

Slow a Leak

Thick rubber bands wrapped around a leaky hose or pipe can buy you a little time (and save money) as a temporary fix.

MAKE A GRIP

Wrap rubber bands around pens and pencils, tools, walking sticks, and sports equipment to create a more comfortable hold. Super-helpful for those with arthritis!

Hold Lids in Transport

Bringing a dish of food to a party or potluck? Rubber bands can help you secure lids to a slow cooker or other dish. If there is a knob in the center of your lid, simply loop a rubber band from the knob to each side handle.

Tidy Up Cords

From blow-dryers to blenders to electric shavers, most small electrical appliances have cords that can get a little unwieldy. Under your desk is another area that can get chaotic with wires. Keep them neat and out of the way with rubber bands or ponytail holders, or fold up detachable cords and store them in paper towel tubes—color-code the bands and label the tubes to remind yourself which cord belongs to which appliance.

Keep a Candle (and Wax!) in Place

Candle not quite fitting snugly into its holder? Wrap a rubber band around the candle's base for a tighter fit. Secure a band a little higher up to stop any wax drips from moving past the candle onto your furniture.

Corral Craft Ribbon

If you have rolls of ribbon around for crafting or wrapping gifts, you know how difficult it is to keep them from unspooling. Solution: Wrap them with a rubber band to keep the ribbon in its place on the spool until you need it.

Save Your Chargers

Charging cords for phones or other devices starting to wear? Wrap a rubber band around the cord to protect the vulnerable spots and stop wires from fraying more. You can also slip a colored rubber band or two around the main part of a charger to spot it as yours versus your spouse's or kid's.

Make Your Own Super Bands

When you're ready to throw them out, cut rubber gloves into strips with extra-sharp scissors to make rubber bands! The fingers will provide you with small bands and the palm section will give you giant rubber bands with tons of household uses—from securing kindling wood to keeping sports equipment together.

Build an Eraser

Create a small rubber band ball by wrapping bands. Once it's sturdy enough to rub on paper, it will erase pencil just as well as your standard eraser. Bonus: It makes a great stress ball to squeeze!

Glide Through Papers

Counting or sorting a large stack of papers? A few rubber bands wrapped comfortably around the tips of your fingers will make the job a lot easier. This little tip will help prevent paper cuts, too. Try it when reading an old book with not-so-crisp pages as well.

Easier Paint Cleanup

Don't get your paint can rim all mucked up with paint! For the times you want to brush off drips, wrap a rubber band around the can from top to bottom, going across the middle of the can opening. Then tap the brush against the rubber band and the excess paint will fall cleanly back into the can.

New Life for an Old Broom

Don't throw it away quite yet! If the bristles are starting to feel tattered, tighten them up by wrapping large rubber bands halfway up the bristles.

Make a Mop or Broom Work Harder

With a large rubber band, secure a dust cloth to a long-handled broom or mop to clean high places. It's an amazing tool that works just as well as expensive store-bought contraptions!

Protect TP Rolls

If your toddler or fur baby likes to unroll or shred your toilet paper, you're not alone. Simply slipping a rubber band around the roll will keep it safe from curious hands and paws.

JEANNE SAYS

Try This
Spoon Solution

At our house, all of our wooden mixing spoons have a rubber band wrapped tightly around the top of the handle. Why? You can safely rest the spoon on the side of the bowl without it slipping.

WHO KNEW?

READERS' FAVORITE

Prevent a Door from Locking

Wrap a large rubber band around the knobs on each side of the door, crisscrossing the band at the side edge of the door to cover the lock. This tip may come in handy if you have kids or pets who could accidentally trigger a lock.

Loosen Up a Baseball Glove

New gloves can be super-stiff—especially for a child's hand. Just a little loosening up can help a lot. After conditioning with olive oil or petroleum jelly (two of our Who Knew? Heroes), place a baseball inside the glove's pocket. Then wrap a big rubber band around the glove to hold the ball in place. Simply let it sit or tuck it under your mattress overnight. Use the glove daily, and repeat the process of oiling and banding for about a week, until the glove is more flexible.

DECORATING AND ENTERTAINING ON A DIME

ID Wineglasses

Having a party? Put rubber bands in different colors (or even shapes) to good use! These are perfect for slipping around the stems of wineglasses so your guests can tell whose glass is whose. Slip in a flower or small charm as a decoration or party favor.

Better Flower Arranging

To help keep flowers where you put them, simply group with rubber bands around the stems.

Decorate a Jar or Tin

Wrap multicolored rubber bands around an old can or jar. Use it to hold flowers, pens, or even hardware—whatever you want to contain in a fun way. You can also space out some bands a bit and tuck in little touches such as dried flowers or cinnamon sticks.

Easy Curtain Pullbacks

Use a rubber band that matches the color of your curtains to keep them pulled aside.

Elevate Your Egg Decorating

If you enjoy dyeing Easter eggs, here's a simple way to add patterns: Just wrap rubber bands around them before dipping into the dye. Wherever you place a rubber band will remain white. Try stripe and plaid patterns. This trick works for any kind of craft painting as well.

ON-THE-GO SOLUTIONS

Hands-Free Phone Holder

Thread a rubber band through the top of your car's AC vent, then pull it out through the bottom. Secure both ends around your phone at the top and bottom. The bands will hold the phone in place, ready to view for driving directions.

Turn a Visor into an Organizer

Turn your car's visor into a handy place to store paper and other flat items by using rubber bands. Wrap several rubber bands snugly around the visor, then slip papers, parking stubs, CDs, or anything else under the rubber bands.

The Smartest Packing Technique

The secret frequent travelers use: To fit the most in your luggage without smashing and wrinkling, roll your clothing and secure with rubber bands.

DIY Tripod

Crisscrossed rubber bands can fasten your phone to a chair, bicycle handlebars, or wherever you'd like to enable fun photos or video.

Protect Books

Whether in your bag or your kids' backpack, books can get damaged when pages fly open. Keep books closed by wrapping a rubber band around them.

CREATE A WRIST STRAP
Flashlight, camera, or other item missing a strap? Simply loop and tie a rubber band to make one.

Makeshift Splint

Use a rubber band to firmly secure an injured finger to a support you have on hand, such as a stick.

COSMETICS AND CLOTHING

Slow Pumpables for Kids

Pumps that dispense soap, shampoo, and lotion can make it too easy for kids to take too much. To reduce the amount, just wind a rubber band around the neck. This simple step will control how far the pump can move and how much it dispenses—and stop the sink mess.

No More Shower Drops

Shampoo bottles and bars of soap can get slippery to handle in the shower. Wrapping a rubber band or two around them will give you a better place to grip.

Simple Nail Template

You can give yourself a French manicure without a lot of fuss and save the $20 to $40 salon charge. Wrap part of a rubber band over your nail to use as a guide, leaving just the nail tip exposed to paint.

Eyeglasses Prone to Slipping?

Looping a rubber band around the end of each side can help them grip better and stay in place.

Get a Little More Give in Jeans

Make the waist of your jeans stretch a little farther by looping a rubber band through the buttonhole and over the button. It's a great quick fix for early pregnancy months or even just after a big dinner.

CLEAN LIVING

You can keep your living spaces looking gorgeous without a lot of chemicals or expensive commercial cleaners. All it takes are these DIY solutions!

SOLVE DUSTING DILEMMAS

Slash Your Dusting Time

To easily clean your coffee table and keep dust away for good, dampen a rag with warm water mixed with a drop or two of liquid fabric softener. Wipe down the tabletop. The fabric softener will repel future dust while getting your table sparking clean.

Replace Your Rags

Instead, wear a pair of old socks on your hands to dust. It's efficient (you're using both hands) and cheap (remember, these are old socks), and you can wash and reuse them. You can also use socks on your duster and sweeper handles instead of buying disposable refills and pads. Those fuzzy socks you see on sale everywhere during the holiday season work especially well.

Open That Umbrella

Some may say that opening an umbrella in the house is bad luck, but you won't mind the risk when you see how much easier it makes cleaning high areas in your home, such as a ceiling fan or chandelier. Just hook the handle of an upside-down, open umbrella near where you're cleaning, then let the dust that you wipe off fall inside. Close it up when you're done and carefully take outside to dump out the dust.

DIY Dusting Cloths

Here's a fresh idea: Whether you use socks or cloths, keep them ready to go to dusting work and deliver a lovely lemon scent around your house. It's simple. In a large bowl, add equal parts water and white vinegar. Add a few drops of olive oil. Soak your clean socks or cloths in the solution until saturated. While they're soaking, peel lemon rinds in good-size pieces. When ready, wring out each sock or cloth until just damp. Spread out the cloths on a counter, and roll a few lemon rinds into each. Store in an airtight glass container so the cloths stay moist until you're ready to put them to work. Launder used cloths and repeat the process as needed.

Amazing Spray

Prefer to have your dust and shine solution in spray form? Avoid the cost of (and chemicals in) commercial sprays! Just tweak the ingredient proportions above. We recommend mixing in a spray bottle 1 cup water, ¼ cup vinegar, 2 teaspoons olive oil, and 10 drops lemon essential oil.

Clear Dust from Ceiling Fans

To easily clean a ceiling fan, spray glass cleaner or a mixture of half vinegar and half water on the inside of a pillowcase. Put the pillowcase over one arm of the fan, then pull it off while applying gentle pressure toward the floor. The pillowcase will wipe the top of the blade clean.

Clobber Cobwebs

Here's an easy way to clean cobwebs from corners: Cover the head of your mop or broom with a pillowcase dampened with water, vinegar, or your preferred cleaning solution, then secure it with a rubber band and go to it.

Reach Easily Between Blinds

Is there any chore more annoying than dusting your venetian blinds? To make the job go more quickly, and to reach every last slat, fasten a cloth around each edge of a set of tongs with rubber bands. Then tackle those slats two at a time! Another crazy but effective option: use bread crusts. Just hold a piece of crust around each slat and run it along the length of the blinds. An old paintbrush will also do the trick, or you can use the brush attachment on your vacuum cleaner. Whatever your tool of choice, make sure you won't have to dust again for a while. Finish by spraying Static Guard (usually used for clothing) onto your blinds to repel dust!

Chase Dust Gently

Forget the feather duster. The easiest way to get loose dust off your knickknacks—and other delicate areas—is to blow it away with a hair dryer. Or spray them with air from a compressed air can (usually used to clean electronics and computer keyboards).

Citrus for Ceramic

To clean dust off ceramic figurines, simply rub them with the cut side of a lemon wedge. Leave the lemon juice on for 15 minutes, then polish up with a soft, dry cloth.

Make Light of Lampshades

The trick to cleaning a pleated lampshade is finding the right tool. Stroke each pleat from top to bottom with a dry, clean paintbrush. Or use a rolling lint remover for a quicker clean. If you dust your shades with a fabric softener sheet, its static-fighting properties will keep them cleaner for longer.

Don't Forget the Bulbs

Clear off that coating of dust from your light bulbs so they can shine bright! All it takes is a cloth dabbed in rubbing alcohol. Make sure your lights are off and the bulbs are cool to the touch first.

Restore Your Radiator

Dread cleaning your radiator? Here's a simple way to get the job done. Hang a damp cloth or damp newspapers on the wall behind it, then use your hair dryer to blow the dust off it. The dust will stick to the wet surface behind it, and then you can simply throw away the cloth or paper.

SHINE WITH MAYO

Artificial plants looking a little lackluster and dusty? Bring back shiny leaves by rubbing on a dab of mayo with a cloth. Baby wipes work well to clean, too.

WHO KNEW?

READERS' FAVORITE

Clean Up with Bread

Bread can clean wallpaper! Eliminate fingerprints, light stains, and even ballpoint ink by simply rubbing a piece of white bread vigorously over the spot. It works magic for precious oil paintings, too. White bread has the perfect amount of moisture to easily pick up dust, without being so wet that it will ruin your painting.

Dust Down Under

Wrap old pantyhose around the head of a broom, then let the handle help you reach underneath a couch or cabinet. The static cling from the stocking acts like a magnet for dust.

SMART WAYS WITH WOOD

Erase Water Rings

Does your wood furniture have white rings left from wet glasses? Remove them with a mixture of 2 tablespoons corn oil and enough baking soda to make a paste. Apply the paste to the rings and let sit for at least 1 hour before rubbing the area gently. Or give mayonnaise a shot: Rub a tiny bit (½ teaspoon) on the ring and let it sit overnight. In the morning, just wipe with a damp cloth and the ring should be gone!

Give Old Wood New Life

We love the antique look of old wooden furniture. But sometimes "old" just looks, well, old rather than "antique." Get wood gleaming again and smooth away any imperfections and scratches with an easy trick that is amazingly effective. You only need two items that you probably already have in your kitchen: oil and vinegar. (Yep, like the salad dressing!) Mix ¼ cup white or apple cider vinegar with ¾ cup olive or vegetable oil. Dip a soft cloth in the solution and rub on for a brand-new look. You can choose to add 8 to 10 drops of an essential oil (we like lemon, orange, or tangerine) for a sweet scent.

Prevent Polish Buildup

Excess polish can leave a dull finish on wooden furniture. To remove it, mix together 2 tablespoons white vinegar and 2 tablespoons water. Apply to the surface and wipe right off. Cornstarch will also do the trick: Sprinkle a little on the furniture and polish with a soft cloth.

Foil Those Fingerprints

You just bought the coffee table of your dreams, but when it was sitting in the store you didn't realize it would attract fingerprints like bees to honey. To get rid of a persistent fingerprint problem, rub down the tabletop with cornstarch. The surface will absorb the cornstarch, which will repel prints.

REACH TIGHT PLACES Wrap a dusting cloth around a ruler or kitchen spatula with rubber bands. The handle will give you an extended reach. Need to reach even farther? Try a heavy-duty sock on a yardstick.

8 TIPS TO ERASE WOOD SCRATCHES AND DENTS

We like furniture with history—just not too much! If you have wood that's damaged, don't despair. There are some simple, extremely low-cost tricks you can use to bring back the beauty and integrity of your wood furniture and floors.

Head to the kitchen for a solution. For tiny scratches in your wooden table or floor, rub vegetable or canola oil into the surface. The oil will darken the area and help it blend in.

Jelly up scratches. Coat scratches with petroleum jelly, let sit for 24 hours, rub into wood, wipe away excess, and polish as usual.

Steal a secret from your shoes. Does your wooden coffee table, dresser, or dining room furniture have visible scratches? No sweat! Use a similarly hued shoe polish to fill in the offending marks.

Make repair child's play. A crayon can work to repair scratches in your wood furniture. Just find a color that's a close match to the wood, then rub the crayon into the scratch. Wipe off any excess wax with a credit card edge, then buff with a cotton cloth.

Go nutty—it works! If you notice a scratch, try this crafty (and delicious!) solution. Find a nut that matches the color of the wood; the most common types for this purpose are pecans, walnuts, and hazelnuts. Rub the scratched area gently with the broken edges of the nuts—using the insides, not the shells. When you're all done, enjoy a snack break.

Bring makeup to the rescue. To fix tiny furniture scratches, use eyeliner in a matching color to fill in the hole.

Cover up with coffee. Would you ever imagine coffee stains could be a good thing? For your damaged wood furniture or floors, they are. Just brew a very strong pot, and then use a cotton ball or rag to apply the coffee over the scratch. It works as a stain, and will blend in the scratch in no time!

Iron out dents. As long as the wood hasn't broken apart underneath, you may be able to fix dents in wooden furniture or floors. Here's how: Run a rag under warm water and wring it out, then place it on top of the dent. Apply an iron set on medium heat to the rag until the rag dries out. Repeat this process until your dent is gone.

Not-So-Permanent Marker

If your kids (or you) get a permanent marker stain on furniture or the floor, don't despair! There may be hope in the form of rubbing alcohol. Test an inconspicuous area first to make sure it won't harm the finish, then apply directly to the stain with a rag or paper towel. Rub until it disappears, then wipe with a clean cloth moistened with water.

Protect with a Band

If you have lots of dings and nicks in your coffee table, the TV remote may be to blame. To make sure hard plastic remotes don't dent your furniture in the future, simply wrap a rubber band around each end. The soft rubber will give your furniture a cushion.

SHINING SOLUTIONS

Clean a Crystal Chandelier

If you have a crystal chandelier, don't dread cleaning it any longer! First, make sure the light switch is off. Next, lay a blanket or upside-down umbrella underneath the chandelier to catch any drips or falling pieces. Now mix ½ cup rubbing alcohol with 1½ cups water in a jar. The crystals clean themselves—all you have to do is bring the jar up to each one and dip it in, then let it air-dry. You can use a little bit of the solution on a clean cotton rag to wipe areas that can't be dipped.

Whip Up Window Cleaner

You don't need expensive cleaners to wash your windows! For a cheap, effective glass cleaner, fill a spray bottle with ½ teaspoon dishwashing liquid, 3 tablespoons white vinegar, and 2 cups warm water. If you're washing something that's very dirty, use more liquid soap.

Reach for a Coffee Filter

We always prefer to clean our windows with something reusable, like an old rag. But if you like to go the disposable route, try coffee filters instead of paper towels. They won't leave behind any lint or paper pieces. Coffee filters work great for electronic screens as well—they grab dust without scratching or leaving streaks.

JEANNE SAYS

Try a Sweet Solution for Polish Spills

Nail polish bottles are notoriously easy to knock over. Quick damage control: Sprinkle sugar on the polish to absorb it from hard surfaces like tile or wood. You can use this trick on carpet too, but you'll need to follow with at least one application of hair spray to remove the fabric stain.

Steam It Streak-Free

A handheld clothes steamer can help you sanitize and get a streak-free shine on your mirrors and windows. Just steam from top to bottom, then simply squeegee downward.

Get Sparkling Vases

Alka-Seltzer is loaded with baking soda and citrus acid, which are natural cleansers. To make your vases sparkle and target hard-to-reach stains, add warm water and pop in two Alka-Seltzer tablets. The vase should soak for about an hour; then rinse.

SPRUCE UP SOFAS AND CHAIRS

Clear the Cushions

Upholstered sofas and chairs often get a musty odor from day-to-day wear, especially if your kids and pets romp around in the cushions. For a simple freshening up, sprinkle a bit of baking soda over the upholstery, between and underneath the cushions. Let sit for a few hours or up to a day, then suck up the remaining soda and debris with a vacuum.

BRUCE SAYS

Ketchup on Polishing

Here's an unlikely cleaning tool: ketchup. It works great on copper. Simply rub on with a soft cloth, let sit for 30 to 45 minutes, then rinse off with hot water and wipe dry.

Cornmeal Cure

Cornmeal absorbs grease stains on light-colored fabric or upholstery. Pour on enough to cover the soiled area and let it sit for 15 to 30 minutes, then vacuum. The stain will be gone!

Magic for Microfiber

Microfiber furniture looks beautiful and elegant thanks to its tiny, shiny fibers that can resemble suede or leather. The big downside: It can be hard to clean. Check the tag on your microfiber item. If there's a "W" on the tag, you can go ahead and use water and soap to clean it; if there's an "S," you'll need to use a solvent-based cleaner, because water could stain the fabric. If you have an "S," here's what to do: First, vacuum the area using a soft brush attachment to suck up any dirt and debris. Then spray rubbing alcohol over the soiled area using a spray bottle. Scrub using a rough sponge or an old toothbrush, and the stains will lift right off. The fabric should dry quickly, but if it seems hardened or discolored afterward, simply stroke it with a toothbrush or soft scrub brush until it's back to its velvety form.

Love Your Leather

You can rub down treated leather with a damp cloth, and an occasional date with warm soapy water won't harm it. If you get a spot on leather furniture, try removing it by rubbing it with artist's gum—a super powerful eraser that can be found at art supply stores. If you accidentally get a liquid that badly stains on your leather, blot up as much as you can, then apply hydrogen peroxide with a cotton ball to wipe it up.

KITCHEN RESCUES

It might be the hardest-working room in your home, but you don't need to work hard to keep it clean and inviting. Here are the tricks you need to know.

EASY OVEN CLEANING

Steam It Clean

A simple, natural way to clean your oven is to place an oven-safe pot or bowl filled with water inside. Heat on 450°F for 20 minutes, and steam will loosen the dirt and grease. Once your oven is cool, wipe off the condensation and the grease will come with it. When you're done, make a paste of water and baking soda and smear it on any enamel. The paste will dry into a protective layer that will absorb grease as you cook.

Chase Caked-On Food

Make the job a bit easier with this solvent. Blend ¼ cup ammonia with a box of baking soda to make a soft paste. Apply this mixture to the stained, cooked-on spots inside your oven and let it sit overnight. Rinse well with regular water the next day, and your oven will look as good as new.

Renew Your Oven Racks

The surprising secret to help lift grime from your oven racks: antistatic dryer sheets. Line your bathtub or a utility sink with four to six dryer sheets. Set the racks on top, and fill the tub with enough hot water to cover. You can add grease-fighting dish detergent for extra cleaning power. Let sit for at least a few hours and preferably overnight, then wipe clean and rinse.

Speed Away Grease

You can loosen grease and grime in an instant with a handheld clothes steamer. Just point the steam to where you need a little extra help, then wipe oven crud away.

Citrus Solution

A self-cleaning oven can leave an odor after it has done its work. Eliminate the lingering smell by turning down the oven to 350°F after the cleaning cycle, then place a baking sheet lined with orange peels on the middle rack. Cook the peels for half an hour, and not only will the oven smell fresh, but your whole kitchen will, too!

Breathe Easy with Baking Soda

To reduce fumes after you've used a powerful oven cleaner, break out the baking soda. Place a freshly opened box on the middle rack of your over and let it sit overnight to help neutralize the cleaner.

Degrease the Fan Cover

Oven fans are magnets for grease. The simplest way to clean the resulting mess is to pop out the fan filter, then run it through your dishwasher on the top shelf. If it's very greasy, run it with pots and pans or by itself.

Fight Oil with Oil

Clean oily splatters on your stove or range hood with . . . oil! Though it seems a bit counterintuitive, this trick works like a dream. Place some mineral oil on a paper towel and rub away stove splatters (if you don't have mineral oil, olive oil will also work). The oil will pick up the dirt and leave behind a protective film so that it's easier to clean next time. If you are using oil to clean a glass stovetop, however, be sure to wash it off afterward so that the oil doesn't burn when you next turn on the stove.

Hair Dryer Trick

If you're having trouble cleaning off the baked-on grease and grime on your range's hood or other areas around your stove, make your job easier without the help of harsh commercial cleaners. Instead, warm it up by blasting it with your hair dryer. Once it's warm, it will wipe right off with a damp cloth.

JEANNE SAYS

One Simple Step to Less Cleaning

Save on household cleaners by keeping your stove neater. How? When cooking, cover unused burners with a baking sheet or pizza pans. The pans will catch all the splatter, and they're easy to stick in the dishwasher afterward!

Great Cleaner for Gas Burner Grates

Removing caked-on grime is easy, but it requires calling in the big guns: household ammonia. Pour ¼ cup into a large resealable bag, place two burner grates inside, and seal. Let the fumes work overnight, then rinse and rub with a rag or paper towel. Stovetop perfection!

Microwave Cleaning Made Easy

With all the use they get, microwaves can get grimy fast. Time for freshening up? Soak a sponge in water until it's completely saturated, then set it in the microwave. In a spray bottle, mix 1 to 2 drops of lemon essential oil per ounce of water. Spray the mixture all over the inside of your microwave. Run the microwave on high for 2 to 3 minutes. The steam will help release the built-up dirt. Once the sponge is cool, you can use it to easily wipe down the interior and exterior of the microwave. Another approach: In a microwavable bowl, combine ½ cup vinegar and 1 cup water. (You can also add a few drops of lemon juice, if you like.) Microwave for 3 to 5 minutes, then let sit for a few minutes while the steam goes to work. Either way, your microwave will be fresh and clean again!

Clear a Toaster Oven Window

How will you get the toast just right if you can't see it? To clean the smudged, greasy, food-flecked window of your toaster oven, use ashes from your fireplace. Rub them onto the window with a wet rag, then rinse clean. You won't believe how well they work! Don't have a fireplace? Mix 4 parts white vinegar with 4 parts hydrogen peroxide and 2 parts dishwashing liquid. You can wipe it down immediately with paper towels, or spray it on, let it sit for about an hour, and then wipe clean.

UNCLOG GAS BURNERS

Thanks to a spill, the burners on your gas range are clogged with last night's dinner. Open up the holes with one of your child's pipe cleaners.

WHO KNEW? READERS' FAVORITE

Leave No Crumb Behind!

Crumbs and dirt can get everywhere in the kitchen—but the worst of all are those sneaky rascals that scatter beneath the fridge and oven. To nab that hard-to-reach dirt, use a snowbrush that's intended for the car. The narrow brush is a perfect fit for the tight space, and its long handle reaches way back to the wall.

De-Gunk the Entire Toaster

With all of its small parts, the toaster oven can be a tricky appliance to keep clean. Make the process easier with this tip: Fill a small, oven-safe baking dish with water and place it inside the toaster oven. Heat the oven to 350°F, and leave for 10 to 15 minutes. The water will convert to steam, helping to soften the crumbs and burned-on food so that you can wipe it down. Just be sure to unplug it and let it cool down before you start cleaning!

Remove Melted Plastic

We've all done it: You place a package of bread on top of a still-hot toaster oven, and a piece of the plastic bag melts onto the metal. Luckily, there's an easy way to remove it: Rub a bit of petroleum jelly on the stuck plastic and turn on the toaster to warm up. Then scrub the area with a sponge until the plastic comes off.

FAST FRIDGE FIXES

All-Purpose Orange Cleaner

We love this go-to orange cleaner—it works great on all kinds of surfaces, like fridge interiors, countertops, sinks, and greasy stoves. All you need are the peels of several oranges, plain white vinegar, water, a spray bottle, and a glass jar with screw-top lid (a mason jar works perfectly). Place the orange peels into the glass jar, cover with vinegar, and leave for several weeks in a cool spot. Then transfer some of the mixture to a spray bottle and add 2 parts water. Shake to combine, and it's ready to use. Your family will love the scent!

Repurpose Plastic Place Mats

For easy-to-clean fridge shelves and drawers, line them with plastic place mats you've cut to size. That way, when you need to clean (for example, when you've found a fuzzy orange!), you can just remove the place mats and wipe them down. It's much easier than trying to remove shelves and clean each groove at the bottom of the drawer. Shelf liner or even simply plastic wrap is another option.

The Fishy Way to Freshen

Head to the fish section of any pet store and pick up a container of activated carbon (used in aquarium filters). An open container will work even better than baking soda to deodorize your fridge.

> **BRUCE SAYS**
>
> **Attack Dried-On Mess**
>
> If someone didn't spot and wipe up a fridge spill right away ("not me!"), don't worry—you can still lift it away easily. Make a paste of baking powder and water, then rub over the spill to make cleanup a cinch.

8 SIMPLE STAINLESS STEEL CLEANERS

You can break your budget at almost $1 an ounce for a stainless steel cleaner that doesn't go very far in your house and still leaves smudges. Why not try one of these simple ideas you probably already have on hand?

Take a shine to vodka. Place a little on a sponge or paper towel, then wipe. Your faucet, sink, and other stainless steel will soon be sparkling again, so pour yourself a little glass to celebrate!

Run on rubbing alcohol. Polish a stainless steel sink and kill germs by rubbing it down with rubbing alcohol. The alcohol is great at removing water spots.

Chase away smudges. Keep some vinegar in a spray bottle for easy stainless shining anywhere, anytime. After wiping clean, dip the cloth in a little olive oil and smooth onto the surface in the direction of the grain.

Baby your sink. For the shiniest sink you've ever seen, finish off your cleaning session by buffing the sink to a sleek shine with a touch of baby oil on a soft cloth.

Say yes to soda. Club soda is a terrific way to clean stainless steel sinks, dishwashers, ranges, and other appliances. The least expensive club soda works as well as the pricey brands; flat club soda is effective, too. Add a little flour for really stubborn stains.

Make a simple paste. To get the cleanest fixtures you've ever seen, apply a paste of vinegar and baking soda to stainless steel faucets, knobs, and bars. Lay old towels or rags on top and wait 1 hour, then buff off. Rinse the fixtures and then let them dry, and you'll have sparkling fixtures without a hint of water marks.

Pledge to shine. You already know Pledge has many household uses, but did you know that one of the best ones is keeping a stainless steel sink clean? Wipe the wood cleaner over it after you wash it out. If you do this at least once a month, the cleaner will keep your sink shiny by preventing water and food stains from taking hold.

Try a good fix for a bad sink. For a stainless steel sink that's been scratched, stained, and treated with every harsh chemical in the book, it might be time for a face-lift. Use chrome polish to buff it back to life.

Foods That Chase Odors

Besides baking soda and vinegar, a number of foods are capable of removing odors. Pour a little vanilla extract into a bottle cap and set it in the refrigerator to absorb odors. Or hollow out a grapefruit or an orange, fill it with salt, and place it in the back of the fridge. Leave it there until the salt gets completely damp, and then throw the whole thing out and replace.

Immaculate Magnets

Clean refrigerator magnets in seconds with help from some old pantyhose. Cut the foot off an old pair and place the magnets inside, then tie the pantyhose shut. Place in the utensil compartment of your dishwasher and the nylon will protect your magnets while still allowing the warm suds through.

CABINET CARE

Two-Ingredient DIY Cleaner

If you're looking for an alternative to commercial cleaners, try this inexpensive, eco-friendly spray. Simply mix a 50/50 solution of vinegar and water. Spray on, let sit for a minute or two on extra grimy areas, then wipe with a clean cloth or paper towel. If you like, slip in a few drops of liquid dish detergent for extra power against grease.

Deep Clean and Shine

Your wooden kitchen cabinets may look clean, but over time, they can develop a sticky film. To eliminate it, mix 1 part vegetable or coconut oil with 2 parts baking soda, and rub on the cabinets. Remove the paste with a damp cloth, and then dry with a clean rag. You'll be surprised at how much brighter they look!

Erase Marker with Toothpaste

If your child happens to get permanent marker on the kitchen cabinets, don't fret quite yet. You may be able to remove it with toothpaste. Add a little of the paste (the non-gel variety works best) to the spot and scrub until the marker disappears. Wipe the area with a clean, damp cloth and no one will ever know that the permanent marker fell into the wrong hands.

COUNTER SOLUTIONS

Give Your Kitchen a Drink

For a scratch-free cleaner that will make your countertops, sink, and any stainless steel sparkle, apply club soda with a moist sponge or soft cloth. You don't even need to rinse off!

Say Goodbye to Stains

You can remove stubborn stains from your countertop by applying a baking soda paste and rubbing with a warm, damp cloth. If the stain remains, consider using a drop of bleach, but be careful—it can fade your countertop along with the stain!

No More Marker

To remove a marker stain (even from permanent marker) from a countertop, use an orange peel. First, rub the outside with your fingers to bring the orange oil to the surface, then rub the peel directly on the marker stain. You may need to use a little elbow grease, but it will come out!

Clean Stone

To remove stains on stone countertops, make a mixture of warm water with a few drops of both hydrogen peroxide and ammonia. Rub it into the stain, wait a few minutes, then rinse with warm water. To eliminate small scratches, you can buff with superfine steel wool.

Marble Maintenance

Marble countertops add a touch of elegance to a home, but unfortunately, they can't be cleaned with most commercial products. We recommend the old-fashioned route. First, fill a small basin or your sink with warm water and add a drop or two of dishwashing liquid. With a sponge, use the soapy water to wipe down the countertop, then rinse and dry the area. If you notice a stain, add a few drops of bleach to baking soda until you've made a paste, cover the stain with it, and leave overnight. The next day, wet the area and remove the paste, being sure to rinse the area thoroughly.

Squeegee Smarts

Using the spongy side of a squeegee, clean marble counters with warm, sudsy water, then remove excess water with the rubber blade. You can also try the squeegee with stainless steel. It's perfect for surfaces that easily get water marks!

PREVENT SINK-SIDE MOLD AND MILDEW

Instead of placing a used sponge on the rim of your sink, where it'll cultivate yucky mildew and mold buildup, attach a binder clip to the sponge's end. Then, keeping the metal prongs extended, allow them to work as props to keep your sponge standing—and airing out much better.

CLEAN IN A CYCLE!

8 SURPRISING ITEMS TO PUT IN YOUR DISHWASHER

Your dishwasher can handle so much more than dishes! (We've already mentioned fridge magnets and oven fan covers.) Make cleaning easy and effective by letting this hardworking appliance do the job. For all of the items below, keep the cleaning separate—do not place dishes in the same load.

De-stink sports equipment. If you've got little linebackers, goalies, and sluggers in the family, you know how funky their equipment can get. Luckily, the dishwasher can work miracles on even the foulest sports gear. Toss kneepads, shin guards, and hockey pads into the top rack, squeeze some lemon juice into where you'd normally put the detergent, and run a normal wash cycle.

Throw in golf balls. In that same sports load, you can toss in golf balls. First place them in a small mesh laundry bag (the kind used for delicates) to contain them.

Shine rubber shoes. Add a bit of baking soda along with your usual dish detergent, and place flip-flops, Crocs, and even rubber boots in the machine for a hot wash. Be sure to remove lining inserts and laces beforehand—laces can go into the regular washing machine and then hang to air-dry.

Sanitize pet toys and collars. Toss them into the dishwasher once a month. Skip the detergent; high heat plus the water pressure will be enough to do the job and keep your pet safe. Place them on the top rack.

Get help with hubcaps and wheel covers. Add a cup of white vinegar to your normal detergent. Then turn the machine to the pots-and-pans wash cycle to get your wheels sparkling clean.

Freshen hair accessories. These items can accumulate dirt and oils left by sprays, gels, and other products as well as your natural oils and sweat. To keep clips, combs, brushes, bobby pins, barrettes, and ties in tip-top shape, wash them regularly in the dishwasher's silverware basket. Be sure to remove any hair first—a wide-tooth comb works well for this purpose.

Clean beauty and grooming tools. Makeup brushes perform best when they're clean. These will hold up best on a low-heat setting. Toss nail clippers into the silverware basket.

Scrub baseball caps. Wash a baseball cap on the top rack of your dishwasher, and remove while still wet. Then, place the cap over a bowl to regain its shape, and dry it away from direct sunlight.

A FRESH DISHWASHER AND DISPOSAL

Deep-Clean the Dishwasher

Give this super-powered cleaning machine its own well-deserved day at the spa: Pour 1 cup white vinegar into an open dishwasher-safe container (any cup will do). Place it in the top rack of the machine and start the hot cycle. For round two, pour baking soda along the bottom of the dishwasher and start a short wash cycle. The double-duty wash will leave it fresh, shiny, and ready for action!

Tackle Tough Stains

To get rid of mineral deposits and iron stains in your dishwasher, run it through an empty wash cycle using powdered lemonade mix instead of detergent. The citric acid in the mix will eliminate your problem.

Beat Bacteria

Step up your dishwasher's game with a little bacteria-fighting hydrogen peroxide. Combine 2 ounces peroxide with your usual detergent—not only will it kill germs, but also your dishes and glasses will sparkle like never before!

Kill the Disposal's Bad Breath

Odors coming from your garbage disposal? Pour about 4 ounces of a minty mouthwash down the drain. Rinse and repeat as needed.

NEED JUST A QUICK CLEAN?

Fill your dishwasher's soap dispenser with lemon juice or baking soda, and run it on the rinse cycle. It will be just the refresher it needs.

BATHROOM MAKEOVERS

A clean bathroom is a must, but you don't need to turn to harsh products with strong fumes to get the job done. You'll be surprised by how many smart solutions you have on hand.

SPARKLING SHOWERS AND TUBS

Another Use for Vodka

For a free mold and mildew fighter, try vodka! It works especially well on the caulking around your tub. Just spray on, leave for 10 minutes, and wipe clean.

Ceramic Shine

To keep ceramic tile sparkling, wipe it regularly with a sponge damped with water and a splash of vinegar. Or use rubbing alcohol—just pour it straight on, and mop or wipe until it dries. Avoid soapy or oily cleaners, and never use abrasives, which will dull the finish and make glazed tiles more prone to dirt.

Simply Clean Tiles

For an easy, natural tile cleaner, mix together ¼ cup baking soda and 1 gallon warm water. Scrub with a sponge or mop, then rinse. For tough stains, wait 10 to 15 before rinsing.

Never Clean a Soap Dish Again

Instead of letting your soap sit in standing water in your soap dish, put it in a mesh bag (like the kind you would get a bunch of onions in) and tie it to your faucet or an in-shower towel rod. The water will run right through.

Spick-and-Span Shower Doors

Need to clean those dirty glass shower doors? You can wipe them down with leftover white wine (if you haven't finished it off!). The wine contains the perfect amount of alcohol to battle soap scum and lime. Apply with a damp sponge, leave for 5 minutes, then rinse off. Finish by quickly buffing with a clean, dry cloth.

Stop Dirt in Its Tracks

If you've ever wondered what's the best way to clean your shower door's tracks, we've got it right here. First spray the inside of the tracks with your favorite bathroom cleaner and let it sit for a few minutes to loosen the dirt and mildew. Then wrap a rag or paper towel around the pointed end of a screwdriver and use it to scrub the inside of the tracks. Rinse with water, and marvel at the results!

Steam Out a Nasty Bathroom

If you've let the bathroom get so dirty that it now resembles a gas station restroom, turn on the hot water in the shower for 10 minutes with the door closed. The steam will loosen the buildup of mildew and mold. Then get in there and clean!

Beat Bathtub Ring

The grimy ring around the bathtub is one of the most dreaded and persistent enemies in the fight between clean and evil. That potent mixture of dead skin cells, body grease, oils, and soap has sticky superpowers on your tub's surface. Instead of worrying about the bathtub ring after it's already pasted onto the tub, take this easy step to prevent it in the first place: Simply drop a bit of baby oil into the water at bath time. It will keep dirt from clinging to the sides and send it down the drain instead.

Rub for Your Tub

No matter how hard we scrub, we never seem to get the corners of our tub clean. The solution: Soak cotton balls in your tub cleaner (or just some rubbing alcohol) and leave one in each corner of your tub overnight. By morning, they'll be as clear as day.

Get Rid of Copper Stains

Removing blue-green stains caused by high copper content in your water can be challenging, even with the help of bleach. Try treating your shower or tub with a paste of equal parts cream of tartar and baking soda. Rub into the stains, leave for half an hour, and rinse well with water. Repeat if necessary.

SHEAR SHOWER GENIUS

Cut the bottom of your shower curtain liner with pinking shears (scissors with a zigzag edge used in sewing). The uneven hem allows water to more easily slide off, making bottom-of-the-curtain mildew a thing of the past.

Blast Through Soap Scum

That combination of mildew, soap residue, mineral deposits, hard water, and oils from your skin is one of our most challenging household foes. To conquer the scum, use cooking spray or vegetable oil. The oil helps break up the slimy coating of soap scum. Spray the oil all over the grimy areas, let sit for 5 minutes, then wash off with soap and water and dry. Just be sure not to get it on the floor or tub, as it can be very slippery!

Sweep Your Tub Clean

This trick requires a clean broom, but it's worth the small investment to make a dreaded chore easier. Here's what to do: Squirt the tub cleaner of your choice (or just dishwashing liquid) onto the sides and bottom of your bathtub. Then use the broom to simply scrub and brush away all the dirt, grime, and soap scum—even in hard-to-reach places! Use a pitcher, bucket, or shower extension to rinse.

Cut Down on Cleaning

You've just spent what seemed like an entire day cleaning your bathrooms. Keep them that way by applying mineral oil all over shower doors and tiled surfaces. This will delay mineral buildup and cut down on future cleaning time.

NO MORE GROSS GROUT

Guard Against Mold and Mildew

Have a stash of broken white candles that you've been wondering what to do with? It may not be the romantic image you had in mind when you bought the candles, but rubbing the wax onto your bathroom grout will help protect it from growing mold, mildew, and other stains.

Get Glistening Again

If your bathtub grout is looking more gloomy-gray than like-new bright white, mildew and mold are the likely disgusting (and dangerous) culprits. To fight these bathroom foes, try this ultra-potent cleaning trick. Pour hydrogen peroxide into a spray bottle. Dry the tub area completely, then spray with the peroxide and let it get to work. Wait a bit, then hit the grimy grout with an old toothbrush. This will take a little elbow grease and maybe a few attempts, but your tub will be back to prime form in no time!

JEANNE SAYS

Store Soap Here

If you've just purchased a new bar of soap, take it out of its box or wrapper and place it in your linen closet. The exposure to the air will harden the soap slightly, which will help it last longer. Meanwhile, it will freshen your closet while it's waiting to be used in the shower.

Shave Time Off Cleaning

We're all for spending less time cleaning, especially when it comes to the "big jobs." So here's a great new way to get rid of grout stains in your shower and tub—shaving cream! After the last person of the day has showered, apply shaving foam to the grout, whose stains have already started to loosen thanks to the steamy shower. After that, it's as easy as leaving on until the first shower the next day! Repeat for a day or two and your grout stains will be gone. Best of all, shaving cream doesn't contain bleach, so it's less harsh on your grout!

Brighten White Grout

Moldy buildup on your grout can spoil an otherwise spotless space, and the mildew and dirt are notoriously hard to get rid of completely. But if you tried milder cleaners with no results, your best solution might be in your laundry room. Simply trace over your grout lines with a bleach pen intended for laundry stains and leave for 20 to 30 minutes. Wipe clean with a dampened towel, and *voilà*— your bathroom will be instantly brighter!

TOILET CLEANERS

Make Your Bowl Smile

For a cheap and easy way to clean your toilet, use mouthwash. Just as it cleans away germs in your mouth, it will do the same in your toilet bowl. Pour 1 capful into the bowl, leave for 10 to 15 minutes, and wipe clean with your toilet brush.

Reach Under the Rim

Clearing away dirt and deposits under the rim can be tricky. But a smart tool can help. Purchase a package of those cotton coils used for perms (you can find them at a beauty supply store). Soak the coil in a basin with vinegar. You might want to do this right in the shower to avoid drips. Then stuff the toilet's rim with the coil. Allow the vinegar to work on the stains overnight, then remove and throw away the coil, and flush the toilet to rinse.

Speedy Toilet-Cleaning Relief

To make this nasty chore easier on your gag reflex, drop two Alka-Seltzer tablets into the bowl twice a week. (A fizzy denture tablet works well too.) After 15 minutes, swipe around the bowl with a toilet brush. Your toilet will be spotless!

Take Soda to the Can

Cola contains phosphoric acid, which can lift stubborn stains such as rust. That makes it a good toilet cleaner: Pour the cola directly into the bowl, leave it for an hour, and then flush.

Lift with Lemonade Mix

Instant lemonade mixes like Kool-Aid contain citric acid, which works great to battle mineral deposits. Sprinkle the powder around your toilet bowl, let sit for a minute or two, then scrub with a toilet brush.

Trick to Dry a Toilet Brush

It's gross to stick that brush back into the holder wet. But what's the solution? Close the seat on top of the brush's handle so it's sandwiched and secure, with the brush in position to drip-dry over the toilet bowl. Come back later when it's dry and ready to stash away with much less ick. You can also add a little mouthwash to the holder to fight germs while the brush is in storage.

CLEAR THE FILM

Cleaning agents can leave a thin film on mirrors. Brighten them by rubbing with a cloth dampened with alcohol.

MIRROR MIRACLES

A Brilliant Solution

Turn to one of our Who Knew? Heroes: vinegar! Use old newspapers to wipe mirrors with a solution of equal parts of vinegar and water. You can add extra shine by rubbing with a clean dry-erase or blackboard eraser.

Cleaner in a Teacup

Here's an all-natural way to clean your mirror that will also give it a spotless shine: Wipe the mirror with a clean cloth dipped in strong, cool tea. Buff with a dry cloth and you're done!

Shine You Can Smell

For a unique cleaner for the mirrors around your home, use aerosol air freshener. It will bring your mirrors to a glossy shine and will have people wondering where that flowery scent is coming from.

Stop the Streaks

If you've ever noticed streaks in your bathroom mirror the day after you clean it, you'll love this tip. When cleaning the bathroom, always wear a dark shirt. Streaks are much easier to spot when the mirror is reflecting something dark.

ALL-AROUND SOLUTIONS

Get Rid of Caked-On Hair Spray

If your beauty routine includes spraying your entire 'do to keep it in place, you probably have a film of hair spray on your bathroom vanity and walls. Remove it easily with a solution of 2 parts water to 1 part liquid fabric softener. Wipe on with a damp cloth, then rub off with a clean one.

Handle Your Sink in a Swipe

Here's a quick and easy way to clean your bathroom sink: Just dampen a cotton rag or a bit of toilet paper with hydrogen peroxide and give it a few swipes!

Whiten Away Rust

Rust attacked spots on your white sink? Make a paste by mixing 1 teaspoon cream of tartar with ¼ cup baking soda. Add a little hydrogen peroxide to form a paste. Rub on the rust spot, let it sit for 30 minutes, and then clean with a damp sponge.

Shine with a Sheet

To clean chrome-plated fixtures in your bathroom instantly, always keep fabric softener sheets handy. Just wipe, and the chrome will sparkle. Rubbing alcohol and baby oil also do the trick.

Polish with Toothpaste

Believe it or not, toothpaste makes a great polish for your faucets. Just rub on and buff off with soft cloth. The white, non-gel variety works best.

Clear That Exhaust Fan

Don't struggle to stretch your vacuum's attachments! Blast out dust and dirt with a can of compressed air instead. Lay a large garbage bag or old sheet underneath the area, so cleanup is simple.

Hardest-Working Homemade Cleaner

A good all-purpose cleaner is essential to any well-run home. Keep this one on hand at all times (but out of reach of the kiddos). Start with 1 quart water and mix in ½ cup rubbing alcohol, a squirt of dishwashing liquid, and ¼ tablespoon ammonia (nonsudsy). Fill a spray bottle and you're ready to go.

Keep Chrome Clean

Keep your chrome fixtures looking cleaner longer by polishing them with car wax. The wax will create a barrier against water spots, soap scum, and other stains so that cleaning will be easier next time. Just rub the wax onto your fixtures like they are cars!

Be Your Own Mr. Clean

Do you love Mr. Clean Magic Erasers? These costly wonders are made from a material called melamine foam. Melamine foam has been used for decades as an insulator and sound-proofer, which means you can buy large sheets of it for less than the cost of a single box of "magic sponges." Buy some online (search for "melamine foam" on Amazon) or at a hardware store, then cut them down to size! They'll cost you less than 30¢ each.

BRUCE SAYS

All You Need: 2 Minutes!

Trying to clean up your bathroom fast, before guests arrive? Here's how to do it in 2 minutes or less: Apply a touch of baby shampoo to a wet sponge and wipe down your sink, fixtures, tiles, and bathtub. It cuts through oily residue, and it smells good, too.

ALL-OVER ODOR ELIMINATION

When company comes, their first impression of your home may be the scent that greets them when they open the door. Make the scent of home pleasant for you and your guests with these tips.

COMMON-SCENTS SECRETS

Take Vanilla Out of the Kitchen

When it's too cold to open the windows, freshen your whole house fast by placing a few drops of vanilla extract on your furnace's filter. Your house's heating system will do the rest of the work for you. To scent one particular area, take a small jar and place several cotton balls inside. Dab a few drops of vanilla extract onto the cotton balls. Before putting the cover on the jar, use a nail to puncture a few holes into it for your very own vanilla air freshener.

Freshen with Fruit

Make a great homemade air freshener you can use anywhere with an orange: Just cut it in half, remove the pulp, and fill with salt. It's easy, effective, and cheap!

Share Some Coffee

Here's an ingenious idea for an elegant-looking decoration that also smells wonderful! Place coffee beans in votive holders or small bowls, then add tea light candles. They'll cast a pretty glow and make your home smell like coffee. Try vanilla-scented tea lights if you love the smell of French vanilla coffee.

Soften the Air

After you pull your clothes out of the dryer, save the fabric softener sheet! Tape it to your heating or air-conditioning vent and it will freshen the whole room.

DIY Natural Room Freshener

In a spray bottle, combine 1 cup distilled water, 1 cup rubbing alcohol, and a few drops of your favorite essential oil (lemon, lavender, and peppermint would be good choices here). Shake well before each use. It's cheaper than Febreze and works just as well!

Neutralizing Spray

Here's an easy spray that will completely neutralize household odors for mere pennies. Fill a 2-cup spray bottle with water and add 2 tablespoons baking soda. Shake before spritzing. You can also add your favorite essential oil for a fresh scent!

Lift Odor from Carpets

Pet odors especially can lock into carpets. But you can freshen your rugs, which will improve the scent of the whole room, with a simple remedy. In a mason jar, combine 1½ cups baking soda and 10 drops of your favorite essential oil; mix to break up any clumps. With a nail, punch some holes in the tin lid before placing it on the jar. Then shake the scented powder on your carpet and let it go to work for about 30 minutes before vacuuming. It's a simple, natural way to shake out odors!

Erase Stink with Your Vacuum

To rid your house of pet, cooking, or other smells, put a handful of potpourri or a cotton ball soaked in vanilla or lavender oil into your vacuum cleaner bag. Now when you turn your vacuum on, you'll release a lovely scent into the air, making odors a thing of the past.

Stop Smoky Smells

Did you know that a bowl of sliced apples will remove the smell of cigarette smoke in an enclosed space? The next time you have a smoky party, cut up some apples and leave them around the house before you go to bed.

JEANNE SAYS

Refresh Potpourri

If your favorite potpourri loses its scent, it's easy to revive—with vodka. Yep, you read that right. Just pour a little vodka into a spray bottle and spritz the potpourri, mixing it up so each piece is saturated.

Zap Fabric Odors

To freshen up fabric and upholstery, you don't have to buy a bottle of chemical-filled commercial deodorizer. Just mix together 1 cup vodka and 1 cup water in a spray bottle, and spritz away. Then let it sit for several minutes until the mixture evaporates. The ethanol in vodka helps zap unpleasant odors, and once it evaporates it will be odorless!

FRESHEN THE KITCHEN

Eliminate Odors with Oatmeal

Out of baking soda and need to freshen up the fridge? Try oatmeal! An open container of dry oats in the fridge will neutralize odors just as well as baking soda does.

Freeze Out Funk

Add a shallow bowl of freshly ground coffee, uncovered, to your freezer. Leave for a few days and any funky freezer odors will disappear.

Citrus to the Rescue

Smelly dishwasher? Just squeeze the juice of a lemon or orange into the liquid detergent compartment and run the dishwasher while it's empty, setting it to "steam dry." The citric acid will neutralize the odors caused by food-particle buildup. Now you can invite your guests into the kitchen without embarrassment!

Vanquish Smells with Vinegar

If you've burned dinner, welcome to the club. To get rid of the smoky scent (or any other strong kitchen odor), simply boil 1 cup vinegar in 2 cups water. In 15 minutes, the smell should be gone. Or just dampen a cloth with a mixture of equal parts vinegar and water. Drape it over the cooking pot, taking care that the edges are far from the flame or intense heat.

WHO KNEW? READERS' FAVORITE

Clean Up from Cleaning Up

Cleaning before company arrives? To remove the fragrance of bleach (and other cleaning materials) from your hands, pour lemon juice over them and rinse. Bleach is alkaline and lemon is acidic. Together they cancel each other out and balance out the pH of your skin.

Make It Spicy

To easily deodorize your kitchen, put a cinnamon stick and other favorite spices (such as cloves or ginger) in a mug of water and microwave it for 2 minutes. Remove the mug and set it on the counter so that the aroma can fill the kitchen. This trick is great for winter, to create a warm, cozy atmosphere.

BEAT BATHROOM BEASTS

Make Your Own Poo-Pourri

Know those odor fighters designed to spray into the toilet before you . . . well, do what you need to do? You can save money by making your own! In a 1.5- or 2-ounce spray bottle, add 15 to 30 drops of your favorite scented essential oil or oil blend. Add witch hazel to fill, put on the lid, and shake before each use. The oils form a film on top of the toilet water, which traps odors.

Natural Lemon Spray

Avoid all the chemicals in store-bought air freshener sprays with this homemade version made with lemon juice. Lemons are natural deodorizers and will give your home a pleasing scent while keeping the air safe for children, pets, and plants. Combine 1 teaspoon baking soda with 2 teaspoons lemon juice in a spray bottle. Add 2 cups hot water and shake the mixture until the baking soda dissolves. Let cool. Spray as needed when things get stinky!

DIY Reed Diffuser

Love the look of a sophisticated reed diffuser in the bathroom but hate the cost? Make your own and save some serious cash with this easy recipe. Find a small vase or container you like and buy a packet of diffuser reeds—often sold as "refills." First, pour ¼ cup mineral oil into a small bowl. Next, add a couple of tablespoons of vodka and mix well. Then, add about 10 drops of your favorite essential oil and stir thoroughly. Finally, pour the mixture into the vase and put in 5 or 6 reeds. After a few hours, flip the reeds over, and flip them again every few days.

Just Gel It

Make your own gel air fresheners at home with this simple recipe: Boil 1 cup of water, then mix in 1 packet gelatin, 1 tablespoon salt, 15 drops of your favorite essential oil, and several drops of food coloring. Once the gelatin dissolves, pour into a glass cup or jar to set. Keep away from kids and pets, and enjoy the scent for a month or more!

Bring in the Charcoal

Hide a charcoal briquette somewhere in your bathroom to absorb foul odors. Charcoal absorbs moisture, which will also help stop mold and mildew buildup in the bathroom. Be sure to use briquettes that haven't been soaked in lighter fluid, and enjoy your newly odor-free bathroom!

TAME THE TRASH

Keep Kitchen Cans Clean

When cleaning your kitchen garbage can, sprinkle a little scouring powder at the bottom. This simple addition will soak up any liquids if your bag leaks, and will also repel mildew and keep your bin smelling fresh.

Deodorize Naturally

Wash and deodorize trash cans with a solution of 1 teaspoon lemon juice mixed with 1 quart water. Sprinkling baking soda into the base of every garbage bag will also help keep odors at bay.

FLOOR & CARPET CARE

Our floors take quite a beating! But you can bring them back to like-new condition and save yourself the cost of expensive pro cleaners or replacement.

GOOD FOR WOOD

Shine Floors Naturally

Keep your hardwood floors looking their best with black tea! Put 1 quart boiling water into a bucket with several bags of black tea. Allow the mixture to steep for 10 minutes, then remove the bags. Lightly dampen a cloth with the mixture and rub it on the floor. When it dries, wash the floor as usual to reveal an amazing shine.

Get DIY Clean and Gleam

There's no need to buy a special cleaner for your wood floors. Simply mix equal parts vegetable oil and white vinegar in a spray bottle, and apply. Shine with a clean cloth until the solution is gone.

Oil Away Scratches

The same everyday wood cleaner recommended above can be transformed to remove floor scratches by simply switching up the ingredient ratios. Go for a mixture of 1 part vinegar and 3 parts vegetable oil. Gently rub into the scratch; no need to rinse off.

STOP THE CREAK

Soothe creaky wood floors with baby powder! With a paintbrush or toothbrush, work a generous dusting into the cracks until the floor is no longer noisy.

Boost the Cleaning Power

Grimy wood floors calling for a slightly stronger cleaner? No need to turn to toxic cleaners! Here's another DIY solution: In a clean milk jug, add ¼ cup vinegar, ½ cup liquid castile soap, and 30 drops of a citrus essential oil (try lemon or orange). Secure the lid on the jug and shake to mix. When you're ready to mop, simply add 1 cup of the solution to 1 gallon of hot water in a bucket.

Nail Polish Spill? Try These Saves

If you've just dumped nail polish on your wood floor (or table), don't despair. You may be able to remove it with shaving cream. Using a soft cloth, rub shaving cream on the nail polish, leave for several minutes, and wipe off. Another option: Grab a bottle of hair spray and apply generously over your polish stain, leave for 20 seconds, and wipe away. Repeat as many times as it takes to abolish the polish! (Hair spray works wonderfully on clothes and carpets, too.) Just be sure to test an inconspicuous patch before you treat the material. Do not reach for the polish remover, which can leave even uglier stains on wood.

Paste Away Marks

Scuffs or even permanent marker marring your wood floors? Try rubbing on a dab of toothpaste with a damp cloth. Toothpaste is one of the mildest abrasives around to do the hard work without damage!

Wax Off!

Removing candle wax from your wood floor is easy: First soften the wax with a hair dryer, then wipe with a towel soaked in vinegar and water.

Iron Out Dents

Every household has its share of daily drops, which take a toll on wood floors. To undo the damage, dab a bit of water on the area and cover with a cloth. Then with your iron on its highest setting, gently move the iron over the cloth in a circular motion, keeping it moving until the cloth is dry. Add more water and repeat the process as needed. The dent should lift up like magic!

EASY CARPET CLEANING

Quick Carpet Cleanser

If you've got guests coming over and need to clean your dirty carpet fast, mix 1 cup ammonia with 1 quart water. Use a mop to rub this solution onto the carpet, and it'll help remove the grime. You might want to test this method beforehand on an unseen area, such as underneath a chair. Do not use this mixture on wool carpets.

Cast Out Carpet Stains

Notice a new spot on the carpet? Don't panic: There's no need to hire a professional carpet cleaner just yet. Simply combine equal amounts of hot water and ammonia and pour over the stain. Place a white towel on top, then iron over the covered spot. The cleaning powers of ammonia combined with the extreme heat will steam out the stain in no time!

Magic for Mud

The kids were out playing in the mud, and—lucky you—they forgot to take off their shoes before traipsing on the carpet. Don't worry; it's not impossible to get rid of those muddy footprints. First, let the area dry, and vacuum up as much dirt as you can. Then, using the cut side of a raw potato, rub the stains. The enzymes in the potato will help dissolve the dirt. Allow the area to dry again, and then blot with a wet rag.

Make This Easy Deodorizer

Want your home to smell fresh? Start from the bottom up—your carpets! In a glass container or canister, simply mix 16 ounces baking soda (your standard-sized box) with 20 drops of any essential oil scent you like. To put it to work for you, shake the mixture on your carpet, wait 30 minutes, and then vacuum.

Carpet Cleaning Work-Around

Finally getting around to shampooing your carpet? You don't have to remove all your furniture. Slip plastic bags over the feet of tables and chairs and secure them with rubber bands. You can clean underneath, then shift the furniture a bit and wash where its legs were. The plastic will keep the furniture from getting wet.

A COMB-OVER YOU'LL LOVE

Dent in your carpet where a piece of furniture used to be? Here's a simple solution: Just fluff it back up with the help of a fine-toothed comb. Or try a fork.

8 SOLUTIONS FOR THE TOUGHEST CARPET STAINS

Sudden spills can bring on panic. But you (and your rugs!) can rest easy when you know these ways to wage war on even the most stubborn substances that meet your floors.

Erase ink stains. Make a paste of cream of tartar and lemon juice, and dab at the stain. Let it sit for 5 minutes or so, then clean with a damp cloth.

Give the rub to gum. Turn to methyl salicylate, which you can find in analgesic heat rubs like Bengay. Put it on the gum, then apply heat with your hair dryer set on low. Press a plastic sandwich bag on the gum and it should pull away easily. Be sure to wash the area afterward.

Get help from egg. Another way to get gum out: Beat an egg white, rub or brush into the gum, let sit for up to half an hour, then wipe off. The egg white breaks down the gum and makes it easy to remove.

Clean up coffee. Blot the stain with a solution of 1 part vinegar and 1 part water, then let it sit for 10 minutes. Dab with a clean paper towel and repeat with the vinegar mixture until the stain is lifted.

Cut grease like lightning. Resist the urge to wipe! Instead, pour on a large amount of cornstarch and gently stir it with your finger. Let it sit for a day, then vacuum it up with the hose attachment. The stain should be mostly gone, but you can repeat the steps as needed. Then use the brush attachment to vacuum away the last remnants of cornstarch.

Remove red wine spills. Try applying a bit of shaving cream (after checking that the carpet is colorfast), and letting it sit for a minute before wiping away. Shaving cream will also work on grease stains.

Deodorize pet stains. Treat the spot with club soda, which contains odor-fighting minerals. Pour some on the area, leave it for 5 minutes, then blot and allow to dry.

Fix paint spills. Head to the kitchen to mix together 1 tablespoon vinegar, 1 tablespoon dishwashing liquid, and 1 quart warm water. Douse the area with this mixture and try rubbing it away. If that doesn't work, wait for the paint to dry and snip off the areas with paint—your carpet's "hair cut" will be less noticeable than a giant paint stain.

No-Slip Substitution

Don't spend money on a no-slip mat for underneath your rug. Grab a caulking gun (or a friend who has one) and apply acrylic-latex caulk to the underside. Apply the caulk in lines that run the width of the rug and are about 6 inches apart and it will never slip again!

Save Money on Shampoo

The commercial cleaners sold for carpet shampooers can be pricey. Did you know that you can make your own nontoxic solution with ingredients you likely have around the house already? Mix together ¾ cup hydrogen peroxide, ¼ cup white vinegar, 2 tablespoons dish soap, 2 tablespoons fabric softener, and 5 drops essential oil (any scent you like). Add the mixture to 1 gallon hot (not boiling) water. You'll never need store-bought again!

A Shocking Solution

If you can't escape static electricity on your carpet, here's an easy fix. Mix 3 cups water with ½ cup liquid fabric softener, put it in a spray bottle, and apply to your carpet. Not only will the static electricity disappear, but the mixture will serve as a carpet deodorizer, too.

Erase Vacuuming Mistakes

Cover the edges of your vacuum head with masking tape so you don't leave behind dark smudges from the metal when you inevitably bump baseboards and walls.

TIPS FOR TILE AND MORE

Simple DIY Floor Cleaner

You don't need a commercial cleaner for vinyl or ceramic floors. Simply use ½ cup white vinegar added to 1 gallon warm water.

Spill Some Club Soda

If you have some leftover club soda after a party, did you know that you can mop your tile floor with it? The carbonation in the club soda will help dissolve dirt. Just pour into a pail and use it as you would a mild soap solution.

Go Up Against Germs

Tea tree oil is another little-known cleaning heavyweight—a natural nontoxic antiseptic, it will kill any lingering germs, bacteria, and fungi on linoleum countertops and floors. Add a few drops of tea tree oil to hydrogen peroxide when attacking linoleum kitchen floors.

The Secret Is Baby Shampoo

The secret to shiny laminated floors is baby shampoo. Just mix a spoonful of baby shampoo with a gallon of warm water and mop as usual!

Another Secret from the Baby Aisle

A bit of baby oil can shine your vinyl floor. Add a couple of drops of baby oil to a cleaning solution of 1 cup vinegar and 1 gallon hot water. Apply with a damp mop, and done.

Toothpaste for Tile Touch-Ups

Scuffs and scratches on the linoleum tiles got you down? A simple solution is at your fingertips: Reach into the bathroom cabinet for some white toothpaste, and apply to the scuffs using a soft cloth. Wipe away with a clean, dampened cloth.

SIMPLE FLOOR SAVER

To keep your home clean during bad weather, place the side of a large cardboard box near your door so family members can pile their boots and gear on top of it.

Tough on Scuffs

More easy ways to remove scuff marks from a vinyl floor? Just use a pencil eraser or even a tennis ball to buff the scuff away.

Super-Stubborn Mark?

For stubborn scuffs on vinyl floors, try WD-40 lubricant or jojoba oil. Dab on a soft cloth and rub away marks. Follow with a vinegar-and-water cleaning solution to remove any extra oil.

Say Goodbye to Gum and Glue

To lift gum from your hard-surface floor, first freeze it with an ice cube. Then use an old plastic gift or credit card to nudge it off. The same method also works to remove glue or adhesive.

Clean a Spot with Cat Litter

If your car has leaked oil onto the floor of your garage, easily clean it up by applying some cat litter to the area (preferably the non-scoopable kind). Its super-absorbing properties will make the stain disappear in a day.

MAGIC MOPS AND BROOMS

Another Use for Baby Wipes

If you own a mop that requires replacement cloths, substitute baby wipes instead of buying packs of those pricey cloths. Rinse off the wipes before using, and they'll get your floors just as clean. Sturdy paper towels are another solid option for ready mops—just rip small holes in the towel so the cleaning liquid sprays through.

Minimize the Dust Trail

Fill a spray bottle with 3 parts water and 1 part liquid fabric softener, and spray your broom before sweeping. The spritz makes the broom bristles more pliable and helps them collect dirt more efficiently.

Upgrade Your Dustpan

Every time you break out the dustpan, there's that little line of grit that refuses to get swept up. Solve the problem with a bit of double-sided tape. Just tape along the edge, then replace the tape every few times you use the dustpan. The fine line of dust will stick to the tape, and you'll never do the "back up and sweep a little more" shuffle again!

Make a Broom Last Longer

There are all kinds of new products available to get your floor clean, but sometimes a simple straw broom is your best bet. Soak the broom's bristles in a bucket of warm salt water for half an hour and then let dry. This little step will prolong your broom's life.

JEANNE SAYS

Repurpose Wine Corks

Slice old corks into thin disks, then glue them to the feet of your heavy furniture. It's a great way to protect your floors, and makes moving the furniture a bit easier when it's time to clean or rearrange for a change.

LAUNDRY LIFESAVERS

The average household does 416 loads of laundry per year. But you can make those loads take less time, money, and hassle with smart strategies!

MONEY-SAVING SECRETS

DIY Detergent Pods

Pods help anyone in your household use just the right amount of detergent to get the job done, which saves money, your clothes, and oversudsing your machine. How to make your own: Grate a bar of pure soap (such as Ivory) until you have ½ cup grated soap. (Or you can purchase soap flakes.) In a glass mixing bowl, combine the grated soap, 1½ cups washing soda, and 2 tablespoons Epsom salts. Mix in 3 tablespoons 3 percent hydrogen peroxide and ¼ cup vinegar. Scoop the mixture by heaping tablespoons onto a baking sheet lined with wax or parchment paper. You should have enough for 24. Give the piles-to-become-pods a little spritz of water to set, and allow to dry (about 12 hours). Once dry, store the pods in an airtight container. Like your laundry to smell fresh? You can add 10 to 20 drops of your favorite essential oil when you add the peroxide and vinegar.

Less-Expensive Laundry Gizmo

The secret, low-cost alternative to one of those balls that releases fabric softener during your laundry load? A clean kitchen sponge dampened with liquid fabric softener. Just put it in the washing machine once it's filled with water at the beginning of the load. It will slowly release the softener just like the plastic balls do!

Make a Bleach Pen

Bleach pens can be a godsend for laundry stains. But for a fraction of the price of the ones you find at the store, you can make a do-it-yourself version. All you need are a few ingredients you probably already have on hand. Grab a small squeeze bottle with a narrow dispensing hole at the top, cornstarch, and bleach. In a small pan, combine ½ cup cold water and 1 tablespoon cornstarch. Stir until the cornstarch is combined. Bring the mixture to a boil so that the cornstarch thickens, then remove from the heat. Once it's cool, stir in 2 to 3 tablespoons bleach, and transfer the mixture to the squeeze bottle. To use, squeeze a little bit out on your worst stains and spots!

Make Fabric Softener Go Farther

Save on laundry products while you're saving the environment. Instead of buying fabric softener sheets, pick up a bottle of the liquid kind. Mix a solution of 1 part fabric softener and 1 part water, and put it into a spray bottle. For every laundry load, spritz onto a cloth and toss it in the dryer. A small amount (several sprays) will go a long way.

Cut Your Sheet to Cut Costs

Cut your dryer sheets in half (or in quarters). You won't be able to tell the difference in your clothes, but your wallet will.

A Dryer-Sheet Alternative

Out of dryer sheets on laundry day? No problem! Try using aluminum foil instead: Just crumple a strip of foil into a ball and toss it in the dryer with your laundry. Not only does it eliminate static, but the foil is also reusable for future loads.

AMAZING STAIN REMOVERS

Armpits: Don't Sweat Stains!

You don't have to throw out shirts with embarrassing yellow stains under the arms. Turn to vinegar! Soak underarm areas in vinegar for 10 minutes before washing, and the yellow stain (and the smell) will be gone by the rinse cycle. If this strategy doesn't work, you can also try rubbing a paste of baking soda and vinegar into the stains before washing the usual way. If the stain remains, repeat with rubbing alcohol, then launder.

FABRIC SOFTENER SWAP TO SAVE

Skip buying liquid fabric softener! Use the same proportions of white vinegar—it's much cheaper and just as effective.

Berries: Your Best Bet

Super-juicy berries are the best . . . until the juice hits your shirt! If you got berries on your clothes, soak the stain overnight in equal parts milk and white vinegar, then launder as usual.

Blood: Stains Meat Their Match

Don't give up on that bloodstain! Head to the kitchen for unseasoned meat tenderizer—it's amazing for treating even set-in bloodstains. Make a paste by mixing a tablespoon or two (more for larger stains) in a bowl with enough water to make a thick paste. Spread it on the stain and allow it to sit for an hour before rinsing with cold water and washing in the laundry. Your garment should come back to stain-free life!

Chocolate: Iron Away

Who knew your iron could help you remove chocolate stains? First, allow the stain to dry and gently scrape off what you can with a spoon. Then cover the stain with a paper towel, turn your iron on low, and iron over the paper towel. The chocolate will melt and transfer to the towel, and you can then launder your item as usual.

Coffee: Try Toothpaste

Get rid of coffee stains on clothes with toothpaste! Massage a little of the white (not gel) variety into the stains, then rinse and repeat if needed. Give it a try on wine as well.

Dirt: Shampoo It Out

If your kid has been playing in the mud again, rub shampoo over the soiled area and let sit for 5 minutes before washing. For tougher stains that need a little extra cleaning oomph, try presoaking in a mixture of 1 part warm water, 1 part ammonia, and 1 part laundry detergent.

Gasoline: Fight Oil with Oil

Got a grease monkey? Removing gasoline stains from clothing can be tricky. The most effective way we know of is to apply baby oil to the stain, then launder as usual. Because gasoline is an oil-based product, it takes another oil to pull out the stain and smell.

Grass: Use Paste Power

You can get rid of grass stains with toothpaste. Scrub it into the fabric with a toothbrush before washing. The white (non-gel) kind works best. Stubborn stain? Soak the item in a mixture of 1 part hydrogen peroxide to 1 part water for 30 minutes, then rinse and launder as usual. Hydrogen peroxide is a gentle bleaching agent that helps loosen stains in fabric.

Gum: Sticky Solutions

Rub gum stuck on clothes with ice until the gum hardens, then carefully remove it with a dull knife before laundering. If that doesn't work, you can also try placing a piece of wax paper on the affected area, then ironing the wax paper. The gum should transfer from the cloth to the paper. Still stuck? Warm a cup of vinegar in the microwave. Dip a toothbrush in the vinegar and brush the gum until it comes out.

Ink: Make It Invisible

Trying to get an ink stain out? Spray ultra-stiffening hair spray on the spot, then launder as usual. Hair spray will usually remove the stain. A more offbeat but equally effective idea: Rub the area with a cut, raw onion, letting the onion juice soak in. Let sit for 2 to 3 hours before laundering.

Juice: Call a Truce

To get juice stains off of your clothes, just use boiling water. Hold the garment over the tub and very carefully pour boiling water through the fabric where the stain is. It will remove the stain and you won't have to put your clothes through the hot cycle in the washing machine.

Ketchup: Get the Red Out

Remove excess ketchup (or any other tomato product) with a dull knife, then dab with a damp, warm sponge. Apply a bit of shaving cream to the stain, and let it dry before laundering as usual.

Lipstick: Lift It Off

Lipstick can be one of hardest stains to remove—if you don't use the right stain remover. The grease in lipstick makes it hard to get out of the fibers in fabric, but rubbing alcohol breaks through it nicely. Just apply rubbing alcohol with a damp cloth to the stain, and dab until the lipstick starts to come off, applying more alcohol as necessary. Then launder as usual.

JEANNE SAYS

Baby Your Clothes
Forget expensive stain pretreatments for your laundry—just reach for the baby shampoo! Use as you would a pretreater and it will work just as well for a fraction of the cost.

7 GO-TO GREASE STAIN REMOVERS

Grease just might be our biggest laundry nemesis. It's a tough stain to remove, but you can be tougher with these laundry techniques—all using things you probably already have around the house.

Try this on-the-go solution. Need a legit reason to stash some pink packets in your purse or pocket? Applying artificial sweetener to a grease stain will absorb the oil, making washing easier once you get home.

Take a tip from your dishes. You rely on dishwashing liquid to remove grease from your dishes and pans. Why not try it on your clothes as well? For grease stains, rub a little dishwashing liquid into the fabric (a toothbrush makes this easy work!), then launder as usual.

Crack open a can for grease monkeys. Have a car enthusiast in your household? Add a can of cola to the washing machine, along with detergent, to remove oil and grease stains from their clothes.

Use powder power. First, blot with a paper towel to remove any excess grease, then cover the area with talcum or baking powder. Don't be shy here—you really want to coat the stains. The powder will absorb the grease. Wait a few hours before shaking it off and washing as usual. You can follow this tip with the dishwashing liquid treatment we shared in the second tip for double-duty stain fighting.

Grab the shampoo. Remove stains from cooking oil (olive, vegetable, canola, etc.) with regular shampoo. Just make sure it doesn't have a built-in conditioner.

Save the day with cornstarch. Grease stains on delicates (including silk and suede) can set off your panic button. But you can stay calm and confident with cornstarch. Just lay the garment flat, cover the stain with this simple ingredient, and set it aside it to do its absorbing work for 24 hours. Dump the spent cornstarch into the trash, and repeat with fresh cornstarch if there is still stain-removing work to do.

Vinegar to the rescue! Another way to attack a grease stain on suede: Simply dip an old toothbrush in white vinegar and gently brush over the grease.

Marker: Sanitize Stains

Yes, there's even hope for permanent marker stains, and it comes in the form of something you already have in your bag: hand sanitizer. Squirt it around the edges of the stain and then work it in; let it sit for 5 minutes before laundering. Just make sure you test the material for colorfastness, as hand sanitizer can discolor it.

Mustard: Make It History

Hydrogen peroxide is effective at getting rid of mustard stains. After making sure the fabric is colorfast, apply a small amount to the stain and let set for several minutes before laundering.

Nail Polish: Run to the Remover

Unfortunately, the only thing that can remove nail polish is nail-polish remover. If the fabric can withstand this harsh chemical, work it in from the inside of the fabric by pressing it gently with a paper towel.

Paint: Act Fast

Treat a paint stain while it is still wet; latex, acrylic, and water-based paints cannot be removed once dried. While the paint is wet, rinse in warm water to flush the paint out, then launder. Oil-based paints can be removed with a solvent; your best bet will be to use one recommended on the paint can. Got dried paint on your clothes? Unfortunately, it's often impossible to remove. Before you give up completely, however, try saturating the stain in 1 part ammonia and 1 part turpentine, then washing as usual.

Rust: Try Lemon Aid

Remove rust stains by wetting the spots with lemon juice, then sprinkling with salt. Let the fabric stand in direct sunlight for 30 to 45 minutes.

Scorch Marks: Cut an Onion

If you have a scorch mark on fabric, your quest to remove it begins in the kitchen. Cut the end off of an onion and grate about a fourth of it into a bowl. Rub the stain with the grated onion, blotting it with as much of the onion juice as you can. Let it sit for 8 to 10 minutes, and if necessary, reapply the onion juice. Once the stain is gone, launder as usual.

BRUCE SAYS

Say Goodbye to Ring Around the Collar

Dress shirts getting stained around the collar? Swipe the back of your neck with an alcohol-based astringent before you get dressed in the morning. The alcohol will prevent your sweat from leaving a stain.

Tea: Treat to Lemon

Tea and lemon are best friends—even in the laundry room. Rub a tea stain with equal parts lemon juice and water. Just make sure the mixture only gets on the stain, using a cotton swab or eyedropper if necessary.

Wine: Win the Stain War

Blot a wine stain with a mixture of 1 part dishwashing liquid and 2 parts hydrogen peroxide. If this doesn't work, apply a paste made from water and cream of tartar and let it sit. One more tactic especially for tough reds: Douse the stain with vodka—the red pigment in wine is dissolvable in higher-proof alcohol.

DEALING WITH DELICATES

A New Spin for Delicates

Do you tend to avoid clothes with "hand wash only" tags when shopping? Here's a game-changer: Wash delicates with ease in a salad spinner. Fill the spinner halfway with cool water. Add a delicate detergent, put on the spinner's lid, and agitate. Next come your delicate clothing items. Soak them for a few minutes, then again place the lid on and give them a few spins. Remove the lid, lift out the inner strainer with the clothing, then pour out the dirty water. Replace with fresh water and spin your clothing again to rinse. Remove the rinse water, and spin one more time to help dry.

Dry Delicates Faster

Hand-washed clothes can stay damp for hours, but trying to wring them out can leave huge wrinkles. Solve this problem with a rolling pin and two towels. Fold the towels and place your wet garment between them. Then roll the rolling pin over the towels several times to get out the water five times faster than air-drying alone.

Sweater Cryogenics

If your favorite cashmere or angora sweater is looking a little worn, put it in a plastic bag and place it in the freezer for half an hour. The cold causes the fibers to expand, making your sweater look new again! Who knew there was such a thing as sweater cryogenics?

Easy Laundry Rack

If you have a toddler or pet safety gate that you no longer need, give it a new life in the laundry room! Lean it against the side of your washer or the wall and it makes the perfect drying rack for delicates and sweaters.

Makeshift Clothesline

If you need to air-dry delicates but don't have a clothesline, hang a long strand of dental floss and place lightweight clothes on it to dry. Floss is sturdy enough to hold underwear, bathing suits, and even tank tops and light T-shirts.

Clean Suede with Stale Bread

The stiff yet gentle texture gives just enough pressure to rub off stains. To contain any crumbs, hover over a trash can as you rub the slice of bread over the spot in a circular motion.

File This Suede Stain Remover

The emery board that you normally use on your nails also can remove small stains from suede. Gently rub the file across the stain a few times to remove the mess.

Erase Pen Marks on Suede

Take a brand-new pencil eraser and rub it in the direction of the grain. The little particles that come off the eraser will get under the surface to remove the stain.

Give Your Leather Some Love

To remove dirt and make your leather goods shine, try cleaning them with egg whites. First beat together an egg white or two, and then rub it into the leather with a soft cloth. (Test first on an inconspicuous area.) Wipe the egg white away and buff with a clean cloth. You won't believe the results!

Best Bet for Lace

Even if you hand-wash it, lace can get easily tangled and torn when cleaning. To prevent this from happening, safety-pin the lace to a sheet or smaller cloth. Wash gently as usual, then unpin when dry.

Gentle Whitening

If you own a lace tablecloth or doily that is beginning to turn yellow, let it soak in a bucket of sour milk for a few hours to return it to its former brilliant white. Just be sure to hand-wash it in mild detergent afterward!

Winning at Linen

If you have white linen that has turned yellow over time, bring it back to its original brightness with baking soda and salt. Just bring a gallon of water to a boil, remove from the heat, stir in ¼ cup each baking soda and salt, and add the fabric. Let it soak for at least 1 hour, then rinse and launder as usual.

Magic for More Than Muffins

Cleaning real or fake fur can be tricky. To get rid of dirt and dinge, treat your fur accents to a little dance with cornmeal. Add the items you want to refresh to a sealable bag with a cup or two of cornmeal, then simply seal and shake. Brush off any leftover cornmeal in the fur when you remove the item from the bag. Trash the bag and remaining cornmeal.

Fix a Shrunken Sweater

If you've accidentally shrunk a sweater in the dryer, there may still be hope. Let it sit in a bucket of water with a generous amount of hair conditioner mixed in. The chemicals in the conditioner can untangle the fibers in your sweater, making them expand back to their original condition. If that doesn't work, it's time to cut up the sweater and make a cozy pillow!

SMART TIMESAVERS

Laundry Room Organizer

Repurpose an old ice cube tray as an organizational tool for your laundry room. It's perfect for keeping buttons that have fallen off your clothes and other small items you may find in your pockets.

THROW IN THE TOWEL

Add a big, dry towel to the clothes dryer when drying jeans and other bulky items. It will cut the drying time significantly.

Help Others Help You

Planning to tag-team laundry? Write any special instructions ("My red sweater doesn't go in the dryer!") right on the washer or dryer with a dry-erase marker.

Sock Sorting the Easy Way

Use a mesh lingerie bag or pillowcase to launder each family member's socks separately. It's an easy way to keep them together so they'll be easier to sort later.

Sock Mystery Solved!

Tired of losing socks every time you do the laundry? To prevent a washing-machine disappearing act, secure sock pairs together with binder clips.

Laundry Slam Dunk

Turn a drawstring laundry bag into an ingenious hanging hamper with an old embroidery hoop. Just slip the opening of the bag through the hoop and it will stay open while you use the drawstrings to hang it from an over-the-door hook or in the closet. Bonus: It looks enough like a basketball hoop that it makes it a tiny bit easier to get our boys to straighten up their rooms!

Ace Clothes Drying

To help your clothing dry faster and reduce static cling naturally, toss a few (clean!) tennis balls into your dryer with your laundry. Tumble dry on low heat. The balls will bounce around, keeping clothes from sticking together.

Quick Lint Disposal

Here's a clever way to get rid of dryer lint: Stick an empty tissue box near your washer and dryer, and simply tuck the lint inside after scooping it out of the dryer. The plastic-lined opening of the tissue box keeps lint from flying away! When the box is full, trash it, use the lint as compost, or toss it into a campfire—lint is a first-rate fire starter.

Freeze Your Jeans

It sounds crazy, but you can save laundry time *and* wear and tear on your jeans by cutting down on the number of times you put them through the washing machine—freeze them instead! The freezer eliminates many of the same odors and bacteria as the washing machine does, so you can cut down on how often you wash your jeans, thus making the fabric last longer. Just shake off any debris, fold the jeans neatly, and put them in a plastic bag. Place in the freezer overnight, and in the morning, they'll be ready to wear. (Of course, you'll need to toss them into the washer for a periodic freshening up, and to remove stains.)

HOME IMPROVEMENT

Hiring professionals to complete painting and repairs can be expensive and stressful. Try these ideas to make DIY household projects manageable and successful.

ALL-AROUND HINTS

Corral Small Parts

An ice cube tray comes in handy when dismantling furniture, electronics, and other items with small parts. As you work, place the parts in the tray's slots to keep them safe, organized, and out of the way.

Save Time with Tape

Where *is* the start of that roll of tape? Attach a paper clip or plastic clip from a bread bag to the end to get started much more easily with duct, painter's, or masking tape.

Make a Handy Holder

If you use tape a lot in your household, make the search for rolls a thing of the past. Attach a toilet paper holder or a wall-mounted paper towel holder to the wall, and you have a great storage spot for tape rolls. Don't want to put out even a little money? Raid your closet for a hanger with a pants bar where the rolls can hang.

Lost Your Ruler?

If you need to measure something and don't have a ruler, grab a dollar bill instead. A dollar is exactly 6¼ inches long.

Safely Remove a Busted Light Bulb

To remove a broken light bulb from the socket, first turn off the electricity or unplug the lamp, and then push half of a raw potato or small apple into the broken bulb's base. Turn it to unscrew the base.

PAINTING POINTERS

Make Cleanup Easier

Slather on some hand moisturizer or cooking oil before painting. It will prevent paint from seeping into your skin, making cleanup easier.

Revive Old Paintbrushes

Brushes can take a beating after just one painting project. But who can afford to buy new ones all the time? No need! Bring old brushes back to new life by soaking them in hot vinegar for 30 minutes. Afterward, wash them in hot, soapy water, brushing off paint as needed, then rinse and let dry before you put them to work again.

When You Want Split Ends

When it does come time to make a purchase, we'll usually tell you to go for the cheapest option. But with paintbrushes, quality matters. To make sure you're buying a high-quality brush, look at the tips of the bristles. If they have a lot of split ends, they'll spread paint more evenly.

Protect While Painting

Before you begin that big painting project, cover doorknobs, drawer pulls, and any other small object you're worried about catching spills with aluminum foil. The foil easily molds to any shape and comes off when you're done. Another easy protector: petroleum jelly—it will keep paint from adhering to surfaces such as door hinges. Just paint some on with a small paintbrush, then wipe away any stray paint easily!

Old Tape? Don't Toss It!

If you haven't used your painter's tape in a while, it may have dried out a bit. You'll know if it begins to peel instead of rolling freely. The solution: Soften the adhesive in the microwave for 10 seconds.

BETTER THAN A DROP CLOTH

The side of a large cardboard box will fit more tightly against your baseboards and slide more easily to your next needed location for painting protection.

Speed a Paint Job

Quicken your interior paint jobs by mixing a quart of semigloss latex paint into a gallon of flat latex paint. The finish won't shine any more than it would with straight flat paint, but the paint will glide on and cover much more easily.

Make the Smell More Pleasant

Many paints have moved to low-odor formulas, but they're still not *no*-odor. To make your time painting more pleasant to your nose, add 1 tablespoon vanilla extract per gallon of paint and stir to mix well. It won't affect the performance of the paint in any way!

Create a Painting Carryall

The cardboard that bottled water cases come in makes a great organizing tray to hold a can of paint and all of your other painting supplies. The makeshift tray will also keep areas underneath free from paint drips. And you can simply toss when you're done.

Keep It Smooth

Did you know that enamel paint spreads more smoothly when it's warm? To get it up to a higher temperature, place it in a warm bath before you use it.

Foil Those Fuzzies

Affordable paint roller refills may cost you in another way: little fuzzies that can come off in your first few rolls. Take a second to run a lint roller over your new roller before you start—you'll be glad you did when you're not trying to pull little pieces off your wall.

Strain Out Lumpy Paint

Lumpy paint? No problem. Use the lid of the paint can as a stencil to cut a circle out of a screen that will fit perfectly inside the container. Push it down with a stir stick as far as it will go so the lumps will be out of the way at the bottom.

Add Marbles for Easy Mixing

Before stirring paint, place a few marbles in the can. They'll stir the paint so well you should just be able to give it a good shake to remix before its next use.

Create a Rim Drain

Make several holes in the bottom of the rim of your paint can with a small nail and hammer. Now the paint will drip back into the can rather than running down the side.

Tap, Don't Wipe

When painting, instead of wiping the brush on the can or bucket, tap it on either side. That will allow the excess paint to fall away while leaving the brush evenly coated.

Rubber Band Trick

Another way to make painting neater is to wrap a wide rubber band around your open paint can from top to bottom. The rubber band will run right over the opening of the can, and you can use it to wipe the excess paint from your brush instead of using the edge of the can. Then when you're done painting, wrap the band around the paint can the other way, at the exact level that the paint is at inside. That way, you won't have to open the can to see how much paint is left.

Save on Pan Liners

There's no need to spend your money on disposable liners for your roller pan. It's just as easy to line the pan with aluminum foil—and a lot cheaper, too.

Guard Against Drips

To catch drips while you paint, try this makeshift drip cup: Cut a tennis ball in half and slice a thin slot in the bottom bowl of one half. Then slide your brush handle through the slot so the bristles stick out of the open side. A small paper plate or cup works, too.

Skip Steps

When painting steps, paint every other one as you work your way down. When those are dry, go back and paint the rest. This way, you'll still be able to use the stairs while your paint is drying (as long as you're careful!).

Use Heat to Remove Painter's Tape

To be extra careful when removing painter's tape, run a hair dryer over it for a few seconds before pulling it away. It will help loosen the glue so that your new paint job doesn't chip.

SPICE UP YOUR OLD WHITE

To tint white paint, add food coloring or a packet of powdered drink mix in the color you'd like directly to the paint and mix well.

An Edgy Solution

When painting a windowsill, forget the edging tape: It's expensive, and it can pull up the paint you already have on the sill. So instead, use strips of newspaper. Dampen them and wring out as much excess moisture as you can without ruining the paper, then use them in lieu of tape. They'll stick as long as they're wet, but won't pull up any paint when you're done.

Get Paint Off Glass

Accidentally paint the edge of your windowpane while doing some remodeling? Hot vinegar can be used to remove paint from glass. Just microwave a cup of vinegar until hot (1 to 2 minutes), then dip a cloth in it and wipe the offending paint away. Next time, just apply lip balm with a cotton swab along the glass next to the trim, and you can wipe away any paint that gets on that portion—it won't stick to the balm.

Make It Stick to Tricky Places

Paint can be stubborn on certain materials. To help paint stick to metal surfaces, rub a soft cloth dampened with vinegar over the surface to be painted. Vinegar also comes to the rescue when painting concrete; apply a coat of white vinegar to the surface before the paint. To help paint stick to plastic surfaces, rub the surface with a fabric-softener sheet before applying.

Bring Out the White-Out

If you still keep old-fashioned correction fluid around, use it as touch-up paint for white appliances, like your refrigerator. If your fridge has a ding but it's not white, try buying a small amount of touch-up paint from a car detailer.

Clear the Odor

To absorb that overwhelming paint odor, place a bowl of onion slices in the room. The old standby bowl of vinegar works as well.

WHO KNEW?
READERS' FAVORITE

A Twist on Storing Paint

Want to know an easy way to store leftover paint in the can? First, place a piece of plastic wrap under the paint can's lid, make certain the lid is on tight, and turn the can over. The paint is exposed to less oxygen this way and will last much, much longer.

EXPERT WALLS

9 INSIDER HINTS FOR HANGING

Now that you've painted your walls with ease and know-how, you're ready to add the finishing touches. Make it clean and simple with these tips.

DIY sticky tack. A terrific way to hang posters in your kid's room without leaving holes or stains is with white, non-gel toothpaste. Just put a generous drop on the back of each corner, press to the wall, and watch it stick.

Make easy entry. Coat a nail or screw with a light layer of lip balm to ease it into the wall before hanging a picture or shelf.

Protect walls with tape. Before you hammer a nail into your wall, cover the spot with clear tape to prevent the paint from chipping.

Free up frames. Protect your walls from the dings and scratches picture frames can leave behind. Whenever you hang a frame, grab two packing peanuts and slice them in half lengthwise. Then glue them to the corners on the back of the frame. The Styrofoam will protect your walls from scratches every time you adjust the frame (or bump into it on your way down the hallway).

Find a stud. Looking for a stud and don't have a stud finder? Use an electric razor instead. Most razors will change slightly in tone when going over a stud in the wall.

Get picture perfect. Hanging a picture frame or other item? Here's a clever trick to make sure you drill the holes exactly where you want them. Photocopy the back of the item you want to hang, and tape it on the wall. Then just drill into the paper wherever the hook or hole is on the photocopy!

Hang pictures easily. To get rid of the guesswork that comes with putting a nail in the wall to hang a picture, try this easy trick. Place a dab of toothpaste on the hook or string (whatever will touch the nail) on the back of the frame. Then hold the frame up to the wall, position it carefully, and press it against the wall. The toothpaste will leave a mark that you can hammer a nail through, then wipe away.

Don't worry about wire. To hang lightweight artwork that's not in a heavy frame, there's no need to buy picture wire. Dental floss will do the trick.

Fix a tilted frame. When a picture refuses to hang straight, wrap clear tape around the center of the wire to prevent it from slipping sideways.

No Cleaning Necessary (for Now)

If you want to avoid cleaning a paint roller or brush (for now), wrap it in foil or a plastic bag and place it in the refrigerator. Or if you're wearing gloves while painting, just hold the brush by the bristles and pull the glove off inside out and over the brush; tie closed at the handle. The covering will keep paint tools moist and usable for a few days so you can finish where you left off later.

Best Brush Cleaner

The fastest way to clean a paintbrush is in a solution of ½ cup liquid fabric softener and 1 gallon warm water. Stick the brush in a bucket of this solution, then swirl it vigorously for 20 seconds.

JEANNE SAYS

Lighter Paint Saves Money

If you're trying to decide between deep or baby blue for your walls, you should know that lighter colors of paint will help you use less energy. They reflect the light and heat in a room better than darker hues.

Soften Stiff Bristles

Even if you clean your paintbrush thoroughly, the bristles are likely to be stiff after they dry. Keep them soft and flexible with ordinary hair conditioner. Just add a tablespoon of conditioner to a pint of warm water, and after cleaning the brush, dip it in the solution for a few minutes.

Keep Your Paint Fresh for Longer

Leftover paint? Prevent it from drying up with this crafty maneuver: Blow up a balloon until it's about the size of the remaining space in the can. Then put it inside the can and close the lid. This will reduce the amount of air in the can, thus prolonging the paint's freshness.

REPAIRS MADE EASY

Chill Out to Smooth Caulk

Caulking can be tricky business—it's hard to get perfect lines, but if you try smoothing them down with your finger, it sticks, creating an even uglier sight. When you need to smooth down caulk, try using an ice cube instead. The cold will help set the line, and it won't stick to the ice.

Easy Wall Repair

You're moving out of an apartment and need to fill in the holes in the wall caused by nails. Just grab a bar of white soap and rub across the hole until the soap fills it. It's not a permanent fix, but it will make the walls look clean until they can be repainted.

Putty from Your Kitchen

To make a putty for quick patches, combine 1 tablespoon salt with 1 tablespoon cornstarch. Mix them together with just enough water to make a paste. Apply while still wet.

Fill a Hole

Before spackling small holes in your wall caused by nails, first cut a cotton swab in half and insert in the hole, stick end first. Then spackle as you normally would. The swab will completely fill the hole and ensure you won't have to go back for a second pass.

Crack Goes the Ceiling

If you have a crack in your ceiling, but you can't afford to replaster yet, you can fake it with some readily available household supplies. Take 1 part white glue and 1 part baking soda, mix them together thoroughly, and then dab the paste onto the crack using your fingers, a cotton swab, or a similar object. If your ceiling isn't white, you can try mixing different food colorings into the paste until you get exactly the right shade.

Perfect Wood Patch

If you need to repair a hole in a piece of wood, add a small amount of instant coffee to the spackle, or to a thick paste made from laundry starch and warm water. The coffee tints the paste to camouflage the patched-up spot.

Fix a Loose Knob

Are the knobs to your drawers and cabinets coming loose? To fix the problem forever, remove the knob and coat the end of the screw with nail polish (use clear if you're a bit messy), then screw the knob back on before the polish dries.

STEADY THAT LADDER

Here's another use for old coffee cans: If you're using a ladder on soft ground, set each of the legs inside an empty can. The cans will help keep the ladder steady as you climb it.

WHO KNEW?

READERS' FAVORITE

Temporary Screen Fix

Don't leave a hole in your screen door just because you don't have the right tools to fix it. Instead, use rubber cement to affix a small piece of pantyhose around the area. It's easy to remove but will keep flying things out of your house in the meantime.

Stop a Door from Sticking

Your bedroom door has expanded, and realigning the hinges didn't work. Instead of taking the entire door down to sand the bottom, try this trick instead. Place enough newspaper under the door until it can just barely close on top of it. Then tape a piece of coarse sandpaper on top of the newspaper, and open and close the door until it glides over the floor without a noise.

Silence Squeaky Hinges

Who needs WD-40 when you have vegetable oil? Simply rub it on squeaky hinges with a cloth, letting the oil run down the sides of each hinge. Or just spritz nonstick cooking spray right on them. Rubbing on a bit of hair conditioner can also tame squeaks.

Stuck Drawer?

If you've been fussing with a drawer that won't open, it's probably expanded due to humidity. Dry it out with a hair dryer set on low heat, or place a work lamp with a 60-watt bulb inside and leave for 30 minutes. The drawer will contract, and you'll be able to move it easily again.

Make a Drain Volcano

Most people know the old science fair project of mixing vinegar and baking soda to cause a chemical reaction worthy of a model volcano, but not many know that this powerful combination is also a great drain cleaner. Baking soda and vinegar break down fatty acids from grease, food, and soap buildup into simpler substances that can be more easily flushed down the drain. Here's how to do it: Pour 2 ounces baking soda and 5 ounces vinegar into your drain. Cover with a towel or dishrag while the solution fizzes. Wait 5 to 10 minutes, then flush the drain with very hot water. Repeat until your drain is clear.

Surprising Declogger

Kitchen sink clogged up? Skip the commercial drain cleaners, which contain harsh chemicals that can destroy your pipes. Instead, slip three Alka-Seltzer tablets down the drain and turn on the hot water for just a few seconds. The tablets will fizz up and get to work on the clog. After 15 minutes, run the water again and the drain should be clog-free.

Protect Your Fingers

How many times have you hit your fingers while hammering in a nail? Next time you're hanging pictures, put the nail between the tines of a fork or a thick plastic comb before hammering. Your fingers will thank you, and your kids won't have to hear you swear.

Loosen a Rusty Nut or Bolt

To remove that pesky rusted nut or bolt, put a few drops of ammonia or hydrogen peroxide on it, and wait 30 minutes. If you're out of both, try a little bit of cola instead.

Simple Rust Removal

To remove rust from nuts, bolts, screws, nails, or hinges, place them in a container and cover with vinegar. Seal the container, shake it, and let it stand overnight. Dry the objects to prevent corrosion. Dip screws or anything else that needs de-rusting into cola and leave for several minutes. Then scrub away the black substance that remains and repeat if necessary.

Hold Screws More Tightly

If you're using a flat-head screwdriver and are having trouble keeping the screw on the end, try rubbing each side of the screwdriver with a piece of chalk. The chalk will increase the friction and give you a tighter hold.

Stripped Screw Saver

Help a stripped screw get some traction with a rubber band. Just place the rubber band over the top of the screw and press it into the groove with your screwdriver. Its grippy, flexible surface will fill in where the screw has been stripped and help the screwdriver turn it.

CLEVER STORAGE

Save your credit card from those trendy container stores! You can corral clutter in some of the trickiest areas with simple tools to keep your home organized.

ORGANIZED ANYWHERE

Shoe-In for All-Purpose Storage

Those over-the-door hanging shoe organizers aren't *just* for shoes! Keep them all over the house—their handy cubicles will hold anything, from accessories to toiletries to spices to remote controls and video games. In kids' rooms, the easy-to-reach pockets make toy cleanup a cinch for little ones.

A Basket Beyond the Kitchen

A hanging fruit basket can hold much more than simply fruit. Try using it in the bathroom to keep washcloths and bath toys handy—you can hang it right over the shower bar. Or put it to work storing old rags in the garage or basement. Fill it with balls of yarn in an area where you knit or crochet. Have it hold hats and gloves near an entryway.

An Attractive Solution

Magnetic knife strips are a handy kitchen idea, but they can stretch a lot farther. They'll grab keys near the door, matchbox cars in the playroom, nail clippers and bobby pins in the bathroom, and all kinds of tools in the garage.

Make Removable Labels

Not ready to commit to sticky labels? Just use plastic wrap! You can write right on the wrap secured around the item.

Gift Wrap Contained

Have an old hamper you no longer need? Repurpose it as a place to store gift wrap! Rolls of wrapping paper fit perfectly inside, and you can hang door hooks over the edges for rolls of ribbon and gift bags.

Create a Dropbox

There's one place in every household that gathers clutter like a magnet: gloves, scarves, and hats in the wintertime; sunglasses, sunscreen, and baseball caps in the summertime; house keys, gum, and cell phones all the time. Maybe it's your entryway or the bottom of your stairs? Make a plan to contain it all! Place a small galvanized tub or other container in that hot spot, and divide it into compartments using strips of cardboard or foam core. Each family member gets a compartment to stick go-to on-the-go items inside.

Soap Dish Key Holder

Tired of searching for your house keys every time you're getting ready to step out the door? Install a mountable soap dish on a wall near the entryway, and stick your keys in the dish when you enter the house. Problem solved!

JEANNE SAYS

Try a Toolbox Carryall

Toolboxes are perfect for all-around storage—we use one to store craft supplies, another for extra school supplies, and yet another to actually hold our tools. As a bonus, they're super-portable, so you can use them for any activity that requires you to travel.

CLEAN CLOSETS AND DRAWERS

Shoebox Dividers

Keep your bureau drawers under control by using shoeboxes to separate underwear, socks, tights, and whatever else gets quickly stuffed in there when company comes.

Make Your Own Closet

You're in desperate need of more closet space, but you can't afford a fancy armoire. Here's what to do: Find two old doors at a yard sale or scrap yard. Paint or decorate them how you please, then hinge them together. Place the doors in the corner of the room at a 90-degree angle to each other so they make a box. Use one as the door of your new closet and the other to hang shelves and attach a bar to. (Drill into the wall or bolt to the floor for more stability—just don't tell your landlord we put you up to it!) Suspend a clothesline between them for additional hanging. It may not be fancy, but we bet your friends will be impressed!

File Your Flip-Flops

Flip-flops and sandals store neatly inside a letter organizer or magazine holder. They'll stay nice and tight out of the way—yet easy to grab when you need them.

More Storage Space for Kids

If a child's room has a super-small closet or no closet at all, there's a fun and simple solution. Simply loft the bed, then attach a clothing bar to the wall in the space beneath. Enclose the area with curtains to create a mini-dressing room (according to Mom and Dad) or a secret hiding place (so says your kid).

Better Boot Storage

Boots never seem to fit quite right into any organizer designed to hold shoes. But you can keep your boots from just hanging out on the floor by clipping them with pant hangers! You can prevent the hangers from leaving marks on your boots by placing a thick piece of fabric or newspaper around the top of the boots before hanging them.

When the Wine Runs Out . . .

Got an empty wine carton left over from your last boozy gathering? Instead of tossing it, reuse the box for shoe storage—place all of your out-of-season footwear into the sizable container and tuck it away until next year.

Frame Your Shoes

Have space under a bed or dresser for storage? Stash shoes there with easy access. Simply organize them on top of the glass of a large old picture frame to create a shoe tray that slides easily.

Wrangle with Rings

If you have one of those plastic rings used to hold together six-packs of soda, save it for your closet! It's perfect for organizing scarves, belts, ties, or anything else you can thread through the plastic holes. Just hang one ring from the six-pack plastic over the top of a hanger and use the other five to neatly hang your accessories.

From Shower to Closet

Got new curtain rings? Use the old ones to organize your coat closet. Hammer a nail into the wall, then hang a couple of curtain rings on it. They can be used to grasp items like gloves and hats, or you can run a scarf through one.

PILLOWCASE IT

Never misplace part of a sheet set. After washing and folding the pieces, put the whole set right inside one of the pillowcases—it's a convenient way to make sure everything stays in one place.

A Hanging Accessory Board

If your accessories live in a jumbled pile on a shelf or inside a drawer, consider this crafty hanging setup. Mount a pegboard to a wall inside your closet, then hang accessories like belts, scarves, purses, hats, and gloves on the pegs. They'll be organized and out of sight!

No-Cost, No-Slip Hangers

Tired of finding clothes on the floor, but not so keen on the prospect of buying all new padded hangers? Make your own: All you need is a hot glue gun! Dab glue onto the shoulders or bottom rung of the hangers. Let it dry, then remove any flyaways around the spots of glue. Once the hangers are completely cool, hang your clothes and *voilà!* Shirts, dresses, and pants stay put. Another option: Wrap pipe cleaners around instead of gluing at those spots—the friction will help clothing stay put.

Closet Space Saver

The next time you get a free keychain, use it to create more space in your closet! Just run the head of a hanger through the key ring, then hang another hanger from it. This trick creates a cascading hanger system. S-hooks and even soda can tabs can accomplish the same purpose if you don't have keychains already on hand.

Screen Your Jewelry

Necklaces getting in a tangle or hidden away where you forget about them? Create a clever display to keep jewelry organized and front and center. All you need is a large picture frame (no glass), a few nails and a hammer, and either chicken wire or window screening. Attach the wire or screen across the back of the frame, then use the grid to hang necklaces and bracelets and even dangle earrings. Simple storage that looks gorgeous, too!

Home Base for Bracelets

A smart way to showcase bracelets: Use a wall-mounted paper towel holder! Install it near your dressing area or vanity and your colorful bangles will be organized and easy to find.

Tuck into a Tray

Store small jewelry in the compartments of an ice cube tray and stick it inside a drawer. If you need multiple trays, stack one on top of the other to save space. Egg cartons work, too.

DIY Earring Organizer

Love to repurpose old stuff? Turn an unneeded box grater into a holder for your earrings! The larger holes are perfect for hanging earrings by their hooks, while the smaller holes can hold studs with detachable backs. You'll have a much better way of viewing and selecting your jewelry if it's hanging together in an orderly fashion. Plus, the DIY shabby-chic effect is totally charming.

NO MORE CRAFT CLUTTER

Scrapbook Storage in Unexpected Places

Love scrapbooking? Store the large pages and any other artwork in a cardboard pizza box! Not only are they sturdy and easy to stack and store, but they're also free—the best perk of all. Ask a nearby pizza joint if they can spare any extras.

Portable Beads

An old CD jewel case lined with double-sided tape can be used to store beads for arts and crafts projects. This storage option is especially handy if you like to bring supplies with you to beading groups or on vacation.

Chip Cans for Crafting

Need somewhere to store knitting needles, paintbrushes, utility knives, and other tall craft tools? Reuse empty Pringles cans! They should be just the right height, and you can cover your tools with the plastic lid when not in use.

Beautiful Boxes for Beads and Ribbons

Here's a handy storage solution for ribbons, beads, and other decorative sewing or gift-wrapping supplies: old wooden tea boxes! Their individual compartments are perfect for sorting beads, buttons, pins, and ribbons. And, maybe best of all, they're stylish and elegant.

WHO KNEW?
READERS' FAVORITE

Sophisticated Art Supply Display

Is your marker and crayon collection overrunning your house? Try this clever storage solution: Turn an unused wine rack into a home for your art supplies! Place clear plastic drinking glasses into each bottle holder, then fill with markers, crayons, pens, pencils, and paintbrushes. Organize by color for a fun decorative touch! A wine rack can also hold yarn in a fun display.

Fresh Ribbon Dispenser

The containers for Tic Tacs and other breath mints are perfect for storing tiny items like pins, needles, buttons, and beads. And they're even better for smoothly dispensing small spools of ribbon. Remove the lid to insert the ribbon roll, then pull the tail of the ribbon out through the lid's opening before you close it. You can even glue multiple containers side by side to create a long dispenser with compartments. Bonus: Your craft time will smell minty fresh!

Keep Yarn Untangled

Here's a crafty idea for keeping your yarn in order: Place one ball of yarn inside a baby wipes container and pull the loose end through the opening at the top. No tangles, no knots!

Make the Most of a Muffin Tin

Repurpose an old muffin tin for craft supply storage. Glue some magnets to the bottom of plastic containers (such as yogurt cups or clear plastic cups) and stick them in the hollows of the muffin tin to create a stable base. Then fill each cup with markers, pencils, paintbrushes, or whatever else you're looking to organize. You'll easily be able to take the cups out, but they'll snap right back into place.

CREATE A DISPLAY TRAY

A home air vent placed facing up can transform into a tray to hold and showcase crafting supplies like stamps, embroidery floss, or small tiles for mosaics.

Another Solution from the Kitchen

Wrangle washi tape into fun and organized storage by hanging the rolls on the spools of a mug tree. Mug trees pop up at yard sales all the time, if you don't have one handy.

Just What the Craft Doctor Ordered

Pillboxes with daily compartments are super-handy for small crafting accents—buttons, jewelry pieces, and more. They're easy to stack and take on the go, too!

Portable Ribbon Holder

Try this creative idea for storing all your spools of colorful ribbon: Pile them onto a standing paper towel holder! Find one with a handle at the top so it's easy to carry around and take with you from room to room. Or reuse a pants hanger as a ribbon organizer. Place the spools along the rungs of the hanger, then hang in a closet for efficient off-the-floor storage.

Pull Together Fabric

Craft with fabric for quilting or sewing? Keep your selections under control and easy to sort by tucking them into hanging magazine racks with slots or housing them on hangers with multiple pants bars. So much better than piles to pull from!

HARDWORKING GARAGE

Bucket It

Hanging buckets or paint cans make easy, inexpensive organizers. Use them to store all your car washing supplies together and tucked away. A hanging bucket also works well to hold a hose and sprinkler: Wrap the hose around the outside and tuck the sprinkler inside.

Window of Opportunity

A plastic window-box planter is another great on-the-wall organizer. Try gathering your garden or auto tools inside to store and carry where you need them. The planters are also the perfect size to hold cans of spray paint.

Gardening Command Center

Those hanging vinyl shoe holders can store much more than shoes! Repurpose an old shoe organizer as a storage center for your gardening tools. Just tack it up on the wall in your garage and you'll have organized storage for all of your small items.

BRUCE SAYS

Keep That Carton

Don't discard that partitioned wine or liquor carton! Instead, cut the top off and keep it in the garage for storage of sporting goods, fishing poles, and other sundries.

Organization in the Bag

Make your neighbors think you're a golfer! Look for a cheap golf bag at a yard sale. It's perfect to stash in a garage corner as an organizer. Stuff long-handled tools like rakes and shovels in the main compartment. Pockets can house work gloves and smaller hand tools.

Repurpose an Old Filing Cabinet

Storing more files electronically these days? Move your old filing cabinet to the garage. Turned on its side with the drawers removed, it can hold anything with a long handle. Use the drawers to hang or stack in another place.

Hold More Than Concrete

Cardboard concrete-forming tubes are inexpensive buys from home improvement stores (under $10) that can store tools, sports equipment, and more. Secure each tube to a garage stud with a plumbing strap.

Tame Extension Cords

If your extension cords live in a huge tangled web in the garage, fret not—they *can* be tamed. Once you've untangled the web and wrangled your cords into individual bundles, wrap each one with a stretch of unused copper wire. Simply twist the ends of the wire together to keep your bundled cord intact. Then stack them on a shelf or hang from a sturdy hook.

Clever Pot Solution

You can also keep cords straight by storing them in upside-down plant pots. Stash them underneath the pots in the garage and, when you need one, pull the plug end through the hole in the pot's bottom.

Have a Ton of Hardware?

Cut the tops off laundry detergent containers and use them to organize your nails, screws, bolts, and other hardware. Label the handle side and stash them on a shelf so it's easy to grab what you need. Old jars secured to the underside of shelves by their lids can also contain all those little bits.

Bungees for Balls

Shelving systems work great for garages. But what do you do when it comes to sports balls that want to roll to their escape? If totes or laundry baskets won't fit, simply string a few bungee cords vertically across the open area, from the bottom shelf to the top shelf, to create a ball cage. No more rolling!

SIMPLE SORTER

Don't throw those old egg cartons away! Use them to sort small items like nails, screws, and nuts.

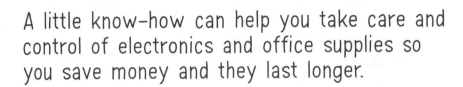

OFFICE & ELECTRONIC SMARTS

A little know-how can help you take care and control of electronics and office supplies so you save money and they last longer.

CLEAN AND PROTECT DEVICES

Simple DIY Screen Cleaner

Sure, you can buy a commercial screen cleaner or cleaning wipes for $10 to $15, or you can make your own at home for pennies. All you need: white vinegar, distilled water, and a spray bottle. In the bottle, mix equal parts vinegar and distilled water. When you're ready to clean your phone, TV, or computer screen, first give it a dusting with a microfiber cloth. Then shake your spray bottle, spritz a little of the mixture on a clean cloth, and bring your screens back to clean!

Dust with Coffee Filters

When your electronic screens need a dusting, use a coffee filter. It'll grab dust without scratching or leaving smudges.

Clean Up Your Keys

The easiest way to clean the gunk and dust between your computer keys is with transparent tape. Slide a 2-inch strip between the rows of your keyboard and the adhesive will pick up any debris. More dust than dirt? Try a small, soft paintbrush. Really tiny crumbs need loosening? Look for cleaning tools in your bathroom. You can brush with a child's toothbrush, and swipe a strand of dental floss between the keys in your computer keyboard. So many simple yet effective options!

Need More Key-Cleaning Power?

Simply dip a cotton swab or cotton ball in hydrogen peroxide or rubbing alcohol and run it between your computer keys. Another surprising solution that works: mouthwash! The same cleaning solutions work for your mouse.

Get Help from Squeeze Bottles

Save plastic squeeze bottles, but not for condiment storage—they make the perfect substitute for bottles of compressed air, which are used to clean out computer keyboards, electronics, and other tiny crevices. This works especially well with squeeze bottles with small spouts, such as lemon juice dispensers. Wash them well and let them dry completely before using. To really power up this repurposed tool, try using just the top of a squeeze bottle as an extension on your wet/dry vacuum to clean nooks on electronic devices.

Refresh Remotes

Remote controls gather a lot of grime and germs from so much handling. Squeeze a drop of hand sanitizer onto a paper towel or cloth to clean remotes. To reach between buttons, use a cotton swab.

Revive a Wet Cell Phone

Here's a trick that could save you hundreds: If your cell phone gets wet, first take the battery out and dry it with a paper towel. Then bury the phone and the battery in a bowl of uncooked rice for 24 hours. The rice will draw the rest of the water out of the phone, and hopefully it will be back in business again.

Carry This Smart Gadget-Saver

Here's a great tip using those silica gel packets that seem to come in everything. Keep your gadgets dry while traveling by tossing a few packets into a zip-tight plastic bag. If any of your techie devices accidentally get wet, stick them in the bag and allow the silica gel to work its moisture-fighting magic. Drop your cell phone or camera in water? First remove the battery, then place the device in the bag and leave it overnight. With any luck, your electronics will be in working order come morning. Just be aware that silica gel is harmful if swallowed, so keep away from kids and pets!

JEANNE SAYS

Don't Track Food on Your Trackpad

If you make a habit of eating while working on your laptop, easily protect your trackpad from sticky and greasy fingers: Cover it temporarily with a Post-it note! You'll still be able to use the trackpad through the piece of paper, and it will stay much cleaner.

Protect Your Phone at the Beach

When you spend a day at the beach, sand can get everywhere—including the nooks of your phone. But you can protect it from scratches, humidity, and other sneaky damage while still keeping it ready for use. Simply wrap it in a layer of plastic wrap. When you're worried about water, you'll need to take the extra step of sliding it into a zip-tight plastic bag. Don't keep it wrapped up for too long or it can overheat.

Keep Cords and Wires in Shape

Thanks to gravity and lots of use, electrical cords tend to fray and break off around their plug ends. Not only is this irritating, but the exposed wiring can also be dangerous. To prevent damaged and frayed cords, try this nifty trick: Dismantle a pen and grab the tiny metal spring inside. Wrap the spring around the end of your cord— this will hold it straight and keep the wire's covering from bending and breaking.

MAKE IT LAST, MAKE IT BETTER

Make That Cartridge Last

You're trying to print out a document but you just ran out of ink! This solution will save you a trip to the store: Take out the ink cartridge, then blow hot air on it with a hair dryer. Once it's warm, put it back in the printer. The heat loosens the ink that is stuck to the side of the cartridge, often giving you enough to finish the job.

Save 30 Percent Ink

Need to print out some helpful but not super-important pages (such as a grocery, chore, or to-do list)? You can conserve ink by changing the font color to gray rather than using the heavier black ink. Also, choose a thinner font. Thinner fonts like Times and Century Gothic will use up to 30 percent less ink than a font like Arial.

Revive a Dead Pen

There's no need to throw away a pen that's stopped writing long before it should have. Just get rid of the dried-up ink clogging its point by boiling water, then removing the water from the heat and dipping the pen tip into it for 10 seconds.

Pump Up the Volume

Have trouble hearing music through your mobile device's speakers? Just place it in a bowl (preferably an aluminum or stainless steel one). The sides of the bowl will amplify the sound.

LONG LIVE THE STAMP PAD
Always store stamp pads upside down. This will ensure that they don't dry out in between uses.

Grab More Battery Juice

You've just realized your cell phone's battery is about to die, but you're at work and don't have your charger. Get a little more talk time by detaching the battery and placing it in your workplace's freezer, then allowing it to come back up to room temperature before you use it. The cold will keep your battery from losing a single drop of juice before you use it. This cool trick works for batteries in your remote, your child's toy, or any small appliance as well.

Power from a Pencil Eraser

If your electronic gadget starts to lose its juice, try this trick before you buy new batteries: Take the batteries out and rub their contacts with a pencil eraser. This will remove small particles of dust and dirt and keep the energy flowing. Put the batteries back in and you'll be surprised at how much longer they last!

Lengthen Laptop Battery Power

If you clean the battery contacts on your laptop and cordless phone, the charge will last longer. Use the tip of a cotton swab dipped in rubbing alcohol to clean the connection points.

Fuzzy TV Signal?

If the picture on your television isn't crystal clear, it may be caused by interference. Place a sheet of aluminum foil between any electronics (like your DVD player, cable box, or TV) that are stacked on top of each other and those wavy lines will be history.

GET ORGANIZED

Declutter Your Desk

If your desk seems cluttered, make sure you're taking advantage of the space above it. Install a shelf or two for books and folders, and attach some hooks on their undersides. Hang small baskets on the hooks and now you have a hiding place for paper clips, pens, glue sticks, tape, and the hundred other things that are taking up room in your office space.

BRUCE SAYS

Take It to the TV

One of the most frustrating things you can do is to forget your phone chargers when you're traveling. From experience, we've learned that most televisions in hotels have small USB ports on their sides. If you have a USB cord but no wall socket, you can often just plug your phone into the TV and watch it charge. Problem solved!

7 TIPS TO CORRAL THOSE CABLES AND CORDS

Your office and other spaces around your home that house electronics don't need to turn into cord jungles! Here's how to bring order.

Bind them in place. You can use supplies you already have on hand in your office to keep cords organized on your desk. Clasp several binder clips to the side of your desk, then slide the cord through the arms and let the plug be held by the narrower end. Instant organization!

Raid the playroom. Lego figurines can give you a hand (literally!) when it comes to holding cords and cables in their places. Look for those little figures that have open hands, and run your cords right through them for fun organization. You can assign roles to remember which character holds which cord—for instance, the firefighter has your computer power cord under control.

Reuse a clever label. Here's a handy way to mark your electrical cords so you know your printer cord from your lamp cord from your clock cord: Use bread bag tags! Write the appliance name (or first initial) on the tag and clip it to the appropriate cord.

Use an upward spiral. When it comes time to part with school notebooks, save the spirals. They work great to collect stray cords and wires. Attach the spiral horizontally to a strip of wood using a hot-glue gun. Place it behind your computer and thread your cables through the rings. They'll stay separate and it will keep them from falling to the floor when not in use.

Make organization more than a pipe dream. Go to the home improvement store and buy some foam pipe insulation. (It usually has a lengthwise slit in it; if not, cut one yourself.) Run the cords through the tube and allow them to come up through the slit wherever needed. Stick the whole thing behind your desk or nightstand, and you won't have to look at unsightly cords again!

Take control with a roll. Don't throw away empty toilet paper or paper towel rolls! Use them to store the millions of cords running behind your entertainment center or desk. The rolls keep the cords untangled, and if you also write which appliances the cords belong to on the rolls, you just might be the most organized person in your neighborhood.

Finally, a use for old telephone cords! Keep cables tidy by running them through an old coiled telephone cord. The coils will keep everything together neatly.

Retrofit a Drawer for Hanging Files

No filing cabinet? No problem! You can turn almost any drawer into one suitable for hanging files. All you need is a drawer that is deep enough to hold hanging files, and two tension rods that are usually used for curtains—the smallest and thinnest you can find. Insert the rods in the drawer parallel to each other and perpendicular to the front and back of the drawer. They should be wide enough apart that the folders' hooks will be able to hang from them (adjust as necessary). Now you're ready to start filing away!

Create a Recycled Inbox

Cereal boxes make great stacking trays for your home office. Carefully cut off the top and back of the box, and you have an inbox waiting to happen. If you don't like the Total, Wheaties, and Chex look, spray the boxes with silver spray paint and let dry before using.

Tame Office Supplies

Does your junk drawer look like a postapocalyptic nightmare? You can keep the mayhem at bay by storing small items—paper clips, staples, tacks, loose change—in an unused ice cube tray. Larger items like pens? Try a cutlery tray in your home office! You'll save yourself the time and stress of having to shuffle around the drawer to find things.

Put Old Cassette Cases to Work

Looking for a container to store earbuds where they won't get tangled? Coil the cord and then place it inside an old cassette case. Your headphones will be safe, and your friends can admire the *Flashdance* soundtrack decoration on the outside. So retro!

INGENIOUS DESK SPACE-SAVER
An old CD rack can be a great organizing tool for your desk. Turn it on its side and it's the perfect place for sorting mail or other small pieces of paper!

WHO KNEW?

READERS' FAVORITE

Charger Home Base

You don't need to buy a charging station for all your electronic devices, even if you want your power strip to remain out of sight. Instead, put the strip in a shoebox and cut a hole in the back for the power cord to reach the outlet. In the lid of the shoebox, cut smaller holes for your charger wires. Plug the chargers in, thread their wires through the holes, and close the lid, taping it on if you'd like.

Safely Store Important Papers

The school year is over, and you need a place to store the kids' artwork and diplomas. Try rolling them tightly in paper towel tubes so they won't crease, then label the outside so you know what's what. The tubes can also be used to store marriage certificates and other important documents.

CLEAR OUT SPACE, GET CASH

Cash for Your Gadgets

Now you can keep your old electronics out of the landfill and possibly get some cash in exchange! Services such as Gazelle.com recycle or refurbish your old castoffs and send you a check in return. Just fill out the easy forms on their websites. They'll make you an offer, and if you accept, they'll send you a box with postage to send your gizmo to them. They take cameras, cell phones, MP3 players, game consoles, personal computers, and more.

Get Money for Ink Cartridges

Got empty cartridges for a printer, copier, or fax machine? TonerBuyer.com will buy them from you, and even pay the shipping! Fill out their online form to find out how much your cartridges are worth, then mail them with their prepaid shipping label and wait for your check in the mail. You can also bring empty printer cartridges into Staples stores, which will give you a $2 credit (up to 10 a month).

Sell Your Books

If you live near a used bookstore, stop in and ask if they buy books. Especially if you have a lot of best sellers, you can get a few dollars or store credit for books. For books so old they'd be considered antiques, you can fetch hundreds! Check out ABEbooks.com, one of the largest marketplaces for used books online, to search for your book and see if it's worth a lot of money. You can also sell any book straight from the site!

CDs and DVDs to Sell?

Sell CDs, DVDs, and video games online at SecondSpin.com and CashforCDs.com. Look up the name of the product you're selling on one of these sites and they'll tell you what they pay and even let you print out free shipping labels!

NATURAL PEST CONTROL

Before you call on expensive exterminators or toxic chemicals, try these natural, DIY routes to rid your house, garden, and outdoor gathering spaces of pesky insects and critters.

KEEP BUGGERS OUT OF THE HOUSE

Pest Control Never Smelled So Sweet

To keep ants, mice, and silverfish at bay, put a few drops of peppermint oil on cotton balls, and place them wherever you've been noticing the pests. You can also smear a bit of mint toothpaste nearby. The peppermint smells good to you, but its odor is repellent to these creatures, and they'll find somewhere else to hang out.

Screen Out Stinkbugs

Keep pesky stinkbugs out of your house by starting with your window screens. Vigorously wipe down the outside of screens with fabric softener sheets, and it will help repel the critters. The fabric softener sticks to the screen, and the stinkbugs hate the smell and the feel.

Spicy Ant Barricade

The arrival of spring brings warm temperatures, breezy open windows, and—unfortunately—an influx of ants. To keep them from sneaking into your home, ditch the store-bought chemicals and reach for the spice rack instead! Mix red pepper flakes and sage, then sprinkle around the pantry and along windowsills and doorways to keep ants from marching in.

Repel Ants with Cucumber

Although it's a salad-bar favorite for us, cucumber is a repellent for ants. Find the spots where they're entering your home, and place some cucumber peels there to make them turn in their tracks.

Make Your Own Ant Traps

Get rid of carpenter ants naturally with this formula: Mix one packet dry yeast with ½ cup molasses and ½ cup sugar, and spread on a piece of cardboard. Leave this sticky trap wherever you see the ants; they will come in droves to the sweet smell. Unfortunately for them, they'll also get stuck. Wait until your molasses mixture is covered with the creepy pests, then throw it away.

Bees Begone

If bees have found their way into your home, don't panic. Fill a wide-mouthed jar with 1 cup sugar and 1½ cups water. They will be attracted to the sugar and will drown in the water trying to get to it.

Spray to Lead Bugs Astray

If flies or bees have invaded your home and you want to get them away from you fast, squirt a little hair spray into the air. They hate the stuff and will go elsewhere.

Kill Roaches the Green Way

Nothing is more revolting than roaches, except perhaps the chemicals we use to kill them. Try using this natural pesticide: Make a mixture of equal parts cornstarch and plaster of Paris, and sprinkle it in the cracks where roaches appear. They'll eat the mixture, it will expand in their stomachs, and they'll die.

Drink to No More Roaches!

Another great method for eliminating cockroaches is to fill a large bowl with cheap wine, then place it under the sink or wherever you see the revolting little bugs. The pests drink the wine, get drunk, and drown.

Relocate Ladybugs

Ladybugs are good bugs in the garden, but if they're swarming your home they can be unwelcome guests! Use a little lemon to get rid of them. Wipe down walls where you see them with a lemon-scented furniture polish and they'll find somewhere else to hang out. You can mix lemon essential oil with water instead.

POWDER POWER!

Ants taking over your house? Try this easy remedy: Sprinkle talcum powder along your baseboards and doorways. It dehydrates their bodies, eventually killing them.

Give Flies the Brush-Off

If you prefer not to use chemicals to get rid of flies, and you're not the most accurate fly swatter, invest in a strong fan. Scientists say that flies' wings are unable to operate in a breeze above 9 mph, so open the windows, turn the fan to full power, and they'll soon buzz off. This is also a great trick for an outdoor party—just aim a few fans at the center of the action instead of spraying down your yard with awful-smelling repellent.

Orange Peel Answer

You may find the smell of oranges delicious, but flies don't! The next time you eat an orange, save the rind and leave it out on your countertop. It will keep flies away.

Fruit Fly Fix

Have a fruit fly problem? Add a couple of drops of dishwashing liquid to a bowl of apple cider vinegar and leave it where you see flies. The smell of the vinegar attracts the flies, while the dish soap breaks the surface tension of the vinegar and causes the little nuisances to drown.

Banish Moths with Basil

There's nothing quite like the sweet smell of basil, right? Not for moths! They hate the smell. Keep some around the house and moths will be a thing of the past.

Make a Moth Trap

Trap moths by mixing 1 part molasses with 2 parts white vinegar and placing the mixture in a bright yellow container. The moths will be attracted to the color and the smell, then drown inside.

Clove's the Way

Silverfish are disgusting, down to each and every one of their legs. An effective, natural way to repel them is with whole cloves. Just sprinkle a few in drawers and other areas where you see them.

Chip Away a Spider Problem

Do you have a spider problem in your home? Just put some cedar chips into a few pairs of old pantyhose and hang them around your house. The spiders will be gone in no time.

A Citrus Solution

Did you know that spiders "taste" food through sensors on the tips of their spidey legs? And one thing they don't like the taste of is citrus. If you're looking to keep spiders out of your home, try making this nontoxic repellent. In a spray bottle, mix together 2 cups water with 1½ teaspoons citrus essential oil (such as orange, lemon, or lime). Spray wherever you see spiders or their webs, and the citrus flavor will send them packing!

Nuts for Spiders

Keep your home spider-free by putting out whole walnuts in their shell in corners, on windowsills, or wherever you tend to see the creepy crawlers. Walnut shells contain a chemical toxic to spiders, and they'll stay away.

Get Rid of Bedbugs

Bedbugs usually require a professional exterminator, but if you have a mild infestation, you might be able to tackle them on your own. With a powerful canister vacuum, vacuum all carpets, baseboards, switch plates, wallpaper seams, appliances, and any cracks you can find. Wash the vacuum canister with hot water to kill any eggs that may be there. Next, hit up these same areas with a substance called diatomaceous earth, which you can find in pet stores or gardening stores. It dehydrates the bedbugs and thereby kills them, so sprinkle it or smear it everywhere you think the bedbugs may be living, including on the floor near your bed, all over your bed frame, and in any cracks in the wall near your bed.

MINTY MAGIC INSECT REPELLENT

Stash mint-flavored gum in the pantry to keep away insects. A few sticks (even wrapped) can do wonders.

WHO KNEW?

READERS' FAVORITE

Best Bait for Mice

If you've seen a lot of Disney movies, you probably think mice live for cheese. But when you're baiting a mousetrap, a better bet is peanut butter. Because peanut butter is sticky, you can be sure the mouse won't grab it and run, and scientists say they love its sweet scent even more than your best piece of Cheddar. If you're squeamish about having to pick up the remains of a rodent you've set a trap for, place the baited trap inside a brown paper lunch bag. Rodents like exploring small spaces, and once the trap has done its trick, you can scoop it right up and throw it away.

Save Houseplants

To get rid of bugs that are harming your houseplant, place the entire plant (pot and all) in a clear plastic dry-cleaning bag. Throw several mothballs in with it, and tie a knot at the top. The sun will still get through, but the bugs will die after a week in seclusion with the mothballs.

Bye-Bye, Buggy Plants

Keep bugs away from your houseplants with garlic. Place a peeled garlic clove, narrow end up, just under the soil of your houseplant. Creepy crawlers will stay away from your plants!

GUARD YOUR GARDEN FROM INSECTS

Stop Wasps

Is there anything worse than coming upon a swarm of wasps when you're enjoying your garden? If you find that wasps are building a nest in the same spot year after year, spray the area with white vinegar several times in the beginning of the spring and they'll find somewhere else to roost.

Keep Plants Pest-Free

When watering outdoor plants, place a few drops of dishwashing liquid into the water, and make sure it gets on your plants' leaves. The detergent will keep bugs away, making sure your plants remain healthy and beautiful.

Aphid Invasion? Go Orange

Place orange peels at the base of the plants that aphids are attacking. A substance found on the peels destroys the insects' waxy outer coating, causing them to suffocate.

Feed the Ants

To get rid of ants for good, sprinkle cornmeal near anthills. They'll eat it, but they can't digest it, and they'll begin to die out. Wait a couple of weeks and see if your ant problem improves.

Put the Pests in Hot Water

If you find an ant nest outside, eliminate it by pouring a pot of boiling water over the area. Make sure you avoid splashing any plants you want to keep, because the water can kill them, too!

A Cure for Cutworms

If you've come outside to find your plants' stems cut as if by a tiny axe, you have a cutworm problem. But you can fix it with a simple toothpick. Place it next to the plant's stem—half in the soil, half above the ground. That bugger won't be able to circle the plant stem and cut it off!

Shell Game

To keep slugs and snails away from your plants, sprinkle some crushed eggshells around the base. This is also a great way of adding needed calcium to the soil. Whenever you use an egg in a recipe, you can rinse out the shell, crush it, and store it in a container for this purpose!

Molasses for Moths and Grubs

Moths and grubs can be a big problem with garden plants like corn, broccoli, cauliflower, and cabbage. To keep them from munching on your plants, make a molasses spray. In a spray bottle combine 4 cups water, 1 tablespoon molasses, and 1 teaspoon dishwashing detergent. Spray this mixture all over the leaves of your plants weekly.

Kill Spider Mites

Do you have trees that are infested with spider mites? You can make a mixture to get rid of them using ingredients already in your kitchen. Take 1 pound flour, 5 gallons water, and 1 cup buttermilk, mix it all together in a large bucket, and put it in a plastic spray bottle. Use it on your trees once a week, and it should keep the mite population under control.

A News Solution for Earwigs

Lure earwigs away from your plants by placing flowerpots filled with crumpled-up newspaper in your garden. The earwigs will hide in the newspaper, and in the morning, you can shake them out into a bucket of hot water, or simply throw the paper away.

Scram, Caterpillars!

Get rid of caterpillars the same way you'd get rid of vampires: with garlic. Mix 1 cup water with 1 tablespoon garlic powder, or 1 minced clove of garlic. Then add a squirt of dishwashing liquid, which will help the concoction stick to leaves and stems. Pour into a spray bottle and spray on plants once every few days to keep caterpillars away.

Stinky Garlic for Stinky Bugs

Like many pests, stinkbugs can't stand the smell of garlic. Crush several cloves of garlic and add to a spray bottle of water. Let sit overnight, then spray onto plants to keep stinkbugs away.

PEST-PROOF YOUR YARD

Peppermint for Pests

Mice, moles, squirrels, gophers, and even rats hate the aroma of peppermint. Try planting mint near your home—chances are you will never see one of these pests again! For a preexisting gopher problem, soak cotton balls in peppermint oil and then drop them down a gopher hole.

Fool a Snake

Believe it or not, snakes dislike humans just as much as we dislike them. To keep snakes out of your yard, it can be as easy as letting them know humans live there! To do this, save the hair from your hairbrush and sprinkle it around the perimeter of your property. Snakes will smell the hair and keep away.

Recycle Dog Hair

Have a dog that sheds like crazy? Save the clumps and poke them into an old grapevine wreath. Hang it (and its repellent scent!) on a stake in the garden to chase away rabbits, raccoons, squirrels, and other unwanted creatures.

A "Fresh" Way to Fight Squirrels

Squirrels can be one of the trickiest garden pests to deal with. They chomp on flower bulbs and other leaves, dig up your favorite plants, and otherwise wreak havoc. Protect your garden by grating some Irish Spring soap around your plants. Squirrels can't stand the smell of it and will stay away.

So Long, Squirrels

If squirrels are making a nuisance of themselves around your home, keep them away with a homemade pepper spray. Take a cup of your favorite hot sauce, add a spoonful of cayenne pepper and a capful of Murphy's Oil Soap, and mix together. Spray the mixture in whatever areas you want the squirrels to steer clear of.

JEANNE SAYS

Hide Away the Sandbox

Cats trying to make a sandbox a litterbox? Design a more protected play area by setting up a small tent, then cover the bottom with sand. Comb a cup or so of ground cinnamon into the sand to keep out ants, centipedes, and other pests, and zip up after each use.

Out with Opossums

If possums are a problem in your yard, mix together camphor oil with enough petroleum jelly to make a paste, and spread it around the base of trees. The smell should keep them away.

Rabbit-Repelling Plants

If rabbits eat your garden year after year, try planting plants that repel them. These include amaryllis, bleeding hearts, daylilies, English ivy, ferns, forget-me-nots, foxglove, impatiens, and pachysandra. Rabbits also hate certain trees, such as cedar, magnolia, maple, oak, pine, and spruce.

Another Bunny Buster

With the help of some vinegar, you can keep rabbits from overrunning your garden. First poke a few holes in the top of a pill bottle, then soak three or four cotton balls with vinegar and place them inside. Bury them just under the soil and the smell will keep rabbits away.

Befuddle Birds

Birds (and their droppings) driving you crazy on your deck? Keep them away with baking or baby powder. Sprinkle it where they like to land, and they'll find somewhere else to go. They hate the feeling of it under their feet!

Call Old CDs into Action

Tie them wherever you want to scare away birds. They're perfect to keep the flocks from feasting on your fruit trees!

So Long, Skunks

Mothballs aren't just for moths. Sprinkle them around your yard and they'll keep skunks away. Just be careful, as they're harmful to your pet should he decide to eat them!

Reclaim Your Yard from Raccoons

Have the raccoons grown rather bold around your backyard and trash cans? Try this equivalent of a phony "Beware of Dog" sign by distributing dog hair around your property. You can also try planting cucumbers, which both skunks and raccoons avoid like the plague.

Keep Pests Out of Your Trash

To keep raccoons, possums, and other critters out of your garbage, regularly spray the side of your cans with a mixture of 1 part ammonia and 1 part water.

Chase Deer with Common Scents

Hanging small pieces of a deodorant bar soap on trees will keep deer from munching on them. Or hang some dryer sheets around your garden. The smell will keep the deer away.

A Not-So-Welcome Mat for Deer

It sounds crazy, but laying old rugs or carpet samples around the outside of your garden in a path about 4 feet wide will turn deer away. They're suspicious of the texture and won't put a hoof on it!

Pet-Proof the Garden

Instead of throwing out orange, lemon, and lime peels, chop them up for use in your garden! If you sprinkle citrus rinds directly on the soil, you'll keep cats, dogs, and other neighborhood animals away from your precious plants.

Foil Pests

If you've ever bitten into a shred of foil that had gotten stuck to a piece of candy, you know how unpleasant the sensation is. Rodents hate the feeling of foil between their teeth, too, so placing strips of foil in your garden mulch will help deter rodents and some bugs. If rodents are eating the bark of your tree, you can also wrap the trunk in foil.

A DEER BARRIER BORDER

Plant thick rows of gladiolas around garden areas you don't want deer to enter. Deer don't eat glads and also won't cross through them—no matter how tempting the plants on the other side.

GREAT OUTDOORS

You can love the time you and your guests spend in your outdoor living spaces even more without breaking your budget or hiring professionals.

BEAUTIFUL NATURAL SPACES

Bring in the Birds

Don't throw out those net bags that onions and citrus fruits come in! In early spring, fill them with anything that might appeal to nest-building birds: pet hair, human hair, lint, plant clippings. Then tie off the bag and hang so birds can help themselves and nest nearby. You can use the same bags to serve suet to your feathered friends in the winter.

STONES FROM A TREE

Having a tree taken down? Put it to good use! Cut some "slices" (about 2 inches thick) to use as stepping-stones.

DIY Birdbath

Want to try a birdbath but don't want the expense and commitment of those heavy commercial types? Simply use a sturdy tomato cage as your base, topped with a round drainage tray for potted plants. It's easy to move and very affordable! Place some colorful marbles or pebbles in the tray before adding water—the brighter the color, the better to attract birds.

The Butterfly Water Cooler

Butterflies like puddles to gather around and drink. Make a butterfly water station out of an old cookie sheet or big saucer lined with gravel. You can also "plant" an old mug up to its rim in the soil, and fill it with water when rainwater doesn't keep it supplied.

Get Reddy for Hummingbirds

These fast fliers are attracted to red. But if your garden color scheme is less fire engine and more pastel, you can fake it. Just wire some red silk flowers around the garden until they discover nectar-filled flowers you've offered in other colors.

Make Your Own Nectar

Don't spend money on hummingbird nectar when it's so simple to make! Dissolve 1 part sugar in 3 parts water, then add a few drops of orange extract or orange juice. Use it immediately, or keep it in the fridge for up to 2 weeks.

Baby Your Garden

Got some old baby gear in the basement or attic? Make your family wonder by getting it out! Then take it outside. Baby gates, spindle cribs, and even the metal springs from cribs make easy trellises you can train flowers or vegetable vines to climb.

Get Amazing Grass

Did you know Epsom salts are one of the best natural lawn fertilizers around? They're composed of magnesium and sulfur, both of which are highly beneficial to grass. Magnesium kick-starts seed germination and is also a player in manufacturing chlorophyll, the substance that plants create from sunlight in order to feed themselves. Sulfur, meanwhile, also helps with chlorophyll, while simultaneously enhancing the effects of other fertilizer ingredients such as nitrogen, phosphorus, and potassium. It also deters certain pests such as ground worms. With all these benefits, it's no wonder that savvy lawn care specialists have been using Epsom salts for years. You can either sprinkle the salts on your lawn using a spreader or make a liquid solution out of them by adding some water and putting the mixture in a spray bottle.

OUTDOOR PROBLEMS SOLVED!

Stains on Stones?

If you have stains on paving stones or a concrete patio, sometimes the solution is simple. Try pouring hot water from several feet above the stone onto the stain. Repeat several times, and your stain may just disappear. If this doesn't work, try rubbing some dishwashing liquid into the spot with a toothbrush, then rinsing off. For really tough stains, add a bit of ammonia to the water.

JEANNE SAYS

Mulch with Souvenirs

Every beach vacation, we bring home more shells and stones than we can use for decoration around the house. So we now bring many into our outdoor spaces. They make perfect mulch and accents around plants, just like purchased pebbles from home centers (without the steep price)!

A Sweet Concrete Cleaner

Powdered lemonade mix can come to the rescue to help scrub away stains on your concrete! Simply add a few drops of water to the drink mix, just enough to form a paste. Apply the paste to a concrete stain and use a stiff scrub brush to scrub the area clean.

Get Rid of Grease

If your driveway or garage floor has become an easy place to do some Rorschach testing thanks to the grease, oil, and transmission fluid stains all over the place, take heart—clean concrete is only 10 minutes away. Spray any stained areas with oven cleaner, then let it sit for 10 minutes. Rinse off with a hose, and the stains will disappear.

Tidy Up the Driveway and Paths

You can keep paved areas looking spiffy with this trick. To remove unwanted grass or weeds from sidewalk and driveway cracks, squirt them with a solution of 1 gallon vinegar, 1 cup salt, and 8 drops liquid detergent. Another way to stop unwanted grass: Sprinkle a thick layer of baking soda where you don't want it to grow.

A Mildew-Free Deck

If your deck is covered with mildew, try spraying the wood with straight vinegar. Leave it for an hour or so, then rinse off. The acid in the vinegar kills mold and mildew, and will help get your deck clean. Another option is to use hydrogen peroxide: Spray on, let sit for 30 minutes, then rinse.

Gleaming Garden Furniture

Vinegar works on your patio furniture to keep it looking fresh and new. Spray it on and let it sit for a few hours before wiping down with a damp cloth. The vinegar spray will also get rid of any mold or bacteria that's already taken up residence.

Give Plastic a Quick Dip

The laziest way to clean plastic or resin patio furniture? Just toss it in the swimming pool before going to bed, and in the morning it'll be good as new. Meanwhile, your pool's filter will clean up the dirt.

GREAT TRICK FOR WINDOW BOXES

If you keep plants in window boxes, paint the boxes white first. The bright, reflective surface will deter insects and reduce the risk of dry rot. It looks great, too!

Cream It Clean

Another quick and easy way to clean plastic outdoor furniture: Use shaving cream! Apply a layer with a damp rag or sponge to your furniture, let sit for 10 minutes, then spray down with the hose. For super-dirty furniture, rinse before and after applying the shaving cream.

Renew Wood

Your wooden porch furniture may have seen better days, but it will shine again once you polish it using vegetable oil or cooking spray. Rub the oil over the furniture to revitalize the dried-out wood. Buff with a dry cloth for extra polish.

A Wonder for Wicker

If your white wicker deck furniture has turned a grimy brown, you have some work to do. But take heart; it isn't hard! First, vacuum up the freestanding dirt on the seat and arms. Then cover the whole piece with a mixture of 1 gallon warm water and 3 tablespoons ammonia. Scrub it with a brush to get between the fibers, then let it sit in a shady area to dry.

Silence Squeaky Lawn Furniture

If your wicker seems to scream every time you sit in it, it's become too dry. Take off any cushions and spray the wicker with a hose. The water will give it enough moisture to silence the squeaks.

Umbrella Rescue

Your patio umbrella was looking good when you packed it away last fall . . . but now it's a mildewy mess. Here's the easiest way to clean it: Fill a bucket with warm water, then add 2 cups white vinegar and ¼ cup liquid laundry detergent. Use a soft brush to apply to the fabric. Let sit for half an hour, then scrub. Rinse with water and let it dry in the sun. The warmth will kill whatever the vinegar and soap didn't.

Sprinkle Doormats Clean

Your porch's doormat can be cleaned with a sprinkling of baking soda. Brush vigorously and then sweep away the dirt. The next time it rains, the job will be complete.

Block Lock Rust

Have a padlock on your shed or something else outdoors? Keep it from rusting by protecting it from the elements. Slice open the side of a tennis ball (carefully!) and slip it over the lock to protect it.

Modern Light Reflectors

You don't need to purchase light reflectors for your driveway if you have CDs or DVDs that don't work lying around. Hang them up on the trees and fence posts lining your driveway, making sure the shiny side is faced out to catch the car lights. In the daytime they'll glint in the sunlight, appearing to be some sort of modern outdoor sculpture and sure to impress your guests.

No More Kiddie Pool Cleanup

Don't let leaves and grime get into your kiddie pool when your little ones aren't using it—it's easy to make your own cover. With a pair of scissors, cut a small X into each corner of an old plastic shower curtain. Then use wire cutters to cut two wire hangers into two V shapes, and use them as stakes by threading them through each X.

Get Rid of Poison Ivy

When it comes to poison ivy, an ounce of prevention really is worth a pound of cure. So if you've got a patch of this pernicious vine on your property, kill it now. Mix ½ gallon soapy water with 1½ pounds salt, spray the plant, and run in the other direction.

ENTERTAINING IDEAS

Lanterns for Much Less

Trendy outdoor décor stores sell lanterns for a pretty penny. But you can make your own with all kinds and sizes of jars—from baby food and minced garlic to pasta sauce and even large pickle jars. Once it's clean with the labels removed, simply place a votive candle in the jar. You can add pebbles or sand to the jar to raise the height of the candle or steady a taller candle. Want a hanging lantern? Fine-gauge wire can be bent to form a handle, with the rest wrapped around the mouth of the jar to secure it.

Create Your Own Luminarias

Have empty tin cans you can repurpose? Fill them with water and freeze overnight. Once they're frozen solid, you can use a large nail and hammer to punch holes in a decorative design on the cans. Need a guide? Draw the design you want with a dry-erase marker that you can wipe off later. After the design is complete, simply let the water thaw and empty and dry the can. Light a tea light inside for your own custom luminaria!

Color Swatch Your Lights

White string lights can go from simple to sensational with a trip to the paint counter—or maybe even your junk drawer! Collect some paint swatch strips in fabulous bright colors. Curl them into cylinders (with the color sides facing out) and secure with clear tape. Slip one sleeve over each bulb on your light string, and attach it to the wire with tape or a small binder clip. Magical mini lampshades for free!

Ladder Up

Need more serving space while entertaining? Place plywood planks across the rungs of a stepladder. Runners can cover the plywood for a fancier look. Now you have a tiered serving station for food or drinks that tucks away again until the next time you need it!

Protect Those Drinks

Keep bugs out of drinks by supplying cupcake liners. They easily slip over the tops of cans and glasses, and you can pop a straw through them if desired. Put a stack in a mason jar for a pretty display that you can label with the intended use.

Forget the Ice

Replace the ice for your drink cooler, tub, or kiddie pool with frozen water balloons. To make them, fill the balloons two-thirds full and stick in the freezer. When the drinks are gone and the ice has melted at the end of the day, have fun!

Condiment Cleanup

Repurpose inexpensive, clear soap pump dispensers as condiment servers. You'll upgrade your picnic table from plastic bottles, and make topping that burger or hotdog easier, with less mess.

A FRESH WAY TO FIGHT FLIES

Are giant horseflies driving you crazy? Next time you go outside, rub mouthwash on your body and enjoy the serenity of a fly-free experience.

8 CHEMICAL-FREE SOLUTIONS TO CHASE AWAY MOSQUITOES

Don't let bug bites ruin your time outside! Try these effective yet natural ways to keep pesky mosquitoes away.

Plant some relief. If you're looking to repel mosquitoes in your backyard, consider adding any of the following easy-to-grow plants to your landscaping: citronella, catnip, marigolds, floss flowers, basil, tansy, and horsemint.

Dress for success. Mosquitoes are attracted to dark blue clothing in particular. (It's true!) If you usually have trouble with mosquito bites, trying wearing light or pastel-colored clothes when you're outdoors. Almost all bugs are attracted to bright, flowery patterns, so keep that in mind when dressing for an outdoor event.

Soften your approach. Simply keep a fabric softener sheet in each pocket. A chemical in dryer sheets is similar to citronella, which is used in expensive bug-repelling formulas.

Go for catnip. For an effective personal insect repellent, rub fresh catnip leaves over exposed skin—just stay away from cats!

Repel all kinds of bloodsuckers. Citronella candles are great for repelling insects, but they can be pricey. Get the same effect by mixing garlic with water and spraying it near outdoor light bulbs. As the bulbs heat up, they'll spread a garlicky scent, which will keep mosquitoes and other bugs away.

Use peppermint power. Combine a few drops peppermint essential oil with 1 cup water in a spray bottle, shake well, and spray onto skin. Not only will the chemical compounds in peppermint help repel mosquitoes, but you'll also smell minty fresh!

Mix up a natural bug spray. Uncomfortable with all of the unpronounceable ingredients in commercial bug sprays? Try making this natural version. In a spray bottle, add ¼ cup apple cider vinegar, ¼ cup witch hazel, and 20 drops of a combo of any of the following essential oils: rosemary, citronella, tea tree, cedar, eucalyptus, or lemongrass. Shake and spray directly on exposed skin and the bugs will stay away!

Spice up your deck. Use this (almost) all-natural insect spray to repel mosquitoes as well as other insects like flies. Chop 1 small onion and 1 head of garlic. Mix together with 4 cups water, 4 teaspoons cayenne pepper, and 1 tablespoon liquid dish soap. Spray around places where you'll be spending time. This mixture will last a week or so if stored in a jar with a tight-fitting lid and kept in a cool, dark place.

Enjoy a Bug-Free Fire

Keep bugs from crashing your party by throwing some sage into the fire pit. They don't like the odor and will stay away. You can also add sage to your charcoal at a barbecue. It will keep the bugs away and give your food some earthy sage flavor.

S'more Solutions

Is it feeling crowded around the fire, or are flames rising too high for kids to toast s'mores? Line terra-cotta pots with aluminum foil. Then add charcoal and light. These handy little cookers allow each person to have their own fire to toast marshmallows with ease. Sticking with one big fire but need to toast a lot of marshmallows for the hungry masses? Use a clean metal rake to fit them all over the fire at once.

BRUCE SAYS

Keep Flies Away from Your Pool

There's nothing more irritating than having flies and other bugs swarm around you while you're trying to take a dip in the pool. We've had some luck keeping bugs away by applying a liberal amount of vinegar around the perimeter of the pool with a sponge.

PET SOLUTIONS

Little tricks can help keep your pets happy and healthy and save you time, effort, and money when caring for them. Always check with your vet to make sure these tips are smart for your pet.

BEST BEHAVIOR

A Red-Hot Repellent

If your dog finds your shoes more appealing than any of his chew toys, there's a simple way to break the attraction. Mix together a little cayenne pepper and petroleum jelly, then swipe a little on the shoes. The hot pepper will deter him, but it won't cause any health problems.

Shake It Off

Distraction is sometimes the best medicine when it comes to behavior modification for pets. Head off trouble by shaking coins in a metal can when you see your furry friend about to jump headlong into a spot where he shouldn't be or a dinner plate that isn't for him.

Spray Away

Unfortunately, cats rarely respond when you tell them "no." So to make sure they have a reason to not repeat bad behavior, spray them in the face with water from a spray bottle when you catch them being bad. If this doesn't work, try spraying them with air from a compressed air can (usually used to clean electronics and computer keyboards).

Keep Cats Off

Specific piece of furniture you don't want your cat on, or place you don't want him to go? Try this: In a spray bottle, mix together ½ cup water with ⅛ teaspoon cinnamon, and shake to combine. Cats detest the smell of cinnamon, so if you spray this solution where you don't want him to go, he should stay away.

Foil Your Feline

Especially when you're not around, you can also cover any area you want off-limits to cats with double-sided tape or aluminum foil. They can't stand the feeling of the stuff under their paws.

Stop the Scratching

Here's something you probably didn't know: Cats hate hot sauce. So if you can't get your cat to stop clawing at your woodwork, just rub in a little hot sauce, buff it thoroughly, and your cat will stay clear. You can also swipe a bit of VapoRub on scratching targets. Cats can't stand the cough medicine's mentholated smell.

Sour-Puss Chewing Solution

If your cat likes chewing on electrical cords, we know you need a solution, and fast! Here it is: Unplug the electronics, then rub the cords with a wedge of lemon. Once they've dried, you can plug them back in. Cats don't like the taste of lemon and will steer clear.

The Herb That Curbs Plant Digging

If your cat seems to think your potted plant is a fun place to hang out—or worse, a good place to go to the bathroom—use some thyme to help her find some other place to play. Sprinkle dried thyme on the surface of the soil once a week. The strong scent will chase her away.

Better Bathroom Habits

Your cat seems to have taken a vacation from the litter box, and you're finding unpleasant surprises in interesting places like the bathtub. To fix this problem, try placing a bowl of food in the areas where you've found those surprises. Cats don't do their business in the same place that they eat, so she'll hopefully find her way back to the litter box. If not, call your vet to make sure she's not suffering from any health problems.

LONG-LASTING TAGS

Prevent rust on your pet's tags by polishing them with car wax. Reapply every few months and they'll last much longer!

HEALTHY AND HAPPY

Help for Itchy Dogs

If your dog has itchy skin, try this soothing oatmeal scrub. In the food processor, grind 1 to 2 cups oatmeal (the amount depends on the size of your dog). Add enough cool water to make a paste and rub the mixture into his skin. After 5 to 10 minutes, wash it off with warm water, and your pooch should be scratching less often. If not, it's time to check in with the vet.

Soothe Those Paws

After playing in the park, your dog keeps licking his paws. It might be an allergic reaction to something he stepped on outside. In a spray bottle, mix together ¼ cup cider vinegar with ½ cup water and spray the mixture on the bottom of his paws. Vinegar will help neutralize any irritants and soothe the skin. If this tip doesn't work, or if the skin is broken, contact the vet.

Clear Up Ears

If your poor pup is prone to uncomfortable ear infections, try this tip for keeping his ears clean. Twice a month, wipe down the inside of the ears with a cotton ball soaked in witch hazel. The astringent will help loosen wax and reduce the incidence of infection.

Restore Regularity with Banana

It's unpleasant, but it happens: doggy diarrhea. Get your dog's digestive tract back in order with some banana. Mash up two small slices for small dogs, three for medium dogs, and four for large dogs. Check with your vet first to make sure he or she is on board.

WHO KNEW? READERS' FAVORITE

Water on the Go

Out for a walk in hot weather? Bring a plastic shower cap with you. When you fill it with water, it will expand enough that you can hold it out as a bowl. An empty, clean pancake-syrup bottle can also make a great portable, squirtable water bottle. Use a carabiner to attach its handle to a belt loop or backpack for a long hike.

Hot Dog Help

If your dog appears overheated, get him cooled down quickly by wiping his paws with a pad soaked in rubbing alcohol. As the alcohol evaporates, he'll start to cool down. If his condition doesn't improve quickly, call the vet, because he may be at risk for heatstroke.

Teething Relief

If your dog is teething, you can create a cheap chew toy by soaking an old washcloth in water, twisting it into a fun shape, and leaving it in the freezer. Give it to your pup fully frozen, and when it thaws out, simply repeat the process. Be careful with tiny dogs, though, as they can get too cold if they chew on frozen toys too often. Frozen green beans are also soothing for pups.

Fido Being Finicky?

If you've bought a new brand of food and your dog doesn't want to eat it, put a piece of beef jerky in the bag and reseal it. By the next day, the smell will have transferred to the food, making it seem much more appetizing.

Butter Up Pills

If you have trouble getting your cat to swallow pills, try rubbing them in butter first. It will make them taste better to your cat, and they'll slide right down his throat. For a dog, use *peanut* butter. Make him a (tiny) peanut butter sandwich! Cut out two small pieces of bread, around an inch square, and spread with peanut butter. Hide the pill inside, and give it to your dog, who will gobble it up without even noticing he just ate a pill.

EATING TOO FAST?

Place a ball in the middle of your dog's food bowl so your pooch has to work around it and slow down.

Soothe Sensitive Cat Tummies

Cats tend to get upset stomachs from super-cold food. Prevent tummy aches (and, worse, vomiting) by letting the food warm to room temperature before feeding. Another trick to try is pulverizing some mint with some fresh catnip and seeing if she'll eat it—mint is good for calming stomachs.

Eliminate Ear Mites Naturally

Mix together 1 tablespoon olive oil and 2 or 3 drops liquid garlic (found at health food stores). With an ear dropper, apply several drops to each ear daily for a month. The combination of the oil and garlic will smother and kill the mites.

4 BEST TIPS TO BEAT FLEAS—NATURALLY

There are lots of natural ways to send fleas packing. Check with your vet to see if these strategies could work for your particular pet and household.

Treat to a massage. Rub coconut oil in your hands, then massage it onto your pet, down to the skin. Next, run a flea comb through the fur. The little buggers will stick to the comb and pull away. (Some may rush to jump off your pet, so it's best to try this trick outside!) Coconut oil contains lauric acid, which acts as a repellent to fleas (and ticks too). Plus, it's soothing and moisturizing for your pet's coat—and smells amazing! And it's completely safe if he tries to lick it. Massage it in once a week to keep fleas away.

Suck them up. Attack fleas sheltering in upholstery and carpets with a high-powered vacuum cleaner with a bag that seals well. Trash the bag as soon as you finish.

Fight with fragrance. In a spray bottle, combine a few drops of eucalyptus essential oil with 1 cup water. Spray your pet's bed and other flea-prone areas of your home. Fleas detest the scent. Don't use this spray undiluted or directly on your pet.

Try lemon aid. Cut a lemon into quarters, cover with boiling water, add one or two sprigs of rosemary and sage, and let steep overnight. Transfer the strained mixture to a spray bottle and apply to your pet, avoiding her eyes. Target behind her ears, around the base of her tail, and under her legs. Pet not letting you spray? Rub the juice from a freshly squeezed lemon or orange on your dog or cat's fur.

A Simple Flea Test

Your pet's been scratching, but you're not sure if it's fleas. Slip a white sock over your hand and run it over her coat, as well as her bedding. If you find any little black specks on the sock, they're likely flea droppings. Try the tips above to get rid of those pesky fleas.

KEEP IT CLEAN

Best Box Cleaner

If your cat's litter box smells like, well, a litter box, rinse it out and add ½ inch of white vinegar to the box. Let it stand for half an hour, then swish it around, rinse, and dry the box.

Expel Urine Smell

If your pet had an accident on your couch and you just can't get rid of the smell, try this solution. In an empty spray bottle, combine 2 parts water to 1 part mouthwash. Spray the mixture onto the soiled upholstery. Next, lay newspaper over the sprayed area and let dry. The newspaper should absorb the smell completely. If not, repeat the process. Your cushions may smell minty fresh for a few days, but once that wears off the urine smell will be gone!

Erase Pet Odors Permanently

If your pet had an accident on your rug, he'll probably keep going back to the spot if you don't eliminate the odor completely. After blotting the stain, pour some cornmeal on it and let it sit for 2 hours before vacuuming up the grains. The cornmeal will absorb any lingering odors, breaking the cycle of indoor pet accidents.

Pleasant-Smelling Litter

Don't spend extra money on scented cat litter. To keep cat litter fresh smelling, simply mix a bit of baby powder into clean litter.

Feed Odor Control

Sometimes, your pet is just plain stinky. If you're beginning to notice pet odor when you open your front door, it's time to take action. Add a bit of brewer's yeast (1 teaspoon for cats and small dogs and 1 tablespoon for bigger dogs) to your pet's food, and your pet will secrete fewer of those unpleasant odors.

Easy-Cleaning Food Dish

Keep your furry friend's food dish free from yucky stuck-on bits of wet food. Just apply cooking spray to the dish before adding the food, and any leftover clumps will stay loose and easy to clean rather than sticking to the bowl. As a bonus, the oil in the cooking spray will help nourish your pet's coat and protect his skin!

Help Pet Food Stay Put

If your pet's food dish always ends up 3 feet from where it started by the time he's done eating, make it skid-proof. With a glue gun, make a thin strip of glue around the bottom rim. When dry, the glue will prevent the bowl from slipping so much across the floor.

JEANNE SAYS

Keep the Calm with Chamomile

To keep your dog or cat calm on the way to the vet, spray his carrier or seat with some chamomile tea. The scent has a relaxing effect (even for pets!), and you'll be able to spend more time focusing on the road, not on what your fur baby is doing.

Chase Away Ants

Do ants keep sneaking into your pet's food? Secret tip: Ants can't swim! Place the bowl of dog or cat food into a shallow bowl filled with water.

Fix a Water Dish Problem

Lucky you! Your pet's new trick is flipping over the water dish. Get one step ahead of him by putting his water in a heavy glass pie plate or baking dish, which he won't ever be able to lift. Problem solved!

Prevent Pee Spots

Is your dog leaving brown spots on your lawn where he decides to pee? Put a few drops of vinegar into his water bowl every time you refill it and brown spots will be a thing of the past.

Sanitize Pet Toys

Keep your pets' playthings clean and free from bacteria and germs by tossing them into the dishwasher alone (without dishes) once a month. But hold the detergent: Just turn the temperature to hot and the heat plus the water pressure will completely sanitize plastic or rubber toys. And not only will a quick wash help ensure that Fido stays healthy, but it'll prolong the life of the toys and keep your floors, carpets, and furniture clean, too.

Calm Dog Baths

If your dog hates taking baths, try placing a towel at the bottom of the tub before you fill it up. It will be much less slippery under your dog's paws, and that will help keep him calm.

Speedier Rinsing

There's nothing quite like wrestling a sudsy, wet dog in the bathtub! To help rinse the shampoo out of his coat more quickly, rinse him with ½ cup cider vinegar mixed in 5 cups water. It will break down the suds, making your job easier.

DIY Dry Shampoo

Washing a pet can sure be a hassle—especially when dealing with a cat. Save yourself the trouble (and several scratches) by using cornstarch instead. Sprinkle cornstarch on your pet's coat, then work it into her hair. It will soak up grease and odors and even fluff up her fur.

BABY YOUR PET'S BED

To give your pet's bed a quick clean, wipe it down with baby wipes. The alcohol will kill germs and the scent will freshen it up.

Knock Out Skunk Stench

Commercial de-skunking formulas can be pricey—and they're generally not close at hand when you need them. Fortunately, a few common household items can clear the air if your pet gets sprayed. This no-fail way to get a skunk smell out of a pet's fur was developed by a chemist as an industrial cleaner for a sulfur compound, then adapted by his coworker to solve a skunk problem! Pour a 1-quart bottle of 3 percent hydrogen peroxide into a pitcher. Mix in ¼ cup baking soda, then add 1 to 2 teaspoons liquid dish soap. Sponge on your dog's coat, avoiding the eyes. Leave on for 5 minutes before rinsing off. Repeat if needed. Safe and better smelling until next time!

Magic Pet Hair Remover

Don't have the heart to banish your pet from the couch? Here's a solution for easily removing all that hair. Mix 1 part liquid fabric softener with 2 parts water in a spray bottle, then spritz your furniture before vacuuming. The hairs will adhere to the softener, making them much easier to remove. As an added benefit, the room will smell fresh and clean! Don't have fabric softener on hand? Spray hair spray on a clean towel, then use the towel to lift off pet hair from your furniture and clothing.

Car Seat Pet Protectors

Before letting your furry friends into the car, place a bath mat onto the seats for protection from dirty paws and hair pileup. The mat's nonslip rubber underside will help it stay put.

Not Furry in a Hurry!

Uh oh, guests are on their way and you've just realized that your furniture is covered with pet hair! Caught without a lint roller? You can use a dry, unused dish sponge, a pair of rubber gloves, or a squeegee to wipe the hair into a pile with your hand. Discard the hair and then repeat the process. After you've gotten most of the hair, take a sheet of fabric softener from the laundry room and use it to pick up the rest—the hair will be naturally attracted to it. If you have time, use a vacuum cleaner to finish.

BEAT BAD BREATH
If your cat or dog has horrible breath, try adding some fresh chopped parsley to his food.

AUTO ANSWERS

We spend an average of 17,600 minutes behind the wheel each year. But you don't need to spend a lot of time or money to keep your vehicle a pleasure to travel in.

LOOKING LIKE NEW

Clear Tar from Your Car

It's easy to remove tar from your car's exterior. Make a paste of baking soda and water, then apply it to the tar with a soft cloth. Let it dry, then rinse off with warm water. Another tar remedy comes from your fridge: mayonnaise. Wipe it on, wait 5 minutes, then easily wipe off both the mayo and the tar.

Don't Get Stuck with Sap

Tree sap dripping on your car is one of the hazards of summer, but you can remove it easily with butter or margarine. Just rub the butter onto the sap with a soft cloth, and it comes right off.

Condition for Shine

After washing your car, give it a second round just like you would your head—with hair conditioner! You might think we're crazy, but applying conditioner, leaving it on for 5 minutes, and then rinsing it off will give your car a just-waxed shine. As an added bonus, it will more effectively repel water.

Match to Cover the Scratch

Chips in your car's paint job can be expensive to fix, so before you head to the auto body shop, see if you can find a crayon or nail polish that closely matches the color of your car. Fill in the nick, and then buff gently once the color is set. This technique works especially well with minor scratches!

Clean Glass with Cornstarch

To clean dirty windows or your car's windshield, mix 1 tablespoon cornstarch with about 2 quarts warm water, apply to the windows, and dry with a soft cloth. It's amazing how quickly the dirt is removed—and no streaking, either!

No More Scraping Bug Guts

The next time your windshield and headlights are splattered, apply a generous amount of hydrogen peroxide to the stains and let sit. After a couple of minutes, apply peroxide to a paper towel and wipe the gunky spots, which should come off easily, and then wash your car as usual.

Remove Bumper Rust

The best way to clean rust from your car's chrome bumper? Scrub the rusted area with a shiny piece of crumpled aluminum foil that has been dipped in cola.

A Simple but Powerful Polish

Need a chrome polish? It's as simple as vinegar. Apply directly on chrome with a rag for a quick shine.

Make Dashboard Scratches Disappear

Got scuffs and scratches? You can eliminate the marks on dashboard plastic by rubbing them with a bit of baby oil.

Keep Leather Supple

Baby oil to the rescue again! If your car has leather seats, regularly apply a thin layer of baby oil to the leather and let it dry. This little step will prevent the leather from drying out and cracking.

Free Floor Mats

If your car's floor mats need to be replaced, consider going to a carpet store and finding some samples to use instead. You'll always be able to find samples that are gray or another color to match your car's interior, and best of all, they're free!

Lift Parking Stickers

If your windshield is covered with parking permits and inspection stickers from years gone by, you'll love this tip. Pour nail polish remover over the decals until they're soaked. Then scrape with a razor blade, and they'll come off cleanly in seconds.

> **BRUCE SAYS**
>
> **Guard Your Grille**
>
> Hate the smashed-up insects that always seem to cover your car grille in the summer? Try this trick: Before screaming down the highway, apply a light coating of vegetable oil or nonstick cooking spray on your grille, and the revolting bugs will wipe off easily.

Patch Up Your Upholstery

Oh no, your kids tore a hole in your car's seat. (OK, so it wasn't the kids, it was you.) Instead of getting an expensive upholstery replacement, use an iron-on patch. Hold the patch in place with a few straight pins while you iron. If you don't have a long enough extension cord to bring the iron into your car, set the iron on one setting higher than the directions on the patch recommend. When it heats up, unplug it and quickly bring it out to the car.

Whitewall Wonders

Steel-wool pads make excellent whitewall tire cleaners. It's best to use the finest steel-wool pad you can find.

Clean Off Brake Dust

To remove brake dust—that fine, black powder—from your car's tires, apply a bit of cooking spray or vegetable oil, let it sit for 10 minutes, and then wipe off. Then spray them again when you're done. The vegetable oil will reduce the collection of dust in the future, and you'll be able to wipe it off even more easily next time.

Get Help from a Wheel Washer

Cleaning hubcaps and wheel covers can take "getting your hands dirty" to another level. Ditch the elbow grease by sticking these tire parts in the dishwasher instead (but do not place actual dishes in the same load!). Turn the machine to the pots-and-pans wash cycle to get your wheels sparkling clean.

Easy Undercarriage Cleaning

Don't forget to clean under your car, especially if you live in an area where salt and ice assault in winter. A trick for these hard-to-reach areas: Run a lawn sprinkler underneath the car and drive back and forth.

WHO KNEW?

READERS' FAVORITE

Bye-Bye, Bumper Sticker!

Time to get rid of an old bumper sticker? Try this: Set your hair dryer on high and run it back and forth over the sticker until the adhesive softens. Then apply a bit of vegetable oil. Carefully lift a corner with a credit card and peel it off. Or try hand sanitizer— rub it into the sticker and let it sit for 15 minutes. It will help dissolve the glue and will practically wipe right off!

The Perfect Trash Can on the Go

To keep trash from winding up in every compartment and on the floor, your car needs a trash receptacle. A plastic cereal container lined with a plastic grocery bag works well. Or try a large purse or tote lined with a plastic bag—it can hang in the back looped over the headrest of a front seat.

FAST FRESHENING

Save Money with a Sheet

Instead of buying commercial fresheners, repurpose fabric softener sheets to help sweeten the air. Place sheets under the car seats, in door pockets, or in the trunk to keep your car smelling fresh.

Put Your Ashtray to Work

There's an even better use for your car's ashtrays than spent cigarette butts. Fill them with baking soda, and they'll keep your car odor-free. Replace the baking soda every 2 or 3 months. Or try a handful of cloves. Either option will freshen up your car in no time—for pennies!

Hang This Instead of Pine Trees

To give your stuffy car a blast of fresh-scented air whenever you need it, make this air freshener: Simply fill a tea infuser ball with scented bath salts. Whenever you open the car door, you'll be greeted with a wonderful fragrance!

Pin a Hint of Natural Scent

If you prefer a more subtle scent, try applying 3 to 5 drops of your favorite essential oil to a wooden clothespin. Then clip the pin to your car's air vents. When the scent begins to fade, just refresh the pin with more essential oil. It's easy and inexpensive.

SIMPLE SAFETY AND MAINTENANCE

Boost Headlight Visibility

Keep your headlights clear and shining bright with toothpaste. Apply to each headlight with a cloth to polish, then rinse off with warm water. Mild abrasives help clear off any debris and cloudiness. Finish by cleaning and coating the headlights with car wax or furniture polish. Repeat monthly as needed.

RECYCLE OLD OVEN MITTS

Time to retire oven mitts covered in stains? They're great when handling hot engine parts or even as car washing mitts.

Check That Tread

Does your car need new tires? To find out, put Abe Lincoln to work. Place a penny in your tire's shallowest tread, with Abe facing the hubcap. If you can see the hair on top of the president's head, the tread is worn down to the point that you should buy new tires.

Suspect a Leaky Tire?

You suspect your car has a hole in its tire, but you can't figure out where. Use this trick to locate the leak and patch it up: Fill a spray bottle with water and a few squirts of dishwashing liquid. Spray all over your tire in bright light and look carefully for a cluster of air bubbles. They'll point the way to even a tiny hole in your tire.

ERASE FOGGY WINDOWS

To clear windows without leaving a smudgy mess, keep a chalkboard eraser in your car. Also, keep a stocking filled with kitty litter in your car to absorb moisture in the first place.

Cushion Your Parking

If you park in a garage at home, chances are you've bumped a wall in the past—either while pulling in or opening a car door. Affixing pool noodles to the side and back walls of the garage can help protect your car from dents and dings. It's like bumper parking. Cut the noodles in half lengthwise, then glue, nail, or bolt to the walls for simple guardrails.

Fix Smeary Windshield Wipers

Messy wipers are a safety hazard, and they're also pretty annoying. If your wipers are smearing the windows, wipe the blades with some rubbing alcohol.

Coat That Crack

Small chip or crack in your windshield? Try coating it with clear nail polish to stop the spread until you can get it repaired. It will be a lot cheaper and faster to fix if you can contain the damage.

Clear Up Corrosion

Accumulated dirt and corrosion on battery terminals can interfere with its performance. Clean them easily with a thick solution of baking soda and water. Start with 1 tablespoon baking soda in 1 cup hot water; add more baking soda as needed to form a paste. Apply the paste to the terminals with an old toothbrush. Let it stand for 10 to 15 minutes before washing it off. Baking soda is a mild alkali and will neutralize the weak acid on the terminals.

6 SECRETS TO KEEP YOUR CAR FROM FREEZING

It's hard enough to dig out your driveway in wintry weather. If you park outside, a few simple steps can save you the trouble of worrying about car doors freezing shut and the time and hassle of scraping icy windows.

Skip clearing windows and mirrors. Save yourself scraping and wiping time each morning by wrapping your side mirrors and windshield wipers in plastic bags or tube socks. Protect your windshields by placing old bath towels across them. When it's time to drive, simply pull everything off and you're ready to go!

Treat your windshield to vinegar. For even more protection from ice and frost, mix 3 parts vinegar to 1 part water and coat the windows with this solution.

Spray on a little D-fense. Spray WD-40 in the lining of car doors. Once in the beginning of the winter should do it to keep your doors opening easily.

Baby powder to the rescue. Use baby power or baking soda to absorb the moisture that collects on the rubber seal lining your car door. Just wipe the weather strip with a dry cloth before sprinkling on the powder. Repeat every few days in the dead of winter to make sure you can always get into your car.

Lube it up. Rub vegetable oil on the rubber moldings around your doors. Because it's the rubber, not the metal, in your doors that freezes, lubing it with oil should keep it supple.

Block the lock. To keep your car's door locks safe from ice during the cold winter months, place a refrigerator magnet over each lock. You can even take an old magnet (last year's calendar from a local realtor, perhaps) and cut it into pieces that fit perfectly.

Give Terminals a Drink

Another way to attack corrosion: Just pour a can of cola over the battery terminals; let it sit for half an hour, then wipe clean.

Make Your Battery Last Longer

Epsom salts can extend the life of your car battery. Just dissolve 1 ounce Epsom salts in 1½ cups warm, distilled water and fill each battery cell.

Always Carry Aspirin . . . for Your Car

If your car battery has died and you don't have jumper cables, don't get a headache just yet. First, try dropping a couple of aspirin tablets into the battery. The acid in the aspirin can provide it with just enough charge to get you to the nearest service station.

Free Up a Frozen Lock

There are many clever ways to fight freezing before it becomes a problem (see our tips on page 173). But if you're stuck with an already frozen lock or door, rub your key or door handle with a squirt of hand sanitizer. The alcohol it contains will help melt the ice so you can get into your car.

Smart Traction Tool

Not prepared with sand or kitty litter in your car? If your car gets stuck on an icy patch and your wheels aren't getting any traction, help free it by using your car's floor mats. Take them out and place under the tires, then drive to a safe place, retrieve the mats, and be on your way.

The Shovel You Didn't Know You Had

Stuck in the snow (or mud) with no way to dig yourself out? A shovel may be closer than you think. Just remove a hubcap and use it as a makeshift shovel. So smart!

OPEN A KEY RING WITH EASE

Place the teeth of a staple remover between the two rings, then press to separate. Your fingers and nails will thank you!

WHO KNEW?

PART 3

CHEF'S
SECRETS

COOKING ESSENTIALS

Get top flavor in less time and with less trouble when you know these kitchen secrets—from ingredient prep to cooking steps.

MAXIMIZE YOUR INGREDIENTS

Awaken Your Herbs

To get the most impact out of your herbs and spices, whether dried or fresh, rub them between your hands before you add them to a dish. You'll release more of the herb's natural flavor, making for a tastier meal.

Guarantee Flavor

Did you know that dried spices stay fresh for only about 6 months? When you open a new spice, mark the date on the bottle so you can keep track of its shelf life.

Speedy Herb Rescue

Dried spices can lose their flavor quickly. Luckily, it's easy to perk them back up before using them in your dish. Just toast them in a pan for a minute or two and their flavors will be revived.

Spin-Dry for Best Results

You need to wash and dry fresh herbs (just like fruits and veggies) before using. But wet herbs can turn into a mess on your cutting board, and any lingering moisture can dilute their flavor. Of course, you can let herbs dry naturally on a paper towel. Or you can speed the process by tossing them in a salad spinner or giving them some help with a hair dryer.

GO BIG!

When selecting limes or lemons at the market, go for the biggest you can find. They tend to be sweeter than their smaller counterparts.

Shake Up Your Garlic

It can be so simple to remove the skins from garlic! Just break the cloves from the head and place them in a bowl or mug. Place another bowl on top and shake heartily. Even more fun: Use a cocktail shaker! With either approach, the skins will start to come off, making the garlic easy to peel.

Another Easy Peel

Another great trick to make garlic easy to peel? Soak cloves in very hot water for 2 to 3 minutes, or rinse under hot water. This prep should make them easily slip out of their skins.

Squeeze the Most Out of Lemons

Double the amount of juice you get from a lemon or lime simply by putting it in the microwave for 10 to 15 seconds before juicing it. The heat will soften up the flesh, allowing you to extract every last drop of juice. It's an easy way to get more for your money!

Skip the Point

The pointy end of lemons can make them difficult to squeeze by hand or even with a press. Take just a second to trim that end and create a flat edge. The reward: More juice!

DIY Bouillon Cubes

Make your own bouillon cubes by freezing leftover chicken broth in ice-cube trays. Once frozen, the cubes can be stored in the freezer in resealable plastic bags until needed. They are easily defrosted in the microwave—or just toss them into a soup or sauce and they'll melt quickly.

Can the Pam

Never pay for aerosol cooking sprays. Instead, buy a giant jug of vegetable oil and add it to a clean spray bottle as needed. It's the same thing and will cost a fraction of the price.

Better Butter Spread

To make your butter super-spreadable for bread or corn on the cob, take a room-temperature stick of butter and whip it with a small amount of water. Not only does this trick make it light and spreadable, but it will also last longer because it expands in volume!

BRUCE SAYS

Seek Out the Salad Bar

Be sure to keep an eye on the prices at the salad bar. If you only need a few artichoke hearts or mozzarella balls for your recipe, they may be cheaper to buy there by the pound than elsewhere in the store.

MAKIN' BACON?

Always rinse bacon under cold water before frying—it will reduce the amount the bacon shrinks when you cook it.

MASTER SMART TECHNIQUES

Simple Step to Better Bacon

Pan-fried bacon never seems to cook evenly, because we try to cram in slices that don't fit so well. The super-easy solution: Cut the slices in half. They'll lie flatter to cook and fit into sandwiches better to gobble up.

Press Your Breakfast

Have a panini press tucked back in a cabinet? Pull it out to cook breakfast! Just a few minutes in the press cooks bacon crisp and delicious. Or create an omelet: Scatter some chopped veggies on the press, pour two beaten eggs over the top, and close the press to cook for about 2 minutes. Fold the result to serve and eat.

Fab Fried Eggs

Want to get that perfect white film over the yolks of your eggs? Add a couple drops of water and cover the pan just before the eggs are done.

Best-Ever Omelet

To make a great omelet, make sure the eggs are at room temperature. All you need to do is take them out of the fridge 30 minutes beforehand. Cold eggs are too stiff to make a fluffy omelet.

Ring Around the Egg

Don't buy a specialty gadget to make perfect circles out of cooking eggs—just reuse an old tuna can as an egg ring! Remove both ends of the can and wash it very well in warm, sudsy water. Then place some water in a pan. When it starts to simmer, place the can in and crack an egg into it for perfect poaching.

Peel Eggs with Ease

For perfectly peeled hard-boiled eggs, crack the eggs slightly on your counter, then place them in a bowl of cool water. The water will seep in and loosen the egg from its shell, ensuring you don't accidentally take out half the white when you're trying to peel it.

Sandwich Toast That's Tops

When toasting bread for sandwiches, put two slices of bread in one wide toaster slot. That way, the bread gets toasty on the outside but stays soft on the inside. Great for BLTs!

Perfect Pancakes

Short-order cooks and chefs have a host of tricks to make the lightest pancakes. First, don't overmix the batter—you don't want the gluten in the flour to overdevelop and allow the carbon dioxide that makes the little air pockets to escape. It's better to leave a couple of lumps in the batter. To further slow the development of the gluten and the leavening action, refrigerate the mixture for up to 30 minutes.

Restaurant-Style Burger Patties

Ever notice the perfectly round hamburger patties sold at the supermarket? Your homemade burgers can look restaurant-ready too, no fancy "hamburger press" necessary! Just use the lid from a jar as a mold for your ground beef—large lids for Whopper-sized burgers and small lids for sliders. Find a lid that's a bit larger than your buns, cover the underside in a stretch of plastic wrap, and fill it with beef. The plastic wrap makes patty removal super-easy, and you'll have a flawless and completely uniform batch of burgers in no time!

Simmer on Any Stove

Cooking over low heat for any amount of time is super-difficult—especially on a gas stove, where you can only pare back the flames so much. But if you can't take the flames lower, make the burners higher to put more space between the heat source and the pan. How? Simply stack two burner grates.

Pluck Herbs with Less Work

Cooking with certain fresh herbs requires stripping their leaves from their stems. Translation: a lot of work. But you can use an easy trick to save time and still savor the flavor of herbs such as cilantro and dill. The magic tool: a simple colander! Just thread the herbs through the holes of the colander, starting from the inside. Leaves pull away and collect in the bowl of the colander.

You Can Keep a Dried Mushroom Down

Ready to rehydrate? There's a tip you need to know to stop the bob. Those dried mushrooms tend to want to float on the soaking water instead of diving in. The problem: That leaves some mushrooms tough or still crunchy. The solution: Force them down by nesting a smaller liquid measuring glass or bowl inside the larger glass or bowl you're using to soak the mushrooms.

JEANNE SAYS

Shape with a Baster

For perfectly formed pancakes, use a meat baster to squeeze the batter onto the griddle. It gives you so much control you'll finally be able to make those animal-shaped pancakes your kids have been begging you for! Don't have a baster? Thoroughly rinse out and use a squeezable ketchup bottle.

Slice Onions with Ease

Love sliced onions in everything from salads and sandwiches to soups and stews? Slicing them doesn't need to be a messy, stinky chore—with chunky results rather than thin, delicate slices. To get slim onion slices, try a tool that does the job even better than the fanciest of kitchen knives: the potato peeler! Simply shave an onion with the peeler to get restaurant-quality slices.

Make Your Own Mini Pizza Stone

Baking or pizza stones give you crisp cooking results. How they work: Put the stone in the oven to heat before you add the food to bake on top. The only catch is, the stones can be pricey (plus, heavy and large to store) for how much use they get in a typical week. So why not make your own smaller version? All you need are unglazed quarry tiles, which are cheap and easy to pick up at home improvement stores and garden centers. They're small enough to fit in your toaster for cooking and a drawer for storage. Use a few together to cover more cooking area, as needed.

Best Breading Tips

Keeping breading on foods can be a challenge, but here are a couple of tricks to try (other than using superglue, which we don't recommend). First, make sure that the food to be breaded is very dry. As for your eggs, make sure they're at room temperature, and beat them lightly.

Let Chicken Chill

Always refrigerate chicken breasts for at least 15 to 20 minutes after breading but before cooking. The coating will adhere better that way. Also, try adding a teaspoon of baking powder to your batter, and use club soda instead of water for a delicate texture.

PITTING PRACTICE

To easily remove an avocado pit, thrust the blade of a sharp knife into the pit, twist slightly, and the pit will come right out.

WHO KNEW? READERS' FAVORITE

Secret to Speedy Meatballs

Want the fastest way to make meatballs? Surprisingly, don't start with a ball. Instead, shape the meat mixture into a log and then cut off slices, which then roll easily into evenly sized balls.

No More Dry Turkey

If your roasted chicken or turkey tends to be too dry, try stuffing a whole apple inside the bird before roasting. (Just toss the apple afterward.) You can also line the bottom of the pan with lemon and onion slices. They'll give the bird a lovely flavor and make sure it stays moist.

Super-Tender Pork

When roasting a pork loin, cook it with the fat-side down for the first 20 minutes, which will cause the fat to begin to liquefy. Then turn the roast over for the balance of the cooking time, and the fat will baste the meat.

Meat Miracle

All meat (except organ meat and ground beef) should stand at room temperature for a few minutes before cooking. This step allows the meat to brown more evenly, cook faster, remain juicier, and stick less when frying.

The Marinade Secret

Vinegar helps tenderize the tough protein fibers in meats, so using it in marinades and braising liquids makes your dishes even more succulent. Simply add some garlic and your favorite spices to balsamic or wine vinegar and you've got a marvelous marinade!

Say Yes to Yogurt

Coating your meat in yogurt may sound odd, but one taste of the cooked result will convince you otherwise. Yogurt is an amazing tenderizer! Use plain, unstrained yogurt combined with the usual marinade suspects (garlic, lemon, herbs).

Let the Roast Rest

Let a roast stand at room temperature for about 15 minutes before you carve it. This rest gives the juices time to be reabsorbed and distribute evenly. When you cook a roast, the juices tend to be forced to the center as those near the surface are evaporated by the heat. Resting the roast also allows the meat to firm up a bit, making it easier to carve into thinner slices.

BRUCE SAYS

Make Fast Froth

You can froth milk for a café-style latte (or hot chocolate) right in your microwave! Add about ½ cup milk to a mason jar. Secure the lid and shake vigorously until the milk volume is doubled. Remove the lid, and microwave on high for 30 seconds. Spoon on the foam, and enjoy your sip!

Stop Sausage from Splitting

Keep sausages from splitting when cooking them by piercing the skin in one or two places while they are cooking. Rolling them in flour before cooking will reduce shrinkage.

Slow-Cooker Hot Dogs

It may sound surprising, but you can actually cook hot dogs in the slow cooker. If you cook them for 4 hours on low, they'll taste like they were cooked on a roller grill at the ballpark! Don't add any additional water to the cooker, as the hot dogs will release water as they cook. This is a great time-saving tip for a barbecue when you've got hamburgers, salads, toppings, sides . . . so much to prepare!

Don't Lose That Bacon

Bacon that doesn't shrink means more for your money—and more bacon that you get to put in your dish! Keep bacon from shrinking so much by adding it to a cold pan rather than a hot, then cook it over medium heat.

The Measure of Your Fish

It can be tricky to figure out the proper cooking time for fish. If you've ever overcooked an expensive piece of halibut, you know what we mean! To avoid this problem, measure the fish at its thickest part. You can estimate 10 minutes of cooking time for every inch of thickness.

Sensational Shrimp

For the most tender shrimp, cool them down before cooking. Place fresh shrimp in the freezer for 10 to 15 minutes, or set them in a bowl of ice water for about 5 minutes.

AGAINST THE GRAIN

Here's a simple tip to make your meat more tender. When it's ready to slice, cut it against the grain (look for slight lines on the surface).

WHO KNEW?

READERS' FAVORITE

Conserve Cooking Oil

The next time you buy a bottle of cooking oil, don't remove the entire safety seal. Instead, make a small slit in it with a knife and take off only a small sliver. It's like making your own pouring spout! You'll cut back on those greasy drips down the side of the bottle, and since you'll be pouring more slowly, you'll use less.

8 REASONS YOUR HAIR DRYER BELONGS IN THE KITCHEN

We associate lots of appliances with the kitchen. But our hair dryer? If you're not convinced, try these tips.

Prep amazing roasted chicken. The number-one secret to crispy cooked chicken skin is starting with dry skin. Start by patting the chicken dry with paper towels. Then set your hair dryer to high and treat your chicken pieces to the heat for about 2 minutes, or until they appear dry. Now you're ready to roast! This technique works for turkey and duck as well.

Soften or melt chocolate. Need to soften chocolate a bit for easier shavings, or melt just a small amount for decorating or a single-serving treat? Turn to your hair dryer—it's easier to monitor your progress than melting in your microwave. It works to soften butter, too!

Separate frozen foods. Fruits, veggies, and even pieces of meat can freeze into a clump, making it difficult to portion out only what you need for tonight's dinner or your morning fruit smoothie. A quick blast from a hair dryer can help you pull them apart.

Help cakes release. Simply direct heat from the hair dryer to the sides of your pan to help a cake glide out. This tip works especially well for cheesecakes.

Give frosting a pro finish. Making a cake at home is a great way to save money, but if you're not a cake-decorating genius, it never looks as good as store-bought! To give the icing on top of your cake the silky look of a professionally made one, ice it as usual, blow a hair dryer across the frosting until it just starts to melt, then let it cool. The result: a nice gloss.

Ease ice cream scooping. Household can't wait for an ice cream treat? A blast of warm air from your hair dryer can soften ice cream as well as your microwave but with less mess.

Speed-dry tall containers. Want to dry out the bottom of water bottles or vases more quickly? Grab your hair dryer to help clear out the last of the moisture.

Give your sponge a tidy home. Even dryer attachments can help in the kitchen! A lot of us have no need for the add-on diffuser attachment that comes with many hair dryers. But it's the perfect shape and size to hold a kitchen sponge in its spikes when not in use and drying.

Stun a Lobster

If you love the taste of lobster but hate cooking it because you're bothered by the lobster's movements, you're not alone. Just put the lobsters in the freezer for 10 minutes before cooking. The cold will dull their senses and the amount they move will be significantly decreased.

Fluffy Rice How-To

If you like dry, fluffy rice, try this trick as soon as the rice is done cooking: Wrap the lid with a cotton dishtowel and set it on the pot for about 15 minutes. The cloth will absorb the steam.

Keep Pasta Warm

Here's a trick that will keep freshly cooked pasta warm longer. Place a large mixing bowl underneath your colander as you drain the pasta. The hot water will fill the bowl and heat it up. Once the bowl is warm, dump out the water and put the pasta in the bowl instead. Then cover the bowl, and take your time as you finish cooking the rest of your meal.

Veggies in the Bag!

Here's an easy way to get your veggies ready for dinner: Place them in a gallon- or quart-size zip-top bag and cut a ½-inch slit on the side, about 1 inch from the top. Microwave them for 2 to 3 minutes on high and they'll come out perfectly!

Oil, Not Foil, for Baked Potatoes

Did you know that wrapping a potato in foil won't actually make it bake faster? Rubbing it lightly with vegetable oil, however, will.

BAKING MAGIC

From prepping and mixing to baking and serving, smart tips can make baking less work with more delicious, professional results right from your own kitchen.

MAKE IT EASY

Create More Counter Space Instantly

If your kitchen isn't as big as you'd like it to be, you're not alone. You may especially long for more space when you're baking. Where do you put all those cookie sheets as you're scooping out dough? A simple solution that doesn't require a kitchen renovation: Pull out a few kitchen cabinet or island drawers. It's a quick way to create more temporary space upon which to rest sheets.

Improvise a Cooling Rack

If you're baking cookies or pies and don't have a cooling rack, simply line up a bunch of butter knives in alternating directions (first with the blade toward you, then with the blade away from you), and put the baking sheet on top of them. You can also use old egg cartons.

Muffin Pan Hack

Sometimes a muffin or cupcake recipe makes more than one pan but not quite two. Or maybe you've run out of muffin pans. You can create individual muffin pans by placing paper liners inside the rings of mason jar lids. Set them on a baking pan or tray to make them easy to lift in and out of the oven.

JEANNE SAYS

Never Buy Cupcake Liners Again

It's easy to make your own! Just cut parchment paper into 5-inch squares, then mold each one around the bottom of a container that fits inside your pan's muffin cups. A juice glass or small can may work well. Sandwich the paper between the muffin cup and the container. Press the glass or jar down into the tin to flatten the liner's bottom.

End Cookie-Cutter Frustration

To get a sharp edge on your shaped cookies easily, dip the cutter in flour or warm oil occasionally during the cutting.

Try This Tin Tip

Making cupcakes or muffins but don't have enough batter to fill the tin? Before sticking the pan in the oven, fill the empty cups halfway with water. This trick will extend the life of the tin and ensure the muffins bake evenly.

A New Cookie Shortcut

If you can't find or don't own cookie cutters, there's an easy replacement that's probably in your kitchen right now. Pull out your nonstick cooking spray, then pull off the top. Facing down, the lid's edge makes easy cuts into dough to shape perfect-size cookies or biscuits.

Cookies That Can't Be Beat

Making cookies? Spritz the beaters with a little vegetable oil or nonstick cooking spray and you won't have to stop every few seconds to scrape the batter off the beaters and back into the bowl.

The Big Chill

For better cookies, refrigerate your dough for 30 minutes after mixing it. Not only will the dough be easier to work with, but the cookies will also spread more evenly in the oven.

Simple Spoon Saver

Is your cookie dough sticking to everything? It's easy to get a spoonful of cookie dough to drop onto your baking sheet if you first dip the spoon in milk.

WHO KNEW?
READERS' FAVORITE

Creative Use for Coffee Cans

A coffee can is the perfect container for so much more than coffee. You can also bake dough in one! Use it like you would a loaf pan, making sure you grease it first and fill only halfway if you're making bread with yeast in it.

Help Cookie Dough Hold Its Shape

Busy family? It's easy to make big batches of cookie dough ahead of time. Shape the dough into an easy-to-slice roll and pop it in the freezer until you're ready to do the actual baking. No stress, right? Almost! The only problem: The underside of the dough ends up flattened against the bottom of the freezer. To prevent this, use paper-towel tubes to hold the roll of dough and keep it round for cookie-shaped slices. First, wrap the dough in plastic wrap. Make a long cut down the length of a cardboard tube and place the dough log inside. The dough will keep its tube shape, ensuring that your cookies are picture perfect!

Shower Caps in the Kitchen

Plastic wrap is perfect for covering bowls of rising dough. Or you can switch out the plastic wrap for a plastic shower cap—the elastic will fit perfectly over your bowl, and the plastic will stretch enough to allow for expansion.

Plastic Wrap to the Rise Rescue

Most bread recipes require multiple "fold" and "let rise" steps. It's easy to lose track. But all it takes to know just where you are in the process is plastic wrap and a marker. Write notes on the current step and timing on the plastic wrap you use to cover the bowl of rising dough.

Kneading without Mess

If you like to bake from scratch, you can avoid a sticky, doughy mess in your kitchen with this simple trick: Before kneading your dough, place it in a resealable plastic bag. Knead through the plastic, and your hands and countertops will remain stick-free! Alternatively, you can slip plastic bags over your hands to use as makeshift gloves.

Easy Greasing

When you finish a stick of butter, don't throw away the paper wrapper. Instead, fold it in half butter-side in and store it in a plastic bag. Next time you need to butter a bowl or pan, use this paper—it's easy and neat!

Save a Takeout Tool

The next time you get chopsticks with your Chinese takeout, keep a few for your kitchen. Even if you haven't mastered the art of eating with them, they're perfect for leveling off cups of flour and other dry goods.

Perfectly Floured Pans

Recipes for baked goods often call for greased and floured pans, which usually involves oiling the pan, then sprinkling flour inside and shaking until it's equally distributed. However, professional bakers generally don't use this method, which can leave flour on your baked goods or make them cook unevenly. Instead, they mix up a batch of "baker's magic," and now you can, too. Mix ½ cup room-temperature vegetable shortening, ½ cup vegetable oil, and ½ cup all-purpose flour. Blend the mixture well and use it to grease pans. You can refrigerate it in an airtight container for up to 6 months.

FREEZE FOR EASE

Store your rolling pin in the freezer. It's much easier to roll out pastry dough and pie crusts with a frozen rolling pin.

Shelling Secret

Buying whole nuts for baked goods can save you money—preprepared nuts you find in the baking aisle are expensive! But what about the time it takes to get them ready for your batter? A few tricks can help. The easiest way to shell pecans, walnuts, and other nuts is to freeze them first. This simple step shrinks the nut away from the shell and makes the job a breeze. Another easy way to shell nuts is to soak them in boiling water for 15 minutes.

De-salt Your Nuts

Your recipe for peanut butter cookies calls for unsalted nuts, but you only have a can of the salted variety. Make them unsalted by placing them in boiling water for a minute or two, then draining. To eliminate any remaining moisture, spread the nuts on a cookie sheet and bake in a 225°F oven until they're dry, about 5 minutes. Cool, and then use your newly unsalted nuts in your recipe.

Mess-Free Mashing

The quickest way to "chop" nuts is to place them in a sealed plastic bag, then roll over them with a rolling pin. This is also a clean, easy way to break up graham crackers or vanilla wafers to make a pie crust.

Faster Dried-Fruit Prep

If you've ever tried chopping dried fruit, you know it can be a mess because the pieces get stuck to the knife. Make the process easier by sticking the fruit into the freezer for an hour before chopping. You can also try spraying your knife lightly with a nonstick cooking spray.

Cleaner Chocolate Chopping

Chopping chocolate for a sweet recipe can be a real pain, thanks to the tiny shards of chocolate left on your cutting board. Make your job much easier by simply heating the chocolate before you cut it. (One minute in the microwave usually does the trick; heat until the edges start to melt.) The slightly softened chocolate won't splinter as much, ensuring you waste very little!

Icing Secret

To keep icing from hardening, just add a very small amount of white vinegar after it is whipped. You can also add a pinch of baking soda to the confectioners' sugar. This will help the icing retain some moisture, and it won't dry out as quickly.

The Icing on the Cake

Here's a tip that makes icing a cake much easier. To keep the cake from sliding around on the plate as you're icing it, place a dab of frosting in the middle of the plate before you put the cake on top. The icing will keep the cake in place, and by the time you've served all the slices, no one will notice the little bit of extra frosting on the bottom.

Surprising Cake Decorating Tool

Trying to decorate a cookie or write or draw on a cake? Icing bags are still too big and leave you without much control. Try a clean kids' medicine dispenser—the syringe design helps the icing come out slowly at your push.

Trace It with a Toothpick

Here's a great bakers' trick to make it easier to decorate the top of a cake: With a toothpick, trace the pattern, picture, or lettering before you pipe the icing. This guide will help you make fewer mistakes.

CHOPPING NUTS IN A BLENDER?
Try adding a small amount of sugar or flour, which will keep the nut pieces from sticking together.

BEST RESULTS

Stick with the Stick

When baking cookies or other desserts, avoid reduced-fat butters or margarines unless the recipe specifically calls for them. These low-fat products have a higher water content than regular butter or margarine, and the finished product will not turn out properly. Use the stick variety of butter or margarine instead.

5 SMART TESTS TO CHECK YOUR INGREDIENTS

Great baking results start with good ingredients. So how do you know if what you're working with is fresh?

The baking powder test. Did you know baking powder loses potency over time? If you can't remember when you bought yours, run a test before using it. Here's how: Put ½ teaspoon baking powder in a small bowl, then pour in ¼ cup hot tap water. The more vigorously the baking powder bubbles, the fresher it is. (Try this test on a fresh box of baking powder so you know what to look for.) Also, when buying baking powder, be sure to check the expiration date on the box. Once opened, it will remain fresh for about a year.

The baking soda test. If you're not sure how old your baking soda is, test its activity level. Stir ¼ teaspoon baking soda into about 2 teaspoons white vinegar. If it doesn't bubble vigorously, throw it out.

The yeast test. Is your yeast too old? Proof it to be sure it's not ready for retirement. Dissolve a little sugar in some warm water, then sprinkle in the yeast. The mixture should begin bubbling within 5 to 7 minutes. If it doesn't bubble, the yeast is too inactive to provide the leavening function and you should throw it away.

The egg test. In most cases, you'll use eggs before they ever go bad. They have a pretty long shelf life, especially if you turn the container upside down (the way we recommend on page 222). But just to be sure your eggs are good to go, you can give them a simple test. Fill a medium-size bowl with cold water. Then gently place the whole (uncracked) egg in the water. If the egg sinks to the bottom, it's fresh. If it floats to the top, go out and buy some fresh eggs.

The flour test. The best way to test flour is to smell or taste it. Rely on your senses to see if it smells rancid or tastes not quite right. A quick taste can also help when you're not sure whether the flour in your canister is self-rising or all-purpose. Self-rising flour is a bit salty because it contains baking powder.

Drop That Cake

That's right, drop it! After you pour the batter into the pan, smooth the top. Then, from a height of about a foot, drop the pan bottom on your countertop. The drop will magically knock out any air bubbles in the batter for a more professional cake shape and appearance. Do this for cakes leavened with baking soda or baking powder.

Drop Cookies Too

For cookies, the drop comes after you take them out of the oven. Just bang the pan straight down on the stove to force the cookies to settle.

Know the Temperature

When baking cakes and cookies, you should always start with room temperature ingredients, never cold ones. For pastry it is just the opposite—the ingredients should be cold.

Smooth Batter Secret

Having your cake or cookie ingredients (milk, butter, and eggs) at room temperature is the secret to smooth batter. If you haven't planned ahead, you can take the chill off milk and butter quickly in the microwave. But what about those eggs? Give them a warm bath! Place eggs from the fridge in a bowl of warm water. As the water cools, repeat by draining the bowl and refilling it with fresh warm water. Let the eggs sit in warm water for about 5 minutes before cracking and adding to the batter.

Don't Rush to the Oven

Did you know that it takes most ovens up to 15 minutes to preheat? For the best results when baking, always make sure you've given your oven enough time to preheat. If it's not quite hot enough, it can make a big difference with your recipe.

Check the Temp with Flour

If you suspect your oven's temperature doesn't match what's on the dial but you don't have an oven thermometer, try this simple test. Put 1 tablespoon flour on a baking sheet and place it in a preheated oven for 5 minutes. If the flour turns light tan, the temperature is 250° to 325°F. If the flour turns golden brown, the oven is 325° to 400°F. If it turns dark brown, the oven is 400° to 450°F. And an almost black color means the oven is 450° to 525°F. Figure out the disparity between what the temperature really is and what it reads, and make sure to set your oven accordingly in the future.

More Color for Cookies

If your cookies typically don't brown enough, bake them on a higher rack in the oven. Other baking fixes that could help browning are substituting a tablespoon or two of corn syrup for the sugar and using unbleached flour in the recipe.

Flatness Fix

Do your cookies come out thin and flat rather than thick and chewy? Sprinkle some flour on the baking sheet after you grease it but before you put the cookie dough down on top of it. The flour will keep your cookies from spreading out, which can be caused by the slickness of the greasy baking sheet.

Crispy Bread Crust

We love this secret to a perfect, crispy crust, which a baker friend passed along: Put some ice cubes in a shallow pan and place in the oven with your loaf of bread. This will produce a dense steam, and as the water evaporates, the crust will become hard and crispy. The steam will also allow the bread to rise more evenly, giving you a firm and chewy inside.

The Best Pie Crusts

The secret to flaky pie crust? Replace half of the called-for water with vodka! The ethanol in the vodka stops the growth of gluten, which makes the crust tough. Use half vodka for a lighter crust without any difference in taste!

Get Rid of Soggy Bottoms

It's always disappointing when you slice into your carefully prepared pie only to find that the bottom is soggy. If you have a problem with fruit or fruit juices soaking your pie crust and making it too wet, brush the bottom with egg white before adding the filling. This step will seal the crust and solve the problem. If your fruit filling is simply too wet, thicken it up. The best thickener is 3 to 4 tablespoons minute tapioca; mix it with the sugar before adding to the fruit. Other solutions for soggy pie bottoms include prebaking the pie crust, partially cooking the filling, or brushing the crust with jelly before you fill it. When using a cream filling in a pie, sprinkle the crust with granulated sugar before adding to prevent a soggy crust.

Shimmering Pies

Do you want your pies to glisten like those in the bakery? It's easy: Just beat an egg white and brush it over the crust before baking. This works especially well for a pie that has a crust cover, like apple.

Dust Your Nuts

Nuts and dried fruit are the perfect addition to muffins, breads, and other baked goods. But sometimes, after you pour the batter into the pan, they sink to the bottom. To keep this from happening, dredge the mix-ins in flour before stirring them into the batter. That way, they'll stay suspended in the cake and won't all end up at the bottom of the finished product.

Toast Those Oats

Our favorite part of oatmeal cookies, is—naturally—the oatmeal! Boost oatmeal flavor by toasting it lightly before adding it to the batter. Simply sprinkle the oatmeal on a baking sheet and heat it in a 300°F oven for about 10 minutes. The oats should turn a golden-brown.

Batter Up

For best results when baking cakes or cupcakes, follow two top rules: Use a cool pan, and never fill the tin more than two-thirds full. We can't guarantee other mistakes won't happen, but at least you'll have these basics covered!

Privacy for Baked Goods

Every time you open the oven to check on your baking goodies, you lower the temperature inside by about 50°F. Open the door only when you have to; otherwise, use the oven light and look through the window!

Try On-the-Spot Marshmallow Topping

Need a quick, delicious topping for your party cupcakes? Try this: During the final few minutes of baking time, place one large marshmallow on top of each cupcake. As the cooking continues, the marshmallows will melt into a sweet, sticky frosting—they're done when the tops become lightly browned.

Easy Mint-Chocolate Frosting

Here's another last-minute cupcake topping idea, this time using tasty chocolate-covered mints. When your cupcakes have baked and cooled, drop a mint on top of each one. Heat the cupcakes in the microwave, one by one, for just a few seconds. Remove and spread the melted mint-chocolate over the top.

BRUCE SAYS

Free Your Muffins
If you appreciate second uses for household items as much as we do, you'll love this tip. If you're having trouble getting your muffins out of the pan, try using a (clean) shoehorn! The curved shape should help them pop right out.

Bananas for Baking Anytime

Sudden craving for banana muffins or bread but your bunch isn't soft enough yet? You can speed the ripening process along with your oven! Line a baking pan with parchment paper or foil, then place the bananas on it and cook in a 300°F oven for 30 to 40 minutes. Remove them from the oven and let them cool for 20 to 30 minutes. Then peel and get to baking your favorite banana recipes!

Pie-Serving Secret

Pies with graham cracker crusts can be difficult to remove from the pan. However, if you dip the bottom of the pan in warm water for 10 seconds, the pie will come right out without any damage.

No More Muffin Mess

To easily remove muffins or rolls from a pan, set the pan on a damp kitchen towel for about 30 seconds. Repeat using a freshly moistened towel until the muffins can be eased out of the pan. Just be sure not to use your nicest towels—you can sometimes get slight scorch marks or fabric sticking.

Cakes Come Clean

Your beautiful cake is perfect except for one thing—you can't get it out of the pan! Lay out a sheet of wax paper and gently turn the whole thing over. Next, put a dish towel over the pan and press it with a hot steam iron. After a few minutes the pan should be ready for liftoff.

Rescue a Layer Cake

You decided to attempt a three-layer cake, and can't believe how great it looks. The problem? The layers are sliding so much it's starting to look like a Jenga game waiting to topple. Fix your presentation by cutting two straws so they're just shorter than the height of the cake, then insert and frost right over them (use four straws if it's really shaky). If anyone notices your cheat, they'll just be impressed!

Lock in Moisture

Do your cakes seem to dry out as they cool? Keep your cake moist by setting a piece of bread on top until you're ready to frost it. You can secure with a toothpick if you like. The cake will stay fresh and moist even if you let it sit overnight!

Double Your Frosting

You may not have time to make your own frosting, but you can blend store-bought frosting with a hand mixer to double the volume. This simple little trick saves money and calories!

Add a Cupcake Surprise

It's easier than you think to add a creamy center! Once your cupcakes are baked and cooled, poke a hole through the top of each one with a straw. Scoop the frosting of your choice into a zipper-lock plastic bag, and seal it up. Slice a small hole in one corner so you can pipe your frosting through the top of your cupcakes. When you're finished piping, spread frosting over the tops to cover the hole, or hide it with a chocolate chip or other candy.

Easy and Impressive Chocolate Garnish

Want to really impress your guests? Get out the bubble wrap! For an amazing garnish, spread melted chocolate on top of clean bubble wrap. Let it set, turn over, peel off the bubble wrap, and stand in awe of your creation. It's perfect for topping a cake, or you can break it into smaller pieces to garnish cupcakes, cocktails, or coffee.

Shake-On Decorating

Here's a neat tip for those who do a lot of baking: Fill a saltshaker with confectioners' or colored sugar for dusting candy, cakes, and cookies. For the best results, choose one with large holes.

Perfect Cake Slicing

To keep the frosting from sticking to your knife as you cut the cake, dip your knife into a glass of hot water between each cut. It will also keep cake crumbling to a minimum.

WHO KNEW?
READERS' FAVORITE

Take the Cake

You may have heard the old trick to transport a cake without smudging the frosting: inserting toothpicks, skewers, or even strands of uncooked spaghetti into it, then draping plastic wrap on top. But here's an even better twist: Don't just insert toothpicks and cover in plastic. Instead, attach miniature marshmallows to the toothpicks before covering. The sharp ends won't puncture the wrap and create a gooey mess.

6 SIMPLE WAYS TO SOFTEN HARDENED SUGAR

If you find that your sugar has become one giant lump, there are a bunch of simple ways to soften it up and bring it back to its former glory—or even head off the problem in the first place.

Bake the box. Brown sugar hardened in its original box? Forget the scraping with a spoon, and don't even think about tossing it out! Simply wrap the box in a ball of foil and bake it in a 350°F oven for 5 minutes. It will be back to its old self in no time. The sugar will be hot, so be sure to handle it carefully.

Pair it with these foods. Brown sugar loses moisture rather quickly and develops lumps easily. To soften hardened sugar, put it in the microwave with a slice of fresh white bread or half an apple, cover the dish tightly, and heat for 15 to 20 seconds; let it stand for 5 minutes before using. The moisture from the bread or apple will produce enough steam to soften the sugar without melting it. It's an easy solution with ingredients you likely have on hand!

Treat it to a towel. Another way to restore moisture? Give it the warm-towel treatment: Microwave brown sugar in a bowl covered with a damp paper towel in 15- to 20-second increments until soft. Use your fingers or a fork to soften any clumps that remain.

Prick a potato. Wash and dry a potato, then poke a few holes into the potato with a fork. Toss the potato in and seal the sugar container. Your brown sugar will be ready for action the next day, no matter how hard it has become.

Toss in a marshmallow or two. It'll add the moisture your brown sugar needs. You'll never have to throw out a hardened rock of brown sugar again, and you won't have to spend money on a special brown-sugar-keeper disk.

Feed it crackers. Granulated sugar clumps less than brown sugar, but it's still prone to getting lumpy. Keep this from happening by sticking a few salt-free crackers in the canister to absorb the moisture. Replace the crackers every week.

Bar Cookie Perfection

Want to know the secret to perfectly cut bar cookies? As soon as you remove your sweet creation from the oven, make a ¼-inch incision with a knife and outline your bars. Then, once they've cooled, cut all the way. This will ensure that the edges of your bars are as smooth as can be.

Carry Cupcakes Anywhere

Turn a shirt-box into the perfect cupcake carrier. Cut eight Xs equidistant from each other in the lid, then place it on top of the box. The cupcakes will fit snugly into each X, making them easy to take with you.

Keep Leftover Cake Moist

If you have leftover cake, you have more self-control than we do! One of the best methods of keeping the insides of a cake from drying out is to place a piece of fresh white bread next to the exposed surface. The bread can be affixed with a toothpick or a short piece of spaghetti.

Freeze with No Frosting Loss

Want to freeze a cake, but don't want the frosting to stick to the plastic wrap? First, put the cake in the freezer without any wrapping. Once the frosting is frozen, cover the cake with plastic wrap. The cold frosting won't stick to the wrap.

TRY A COOKIE STACK

Cookie bottoms keep burning? Try baking on two sheets stacked one on top of the other.

SECRET INGREDIENTS & SWAPS

Try these simple yet ingenious ways to boost flavor in recipes or replace what you don't have on hand in the kitchen.

FOR SWEETS AND BAKING

Better with Buttermilk

To give your muffins an extra tang and an incredibly light texture, swap out the milk for buttermilk. In addition, for every cup of milk that you substitute, add ½ teaspoon baking soda to the batter. You can also try this tip with plain yogurt. You'll win raves for that extra-special something in your muffins!

DIY Brown Sugar

Out of brown sugar but the recipe calls for it? You can make your own if you have white sugar and molasses. Simply mix in a bowl with a fork (or in a mixer) 1 tablespoon molasses per 1 cup granulated sugar for light brown sugar and 2 tablespoons molasses per 1 cup sugar for dark. Keep mixing until the molasses is fully incorporated—it may not look like it's happening at first, but keep the faith and fork stirring!

Lower-Calorie Sweetener

In spiced recipes like muffins and biscuits, try reducing the amount of sugar in your recipes by half and doubling the cinnamon. Not only will the cinnamon taste help retain sweetness with the fewest calories possible, but it has also been shown to help control blood sugar levels.

CUT THE FAT

When a baking recipe calls for vegetable oil, try substituting half of the oil with applesauce. It's an easy way to reduce the fat content in your food.

No Need for Heavy Cream

Making whipped cream? Save a trip to the store! Heavy cream isn't something we all keep in our fridge stock. You're more likely to have light cream, which can work perfectly fine for whipped cream if you know the trick. To whip light cream into a firm, mousse-like consistency, simply add 1 tablespoon unflavored gelatin dissolved in 1 tablespoon hot water for every 2 cups of cream. After whipping, refrigerate it for 2 hours.

Fast, Easy Fluff

However you make your whipped cream, you can give it more lasting power to hold its shape longer. The secret: Add a little marshmallow spread to the mix.

Two for One in Cakes

When baking a cake, try substituting two egg yolks for one whole egg. The cake will be very rich and dense, because the yolks don't hold as much air as the whites. This isn't exactly a healthy tip, but it sure tastes good!

Keep Your Cake Light

For a light, moist cake, enhance your cake flour by adding 2 tablespoons cornstarch to every 1 cup of cake flour, then sift them together before you add to the mix. You'll be pleasantly surprised by the results!

Spice Up Crusts

Next time you make a pie, add a little flavor to the crust by sprinkling a little ground spice or minced herbs into the flour. Use cinnamon or ginger with an apple or other dessert pie, and try finely chopped parsley with a quiche or meat pie.

Pumpkin Pie Loves Marshmallows

For a unique pumpkin pie, put small marshmallows on the bottom of the pie, just above the crust. As the pie bakes, the air in the marshmallows expands and the marshmallows rise to the top.

Add This for Extra-Rich Brownies

It may sound strange at first, but mashed or pureed avocado can replace oil or butter in many baked goods. It's especially good with chocolate and adds a rich, creamy texture to brownies. Bonus: It has healthy fats!

SENSATIONAL COOKIES

Want to take your classic chocolate chip cookie recipe to the next level? Simply shake on some coarse sea salt before baking.

JEANNE SAYS

Get Perfect Pancakes

If you like brown-on-the-outside pancakes like we do, add a little extra sugar to your batter. The sugar caramelizes, giving a darker color to the pancakes. Also, some people swear by adding a tablespoon of pure maple syrup (the real stuff—no imitations!) into your pancake batter.

Sweet Savings

To save money, purchase solid chocolate candy (usually in bunny or Santa form) after major holidays when it's gone on sale. Store the chocolate in the freezer, then shave off bits with a vegetable peeler to use on top of desserts.

Fix for Firmer Gelatin

If you've ever had a Jell-O salad melt at a picnic, you'll love this tip. When you add the water to any gelatin recipe in hot summer months, mix in a teaspoon of white vinegar to keep salads and desserts firm.

Lemon Extra Touch

Grate some lemon peel and mix it with sugar in a food processor for some delicious "lemon sugar," which is perfect for the tops of cookies and other desserts, as well as the rims of cocktail glasses!

Water Plus

Trying to break free from your soda or juice addiction? Add a couple of slices of lemon or orange (or both) to your filtered water pitcher, and try drinking that instead. Your taste buds will be satiated, and your body will thank you! If you find yourself drinking a lot of soda at work, bring the pitcher with you and place it on your desk. You'll find that you'll normally choose convenience over a run to the vending machine for your sugary fix.

Cup of Joe with a Twist

Flavored coffee is such a treat, but it's also expensive! Luckily, it's easy to add your own flavors with ingredients you have on hand. Orange peel, vanilla extract, cinnamon, allspice, or ground-up roasted nuts can all be mixed into coffee grinds before you brew. To make 6 cups of coffee, you just need ¼ teaspoon of whatever flavor you choose. Experiment to get the proportions exactly to your liking.

Easy, Sweet Coffee

If you love sweetened, flavored coffee, simply mix ¼ teaspoon vanilla extract or 1 teaspoon cinnamon with 1 cup sugar in a food processor until well-blended, then add a little scoop to your next cup. It's usually much cheaper than buying flavored coffees or creamers, and tastes better, too.

WHO KNEW?

READERS' FAVORITE

Enjoy a Full-Flavored Drink

Who doesn't enjoy an iced coffee on a sultry summer day? To make sure melting ice doesn't dilute your drink, make ice cubes using the small amount of coffee left at the bottom of your coffee pot each morning. Use them in your iced coffee and it will never taste watered down. This is also a great tip for iced tea!

9 KITCHEN DILEMMAS DENTAL FLOSS CAN SOLVE

Smart substitutions for kitchen tools are just as helpful to know as ingredient swaps. Here are clever ways that floss you get for free at the dentist's office can be invaluable in the kitchen.

Cut your cake cleanly. If you've got a delicate cake that will fall apart and stick to the knife when you cut it, use dental floss to slice it. Hold a strand of floss at both ends and pull it taut, then slice it through your cake.

Slice a log of cookie dough. Using floss (rather than a knife) to slice will give you clean cookies that don't crumble or smoosh. This technique works well for cinnamon rolls, too.

Free stuck cookies. Cookies stuck to the baking sheet? Work some dental floss between each cookie and the sheet and you should be able to remove them easily.

Slice delicate cheeses. One of the easiest ways to cut cheeses like feta, goat cheese, and even mozzarella into perfect rounds? Use dental floss! Hold the floss tight and move it down with a gentle sawing motion.

Release dough from cutting boards. When you're rolling out dough, it's not hard for it to get stuck. Slide the floss under the dough and lift gently to free it.

Tie and dry herbs. Bundle them using floss and hang them with leaves facing down to dry. It should take about 10 days for leaves to feel dry to the touch—that's your indication that they are ready to use.

Truss with floss. You might know that "trussing" means tying the wings and legs of a bird down for more even cooking. But do you know which is the best string to use for trussing? Dental floss! Not only does it come in a small container that's easy to handle, but it's also very strong and won't burn in high heat.

Cut wraps, burritos, calzones, sushi rolls, and more. A heavy knife will slice but also drag out all the filling. Try a gentler approach with floss.

Enjoy hard-boiled eggs. Always cool a hard-boiled egg before you try to slice it; it will slice more easily and won't fall apart. Your best implement if you don't have an egg slicer? Dental floss! Just hold taut and slice through the egg—it'll work beautifully without crumbling the yolk.

SAVORY SECRETS

Sweet Addition to Chili

Although it may sound unusual, chocolate makes a great addition to chili. Save it for the last hour of cooking. Just chop up one milk chocolate bar and add it to the pot to meld with the flavors. Once you try it, you'll add it every time!

Save Your Rinds

The rinds of hard cheeses like Parmesan are great flavor enhancers for soups. Add a 3-inch square to your next pot of soup, and when you're serving the soup, break up the delicious, softened rind and include a little of it in each bowl. It's completely edible.

A Cottage Cheese Shortcut

When making meatballs, meatloaf, or hamburger patties, try adding ½ cup cottage cheese for every pound of ground meat. Not only does it add flavor and protein, but it will also stretch your recipe to serve a few more people.

Frozen Fish Fix

Pining for fresh fish but stuck with frozen? Try this: Cover the frozen fish in milk until it thaws, then cook. Your family will never know it was frozen!

The Secret to Crispy Chicken

Make your fried chicken super-crispy by adding 3 to 4 teaspoons cornstarch to each cup of flour. Or add 1 teaspoon baking soda to the batter. Then sit back and wait for your fried chicken to win raves!

Beautifully Browned Bird

Try basting your bird with a small amount of white zinfandel or vermouth—it will help crisp the skin, and the alcohol imparts a brown color and glaze to the outside of the meat. Or brush the skin with reduced-sodium soy sauce during the last 30 minutes of cooking to produce a beautiful burnished color.

Your New Favorite Breadcrumbs

Look to the side dishes in your pantry for crisper, more flavorful alternatives to breadcrumbs. Instant mashed potato flakes pair perfectly with fish, and chefs swear by them for frying up amazing onion rings. Or try grinding Arborio rice to use in place of breadcrumbs—it caramelizes beyond compare.

Want Free Breadcrumbs?

Set aside a special jar and pour in the crumbs from the bottom of cracker or low-sugar cereal boxes. Also add crumbs from leftover garlic bread and a few dried herbs, and soon you'll have seasoned breadcrumbs!

Bring Cookies to Dinner

Slow-cooker pot roast is an easy meal for families on the go. But you can make it extra tasty by sprinkling some crushed gingersnaps over the top of the roast. The mix of sweet and spice is perfect. Comfort food with cookies—what could be better?

Shake Up Beef Stew

Making beef stew? Shake up a bottle of Italian dressing and brown the meat in it to infuse flavor. Add about ½ cup per 3 pounds of beef.

Sauté with Sugar

Before sautéing meats, sprinkle a tiny amount of sugar on the surface of the meat. The sugar will react with the juices and then caramelize, causing a deeper browning as well as a tastier result.

Don't Pour That Pickle Juice!

Did you know that the acid in pickle juice acts as a meat tenderizer? Use that juice mixed with garlic and your favorite spices as a marinade for pork, steak, or chicken. Let sit for at least an hour or overnight. You can also use pickle juice to add zing to boiled potatoes—just add a little to the boiling water.

Add This to Pasta and Rice Pots

Keep pots of pasta or rice from boiling over by adding 1 tablespoon butter to the water when you add the pasta or rice.

TAKE TOMATO SAUCE TO A NEW LEVEL

After you've simmered your favorite recipe, remove the sauce from the heat. Then stir in most of the zest from a lemon, reserving some for sprinkling on top.

WHO KNEW?

READERS' FAVORITE

Another Reason to Open a Bottle

Wine corks (the natural kind, not plastic) contain a chemical that, when heated, will help tenderize beef stew. Just throw in three or four corks while cooking your stew, and don't tell anyone your secret!

Starchy Secret

Preparing pasta? If you put a few drops of vinegar into the water as it boils, the starch will be reduced, making the pasta less sticky. This also works with rice: For every cup of uncooked rice, add a splash of vinegar.

SUPER-FLUFFY MASHED POTATOES

Add a pinch or two of baking powder, powdered milk, or even instant potatoes for extra fluff.

Chef's Pasta Trick

Before you drain pasta, scoop out a cup of the cooking water. When you toss the pasta with the sauce, add a little bit of the water. The starchy water will help the sauce cling to the pasta, making for a tastier dish.

The Best Fries Around

For the greatest French fries, soak cut potatoes in ice-cold water in the refrigerator for an hour; this will harden them so that they absorb less fat. Dry them thoroughly, then fry them twice. First cook them for 6 to 7 minutes, drain them well, and sprinkle them lightly with flour (this step makes them extra crispy and crunchy). Then fry them again for 1 to 2 minutes, until they are golden brown.

Delicious Low-Fat Mashed Potatoes

If you're watching your weight but love mashed potatoes, cut out the milk and the butter (or just some of it). Instead, save some of the cooking water from the potatoes and use that instead. Season with freshly ground black pepper and a bit of lemon juice for a no-added-fat, flavorful mash.

Simple Herb Substitution

We've all been in this situation: You want to make a particular recipe, but you only have the dried form of the herb called for. Save yourself a trip to the supermarket with this handy rule of thumb. When using dried, use a third of the amount that's called for of the fresh herb, and vice versa. For example, 1 tablespoon fresh oregano equals 1 teaspoon dried.

No Wine? No Problem

Making a recipe that calls for wine and don't have any on hand (or prefer not to use it)? Try these easy substitutions. Replace red wine with cranberry juice and white wine with white grape or apple juice. Your dish will taste just as good and you'll save money, too!

Quick Thickeners

An easy method for thickening stews, soups, or creamed vegetables is to add a small amount of quick-cooking oats, a grated potato, or some instant mashed potatoes. Never add flour directly, as it will clump. But if you're a particularly prepared cook, you can combine a stick of melted butter with ½ cup flour, then place it in a covered bowl in the refrigerator and let it harden. Then when you want a thickener, simply add some of this special mixture. It melts easily and will thicken without lumps.

Save Your Celery Leaves

Don't throw away celery leaves—while they don't work well with dips, they still have a wonderful flavor similar to parsley. When chopping celery, set the leaves aside on a paper plate, let them dry, and throw them in stuffing, salads, and soups for great extra flavor. You can also keep bacon from splattering all over the stove (and the cook) by adding a few celery leaves to the pan.

Tender, Sweet Corn

Never add salt to the water when boiling corn; table salt contains traces of calcium, which will toughen the kernels. Instead, add a little milk to the cooking water, which will bring out the sweetness of the corn.

Reduce Green Odors

Kale, cabbage, and collard greens are delicious to eat, but can sometimes smell stinky when they're being prepared. Be sure not to overcook them—that's what makes them release odors. Also try placing a few unshelled pecans in the saucepan while cooking, which will help absorb any scents.

Meet Brussels Sprouts' Best Friend

Boiling Brussels sprouts can cause a distinct sulfur odor to pervade your kitchen. To prevent this sour smell, just throw a few celery stalks into the pot with the sprouts—they'll absorb the odor and neutralize the scent.

GRILLING GENIUS

Become a grill master with wallet-friendly ways to keep your barbecue cooking, impress your backyard guests, and speed cleanup.

EASY PREP AND TOOLS

Get Set for BBQ Season

Make sure your outdoor grill is prepped anytime you want to call it into action. Clean the grates by placing them in the tub and covering with very hot water and 1 cup each ammonia and dishwasher detergent. Cover with old fabric softener sheets and soak overnight. The next day, don your rubber gloves, scrub away, and watch the grease dissolve.

PLAY KEEPAWAY

Store charcoal briquettes in airtight plastic bags—charcoal absorbs moisture very easily and won't be as easy to light if exposed to air.

The Cleaner from the Produce Section

Your barbecued chicken was a hit, but your grill is a mess. What to do? Poke half an onion, dipped in vegetable oil, on your grill fork, and scrub it over the hot grates. The onion's enzymes will break down grime, and the oil will help soften the grilled-on gunk.

Grill-Cleaning Muscle for Less

Save on expensive grill cleaners by simply using WD-40 instead. Get rid of charred food stuck to the grill by removing it from the barbecue and spraying it with the oil. Let sit for 5 to 10 minutes, then wipe off and clean with soap and water.

Foil That Mess

When you're done cooking, place a large piece of aluminum foil over the entire grill, then put the top back on and let it sit for 10 to 15 minutes. The caked-on mess from the burgers and hot dogs will turn to ash.

Today's News: A Clean Grill

Another great way to clean your grill is with wet newspaper. After cooking, just place it on a warm grill for 1 hour with the lid closed. You'll be amazed by how easily the grime comes off!

Dress Your Grill

Don't spend big money on a grill cover! Just look for an inexpensive rain poncho at a discount store—it'll do the trick and protect your grill just as well.

Keep the BBQ Going

It's unforgivable to run out of fuel before the last kebab is bobbed! Even without a gas gauge, there is a way to figure out how much fuel you have left. Here's what to do a day or two before the flip-flopped masses are set to arrive. Boil water, then pour it down the side of the tank. Place your hand on the side: the cool part has propane inside, the warm part is empty.

Sugar Solution

Can't get the charcoal going, and don't have any lighter fluid? Try using sugar. Once sugar is exposed to a flame, it decomposes rapidly and releases a fire-friendly chemical that can help ignite that stubborn charcoal. Simply apply a light dusting of sugar to the coals before you light them.

DIY Chimney Starter

Using one of these metal canisters makes getting charcoal good and hot a cinch! You simply place crumpled newspaper at the bottom and pile charcoal on top, then light the newspaper. The upward draft created by the chimney shape helps spread the heat to the charcoal in no time. You can buy one, but it's simple to make your own. All you need to do: remove both ends of a large coffee can with a can opener, and you've got a canister ready for charcoal. A set of pliers helps you lift off the hot chimney and free the coals once the charcoal is ready for cooking.

REUSE THOSE CARTONS

Cardboard egg cartons are great to use when starting fires (in your fireplace or outside). Fill them with bits of wood and paper, like receipts. You can also fill an egg carton with charcoal and use it to start your barbecue grill.

Wood Chips Made Easy

Getting wood chips ready for the grill by soaking them? It's easy to make sure they stay submerged in a zipper-lock bag filled with water. And it's easy to carry the bag right out to the grill.

JEANNE SAYS

Create a Clever Condiment Tray

Preparing condiments for a barbecue? Use a muffin tin! It's the perfect size for toppings like chopped onions, relish, shredded lettuce, pickles, and more. Plus, you'll only have one dish to wash.

Make Your Grill Super-Hot

To get your grill even hotter (making sure the bar marks on your steak are extra impressive), cover it with a large sheet of foil for 10 minutes before cooking. This little step will keep the heat from escaping.

Put Herbs to Work

To get the most out of that grilled flavor everyone loves so much, add a few sprigs of your favorite herbs, such as rosemary, thyme, and savory, directly to the top of the charcoal as you grill. It will infuse whatever you're cooking with mouthwatering flavor. Bonus: Rosemary and sage are mosquito repellents to keep the buggers away from your BBQ crowd!

Food Safety While Saving Dishes

When you're making hamburgers, place a sheet of plastic wrap on your platter before adding the raw patties. Once you've added them to the pan or the grill, you can toss the plastic and the platter underneath will still be clean for the cooked burgers. That way you don't have to wash two dishes, and you protect your family from potentially harmful bacteria.

Add a Warming Rack

While gas grills usually have a built-in warming rack, most charcoal grills don't. But you can create your own by setting a smaller rack on top of two empty tin cans placed on the main grill rack. Now you can keep food warm until you're ready to serve. The lift also gives you control when you want to toast (not burn!) buns.

THE MAIN EVENT

Juicy Burgers Begin with Ice

The secret to a super-juicy burger that will impress your barbecue guests is closer than you think. Just head to your icemaker! Fold an ice cube into the center of each burger patty, or use your thumb to make an indentation and set the ice cube on top. As it cooks, the ice cube melts and locks moisture into the burger.

No More Burger Breakups

Keep your hamburgers from breaking apart on the grill by sticking them in the freezer for 5 minutes before cooking. The brief shock of cold will help them keep their shape.

Barbecued Ribs in 30 Minutes

Love barbecued ribs but don't love the long cooking time required to get that lip-smacking, fall-off-the-bone texture? Make them a weeknight favorite with this secret for getting them on the table in half an hour. Put 2 pounds of meat in a bowl and coat with a cup of your favorite barbecue sauce. Cover the bowl and microwave it for 8 minutes. Then turn the ribs and return them to the microwave for another 8 to 10 minutes. After you pull them out, grill the ribs over high heat for a few minutes per side until beautifully burnished.

Easy Squeeze for Sauce

If you have your own special recipe for barbecue or hot sauce, it's probably a must-have at every cookout. The perfect container for storing and dispensing it is a water bottle with a squirt top. Buy water in one of these types of bottles at the store for a container that's easy to toss out, or use a reusable one with your favorite team's logo when tailgating or watching the game at home.

Give Meat a Spritz

While you're grilling, keep some apple juice in a spray bottle nearby. Periodically spritz your meat for more flavor and tenderness and better color. So simple! Just resist the urge to spray your guests.

Mayo Magic for Fish

Fish on the grill is delicious and super-nutritious. The tricky part? Fish tends to stick to the hot grill grates, leaving you with grilled fish scraps rather than plump fillets. For extra lubrication, try coating the fish in mayonnaise instead of oil—the thicker texture makes it harder for the flesh to grip the metal. Plus, mayo adds a new layer of yummy seasoning.

Think Thick for Grilling Fish

If you plan on grilling fish, be sure to purchase steaks that are at least 1 inch thick. Fish dries out very quickly on the grill, so the thicker it is, the better. The skin should be left on fillets while grilling and removed after they are cooked.

BRUCE SAYS

Grill Vacancy Can Save Dinner

It's tempting to squeeze as much good food as you can onto the grill. But it's smarter to always leave 30 percent of your grill empty when cooking. Next time a flare-up occurs, it's easy to move your dinner out of harm's way and prevent charring.

No-Stick Grilled Scallops

Grilled scallops can be a special treat, but only if you don't leave half of them stuck to your grill's grate! Try this trick at your next barbecue to ensure great results. Whisk together 3 tablespoons oil, 1 tablespoon all-purpose flour, and 1 teaspoon cornstarch. Brush this mixture all over the scallops before grilling and they'll brown without sticking.

Double-Team Your Kebabs

When barbecuing meat and veggies, use two skewers per kebab. It's a simple trick to stop food pieces from spinning when you rotate the skewers. Be sure to soak wooden skewers in water for 30 minutes beforehand to keep them from burning.

GRILLING SOMETHING DELICATE?

To prevent food free-fall, place an extra grill rack under the grill and perpendicular to it.

Naturally Seasoned Skewers

Skip the usual wooden or metal skewers, and swap in rosemary sprigs. Look for long sprigs that have especially thick and sturdy stems. Simply remove the leaves from about three-quarters of the sprig to allow room for your kebab ingredients, and set aside the rosemary leaves for another use. No presoaking, plus you add amazing flavor and aroma! They look gorgeous, too.

Perfect Grilled Corn

Doing some grilling? Impress your guests by barbecuing fresh corn to perfection this way: Before grilling, peel all but the innermost layer of husk from the corn, and trim the excess silks as well. Place on the grill and as soon as the husk darkens enough that the outlines of the kernels are visible through it, remove the corn. It will be perfectly cooked and have a wonderful, smoky flavor.

No More Smoke in Your Eyes

The simple secret: Lift the grill's lid away from your face. And make sure that you are not standing downwind from the fire.

Sweet Finale

You've enjoyed your main grilling event and started to shut down the grill. While the heat remains, make a fun dessert: banana boats. Slice deep lengthwise cuts along the curves of unpeeled bananas, being careful not to cut all the way through. Now fill in the banana slits you've created with chocolate chips, mini marshmallows, chopped nuts, or any other topping you dream up. Wrap the bananas in aluminum foil and place on the grill, cut-side up, for 8 to 10 minutes before spooning out the gooey goodness.

FRESHER FOOD LONGER

The average American household throws away up to $2,200 of food each year. Reclaim that money and enjoy fresher meals with these hints!

FRUIT AND VEGETABLE SECRETS

Lasting Lemons

Lemons will stay fresh for up to 3 months if you store them in a bowl of water in the fridge. Just change the water every week. Who knew?

Zest Anytime You Need It

Don't toss those lemons after you've used their juice! Store halves in zipper-lock bags in the freezer until you need their zest for a recipe.

Fresh Apples All Day

Keep sliced apples from browning in your kid's lunchbox with a rubber band! Hold the apple together while slicing (an apple slicer works best), then secure the rubber band around it to hold it together. The cut edges will stay on the inside and until your child takes off the rubber band!

Mold-Free Melons

To keep melons from getting moldy as they ripen, rub the exterior rind with a teaspoon of full-strength vinegar every few days.

JEANNE SAYS

Perk Up Apples

If apples are dry or bland, slice them and put them in a dish, and then pour cold apple juice over them and refrigerate for 30 minutes. OK, so it's kind of a cheat, but it will ensure picky eaters get their nutrients!

**SEND
CUKES TO
THE COUNTER**
Surprise! Cucumbers
will last longer at
room temperature,
whereas keeping
them in the fridge
will accelerate
their decay.

Shake Up Your Pineapple

Did you know that the natural sugars in pineapple have a tendency to settle on the bottom of the fruit? If you don't dig into that pineapple soon enough, you may find mold forming on the bottom. For longer storage, slice off the leaves and turn the fruit upside down on the counter. Flip which side is up every other day or so. That way, the sugars will be evenly distributed throughout the entire pineapple.

Great Grapes

The best way to keep your grapes lasting longer? Keep them unwashed and attached to their stems until you're ready to eat them. This will ensure they don't become waterlogged and susceptible to bacteria.

Berry Bath to Beat Bacteria

Get rid of any mold spores lurking on your berries or greens by rinsing them well in vinegar water before putting them in your fridge. After discarding any berries that show even a bit of mold, put 3 cups cold water and 1 cup white vinegar in a large bowl or salad spinner. Immerse the berries, and swish around for about a minute. Drain the berries, then rinse with clean, cold water until any trace of vinegar aroma or taste is gone. Spread out rinsed berries on a clean cloth or paper towels, and pat and roll lightly with towels to dry them well.

The Gentlest Way to Dry Berries

Berries need to be rinsed, but they taste (and keep) best when they're dry. Here's the best drying technique: Set a dry dish towel on the counter, stretched out lengthwise. After rinsing the berries, place them in the center of the towel. Then fold the towel in as you would a formal letter. Take an end in each hand to hold the towel loosely, then tilt the package gently back and forth to roll the berries dry.

Bring Berries Back

Berries gone soft but not moldy or rotten? Place them in a single layer on a parchment-lined baking sheet and stick in the freezer for 20 minutes. They'll be firm enough again to serve with ice cream or yogurt.

Refrigerate Raisins

Raisins will last for several months at room temperature if they are wrapped tightly in plastic or stored in a plastic bag. They will last even longer (up to a year) if you place the plastic bag in the refrigerator.

Wrap Bananas Right

Bananas are almost as bad as berries when it comes to how quickly they can go from perfect to overripe. It often seems like the blink of an eye! But you can make your bananas last longer without brown spots by simply wrapping the stems in plastic wrap. Why it works: The stems are the hot spot for ethylene gas emission, which brings on the browning. Contain the stems and you minimize the spread to the rest of the banana. Simple and smart!

Keep Figs Fresh Longer

Figs are fragile—they bruise and spoil quickly if left to bump against each other in a bowl or bag. So treat them like another fragile food: eggs. Place figs in an empty egg carton to protect their personal space and help them stay fresh to enjoy longer.

Raisin Rejuvenation

Sad-looking raisins? To plump them up to perfection, place them in a small baking dish with a little water, cover, and bake in a preheated 325°F oven for 6 to 8 minutes. Or pour boiling water over the raisins and let them stand for 10 to 15 minutes, then drain.

Tip-Top Tomatoes

For the best storage, keep tomatoes stem-side down in a cool place on your counter. Because they're fairly delicate, placing tomatoes upside down thwarts air from entering through their stems, which accelerates ripening. If they're stored in the fridge, they'll lose flavor and develop a mealy texture.

Give Your Veggies a Haircut

If you've purchased vegetables with leafy tops, such as beets or carrots, remove the green tops before you store them in the fridge. The greens will leach moisture from the root or bulb and shorten the vegetable's shelf life.

Lasting Lettuce

Your lettuce will last longer if you store it in a bag with a piece of nearly burned toast. Yes, really! The toast will absorb moisture from the lettuce, making it last a long time. Check the toast daily, and replace it once it gets soggy.

NEVER THROW OUT OVERRIPE BANANAS!
Stick them in the freezer once they get completely brown, and you can still use them later for banana bread and other baking projects (just peel them first).

Revive Limp Celery

Have you ever found it hard to use up an entire package of celery before it starts going all rubbery on you? To get the celery crisp again, place it in a bowl of ice water with a few slices of potato, then wait an hour. When you come back to it, it will be ready to use.

Leave the Seeds

When using only part of a red, green, or yellow pepper, cut it from the bottom or the sides, leaving the seeds attached, and it will remain moist for longer. You can put the rest in a resealable plastic bag and use it within 3 to 4 days.

Make the Most of Mushrooms

The best way to store mushrooms in the fridge? Leave them in their original container, uncovered except for a single layer of cheesecloth on top.

Move Mushrooms to the Freezer

Can't use all of your mushrooms? To freeze, wipe them off with a damp paper towel and slice them. Then sauté them in a small amount of butter or olive oil until they are almost done. Remove from the heat, allow them to cool, then place the mushrooms in an airtight plastic bag in the freezer. They should keep for up to 10 to 12 months.

A SWEET TIP FOR A SWEET PEPPER

If you eat pimientos, be sure to cover them in vinegar before storing them in the fridge. They'll last much longer!

Keep Onions Fresh

The sugar content of yellow onions makes them spoil quickly if they are stored closely together. The solution is to store your onions in an old (clean) pair of pantyhose, making knots in the legs so the onions can't touch. It might look a little weird, but it works!

Better with Butter

You've chopped up half an onion and you'd like to save the rest for later. Make sure the onion lasts longer in your fridge by rubbing the cut end with butter, then wrapping in plastic wrap.

Freeze the Green

Have way too many green onions left after using what you need for your recipe? Chop them up and freeze them in an empty water bottle (plastic or glass). They'll be quick to pull out whenever you need to add some to a stew.

Save the White, Too!

Quit wasting money on green onions! Next time you buy fresh green onions, don't toss the white ends. Instead, stick them in a glass of water and place the glass in a sunny window. In a few days, the onions will begin to regrow. Then whenever you have a recipe that calls for green onions, just snip off what you need. Keep the water fresh by changing every so often.

Separate Your Onions and Potatoes

Potatoes hate onions . . . at least until they're cooked together. Onions should never be stored with potatoes, because moisture from the onions can cause potatoes to sprout. Onions also release gases that will alter the flavor of a potato.

Pair Potatoes Right

If you store fresh ginger with potatoes it will help keep them fresh longer. Half an apple stored with potatoes will stop them from sprouting by absorbing moisture before the potato does.

Cool for Corn

Always store corn in a cool, dry location, and keep the ears separated in order to prevent them from becoming moldy. As it warms up, the sugar in corn converts to starch very quickly, so eat as soon as possible for the sweetest corn. But if you can't finish . . .

Freeze Those Cobs

Did you know you could freeze corn on the cob? After shucking the corn, boil it for 5 minutes, then plunge it into ice water and pat dry. Pack the cobs in a freezer bag before freezing. To cook, place the frozen corn in boiling water for 10 to 15 minutes.

Give Guacamole a Sprinkle

You may look good with a tan, but your guacamole sure doesn't! To keep the avocados from oxidizing (which causes the brown color), cut them with a silver or stainless steel knife, and leave the pit in the dip (until serving). Sprinkle lemon juice on the surface of the dip, and cover tightly with plastic wrap until you're ready to eat.

Water Your Asparagus

To make asparagus last longer in the refrigerator, place the stem ends in a container of water, or wrap them in a wet paper towel and put in a plastic bag. Like flowers, the asparagus spears will continue "drinking" the water and stay fresh until they're ready to use.

Hooray for Puree

Fruit or veggies about to go bad? Give them a second life by cutting off any bruised or bad spots, then pureeing and freezing or refrigerating. Pureed fruit works great in muffin recipes or mixed into ice cream, while pureed veggies add nutrients to pasta sauce, stews, and casseroles.

Simple Mold Fighter

It is always a good idea to line the crisper bins of your refrigerator with newspaper or a few paper towels to absorb excess moisture. Mold spores love moisture, but the paper will keep it away.

Keep Fruit Looking Fresh

Even though the taste isn't affected, it's still disappointing to unveil your fruit salad only to discover a thin layer of brown oxidation all over the fruit. A common method for keeping cut fruit looking fresh is to add a bit of lemon juice. However, an even more effective method is to fill a spray bottle with water and a few dissolved vitamin C tablets (usually available in the vitamin and nutritional supplement section of the drugstore). Spray this mixture on the cut fruit and not only will you stop the oxidation but you'll be getting added vitamins as well!

Fresh-Cut Veggies Stay Fresh

If you'll have crudités at your outdoor party, keep those cut veggies fresh and crunchy by storing them properly: Place damp paper towels over the vegetables and wrap everything in plastic wrap. Stick the wrapped veggies in the fridge until it's time to serve. Carrots, broccoli, and peppers will stay bright and crisp for 12 hours.

SAVE HERBS AND SPICES

Sensitive Spices

Both cayenne pepper and paprika are affected by light and heat, and have a shorter shelf life than just about anything else on your spice rack. In fact, take them off your spice rack and store them both in the refrigerator for a longer life.

Best Way to Store Dried

Do your dried herbs and spices lose some of their zest after sitting on your spice rack for years? Spices and dried herbs keep their flavor better if stored in a cupboard away from heat, light, and moisture, all of which impair flavor, change color, and shorten life. Make them last longer by putting half into a sealed, airtight container when you purchase them. Label the container and keep it in your dark cabinet, or better yet, your freezer. When the spice on hand loses its aroma, replace it with some from your stash, and you'll never have to be irritated about throwing away an entire container of mustard seed or marjoram again.

Tuck In Fresh Herbs

Fresh herbs are a wonderful addition to any dinner, but let's face it: They go bad quickly and they're hard to freeze. To keep herbs fresh longer, loosely wrap them in a damp paper towel, store in a plastic bag, and keep in the vegetable crisper of the refrigerator.

Grab a Jar

Fresh herbs like parsley and cilantro will last for at least a couple of weeks if you store them in a jar. Just clip the stems of the herbs and place them in a jar with water in it, like you would with flowers. Cover loosely with a plastic bag and refrigerate.

Go Frozen with Ginger

Keep raw ginger in a sealed plastic bag in the freezer, and it will last pretty much forever. Best of all, you don't need to defrost it before you grate it into stir-fries, sauces, or whatever else you're making.

DIY Drying

Don't throw away fresh herbs if you've got more on hand than you need. Just rinse the leaves, air dry, and place (in a single layer) on a plate with a paper towel. Then microwave them in 30-second intervals until they're crunchy (which can take up to 4 minutes). If you store them in an airtight container, they'll last for a year!

Revive Old Spices

Crushing dried herbs gives them a boost when they're past their flavor prime. Don't have a mortar and pestle? A great way to crush spices is to place them in a pan and press them with the bottom of a smaller pan. A dedicated coffee grinder works well, too.

Better with Butter

For a delicious way to preserve the bounty of summer herbs, try making a compound butter. First, allow a stick of butter to soften on the counter. Meanwhile, chop up some of your favorite herbs. Then blend together the herbs and the softened butter with a food processor or hand mixer. Turn the mixture out onto parchment paper and roll it into a log. Place the log in a freezer bag, and freeze for up to several months. Whenever you want a taste of summer, just cut off a small piece and use on steaks, bread, and sautéed vegetables. Delicious!

Fresh Taste from Frozen

Enjoy fresh herbs from your garden all year round (or preserve expensive herbs before they go bad) with this tip: Just chop clean leaves, pat dry, and freeze in ice cube trays with enough water to cover the leaves. Then pop into dishes for a fresh, summery taste.

BEST TIPS FOR BEVERAGES

Save Your Wine by Losing Your Marbles

How do those boxes of wine last so much longer than open bottles? Their design minimizes air entry, which brings on spoilage and compromises taste. You can create your own wine-saving storage with a mason jar when you have just a little left. Pour the leftover wine into the jar, then add clean marbles until the jar is full with no space for air. Close off with the jar's airtight lid.

Soda That Pops

Yes, there is a way to keep open soda from going flat—not for a month, but for an hour or so. Leave an open can or bottle inside a sealed plastic freezer bag while you run out to do your errands, and it will still be bubbly when you get back.

A Fizzy Trick

To make the bubbles in your soda last longer, decrease the amount of air that the carbon dioxide (which causes the fizz) has to escape into. This is easily accomplished by squeezing in the sides of the bottle after you pour a glass.

SAVOR THOSE SPROUTS

If your head of garlic sprouts, it's still perfectly good to eat. Some of the flavor will go into the sprouts—chop them off and add to salads for a delicious treat!

PANTRY POWER

Perfect Partner for Bread

Bread stays fresh for a longer time if you place it in an airtight bag with a stalk of celery. If you are going to freeze a loaf of bread, make sure you include a paper towel in the package to absorb moisture. This will keep the bread from becoming mushy when thawed.

Bread Gone Stale?

Simply wet your fingers and flick some water on the top and sides of the loaf. Then wrap in foil and heat in a preheated 250°F oven for 10 minutes. It will taste fresh again!

Extend That Bread

If you really want to impress your dinner guests, make some homemade croutons for your salad. After cutting your leftover bread into cubes, fry in olive oil and a little garlic powder (not garlic salt), a pinch of Parmesan cheese, and parsley. Fry until they're brown, then let cool on paper towels. You can also cut the bread into smaller pieces, then chop in a blender or food processor to make breadcrumbs (you may have to cut off the bottom crust first).

Soften Hardened Marshmallows

If you find an old bag of hardened marshmallows, add a slice of very fresh white bread or half an apple to the bag to soften them. Note that this is not a quick fix: You might need to leave the bag for 1 or 2 days until the marshmallows absorb the moisture. But at least you won't have to throw them out! Next time, store them in the freezer, then just cut them apart with scissors dipped in very hot water.

Flip for This PB Tip

All-natural nut butters are healthy and delicious, but it takes a lot of arm action to stir them every time you pull out the jar! The answer: Flip their jars upside down to keep them from separating. Keep the lids screwed on tight, and don't try to do this with a lid that doesn't screw onto the jar.

Secret Ingredient for the Cookie Jar

To keep your cookies soft until the last one is eaten, add half an apple or a slice of white bread to the cookie jar. This will provide just enough moisture to keep the cookies from becoming hard.

Cap That Bag Closed

You can create an airtight, sealed bag with the top part of an old plastic bottle. All you need to do is cut off the top of the bottle and take off the cap. Push the bag through the bottleneck, fold it over the edges, and twist the cap back on. It's much more effective at keeping food fresh than the usual clothespin method.

Make a 2-in-1 Package

You can divide a bag of beans or noodles in half without measuring or moving the food into a separate container. Simply lay the package flat and even out the contents. Then pinch the bag in the center, twist, and secure tightly with a rubber band. It should look like an hourglass but with no space for contents to cross from one side of the bag to the other. To use one portion, snip a corner of the bag open. The rest of the bag remains secure for another time.

FRIDGE AND FREEZER SMARTS

Relocate Milk and Cheese

It's better to store milk on an inside shelf toward the back of the refrigerator, not on the door. Why? All dairy products are very perishable. The optimal refrigeration temperature is actually just over 32°F; however, few refrigerators are ever set at or hold that low a temperature. Most home refrigerators remain around 40°F, and the temperature rises every time the door is opened. Store cheese near the bottom of the refrigerator, where temperature fluctuations are minimal.

PINCH YOUR MILK

Add a pinch of salt to a carton of milk to keep it fresh for a week or so past its expiration date.

Save with a Freeze

When you know your milk is going to go bad before you can use up the rest of it, separate it into a few resealable containers and put them in your freezer. That's right, milk can be frozen! If you use skim milk, it can be thawed and drunk later, and you'll never be able to tell the difference in taste. For other varieties of milk, after thawing, use for sauces or baking. This is a great strategy for when you find milk at a deep discount. Buy as much as you can and freeze for later!

Stop the Clump

Whether you shred your own or use store-bought bags, shredded cheese can clump in its package. A simple trick: Add in a pinch of cornstarch or flour. The addition will coat the shreds and keep them separated.

Sweet Cheese Tip

Cheese will stay mold-free longer if placed in a sealed plastic container with a tight-fitting lid. Wrap it in a cloth dampened in white vinegar. Then add three or four sugar cubes, which will attract any mold if some does form.

Revive Moldy Cheese

Cheese with a little mold on it is still perfectly safe to eat once you remove the offending areas. The easiest way to do this is to take a knife, dip it in vinegar, and slice the mold off. Dip the knife in vinegar after each slice—it kills the mold and prevents it from coming back.

Cheese Freeze

Believe it or not, you can successfully freeze many varieties of cheese without their losing taste or texture. Cut into small blocks, place in sealed plastic bags, and keep in the freezer for when you need them. Cheese varieties that can be successfully frozen are brick, Cheddar, Camembert, Edam, Gouda, mozzarella, Muenster, Parmesan, Port du Salut, Swiss, provolone, and Romano. Small cheeses, such as Camembert, can even be frozen in their original packages. When removed from the freezer, cheese should be put in the refrigerator and used as soon as possible after thawing.

Cottage Cheese Care

Because of its high water content, cottage cheese doesn't last as long as other food products in the refrigerator. To extend its life, store it in the container upside down.

Preserve Sour Cream

Like to keep sour cream on hand as a condiment but annoyed that it goes bad before you can use it all? To help sour cream last longer, add white vinegar right after you open it (1 teaspoon for a small container and 2 tablespoons for a large container). You won't notice the taste, and the sour cream won't go bad as quickly.

Extend Your Eggs

Forget those egg compartments on fridge doors! Always store eggs in their original carton on an inside shelf of the refrigerator. But before you put away that carton, turn the container upside down. Storing eggs with the tapered end down maximizes the distance between the yolk and the air pocket, which may contain bacteria. The yolk is more perishable than the white, so turning the eggs upside down will change their center of gravity, and the yolk will move away from possible contamination. This means your eggs will last even longer!

BRUCE SAYS

Keep Pouring That Ketchup

Ketchup bottle nearly empty? Don't give up—or needlessly bang on the bottom! Simply pour in a bit of vinegar and shake the closed bottle. There'll be no change to the taste, and you'll get more out.

Save Your Yolks

Believe it or not, you can save egg yolks for later use. If you have used egg whites in a recipe and want to save the yolks, slide them into a bowl of water, cover with plastic wrap, and store in the refrigerator for a day or two. It beats throwing them out!

Egg-cellent Move

For eggs that last practically forever, separate them into whites and yolks, then freeze them separately in a lightly oiled ice-cube tray. When frozen, pop them out and store in separate resealable bags in the freezer. These frozen eggs are perfect for baking, and will last longer because they're separated.

Make Condiments Last

It's frustrating to throw out condiments like sour cream, mayonnaise, yogurt, and mustard because you didn't use the entire container before it went bad. However, you can easily combat this by changing containers as you use up the item. Using a smaller container exposes the condiment to less air—and fewer bacteria.

No Ice on Your Ice Cream

It's always disappointing when you remember you have one last bit of ice cream in the freezer, only to open it and find it's covered in ice crystals. To keep this from happening, simply store your ice cream container upside down.

LOVE YOUR LEFTOVERS

Leftover Rice, Longer

Rice can stay delicious in the fridge for a longer amount of time if you store a slice of toast on top of it. The toast will absorb excess moisture and keep the rice fluffy and fresh.

Stock Up on Stock

If you're making a large batch of soup or stock and need to store the leftovers, pour the remaining soup into plastic bags and place them in the freezer so they lay flat. Once they're frozen, stack them on top of one another for optimal storage that'll save you valuable freezer space. Defrost by peeling off the bag and placing the frozen block in a covered casserole dish in the microwave. If you portion each bag to hold approximately 1 cup, you can defrost only what you need and the rest will last longer!

Pick Up the Paste

If you often end up with way more tomato paste than you need for a particular recipe, use this thrifty tip for storing leftovers: Just spoon the remainder into ice-cube trays! Each compartment will hold roughly a 2-tablespoon portion, so you can drop one or two cubes into your recipe as needed.

Saucy Storage

Another idea that gives you flexibility in finding a temporary home for leftover sauce: Store it in a plastic Easter egg. Fill both sides, snap together, then find a little pocket of freezer space to store. If the egg resists opening when you're ready to use, run warm water over it.

Reheat a Roast

When storing a cooked roast in the fridge, place it back into its own juices whenever possible. When reheating sliced meat, place it in a casserole dish with lettuce leaves between each of the slices. The lettuce provides just the right amount of moisture to keep the slices from drying out.

FAST, DELICIOUS PIZZA HEATING

When microwaving pizza, put a small glass of water in the microwave to keep the crust from getting chewy.

KITCHEN PROBLEMS SOLVED!

Don't let little glitches get in the way of your amazing dinner party or create extra work in the kitchen! You can save the meal, contain mess, and more with these solutions.

MEAL RESCUES

Defrost in a Flash

The best way to thaw turkey is on a shallow baking sheet in the refrigerator, in its original packaging, allowing 24 hours for every 5 pounds of bird. But if you've forgotten to stick the bird in the fridge, the fastest, safest method of thawing frozen poultry is to place it—still wrapped in plastic—in a bowl (or bucket) of cold water. Check the water regularly and change it as it warms up—never use hot water for large pieces of meat, as it will promote bacterial growth.

Overdone Spaghetti?

If you forgot about your simmering pot of pasta on the stove, and your noodles are now limp and mushy, try this trick. First run them under the coldest water possible—this will stop the cooking process immediately and make the starch inside them contract. If you're making a dish with tomato sauce, heat them back up directly in the sauce, as the acid will help them hold up even better.

Freshen Up Burned Fish

You went a bit overboard with the blackened catfish, and now it's a little too black. Freshen up burned fish with some chopped parsley. It will help neutralize the burned flavor and may just save dinner!

Rice Repair

If you burned the rice, fear not! It's white bread to the rescue. Get rid of the scorched taste by placing a slice of fresh white bread on top of the rice while it's still hot and covering it for a few minutes.

Underestimated Your Time?

Halve the oven time needed for baked potatoes by placing each medium-size potato on its end in a muffin tin. Turn over after 10 minutes, and they'll be ready in a half hour or less.

Dry Fish Fix

If you're cooking fish and it comes out too dry, brush it with a mixture of equal parts melted butter and lemon juice and some dried or fresh herbs. The butter will help make it moister, and the lemon juice will help it hold together and cause your diners to salivate—perhaps making them less likely to notice your cooking error.

Burned a Roast?

There are few kitchen disasters more disheartening than burning a roast. But there's help! Remove it from the pan and cover it with a towel dampened with hot water for about 5 minutes, which will stop the cooking. Then cut or scrape off any burned areas with a sharp knife, and put the roast back in the oven to reheat if necessary.

Speed Up a Slow Roast

The dinner party guests have eaten their way through the hors d'oeuvres, but the roast you're making still isn't close to being done. Speed up the process by making incisions in the meat every inch or so (don't cut more than halfway down) and then tying the roast together with string. The heat will be better able to penetrate through the incisions, and you'll get dinner on the table sooner.

Make It Lean for Less

For extra-lean ground beef that you don't need to purchase at a steep price, place the cooked meat in a fine mesh strainer and rinse with hot water. You'll eliminate up to half of the fat content!

5 SMART SAVES FOR BEVERAGES

Beverages should be the simple part of entertaining, but even they can trip you up from time to time. Use these little tricks to keep the sipping smooth.

Get cork control. Uh oh, you were uncorking a bottle of wine and didn't do a very good job. You're not above drinking wine that has a little cork floating in it, but you definitely don't want to serve it to guests! Simply hold a coffee filter over a carafe and pour. It will filter out the cork pieces and your reputation will be saved . . . for now.

Make flat soda a thing of the past. When you pour a warm soft drink over ice cubes, the gas escapes from the beverage at a faster rate because the ice cubes contain a greater surface area for the gas bubbles to collect on, thus releasing more of the carbon dioxide. This is the reason that warm beverages go flat rapidly (and sometimes fizz over the glass), and why warm drinks poured over ice go flat even faster. To slow down the process, add ice after you've poured the drink and the bubbles have dissipated.

Cure cloudiness in iced tea. Cloudiness is common in home-brewed iced tea, but it can be easily prevented. Simply let the tea cool to room temperature before refrigerating it. If the tea is still cloudy, try adding a small amount of boiling water to it until it clears up.

Bring out nice ice. Yes, even ice cubes can be perfected. Do yours look like they've melted and refrozen a hundred times? Make them beautiful and clear by using water that you've boiled, cooled, then poured into the ice-cube tray.

Try a rinsing remedy. When ice cubes stay in the freezer tray more than a few days, they tend to pick up odors from foods you have stocked away. Give them a quick rinse before using them to avoid altering the flavor of your beverage.

Free stuck cubes. If you're trying to retrieve a stubborn ice cube from the ice-cube tray, here's a surefire trick. Run your finger under running water for a second, then press it to the center of the cube. The ice will stick to your finger long enough for you to transfer it into your glass.

A Great Use for Stale Bread

If you're broiling steaks or chops, put a few slices of stale bread in the bottom of the broiler pan to absorb fat drippings. This will eliminate smoking fat, and it should also reduce any danger of a grease fire.

Update Your Meat Menu

If your meat turned out dry, rethink your dish. Shred beef or chicken and tuck it into a sauce over pasta or feature it as a taco filling. No one needs to know what was originally on the menu!

Ham Too Salty?

A little salt in ham is a good thing, but if your ham slices are too salty, place them in a dish of low-fat milk for 20 minutes, then rinse them off in cold water and dry them with paper towels before heating. The ham won't pick up the taste of the milk, but it will taste much less salty.

Save That Soup

Have you ever had to throw out a batch of soup because you accidentally oversalted it? Not anymore! Potatoes contain starch, which absorbs salt, so all you need to do is peel a raw potato or two and toss it in the soup. Let the pot simmer for about 15 minutes before removing the potato, and your soup will be almost as good as new.

Balance Out Salt

It's been said that you can always add more salt to a dish, but you can never take it away. While that's true, you can tame down an oversalted dish by adding ¼ teaspoon vinegar and ¼ teaspoon sugar to the food. Mix well, and taste. If it's still too salty, keep adding this combination in small increments until you've balanced out the flavors.

Antidote to Garlic

If you have added too much garlic to your soup or stew, add a small quantity of parsley and simmer for about 10 minutes.

Sweet 'n' Spicy

Overspiced your dinner? Just add a bit of sugar, honey, or maple syrup. The sweet allows your taste buds to handle more hot, saving your meal.

DON'T TOSS THOSE MUFFINS!
Baked goods a little burned on the bottom? Just lightly shave the charred bottoms off them with a box grater or vegetable peeler.

Transform Those Veggies

Cooking dinner and your vegetables turned to mush? Simply add some herbs along with tomato sauce or cream. Then top with cheese and/or breadcrumbs and stick in the oven for 30 minutes. Your diners are sure to be impressed with your new recipe for "vegetables gratin"!

Quick Fix for Curdling

If you've added too much citrus to dairy and caused it to curdle, add an ice cube to the mix and you'll be back in business in no time. The cold will actually reverse the curdling process.

Toppings to the Rescue

Too much dressing can ruin your salad, so if you accidentally add too much, just add more croutons or crunched-up tortilla chips. These salad toppings will soak up the excess.

BETTER PREP

DIY Recipe Stand

Ever find yourself shuffling back and forth between the stove and your recipe directions as you cook? With this quick trick, you will shuffle no more! Slip the bottom of your recipe cards into binder clips turned upside down, then stand the clips on their metal prongs atop your counter.

Keep That Recipe Handy

Don't have room for a countertop cookbook holder? Here's a clever way to keep a recipe within easy view: Attach it to the clips of a pants hanger, then loop the hanger's handle over a top cabinet knob or pull. Your recipe will be right at eye level!

Forgot to Take Out the Meat?

If you're in a rush to get some frozen meat thawed, pour a bit of white vinegar on it. This will help it thaw faster, as well as help tenderize the meat. This technique works great on steaks!

Know the Score

Use this trick to make unfreezing a portion of ground meat easier. Place the meat in a resealable plastic bag, flatten, then score into sections (like a tic-tac-toe board) by pressing a butter knife into the bag. Seal the bag and stick it in the freezer, and when you need just a little ground meat you'll be able to easily break off a chunk.

Simple Meat Slicing

Cutting meat into bite-size pieces for dishes like pastas and stir-fries is easier when it's half frozen. Place fresh meat in the freezer for 2 hours before you start dinner. Or place frozen meat in the microwave and cook on the defrost setting for about 5 minutes (turning once if you don't have a turntable). Your knife will glide right through!

Insta-Peel for Tomatoes

Need to quickly peel tomatoes for a recipe? The easiest way is to place them in a pot of boiling water for a minute. The skins will practically fall off.

Crush Garlic without a Press

Using garlic but short a garlic press? This kitchen trick gets the job done so well, you may not ever have to buy a press again. Use a regular old fork as you would use a grater: Hold it so the tines are pressed against your work surface, then rub a peeled garlic clove across the tines to "crush" it into a paste. This will take some forceful action in your rubbing motion, but you'll get perfectly crushed garlic for your dish.

Spray Away the Stick

You can prevent jars of sticky foods and liquids (jam, honey, syrup) from resisting opening with one little step. After opening them the first time, spray a little nonstick spray around the jar rims before closing up. Spraying in pulses and holding the jar at an angle will help you direct the spray at the rim, not the food.

Fresh Spaghetti in Small Spaces

Homemade pasta doesn't need to take over your entire kitchen. Forget those hefty commercial drying racks. A simple, clean plastic coat hanger hung from a pot rack or cabinet handle can work just as well.

JEANNE SAYS

Get More Pop for Your Money

Soak your popcorn kernels in water for a few minutes before popping. The water helps them pop faster and you end up with fewer unpopped kernels! A money saver!

Decrystallize Honey

There's nothing more sweetly delicious than real honey, but we find it often gets thick and full of crystals after a little while in the cabinet. To get it back to its former consistency, simply place the jar in a bowl of hot water for 5 to 10 minutes, and then stir.

Let It Slide

Cooking with sticky ingredients like syrup or honey? Before you try to pour them into—then out of—measuring cups, fill the measuring cup with hot tap water and let it sit for at least 10 seconds. It will warm up the cup just enough to allow sticky foods to slip right out.

Eggshell Escape?

If you've ever gotten eggshell in your bowl of cracked eggs and tried to fish it out with your finger, you know how hard it can be. A better tool than your finger, and even a spoon? An eggshell half that you were able to break cleanly. The edge cuts through the egg whites more easily than other implements.

AVOID A MESS

No–Drip Pancake Batter

Ladles can still leave quite a mess as you move small amounts of batter repeatedly from the bowl to the griddle. Instead, try pouring a good amount of pancake batter into a clean, quart-size yogurt or cottage cheese container. Bending the flexible sides will give you an easy pour for more portions into the pan.

Slow Down That Syrup

It's easy for anyone, but kids especially, to pour too much syrup on pancakes, waffles, or French toast. So before you pour, attach a liquid pourer (like you see in cruets of oil) to the syrup bottle top. When you're finished, remove, wash, and set aside for your next syrup session.

Easy Ice for Bottles

Trying to fit ice cubes into water bottles is messy and difficult. Make ice-cold, on-the-go water easy by storing bottles filled with a small amount of water in the freezer. The water will become built-in ice for the bottles that you can then finish off with fresh water.

Reduce Roast Beef Splatters

Roast beef has a tendency to splatter both in the oven and all over the stove when you take it out. Keep the splatters and resulting smoke to a minimum by placing some water in the bottom of the pan before it goes in the oven. Monitor it periodically and add more if needed.

Even Better Than Butter

Butter is delicious to use for sautéing, but it burns quickly. To raise butter's smoke point (the temperature at which it burns), add a little vegetable oil to the pan. Vegetable oil is made for cooking at higher temperatures.

Sticky Solution for Shaping

Here's a simple tip: If you wet your hands with cold water before shaping hamburger patties or meatballs, the mixture won't stick to your fingers.

Cleaner Carving

If you've just made a super-juicy roast chicken or turkey, you can congratulate yourself as a cook. But what to do about all of the juices making a mess of your counter as you carve it? Place your cutting board inside a rimmed baking sheet before you cut, and you'll have not only an easy cleanup but also some rich drippings you can use in gravy or broth.

Perfectly Cooked Pasta

Stop your pasta water from spilling over with this trick: Add a long metal spoon to the pot, and it will absorb the excess heat and let your pasta cook at the correct boiling point. Just be careful, because the spoon will get quite hot!

BRUCE SAYS

PERFECT YOUR POUR

Poke holes in the foil seals of oil, salad dressing, and marinade bottles with a fork to control the flow of the liquid. The shirt you're wearing will thank you for this one!

WHO KNEW? READERS' FAVORITE

When Movie Night Goes Wrong

If you've ever burned popcorn in your microwave, you know that the stink permeates the entire house. Make it smell fresh again by stuffing the microwave with crumpled newspaper—leaving the microwave off, of course! After a few hours have gone by, remove the paper. Smell still there? In a bowl, mix 2 tablespoons coffee grounds with ½ cup water and heat on high in the microwave for 3 minutes.

Avoid a Boiling Blunder

To keep a pot from boiling over, stick a toothpick between the lid and the pot. Other tricks include placing a wooden spoon across the top of the uncovered pot or rubbing butter around the inside lip of the pot.

For More Than Muffins

Baking stuffed bell peppers or tomatoes in a well-greased muffin tin will help them hold their shape—and make sure they don't tip over when you take them out of the oven.

Easy Herb Lift

If you're cooking with herbs that will need to be removed before eating, make them easy to remove by putting them all in a tea infuser before you add them to your dish.

Garlic Be Gone

You've been cooking with garlic, and now you can't get the smell off your hands! To get rid of this or any other kitchen odor, just dab your hands with a bit of toothpaste (the white, non-gel kind works best). Then rub them together and wash off.

EASY CLEANUP & ORGANIZATION

You can tame your kitchen jungle with ease. Simple steps help you love time spent in your kitchen again—and get out quickly when the cooking is done!

SAVE YOUR SPACE

Splatter-Proof Your Stovetop

When cooking on your stovetop, it's not uncommon for grease to go everywhere. But you can minimize the mess by covering unused burners with square floor tiles. The tiles are much easier to clean than burners, plus they can give you added counter space. Win-win!

Block the Spray

Nonstick cooking spray is incredibly useful. The downside: It can wind up coating more than your cookware when you push the button. But there's a simple solution! Spray your nonstick cooking spray over your open dishwasher, where it will be easily (and automatically) washed away.

DIY Mixer Guard

You can turn a simple paper plate into a splatter guard for your stand mixer. First, remove the blade or beaters. Then poke the top portion of the beater through a paper plate. Reattach and you're ready for your next recipe!

Another No-Mess Mixer Trick

To prevent messes when using a stand mixer, stick a serving tray underneath it before you begin. The tray will catch drips and splashes of food as you blend, and all you'll need to clean is the tray itself, rather than your countertops.

Keep the Can at Hand

If you're making a recipe that calls for an entire can of an ingredient, don't rush that empty can into your recycling bin. Set it up as a spoon rest while you finish cooking. It'll hold your utensils ready at hand and keep your counter clean from drips.

Contain Cutting-Board Overflow

Whether you're slicing seeded bagels or peeling potatoes, kitchen prep around a cutting board can get messy beyond the board. Before you start, slip a sheet of newspaper under the board to help make cleanup of the area as easy as crumpling and trashing the newspaper.

Clean Your Hands

Your hands can take a beating while you're preparing and cooking food. But a simple solution from your pantry can help. To remove food stains from your hands, rub a peeled, raw potato over them. Your hands will come clean like magic!

Freshen Up

Chopping up garlic or doing other smelly kitchen chores doesn't have to leave your hands smelling bad! Just pour a few tablespoons of mouthwash into your palms and rub your hands together, and the odor will disappear. Another simple way to get food odors off your hands is to rub them on the back of a stainless steel spoon.

WHO KNEW?
READERS' FAVORITE

Make Any Bag the Perfect Fit

Whether it's a bag you're reusing to collect food scraps for compost, recycling materials, or just everyday trash, you can make the bag fit your container snugly and stay open at the top with a simple clip. If you have a binder clip or clothespin, that will work. But even better: Reuse one of those notched clips that come on bread bags. There's a reuse for everything!

Grounds for Removal

Don't throw away used coffee grounds—instead, keep them in a can near the sink. Rub a small amount over your hands after handling fish or chopping pungent foods like garlic and onions. The grounds will remove odors on your hands.

DISHES BE DONE!

Good Measure, Fewer Dishes

To use the fewest cooking utensils possible, first measure out all the dry ingredients, then the wet ingredients. This way, you can reuse the measuring spoons or cups, and only have to wash them once.

Clean Utensils as You Go

Make cooking a little more like a kindergarten paint session to save yourself some time! Just keep a jar with warm soapy water on your counter and place whatever knife or other utensil you're working with in it when you're done with that part of the recipe. When you need it again, you don't have to stop what you're doing to wash it. A quick rinse will do.

JEANNE SAYS

It's in the Bag!
You don't need to dirty a colander to thaw frozen shrimp. Just poke or cut a few small holes into the bottom of the shrimp's bag, then open at the top and run water through.

No More Dough Dread

How do you clean sticky dough from your mixing bowls? Taking a dish brush or cloth to it makes a complete mess! Instead, try first getting off the worst of the dough with a crumpled piece of aluminum foil. Then you can simply toss the foil and clean the bowl the rest of the way (much more easily!) with dish soap and hot water.

Drying Rack at the Ready

Need extra dish-drying space? Reach for your roasting pan's rack. Once it's turned upside down, it can hold large, thin items (think: baking sheets) steady in the slots while they air-dry.

Sort Now, Save Later

It takes less time and effort to group your spoons, forks, and knives together now when you can see them easily than after they've gone through the dishwasher. Mentally assign slots for each in your silverware basket.

8 WAYS FUNDRAISING BRACELETS WORK HARD IN THE KITCHEN, TOO

You've just bought yet another silicone bracelet to support a good cause. But what can you possibly do with so many bracelets? Put them to work in the kitchen to help you stay organized!

Keep it together. Loop the bracelets around baking mats, flexible cutting boards, sets of utensils you'd like to group, rolls of trash bags, and much more.

Get a grip. Loop bracelets around the lids of glass jars or plastic bottles that are difficult to open. They'll give you an easy grip for a better twist—without the added cost of buying yet another kitchen tool.

Seal it up. Use bracelets as you would large rubber bands to close off bags of snacks, cereal, and frozen veggies.

Clear clutter. Count the number of cords just hanging out in your kitchen. Bracelets can help you corral all that clutter and clear more counter space. Just wind up all the hanging cords and loop a bracelet around that surplus to keep it out of the way.

Stop the slide. Cutting boards that lack grips tend to take a walk across the counter, which is annoying and also very unsafe. Stretch a bracelet around each end of a cutting board to grip your counter and keep your board right where you need it.

Label your herbs. Taking advantage of a kitchen herb garden is easier when your pots are labeled. Colorful bracelets around the small pots give you an easy place to write the herb's name—just use the side without any writing, and label it with a permanent marker.

Mark the level. When storing foods in opaque containers, such as oatmeal, coffee, flour, and other dry goods, place a bracelet around the outside of the container marking the level of the remaining contents. (Then simply move the band down as the level goes down.) It will serve as an easy visual reminder to know when you need to go shopping for that item again.

Make a drink display. Filling up a travel mug with hot coffee or tea? Slip a bracelet or two around your mug for a simple grip that displays the causes you support. You can also loop them around sippy cups to ID which child they belong to—simply color-code or write the child's name on the bracelet. Use them in the same way for beverage bottles or cans at a party.

Don't Lose Those Lids

Keep track of small lids and utensils in the dishwasher by containing them in a small mesh laundry bag—the kind used for delicate items. Load the bag in the top of the dishwasher.

STORAGE SOLUTIONS

Nonskid Drawers

A nonskid rug pad is a terrific liner for your kitchen drawers. The tacky surface prevents utensils from slipping around.

Double-Decker Utensil Drawers

Use your drawer space as efficiently as possible, especially if yours are extra deep. Stack two utensil trays on top of one another, then store your frequently used utensils—forks, spoons, knives, can openers—in the top tray, and those less often used in the bottom. Simply lift off the top tray whenever you need your chopsticks, skewers, ladles, and garlic press.

Cookie Cutter Holder

Here's another great tip for saving precious space in your kitchen drawers. Keep cookie cutters organized and easy to find by slipping them over a cardboard paper towel tube and standing them upright in the pantry.

Win at Match Game

So many plastic food storage containers and lids, so little time you have to spend finding the matches! Sound like your kitchen? Try labeling container and lid pairs with a permanent marker. You can use letters of the alphabet, numbers, or even symbols like hearts and stars. Then simply match container A with lid A when you need them—or even better, get the kids or grandkids to help!

This Tip Will Stick

Plastic wrap can be fussy about sticking to certain surfaces (such as metal) for a tight seal. Try dabbing just a bit of water around the sides of the container before asking the plastic to stick.

> **BRUCE SAYS**
>
> **Cover That Corkscrew**
>
> Ever reach into a drawer only to have something stab you back? Keep a cork on the point of a corkscrew or other sharp utensils to protect your hand—and have an extra cork at the ready.

Wrap Not Rolling? Anchor It

Stuck at getting the plastic wrap (or foil, wax paper, or parchment paper) to stay and roll smoothly from the box? Add more weight to the wrap's tube by sliding something long with a little heft inside—try a stainless steel turkey baster or honing steel. It'll act as an anchor so the wrap rolls and tears more smoothly.

Cover That Can

Only need a little bit from that can of broth or tomatoes? Make a lid by covering with plastic wrap and securing on the sides with a rubber band.

The Solution Is in the Bag

Opening a new bag of frozen fruit, vegetables, or bagels? Don't leave those frozen peas to spill while you scramble for a twist tie or rubber band. When you open the bag, cut or rip a strip right across the top, then use that plastic strip to tie the bag closed. So simple!

Free Up Freezer Space

What's hiding at the bottom of your freezer? Freezers seem to have dead zones where bags of frozen vegetables try to hide—and ultimately die a slow death of freezer burn. Try stacking plastic magazine holders on their sides in an upright freezer, or vertically in a bottom freezer, to create makeshift shelves that help you separate and see everything that's there.

Don't Let Them Slide

Ever been reaching for something in a cabinet and accidentally moved something else close to or over the edge? To avoid a mess from falling glass containers, set up a guardrail. All it takes are eye hooks screwed into the sides of the cabinet with a bungee cord strapped across.

Add an Extra Lazy Susan

If you have a lazy Susan in one of your kitchen cabinets, you know that it makes accessing all of the items in the cabinet so simple. Why not try the same concept elsewhere? Buy another one and use it in the refrigerator to store condiments. Spin it around to grab ketchup, barbecue sauce, mustard, or whatever else is normally at the back of the fridge.

ANOTHER EXCUSE TO BUY WINE

The cardboard inserts from boxes of wine make great dividers for organizing boxes of foil, plastic wrap, plastic bags, and more.

Slim, Secure Storage for Baking Ingredients

Bags of flour and sugar can easily tear if kept in the paper bags they come in. But not everyone has room in their kitchen for hefty canisters or big storage containers. Keep your ingredients streamlined and secure by storing them in gallon-size, zipper-lock plastic bags. Just label the bags with a permanent marker. Bonus: The bags open wide, making it easy for measuring cups to fit in.

A Place for Place Mats

If you have limited storage space in your kitchen, a binder clip can come in handy for storing place mats. Take a binder clip and open the little "wings." Tack one side of the wings against the inside of a kitchen cabinet, or hang it on a nail. Then simply clip to hang your place mats in place!

Extra Shelves Made Easy

Add a shelf to your kitchen cabinet without spending cash or installing any hardware—just use a serving tray! Line the tray with no-skid shelf liner, which will keep your glasses and dishware from slipping around. Set your larger glasses on the bottom of the cabinet, then place the tray on top and set smaller glasses on your new "shelf."

WHO KNEW?

PART 4

HEALTH & BEAUTY BOOSTS

DIY SPA TREATMENTS

These all-natural splurges will leave you saying *ahh!* without making an appointment outside your home. Get ready to feel and look your best!

AMAZING SCRUBS

Apricot–Sea Salt Scrub

Here's a great scrub for smoothing out rough spots on elbows, hands, feet, or wherever you need a little extra help.

- ¼ cup sea salt
- 2 tablespoons apricot kernel oil
- 5 drops apricot essential oil

Mix together all of the ingredients, then rub onto the skin. Rinse with warm water.

Light Sugar Scrub

Dry, itchy skin bothering you? Try this super-moisturizing light scrub.

- 3 tablespoons baby oil
- 2 tablespoons yogurt
- 4 teaspoons brown sugar

Mix together the ingredients, being sure to break up any lumps in the brown sugar. Massage immediately into skin, as the sugar will begin to dissolve. Rinse with warm water.

Minty Morning Wake-Up

This invigorating scrub is great for sleepy mornings. For best results, make it the night before and store in the refrigerator until morning.

    1 cup rice
    6-ounce container plain yogurt
    5 sprigs mint
    3 drops peppermint essential oil

In a food processor, add the rice and pulse until ground. Transfer the contents to a bowl. Then process the yogurt and mint together and add to the ground rice. Add the essential oil, stir well, and refrigerate. Then, during your morning shower, rub the mixture into your skin. You'll feel it working!

Ginger Face and Body Polish

For beach-ready skin, try this body polish. Ginger will help stimulate the skin, salt and sugar will rub away dead skin cells, and the combination of coconut and olive oils will provide deep hydration.

    ¼ cup coconut oil
    2 tablespoons grated fresh ginger
    ¼ cup olive oil
    ¾ cup raw sugar
    ¼ cup sea salt

In a small saucepan, add the coconut oil and grated ginger, and heat on low until the oil melts and the ginger has infused it. Strain into a bowl. Stir in the olive oil, sugar, and sea salt, and allow the mixture to cool. Transfer to a cosmetics jar. To use, massage a little into the face and body, and leave for 5 minutes before rinsing under warm water.

Strawberry Treat for Hands and Feet

Take advantage of the natural fruit acids in strawberries to make an effective scrub for the hands and feet.

    7–8 fresh strawberries
    2 tablespoons olive oil
    1 teaspoon coarse salt

In a small bowl, mash the strawberries with a fork. Stir in the olive oil and salt. Rub onto hands and feet, rinse, and dry.

Mint for Your Lips

Nothing's worse than chapped lips in winter. Here's a minty scrub that tackles the problem at the source—and smells fantastic.

1 tablespoon brown sugar
1 tablespoon sugar
Sweet almond oil (or vitamin E oil)
Peppermint essential oil

In a small bowl, stir together the two sugars, and start drizzling in the sweet almond or vitamin E oil until the mixture is a little runny. Add a few drops of peppermint essential oil and stir well. To use, take a small amount and rub gently on your lips for 30 seconds. Rinse and apply lip balm as usual. Store the excess in a jar in the refrigerator for whenever you need a little extra pampering.

JEANNE SAYS

Sweeten Those Rough Patches

Is the skin on your elbows looking a bit rough? Here's an easy treatment: Cut a lemon or lime in half, then sprinkle it with brown sugar. Bend your elbow and shove it right into the citrus, then twist the fruit back and forth. The fruit's acid will slough off dead skin with the help of the sugar.

Peppermint Foot Scrub

Some days it seems we never have a chance to sit down! Here's a great scrub that will both soothe and exfoliate those tired, aching feet.

1 cup sugar
2–3 tablespoons grapeseed oil
5 drops peppermint essential oil

In a small bowl, add the sugar and begin drizzling in the oil until you have a coarse, damp mixture. Stir in the peppermint oil until well blended. Rub a tablespoon or two onto the soles of your feet. Store any remaining scrub in a resealable jar.

Citrus Hand Scrub

This freshly scented hand (or foot) scrub gets a boost from citrus zest. It's perfect to help remove stains and food odors, or just for a simple exfoliation.

¾ cup sugar
3 tablespoons coarse salt
½ cup olive oil
Zest of a lemon or orange

In a medium bowl, mix together all of the ingredients. Massage into your hands. Store any remaining scrub in a resealable jar.

ALL-NATURAL MASKS

Veggie Revitalizer

This powerhouse of a body mask is loaded with vital nutrients to help rejuvenate and revitalize skin.

- 2 ripe avocados, peeled and pitted
- 2 carrots, thinly sliced and steamed until soft
- ½ cup milk
- 2 eggs, lightly beaten
- ¼ cup honey

Mash together the avocados and carrots in a medium bowl. Stir in the milk, lightly beaten eggs, and honey. Apply the mixture to damp skin, then leave on for 10 to 15 minutes. Rinse with lukewarm water.

Yogurt Soother

Try this body mask to help soothe irritated skin. The lactic acid in the yogurt gently breaks down dry skin cells, and turmeric is a well-known anti-inflammatory.

- 1 cup plain yogurt
- 1 teaspoon turmeric

Combine the yogurt and the turmeric, blending well. Apply to damp skin and leave on for 10 minutes. Rinse with lukewarm water, then moisturize.

Strawberry Body Mask

This body mask is great for summer, when strawberries are in season, and when skin tends to be a little oilier. After using, your skin will feel tighter and smoother!

- 1 cup strawberries, pureed
- 2 egg whites
- 2 teaspoons honey
- 1 teaspoon lemon juice

Whisk the egg whites for a minute or two, then stir in the pureed strawberries. Add the honey and lemon juice and stir well. Apply to wet skin in the shower, and wait 15 minutes so that the enzymes in the fruit can work. Rinse with cool water.

BRUCE SAYS

Toast This!

Have a teeny bit of Champagne or white wine left after a party? Make a face scrub with it! Wine contains tartaric acid, a terrific exfoliant. Mix a few teaspoons sugar with enough wine to make a paste, then massage into clean skin.

International Age-Eraser

Turmeric and besan (also called chickpea flour or gram flour) are centuries-old magic ingredients in the Indian woman's skincare regimen. They brighten skin tone, clear up acne and redness, and help reduce signs of aging. They're also easily found in Indian grocery stores.

1 tablespoon chickpea flour
1 tablespoon milk
⅛ teaspoon turmeric

Combine the chickpea flour, milk, and turmeric. Apply to your face and leave on for 15 minutes. Rinse with warm water.

Better with Banana

In need of a calming facial mask at the end of a long day? This mask is especially good for acne-prone skin because of the toning properties of the lemon.

1 ripe banana
Honey
1 teaspoon lemon juice

Mash a ripe banana in a bowl with a drizzle of honey, and add the lemon juice to stop the mixture from browning. Apply to your face and leave on for 15 minutes. Rinse with warm water. If you're headed out after your facial, be sure to apply moisturizer with sunscreen—your skin may be a bit more sun-sensitive due to the lemon juice.

Skin-Balancing Facial

Do you have acne scars or other dark spots on your face? You can use the enzymes in certain foods to help lighten them! Here's a soothing mask to try.

1 teaspoon lemon juice
1 teaspoon honey
2 teaspoons plain yogurt

Stir together the lemon juice, honey, and yogurt in a small bowl. Apply to your face and leave on for about 10 minutes. Rinse with warm water.

Pumpkin Pampering

For clean, soft skin—and a clever way to use up that can of pumpkin that's been gathering dust in your pantry since Thanksgiving—try this facial mask.

1 (15-ounce) can pumpkin puree (not pumpkin pie filling)
¼ cup plain yogurt
¼ cup honey
¼ ground almonds
Olive oil

Mix together the canned pumpkin with the yogurt, honey, ground almonds, and a drizzle of olive oil. Apply to skin, and take a hot bath to let the steam and enzymes in the mask do their work. After 10 minutes, rinse and apply your normal moisturizer. Refrigerate any leftovers and use within a week.

Clarifying Facial

If you have oily skin, try this sweetly scented scrub. The clay will help remove impurities and excess oil while the oats and almonds exfoliate and soothe skin. As a bonus, lavender is great for stress relief!

1½ cups rolled oats
¾ cup almonds
1 tablespoon dried lavender
¾ cup honey
1¼ cups white kaolin clay

Pulse together the oats, almonds, and dried lavender in a blender. Mix in the honey and white kaolin clay. (You can find the clay online or at stores that carry natural beauty products.) Remove a tablespoon of the scrub and mix with water to make a thick paste. Massage over the face and neck and leave on for 10 to 15 minutes. Store the leftovers in the refrigerator in a closed container.

WHO KNEW?
READERS' FAVORITE

This Face Mask Is the Cat's Meow

Clay cat litter is the same clay that's found in some of the most expensive face masks on the market! Find cat litter labeled "100 percent all-natural clay" and mix it with water until it gets to the consistency you want. Adding a couple of drops of scented oil will also make it seem less like you're applying cat litter to your face. Wash off the mask after it hardens.

Smoothing Hand Mask

Try this overnight hand mask to gently remove dead skin cells.

½ cup buttermilk
1 tablespoon almond oil

In a small bowl, whisk together the buttermilk and almond oil. Submerge your hands completely, remove, and allow to dry. Then cover your hands with cotton gloves and leave on overnight. In the morning, rinse your hands well to reveal brighter skin.

LUXURIOUS BATHS AND MORE

Peppy Peppermint Bath

This peppermint bath is sure to stimulate your senses and get your skin tingling!

½ cup powdered milk
¼ cup cornstarch
1 cup warm water
5 drops peppermint essential oil

Add the powdered milk and cornstarch to the warm water and whisk until thoroughly combined. Stir in the essential oil and pour the entire mixture into your bathwater.

Humectant Honey Bath

For dry, irritated skin, try this moisturizing honey bubble bath.

½ cup grapeseed oil
¼ cup honey
¼ cup liquid castile soap (such as Dr. Bronner's)

Mix together the oil, honey, and soap, being careful not to froth them up too much, then pour the mixture into a squeeze bottle. You may need to shake it up before using. Add a few tablespoons under running bathwater. The leftovers will store well in a cool, dry place.

Soothing Cinnamon–Oatmeal Soak

For soft, smooth skin, try this cinnamon-oatmeal soak.

⅓ cup oatmeal
¾ cup powdered milk
⅓ cup baking soda
2 tablespoons cornstarch
2 teaspoons ground cinnamon

In a food processor, pulse the oatmeal until it's a fine powder. Transfer it to a small bowl and stir in the powdered milk, baking soda, cornstarch, and cinnamon, being sure to break up any lumps. Place in a piece of cheesecloth and tie to secure. Add the sachet to hot bathwater.

Moisturizing Milk Bath

The great thing about this milk bath is that you can make a large quantity of it all at once and then store the rest for multiple uses.

3 cups powdered milk
¼ cup oatmeal
¼ cup almond meal
¼ cup cornstarch

In a food processor, pulse the oatmeal until it is powdery. Pour all of the ingredients into a large zip-top plastic bag, seal, and shake to combine thoroughly. When you want to use it, measure out ½ cup into a cheesecloth or sachet and tie it closed. Add to your hot bathwater. For an extra-moisturizing bath, break open a vitamin E capsule and add to the water.

Simple Bath Salts

To relax sore muscles and soften skin, try these basic bath salts.

1 cup Epsom salts
¼ cup baking soda
¼ cup powdered milk
¼ cup cornstarch
Essential oil (choose your favorite)

Mix together the Epsom salts, baking soda, powdered milk, and cornstarch in a small bowl. Add this mixture to a warm bath along with a few drops of your favorite essential oil.

Da Bomb Bath Fizzies

You've seen those fancy bath bombs in bath and body stores, right? Did you know you can easily make your own? You do need one hard-to-find ingredient, citric acid powder, which you can locate online or at some supermarkets in the canning section. (It's what reacts with the baking soda to make that fizzy sound—kind of like those baking soda and vinegar volcanoes you'd make as a child.)

1 cup citric acid powder
1 cup baking soda
½ cup cornstarch
½ cup grapeseed oil
10 drops essential oil (choose your favorite)
5 drops food coloring (optional)
Cookie cutters, silicone molds, or ice cube trays

Mix together the citric acid, baking soda, cornstarch, and oil until you have a crumbly dough. Stir in the essential oil of your choice and the optional food coloring. Press the mixture firmly into the molds or ice cube trays, and then let dry for 24 hours. Remove carefully. Depending on the size of the bomb, you can use one or two per bath.

Ahhh-mazing Almond Bubble Bath

For a special bath, here are some super-simple bath suds.

1 cup unscented liquid castile soap (such as Dr. Bronner's)
2 tablespoons honey
½ teaspoon almond extract

Mix together the liquid soap, honey, and almond extract in a resealable container. To use, place a tablespoon or two under hot running water.

WHO KNEW? READERS' FAVORITE

Give Your Bathroom a Spa Look

Make apothecary-style jars by gluing dollar-store glasses on top of candlestick holders. Use them in the bathroom to hold supplies like cotton balls. They'll look just as good as the expensive kind without costing you a lot.

SWEET TREATMENTS

4 BEAUTY RECIPES FEATURING CHOCOLATE

Who doesn't want to cover themselves in chocolate? Chocolate contains antioxidants that give skin a firmer, more youthful look. Here are a few of our favorite ways to indulge without calories.

Chocolate–Honey Scrub

½ cup honey
½ cup sea salt
2 tablespoons cocoa powder
1 tablespoon olive oil

Mix together all of the ingredients in a bowl, being sure to break up any lumps in the cocoa powder. Apply this luscious mixture to your skin, rubbing in a circular motion. Leave for 5 minutes, then rinse with warm water. Leftover scrub can be stored in a tightly sealed container in the refrigerator.

Cocoa Bath

½ teaspoon unsweetened cocoa powder
½ cup Epsom salts

In a small bowl, combine the cocoa powder and Epsom salts. Add the mixture to your bath as the water is filling. It will exfoliate dead skin cells while promoting new cell growth at the same time!

Chocolate Body Butter

1 cup coconut oil
¼ cup cocoa powder
¼ teaspoon vanilla powder
1 vitamin E capsule

Place all of the ingredients in a bowl, squeezing out the contents of the vitamin E capsule. With a hand mixer, begin to beat on low. As the cocoa becomes incorporated, increase the speed until the mixture is the texture of whipped butter. Transfer to an airtight container and store in a cool, dry place.

Dessert Facial

1 tablespoon unsweetened cocoa powder
2 tablespoons plain yogurt
Honey

Whisk together the cocoa powder and yogurt, being sure to break up any cocoa lumps. Add a good squirt of honey and stir to combine. Place this incredible-smelling mixture on your face and leave on for 10 minutes. Rinse with cool water to reveal soft, radiant skin.

Bubble Bath Gels

Make some of these incredible bath gels for yourself or give them out as gifts!

1 envelope unflavored gelatin
¾ cup water
½ cup unscented liquid castile soap (such as Dr. Bronner's)
Essential oil (choose your favorite)
Food coloring (optional)

In a small bowl, pour in the gelatin. Bring the water to a boil and pour over the gelatin, stirring until it's fully dissolved. Then stir in the soap and a few drops of the essential oil of your choice. For an extra twist, add a drop or two of food coloring. Pour the mixture into a storage container and refrigerate until the mixture is set. To use, place a tablespoon or so of the gel under running bathwater.

Repurpose Perfume

You can literally bathe in your favorite perfume by making your own scented bath oil. Just add a few drops of perfume to a quart of baby oil, shake well, and add to your bath.

No Ordinary Oil

For an inexpensive, luxuriously fragrant bath oil, combine sunflower oil with crushed lavender or rose petals (or both). Let the mixture stand for a few days before using it.

DIY Coconut Body Butter

If you love coconut-scented body butters, you'll love this all-natural homemade version. To make it, place some pure coconut oil in a bowl, and using a hand mixer, blend it until it's the consistency of whipped butter. Add a few drops of your favorite essential oil, and continue mixing until evenly combined. Transfer the mixture to a glass jar, and it's ready to use anytime your skin needs a little extra help. You'll be amazed at how long the jar of coconut oil lasts, and how nourished your skin feels.

ANTIAGING SECRETS

Creams and serums that promise to take years off your skin can cost hundreds of dollars per month! But you can get great results from natural treatments and smart makeup strategies.

FIGHT WRINKLES

Cream Signs of Aging

Smooth fine lines and wrinkles with this simple moisturizing cream. In a small bowl, mix together 2 teaspoons honey, 2 teaspoons castor oil, and 1 teaspoon lemon juice. Massage into the face and neck and leave on for 5 minutes. Rinse with warm water, and enjoy younger-looking skin!

Take a Deep Breath

Make your nighttime lotion regimen even more effective: Before smoothing on your cream, take five deep breaths to boost levels of oxygen to the skin.

The Goodness of Grapes

You've probably heard about the benefits of resveratrol, the powerful antioxidant in red grapes and red wine. It helps boost the production of collagen, giving your skin a younger look. Try this mask to help minimize fine lines and firm the skin. Combine 5 red grapes, 2 to 3 teaspoons olive oil, and 1 tablespoon honey in a blender. Apply the mask to the face and leave on for 10 to 15 minutes. Rinse with warm water.

INSTANT NIGHT CREAM

Don't buy expensive vitamin E creams! Instead, just use the capsules you find in the vitamin aisle at the drugstore. Break them open and massage the oil into your face before bed.

Wine to Win Against Wrinkles

Drinking red wine is good for the heart because it contains antioxidants such as resveratrol, which strengthens blood vessels and prevents blood clots. But red wine is also great for your skin! Add some to any hydrating face mask and the antioxidants will lend powerful antiaging properties to the treatment.

Kick Wrinkles with Kiwi

Kiwis are rich in vitamin C, which is known for its potential as an antiaging ingredient. Plus, the little black seeds are effective at exfoliating the skin. Mash 2 kiwis (peeled and chopped) in a small bowl, then stir in ¼ cup cornmeal. Massage into skin for a few minutes, then rinse.

Peel Away Years

Papaya is rich in enzymes that help remove dead skin cells. To make a freshening facial peel, combine 2 tablespoons chopped papaya and 1 tablespoon dry oatmeal in a blender or food processor. Pat the mixture onto clean skin and leave for 10 minutes before rinsing off.

Firm with Chocolate

A popular ingredient in expensive antiaging skin products, copper helps to firm and smooth skin, as recent research shows. Fortunately, one of the most copper-rich foods just happens to be chocolate! Here's a great facial mask that takes advantage of the antioxidant and antiaging qualities of chocolate and copper. Plus, it smells divine. Combine 2 tablespoons unsweetened cocoa powder with enough milk or heavy cream to make a paste. Apply to the skin and leave for 15 minutes, then rinse with warm water.

Don't Forget Your Hands

Your hands can give away your age just as much as (or sometimes more than) your face! Buy a small container of pure beeswax online or at a health food store and you can make the very same luxury hand creams you always pine over (for a fraction of the cost). Just combine 1 teaspoon beeswax with 3 tablespoons water, 2 tablespoons olive oil, and 1 tablespoon vegetable shortening or shea butter. Add 2 drops essential oil for a lovely scent.

Eat More Seafood

You can fight wrinkles from the inside out! Fish such as salmon, trout, sardines, and tuna are rich in omega-3 fatty acids that help keep skin supple. Aim to put these antiaging eats on the menu at least twice a week.

Pinch for Relief

Many people hold stress in the area between their eyebrows, and in time, vertical stress lines will develop there. When you feel your brow knit together with concentration or stress, take a moment to pinch the muscle there, working from the center of the brow along the brow line in each direction with a thumb and bent forefinger. Not only will it make you feel better, but it will prevent wrinkles, too!

Turn Back Years with Peppers

Collagen is a protein our bodies make less of as we get older. The problem? It's key to skin's staying elastic to fight off wrinkles and loose skin. The best way to boost your body's own collagen production: get more vitamin C—one of the most important players in the process. Just ½ cup of raw red peppers provides 158 percent of your daily dose of vitamin C. Other good C sources: grapefruit, kiwifruit, green peppers, broccoli, strawberries, and oranges.

Fight Aging in Your Sleep

A surprising but surefire way to bring on signs of aging: Sleep on your stomach. What's the problem with this sleeping position? Gravity! It pulls your face downward and allows fluid to pool in your face. The results are sagging skin around the face and puffy eyes. Try to train yourself to sleep on your back—the best position to fight aging.

KEEP YOUR HANDS LOOKING YOUNG
Put a tube of sunscreen in your purse and apply regularly.

WHO KNEW?
READERS' FAVORITE

Pungent but Powerful to Erase Age Spots

If you're looking to eliminate unsightly age spots, sometimes you have to get serious! Grate a medium onion onto a cheesecloth or sturdy paper towel, then squeeze the onion juice into a bowl. Mix in 1 tablespoon each of white vinegar and hydrogen peroxide. Dab the mixture on the age spots twice a day (keeping away from your eyes), and keep it in the fridge when you're not using it. You should see results in a week or two!

5 WRINKLE-FIGHTING FACIAL EXERCISES

In a pretty fascinating study, women who did daily or almost-daily facial exercises for 20 weeks looked 2 years younger (as concluded by doctors)! Here are some of the study's moves (designed by Happy Face Yoga) that could work for you. Repeat each two to three times.

Cheek Lifter. Open your mouth to form an O, positioning your upper lip over your teeth. Smile to lift your cheek muscles up, placing your index fingers lightly on the top part of cheek. Release your cheek muscles to lower them, then lift back up. Do this 10 times. On the tenth lift, hold your cheek muscles as high as you can and lift your fingers about an inch away from your face and up toward your scalp area. Hold for 20 seconds while looking up at your fingers, then release.

Happy Cheeks Sculpting. Smile without showing your teeth. Purse your lips together, then smile, forcing your cheek muscles up. Place your fingers on the corners of your mouth and slide them up to the top of the cheeks. Hold that for 20 seconds.

Eyebrow Lifter. Smile, then press three fingertips of each hand under your eyebrows to force your eyes open. Keep smiling while trying to frown your eyebrows down against your fingers. Hold for 20 seconds while breathing deeply.

Upper Eyelid Firmer. Smile, then place your index fingers at the outer corner of each eye and your middle fingers at the inner corners. Squeeze your eyes closed tight, and roll your eyeballs up toward the ceiling (still keeping your eyes closed). Hold for 30 seconds.

Jaw and Neck Firmer. Smile, then open your mouth to make an "ahh" sound. Fold your lower lip and the corners of your lips into your mouth and hold them tightly. Extend your lower jaw forward. Using your lower jaw only, scoop up very slowly as you close your mouth. Pull your chin up about an inch each time you scoop, tilting your head backward. Open and close your lower jaw for 10 reps. On the final rep, your chin should be pointed toward the ceiling; hold for 20 seconds.

LOOK YOUNGER NOW

Grab a Glass of Water

When you dry out, so does your skin. Even short-term dehydration leads to skin that looks sunken and wrinkly. The longer you shortchange your skin of moisture, the more it loses elasticity—meaning it doesn't bounce back. Aim for at least six glasses of water a day. It might be the simplest (free!) way to get younger-looking skin!

Get Milk

Need a quick way to get glowing skin? Soak a clean washcloth in cold milk and place it over your face for 10 minutes. You'll get soothing proteins, fats, amino acids, and vitamin A. Plus, the lactic acid in milk exfoliates, so skin looks instantly renewed and younger.

Perk Up Tired Eyes

Your eyes may be calling for caffeine! Soak two tea bags in hot water until they plump, then plunge them into ice water for a few seconds. Squeeze out a bit of excess water and then place the bags on closed eyes for 15 minutes. The caffeine shrinks those dark blood vessels that bring on circles and forces out fluid to de-puff the entire eye area.

Ditch a Double Chin

If a double chin is driving you nuts, use a little makeup to hide it. When applying powder or foundation to your face, use a slightly darker shade under your chin, which will make it appear to recede. Blend toward the back of the jawline to add definition.

Ladies Only

Men, look away while we tell the ladies this secret cleavage tip. To instantly make your chest look more youthful, mix up this treatment and apply to your visible cleavage area: 1 egg white, 1 tablespoon each honey and plain yogurt, and 1 teaspoon olive oil. Rinse off after 10 minutes. It will brighten and tighten the skin and make you feel 10 years younger!

Save the Powder

Face powder tends to settle in the fine lines and crinkles of the skin, so it's best to pass or at least be selective, using it only on smoother areas.

JEANNE SAYS

Take Your Lips Back in Time

Dark or bright lipstick colors can emphasize thinness and fine lines around your mouth. Instead, choose a subtle pink lipstick that's a flashback to the color of your lips when you were younger.

Lift Lashes

Curling your lashes can give the illusion of lifting the whole eye area. But you may be doing it wrong. Set the curler at the root of lashes, then instead of simply holding steady, give three firm, gentle pumps. Release and repeat. For even longer-lasting curl, heat your curler with your blow dryer for 15 seconds first.

Make Forehead Wrinkles Disappear

To take the focus off wrinkles, go for thick, brow-skimming, razor-cut bangs and a low side part right above your pupil (versus a center part).

SKIN SOLUTIONS

You don't need expensive brand-name products to cleanse, exfoliate, and moisturize! Reveal smooth, healthy skin with simple, natural ingredients that work wonders.

GENTLE CLEANSERS

Get Radiant with Rice

Loaded with vitamins B and E, rice smooths and softens skin when used to make a daily face wash. Simply boil ½ cup white rice in 2 cups water. Remove the rice and let the water cool. Use a cloth to massage the rice water onto your skin, then rinse.

Treat Your Pores to Tea

Place three bags of chamomile tea in a medium-size bowl; add several cups boiling water. Cover the bowl with a towel, and allow the tea to steep for 10 minutes. Then remove the towel, place it over your head, and hold your face over the bowl for about 5 minutes. The steam will open your pores, and the chamomile will help unclog them.

Stubborn Makeup or Face Paint?

Turn to olive oil or cold-pressed coconut oil! Simply rub it onto the skin with a dry cloth, then wipe off with a wet cloth.

Calm and Tone with Cucumber

Grate a cucumber on the side of a box grater or in the food processor. Mix in about ½ cup plain yogurt—enough to bind the mixture together. Apply the cooling blend to clean skin, and leave it on for 5 minutes to tighten pores, reduce puffiness, and tone skin. Rinse with cool water.

Brighten with Kiwi

Here's an all-natural facial cleanser that works well for normal to dry skin types. The vitamin C from the kiwi will help brighten skin, and the cornmeal will remove dead skin cells.

    1 kiwifruit, peeled
    2 tablespoons plain yogurt
    1 tablespoon honey
    1 tablespoon olive oil (or almond oil)
    1 teaspoon cornmeal

Puree the peeled kiwifruit with the yogurt, honey, olive oil, and cornmeal. Rub gently into your face and neck, then rinse well.

Cleanse, Soften, and Smooth in One Step

Mix 1 tablespoon baking soda with enough lemon juice to create a paste, then rub all over your face. Leave on for a few minutes so the mild acids in the lemon and baking soda can get to work. Combining the natural disinfectant properties of lemon and the gentle exfoliating powers of baking soda, this easy DIY face wash cleans, tones, and unclogs your pores.

CLEAR SKIN

Peel Away Acne

Try using a banana peel at bedtime! First, wash your face and pat dry. Peel a ripe banana and cut the peel into pieces a few inches long. Rub the pulpy interior side on the affected area of your face for about 10 minutes, or until the peel turns black. Repeat with fresh pieces of peel. Do not rinse until morning; allow the banana peel's nutrients to do their work overnight—they have both anti-inflammatory and antimicrobial properties. For best results, repeat for a few nights.

Beat Blackheads

Mix together 2 tablespoons salt and 2 tablespoons lime juice. Spread the paste onto your skin and allow to dry, then rinse off with warm water. This fresh-smelling toner will not only get rid of blackheads but it will also tighten your pores.

SWEET PIMPLE SOLUTION

Simply apply a drop of honey to the affected area and cover with a small bandage. Honey is loaded with healing enzymes that kill bacteria and toxins and reduce inflammation.

A Sticky Trick for Pores

Don't buy expensive pore strips for blackheads. Raid your child's school-supply box instead! Apply a thin film of white glue to your nose and other problem areas. Allow to dry, and peel off to reveal cleaner pores.

Simple Pimple Fighter

Over-the-counter acne creams are effective, but there's a product in your medicine cabinet that works just as well and is much less expensive: hydrogen peroxide. This miracle worker kills the pimple-producing bacteria living in your skin and oxygenates your pores to prevent new bacteria from setting up shop. First, wash your face to remove dirt, oils, and any makeup. Gently pat dry. Then soak a cotton ball in peroxide and dab it over any blemishes or apply it all over your face. Let sit for about 2 minutes, or until the peroxide stops bubbling, then rinse off.

Egg on Your Face

For eliminating blackheads, egg whites are egg-cellent (sorry, we couldn't resist). Whisk an egg white in a bowl and apply it directly to the face. Cover the area with toilet paper and allow it to dry until the paper becomes stiff. Then peel it away, and rinse with warm water.

Rub on Natural Relief

Try this neat trick to clear up your face. Cut a raw potato in half and rub the flat end over your face. Leave the juice on for 20 minutes before rinsing off. The starch in the potato will help dry out your oily skin.

Calm Skin with Cucumber

Drink it or apply it your skin—or both! Cucumber juice can treat and prevent acne while improving your skin's texture. To make juice, peel a cucumber and thinly slice. Fill a pitcher with cold water, add the cucumber slices, and let sit for about an hour before drinking or dabbing onto your skin with a cotton ball.

Make Blemishes Butt Out

Who knew diaper rash cream could help get rid of pimples? Dab a bit on offending areas, and the zinc oxide in the cream will dry up oil and kill bacteria while the moisturizers soften your skin. Meanwhile, it costs less than most store-bought acne treatments with the same ingredients.

JEANNE SAYS

Make Your Own Pore Strips

Mix together 1 to 2 tablespoons unflavored gelatin with equal parts milk; heat until warm. Spread the mixture on your skin and allow to dry completely. You will be able to peel it off in strips, removing blackheads in the process.

Paste Pimples Away

Fear you're getting a pimple? Dab the offending spot with a little tea tree oil, then cover it with a bit of toothpaste. The tea tree oil is an antiseptic, and the toothpaste has an anti-inflammatory effect.

RENEW AND SMOOTH

Nourish with Nutmeg

This nutmeg-milk facial scrub provides a double whammy of skin nourishment: Nutmeg works as an astringent, exfoliant, and anti-inflammatory (goodbye blackheads and acne), while the milk's lactic acid works as a peel to eliminate dead skin cells. To make the scrub, combine nutmeg and milk until the mixture resembles a paste. After washing your face with a cleanser, massage the nutmeg scrub onto your skin in gentle circular strokes. Let sit for 5 to 10 minutes, then rinse.

BRUCE SAYS

Drop the Pimples

Use eye drops to get rid of pimples! Put a few drops on the back of a metal spoon and place in the freezer. A minute or so later, it should be ready to apply to the blemish. The eye drops take away redness while the cold goes to work to minimize swelling.

Butter Up Your Skin

This facial mask contains two exfoliating powerhouses—oatmeal and buttermilk. Buttermilk contains lactic acid, which helps dissolve dead skin cells to reveal younger-looking skin. Puree 1 tablespoon rolled or instant oats, 1 tablespoon honey, and ¼ cup buttermilk in a blender. Massage gently into the face, and leave on for 10 to 15 minutes. Rinse with lukewarm water.

Honey for Your Hands

Combating severely dry skin can really seem like a losing battle. Whip up this intensive moisturizing cream to start fighting back. In a bowl, stir together ¼ cup shortening (at room temperature), 1 tablespoon honey, and ⅛ teaspoon rosewater. Massage a little into those dry hands (or feet) anytime they need a little extra help. Store the leftovers in a tightly sealed jar.

Try a Little Tenderness

The next time you buy a pineapple at the supermarket, don't just toss the peel. Use it on your feet! Pineapple contains bromelain, a natural meat tenderizer, which is also great at exfoliating rough spots on your skin like your heels and elbows. Rub the fleshy part of the pineapple peel against your skin for several minutes, then rinse.

Smooth Away Cellulite

To reduce the appearance of cellulite while exfoliating, try this brown sugar and coffee scrub. When rubbed against the skin, it helps increase circulation and make the cellulite less noticeable.

½ cup packed brown sugar
2 tablespoons ground coffee
2 tablespoons olive oil
1 tablespoon honey
1 vitamin E capsule

In a small bowl, mix together all of the ingredients. Massage a small amount on damp, clean skin for a few minutes, using circular motions. Rinse with warm water to reveal firmer-looking skin!

Moisturizer from the Microwave

Here's a great idea for chapped winter skin. Place your regular lotion in a microwave-safe bowl and microwave for 5 to 10 seconds. The warm lotion will feel great on cold mornings, and it will absorb faster into your skin than if it were at room temperature.

NAIL KNOW-HOW

Want hands and feet you don't need to hide? Skip the pricey salon visits! Get your nails in top shape with these easy at-home solutions.

HEALTHIER NAILS

Get Strong with Garlic

Do you have dry nails that tend to break? Garlic may be the answer. Add a little chopped garlic—no more than $\frac{1}{8}$ teaspoon—to a bottle of clear nail polish. Let the garlic sit in the bottle for 7 to 10 days before applying. Use as a base coat, top coat, or both. Don't worry about the smell; the top coat will mask it entirely.

Moisturize with Mayo

To keep the cuticles of your nails super-soft, pour mayonnaise into a small bowl and submerge your fingers in it for 5 minutes. Keep the bowl covered in the fridge (just make sure no one uses it for sandwiches) and repeat every day.

Cuticle Cream Cost Cutter

Did you know that cuticle cream contains almost the same ingredients as lip balm? Whether you did or not, you've probably noticed lip balm is much cheaper! Find a scent you like and apply directly to your cuticles to keep them healthy and prevent hangnails—at a fraction of the cost.

Get Rid of Stains

If dark nail polish has stained your fingernails, here's a quick fix: Plop a denture-cleaning tablet into a glass of water and soak your nails for a couple of minutes. The stains will come right off.

At-Home Hot Oil Treatment

Hot oil manicures are hot at nail salons to help revive and condition dry, damaged nails. But you can save money by creating your own at home! All you need to do is mix equal parts sunflower, olive, castor, and almond oils together, then heat the mixture for 15 to 20 seconds. Break open a vitamin E capsule and add it in. Carefully test the mixture to make sure it isn't too warm before dipping your nails in to soak up the moisturizing oils. Enjoy until the oils cool, massage some of the oil into your hands, then rinse.

Paste Your Way to White

Suffering from yellow fingernails or toenails? After removing any polish, bring back their natural luster with some whitening toothpaste! Apply the toothpaste to nails and let sit for an hour (a perfect time to catch up with a good book). Grab an old toothbrush if you need a little extra scrubbing power.

A Handy Massage

Before your next manicure, try this trick for whitening up nails that have been yellowed by polish. In a small bowl, squeeze the juice of a lemon and add in enough baking soda so that you have a loose paste. Massage the mixture into your nails for a few minutes, then rinse.

Fix a Broken Nail

If your nail has broken too low for comfort, you can make a simple patch to cover it until the nail naturally grows out. Just cut a small piece from a tea bag and apply with nail glue.

PERFECT POLISH AND DRYING

Trade Your Shake for a Roll

Did you know that shaking a bottle of nail polish isn't the best way to properly mix it before applying? Shaking can cause air bubbles, which can be a pesky problem when you're trying to paint your nails. Instead, roll the bottle between your palms.

BRUCE SAYS

Do Away with Dirt and Grease

Working in the garden or under the hood of the car? To make nail cleanup easier afterward, scratch your nails on a bar of soap first. An old toothbrush combined with dishwashing liquid works well as a fingernail cleaner after the fact.

6 POWERFUL NAIL FUNGUS FIGHTERS

If you have an unsightly nail fungus that makes you want to hide your hands or feet from view, you'll love these tips that help you clear it up without expensive or prescription treatments.

Sock it to fungus with a soak. Treat your feet or hands while you soak your nails in a mixture of 1 cup vinegar and 2 cups warm water every day for 15 minutes. The acid in the vinegar will attack the fungus, leaving you with lovelier nails. You can also try this tip for athlete's foot.

Try a foot-in-mouth solution. If you have yellow toenails, you may have a fungus problem. Get rid of this affliction by soaking your toes in mouthwash for 10 to 15 minutes each evening. Mouthwash has ingredients such as thymol and menthol that have antifungal properties.

Oil the fungus away. Certain oils have antifungal properties. The best bets for nails: oregano oil and tea tree oil. With a cotton swab, dab a few drops of oil on your nails twice daily.

Rub out fungus. Head to your medicine stash for this remedy: Use a cotton swab to apply a mentholated vapor rub, like Vicks, to the nail twice a day. If used consistently, it should eliminate the fungus. How it works: Rubs like these contain the antifungals camphor and eucalyptus oil.

Kick it with cornmeal. If you're a savvy gardener, you might know that cornmeal has long been used as a way to fight fungal diseases on flowers and lawns. Many people swear by that antifungal action for their nails. And there's no harm in giving this safe, all-natural treatment a try. Just pour some cornmeal into a shallow pan, mix it with water hot enough to dissolve it into a paste or mush, and let it cool for about an hour while you do other things. When you come back to it, add enough water to cover your feet or hands and then soak in it for an hour while you watch Netflix.

Serve your nails a spot of tea. But not just any tea will do! Pau d'arco is the type you need. It's made from the bark of a South American tree that contains antifungal compounds. If you can't find it your local grocery or health food store, Amazon has options. Use two tea bags steeped in warm water to create a nail bath, then soak your feet or hands twice a day for 20 minutes.

Smooth Move

If your polish never seems to glide on as smoothly as a salon application, try this trick. Stick the bottle in the fridge for 15 minutes before you apply.

Grab and Go

To make it easier to grab the polish you want in a hurry, paint a small area of an adhesive label with the color. Then use a hole puncher to create a circle swatch of the color that you can stick to the top of the polish bottle for an at-a-glance color selection.

Stray Polish Solution

You can keep polish from sticking where it's not welcome. All you need to do is apply a little petroleum jelly with a cotton swab to those areas around the edges of your nails. You can use the same trick when removing a dark nail polish so the color doesn't run and stain your hands as you attempt to remove it from your nails.

Want Polish That Lasts Longer?

Grab the vinegar! With a cotton ball, apply white vinegar to your nails to clear away any dirt or residue just before applying the nail polish. It helps your polish make a better seal and go the distance.

Ooh-la-la Manicure

If you've ever wanted to do an at-home French manicure, but had no clue how to get those perfect crescent shapes at the top of your nails, we've got an incredible tip for you! All you need is a plastic bandage wide enough to cover your nail. Stick the end of the bandage on your nail, exposing just the amount you want to paint. Then apply the polish and move the bandage on to the next nail. Now the only thing left to do is wait for your nails to dry—and show them off!

JEANNE SAYS

Top the Tip

When applying a top coat, don't forget to cover the edge of your nails. That's the spot that takes a beating and can open the door to polish chips!

WHO KNEW?

READERS' FAVORITE

Packing Peanuts Turned Beauty Product

Here's another use for those packing peanuts you never seem to be able to get rid of. The next time you're giving yourself a pedicure, insert a peanut between your toes to separate them; painting your toenails will be much easier.

More Is Less

Surprise! It's actually quicker to apply three super-thin layers of polish, letting each dry before applying the next, than forcing on one or two thick layers and waiting a polish eternity for them to dry.

Spray Dry in Your Kitchen

Make your nail polish dry more quickly by spraying your final coat with cooking spray. The oil will help them dry faster, and it will moisturize your cuticles, too!

Gone Dotty

Spice up your manicure with some polka dots! Make them perfect with this fun trick: Unbend a bobby pin, dip one tip into the nail polish, and then dot it on your nails. It's so easy you'll want dotted nails all the time!

Polar Plunge for Polish

Ice is nice when it comes to setting nail polish. Before you start your painting, fill a bowl with ice cubes and run some cold water over the top. Then, when you're ready to speed-dry, dip your nails in the bowl for about a minute. The cold will set the polish, not just on top but all the way through—protecting you from those annoying little chips.

Better with a Bobby

Here's a trick to give you that salon look when painting your own nails: Dip a bobby pin into nail polish remover and dab along the edge of your cuticle when you're done painting for a cleaner line.

FANCY FISHNETS

Cut off a piece of a loofah. After you've applied and dried your base color of choice, use a sponge to dab on a second color over the loofah. You'll get a fishnet effect!

Spit Shine

You just got a perfect pedicure at the salon, and suddenly you bump your toe against the leg of a chair, smudging the polish. Before you get too upset, quickly lick one of your fingers and run it over the smudged nail, applying a bit of pressure if needed. Surprisingly, there's a chemical in saliva that reacts with nail polish and can smooth over these little mishaps.

Neat Nail Polish Remover

Use an old pill bottle as a quick nail polish remover! Place several cotton balls or an old makeup sponge inside and add a bit of nail polish remover. Then when you have to remove old polish, just dip your finger inside the pill container and twist. You can create a similar helper with a mason jar and a rolled-up cleaning sponge.

HEALTHY HAIR

It may sound crazy, but we spend as much as $55,000 in a lifetime on hair products and treatments. Fortunately, you can nurture beautiful hair for much less when you know a few secrets.

EVERYDAY ANSWERS

Protect with a Simple Step

Take just a minute to brush your hair before you wash it. By doing so, you'll evenly distribute the natural oils in the hair, thus reducing breakage. You'll head off damage without expensive treatments!

Break Down Buildup

Using styling products can make your hair look limp, as shampoos don't always take care of the buildup. Every other week mix ¼ cup baking soda with enough water to create a paste. In the shower, rub the paste into your hair, rinse, and then wash and condition as usual. The baking soda takes care of all the product buildup, and there's no need to buy any expensive special shampoo.

Sensational "Salad" Shampoo

It may smell like a salad when you mix it up, but this shampoo formula works wonders to cleanse and clarify your hair! In a spray bottle, simply combine ½ cup water, ½ castile soap, ¼ cup apple cider vinegar, and 2 tablespoons tea tree oil. You can also add a few drops of your favorite essential oil scent. The result will be more liquid than creamy, so it's easiest to wet hair, spritz it on, massage it, and then rinse.

Conditioners from Your Kitchen

Looking for a simple, natural conditioner you can use every day? Try mayonnaise or coconut oil. Leave either white wonder on your hair for a few minutes before rinsing out. If your scalp tends to be greasy, concentrate conditioning on just your ends.

Coconut-Citrus Scalp Rub

To soothe a dry, itchy scalp, try this terrific-smelling treatment. Mix together ¼ cup coconut oil with 3 tablespoons lemon or lime juice. Massage the mixture into your scalp and leave on for 15 to 20 minutes. Rinse, and follow with your regular shampoo and conditioner. You'll love the way your scalp feels, and how your hair smells!

Cold Shine

Extra-shiny hair starts in the shower! Finish your final rinse with a blast of the most freezing cold water you can bear. It closes the hair cuticles so that light bounces off them, resulting in super shiny locks.

Homemade Volumizer

If your hair is looking limp, try this unique trick. Soak ¼ cup rice in 1 cup warm water overnight. In the morning, strain off the liquid into a spray bottle and spritz it on damp hair. The starch will cling to each strand, creating lots of body and volume. And it barely cost pennies!

A Salty Boost

Give fine or thinning hair a volume boost with Epsom salts. In a microwave-safe bowl, stir together 3 tablespoons Epsom salts and 3 tablespoons conditioner. Microwave on 50 percent power until warm. Apply the mixture to clean, damp hair and leave on for 20 minutes. Rinse and style as usual.

DIY Dry Shampoo

Why spend on dry shampoo when you've already got the perfect substitute in your pantry? It's cornstarch. Granted, this tip is a little messy, so stand on a towel, or apply in the shower before turning on the water. Sprinkle a couple of tablespoons of cornstarch on dry hair and massage throughout the hair and scalp. Let it sit for 5 minutes to absorb excess oil, then flip your head upside down and massage or brush it out. Instantly revitalized hair!

Natural Relaxer

Here's a great tip for African American women looking for a natural alternative to those chemical-laden relaxers. In a small bowl, juice 2 limes and stir the juice into 1¾ cups coconut milk. Transfer the mixture to a small saucepan and place over medium heat. Start whisking in a few tablespoons of cornstarch, stirring constantly until the mixture starts to thicken. When it reaches the desired consistency, remove it from the heat and let it cool slightly. Massage thoroughly through your hair, then cover it with a shower cap or plastic wrap. After 45 to 60 minutes, you can rinse it out.

A Saline Solution

Even if you don't have time to properly wash, dry, and style your hair, you can still get rid of oiliness in just a few minutes. Here's another version of a dry shampoo: Take a handful of kosher salt and rub it into the roots and scalp. (You may want to do this in the tub or over a sink to avoid making a mess.) Wait 5 minutes so that the salt can absorb the oil, then shake it out.

Shampoo Less Often

Here's a great trick for those of us with oily hair who want to extend the time between shampoos. Spray freshly shampooed hair with a mixture of equal parts apple cider vinegar and water. Comb it through the hair and wait a few minutes before rinsing it out and styling as usual. The acid in the vinegar helps keep oily hair clean longer!

Get Rid of Static

If brushing your hair makes it practically stand on end, run your brush under cold water before using it on your hair.

Hair Spray Hint

Who knew that unscented hair spray is less sticky than the scented kind? If you need hair spray for your 'do but hate the feel, opt for the unscented variety. Also make sure you keep the can at least 6 inches away from your hair while spraying.

YOUR HAIR WON'T KNOW THE DIFFERENCE!
For a cheap alternative to hair gel, try a light hand lotion instead. With so many scents available, you'll probably find one you like even more than your normal hair-care product!

GET TO THE ROOT OF PROBLEMS

Rehydrate with Hot Oil

There's no need to buy commercial hot oil treatments when you can use oils you've already got at home. Gently heat ¼ cup olive, grapeseed, or almond oil in a saucepan until it's warm. Be careful: You don't want it so hot that it will burn your skin. Massage into damp hair and cover with plastic wrap for 20 minutes before shampooing.

Delicious Hair Mask

For a deep-conditioning hair mask, mash the flesh of an avocado with 1 cup mayonnaise. Rub it into your hair and cover your head with plastic wrap or a shower cap. After 20 minutes, wash it out with your usual shampoo.

Healthier Hair in Your Sleep

No time for hair treatments? Restore your hair while you sleep! Before bed, apply a quarter-size dollop of coconut oil to your hair, comb it, and cover it with a shower cap. In the morning, shampoo as usual and reveal the hair of your dreams.

Thicken Thinning Hair

Feed your hair protein to thicken and strengthen it! One of the best sources: eggs. Simply beat one or two eggs and apply to damp hair, paying special attention to the scalp. After 30 minutes, shampoo out.

Vitamins to Strengthen

We know oranges are full of good stuff for our body, but hair benefits from the vitamin C, acids, and pectin in oranges, too. To transform hair from damaged to silky and strong, puree an orange in the blender (peel included!). Apply the orange hair mask and leave on for 30 minutes before rinsing out.

WHO KNEW?

READERS' FAVORITE

The Power of Powder

Has your perfect day at the beach left you with a ton of sand in your hair? Before shampooing, massage a tablespoon of baby powder into your roots, then brush thoroughly. The powder helps loosen the sand so shampooing will now be easy!

Enjoy a Scalp Massage

It turns out that the person washing your hair at the salon is on to something! When you apply shampoo or conditioner, take a few moments to give yourself a slow fingertip scalp massage. Using gentle circular motions and a little bit of pressure on the scalp will boost blood circulation around the follicles and stimulate regrowth. Similarly, if you want to strengthen your hair, be sure to brush or comb it thoroughly each night. This will increase circulation in your scalp, loosen dry skin, and help moisturize your hair with your body's natural oils.

Get Growing

Looking for a natural solution to thinning hair? Here's a terrific scalp massage that stimulates blood flow in the hair follicles and may spur hair growth. Mix 5 drops lavender essential oil, 5 drops bay essential oil, and 3 tablespoons almond or grapeseed oil. Massage a small amount into the scalp every day and leave for 15 to 20 minutes before rinsing out.

Seal Your Split Ends

Your hair stylist just called to reschedule your appointment, but you've had it with your split ends! This simple moisturizing hair mask will rescue your locks and buy you a few days until you can get yourself into the salon chair. Whisk together an egg yolk with 1 tablespoon grapeseed or olive oil and 1 tablespoon honey. Massage the mixture through damp hair, paying special attention to the ends. Then cover your hair with a towel or plastic wrap and wait 30 minutes. Rinse with warm water.

> ## JEANNE SAYS
>
> ### Save That Fruit!
> Don't toss those brown bananas and overripe avocado! They're perfect to make a nutrient-rich conditioner. Just mash them together and enjoy a tropical hair mask for 15 minutes before washing out.

Stop the Slick

Just like an astringent for your face can control oil, an astringent for your scalp can do the same. And it's simple to make your own formula! Mix equal parts witch hazel and mouthwash, then dab on your scalp with a cotton ball before shampooing as usual.

Clear Up Greasy Hair

Vinegar is not just for the kitchen; it gets grease out of oily hair! Simply shampoo your hair as usual, rinse, then pour ¼ cup vinegar over it and rinse again.

7 DANDRUFF REMEDIES THAT WORK

You don't have to buy expensive, chemical-filled shampoos to get rid of dandruff. Instead, use one or more of these remedies you may already have on hand.

Time for thyme. If your scalp is getting flaky, try treating it with a mixture of 2 tablespoons dried thyme and 1 cup water. Bring the water to a boil in a saucepan, then add the thyme and wait 5 minutes. Remove from the heat and let cool, then strain out the thyme and pour the water on your hair and scalp after you've washed and rinsed it. To let it work, don't rinse it out for 12 hours—but don't worry, your hair will dry fine (and smell delicious)!

Tame it with tea tree oil. Tea tree oil is a natural antiseptic. Just add a few drops to your regular shampoo to give it dandruff-fighting power.

Try an antidandruff diet. You can reduce flakes in your hair by changing your diet. Increase your intake of raw foods that are high in enzymes (fruit, vegetables, and nuts). If your dandruff still doesn't improve, try swallowing 1 to 2 teaspoons flaxseed oil a day.

Reach for vinegar. You can use apple cider vinegar to regulate the acid level on your scalp and clear out the dry skin flakes. Maximize the benefits by adding fresh mint! Heat ¼ cup apple cider vinegar with ½ cup water and a few leaves of fresh mint in the microwave or over low heat on the stove. Let cool, then chill in the fridge overnight. Tomorrow, use it to cover your scalp—massaging the mixture into your hair—and wait a half hour before you shampoo it out.

Open the medicine cabinet. After shampooing your hair, pour a solution of half mouthwash, half water over it. Work into your scalp and let it sit for 5 minutes, then rinse out and condition as usual. Repeat once or twice a week until dandruff is gone.

Cure more than headaches. Aspirin may help reduce dandruff if you crush a couple of tablets and add them to your normal shampoo. Just be sure to let the shampoo sit on your hair for 1 to 2 minutes before washing it out.

Know the citrus solution. Mix 2 tablespoons lemon juice with 2 cups warm water and pour over your head after you rinse out your conditioner. Let it dry in your hair and it will not only keep dandruff away but it will also make your hair smell wonderful.

Get Rid of Lice Naturally

Nothing strikes fear in the hearts of parents like the words "lice outbreak." The harsh chemicals that are used to fight lice are almost as bad as the lice themselves. Luckily, there is a cheaper, more natural alternative. Cover your child's head (or yours, if the little buggers have gotten you!) with a thick conditioner. Put on a Disney movie to keep your kid busy, then get a wide-toothed metal comb. Dip the comb into rubbing alcohol and comb through the hair, staying close to the scalp. Between each swipe, wipe the comb on a white paper towel to make sure you're getting the lice. Dip the comb in the alcohol again and keep going. Cover the hair with baking soda, and then repeat the process with the alcohol and the comb. Wash hair thoroughly when finished, and repeat this procedure each day for a week or until the lice are gone.

COLORING HELPERS

Espresso Your True Colors

If you have dark hair, you can conceal grays without paying for hair coloring. Just rinse your hair with strong coffee (let it cool first!). Let the coffee sit in your hair for 3 minutes, then rinse out. Repeat one or two times as necessary. The coffee will not only provide a subtle tint but it will also get rid of any product buildup on your locks!

Lighten with Lemon

You can go light while leaving the damage of chemical highlights in the bottle! In a spray bottle, mix 2 parts lemon juice with 1 part water, then saturate any area of your hair you want to lighten. Use the natural rays of the sun or heat from your hair dryer to help set the color; leave on for an hour before washing out. Repeat once a week for a month for longer-lasting effects.

Trend Toward Red

Rather see red? In a spray bottle, mix 1 cup beet juice with ½ cup carrot juice. Guard your clothing from tough stains, then saturate any area of your hair where you want to see touches of red. Step into the sun to set the color, or get heat help from your hair dryer. Wash the juices out after an hour. You can repeat once or twice a week for a month for bolder, longer-lasting effects.

KEEP COLOR LASTING

The better moisturized your hair is, the better it holds color. Treat your tresses to some coconut oil—one of the best natural moisturizers.

Sweeten Up Your Hair Dye

If at-home hair coloring irritates your scalp, try adding a little Sweet'N Low to the mixture before applying it. The artificial sweetener helps neutralize any ammonia-based formula. It will be easier on your scalp while still being just as effective.

Simple Root Touchup

Roots sneak up on you? You can blend away any discrepancy in a hurry. All you need is eye shadow! If your roots are darker than the rest of your hair, soften the transition with the help of an eye shadow that's the same shade as your roots. Just apply with a makeup brush or cotton ball to about an inch below your roots to create a better blend. If your roots are lighter than the rest of your hair, apply an eye shadow that is the same color as the length of your hair onto the roots.

When Dye Needs to Die

Uh oh, you just tried dyeing your hair a new color, and it looks bad enough that you don't want to leave the house without a hat. What to do? Just wash it three or four times using an antidandruff shampoo that contains zinc pyrithione. This chemical diminishes dye more quickly, without damaging your hair.

SIMPLE BEAUTY

Fancy beauty counters and chemical-laden products are not what you need to look your best. Feel confident, beautiful, and healthy with these hints!

LOVE YOUR LIPS

Brush to Better Lips

For lips that need a little extra TLC, especially in the winter, try this effective scrub. Mix together 2 teaspoons baking soda with enough lemon juice to make a paste. Gently scrub the mixture over your lips with a dry toothbrush for a minute or two, then rinse and apply some petroleum jelly or your favorite lip balm.

Gentle Lip Scrub

Cut out the "middleman" of expensive lip balms that contain vitamin E and go straight to the source! Buy some vitamin E capsules at a health food or vitamin store and use them directly on your lips. Just squeeze out the contents of the capsule and apply to lips, or make this simple lip scrub that's both exfoliating and moisturizing—ideal for sensitive skin. Mix the contents of a vitamin E capsule with enough sugar to make a paste. Rub onto your lips for 30 seconds, then wait 3 minutes before rinsing with warm water.

Exfoliate Deliciously

Eliminate unsightly rough spots and help lipstick adhere more evenly by applying an exfoliating lip scrub. This homemade version is easy, and so tasty you may just want to eat it! Mash together a strawberry or two with a drizzle of honey. Rub the mixture on your lips in a circular motion and wait 5 minutes before rinsing (or licking!) off.

A SPICY BOOST

Rub your lips with cinnamon! Cinnamon increases blood flow, giving your lips a fuller look. Rinse, and then apply your lipstick as usual.

Sweet and Simple Solution

Send chapped lips packing with coconut oil! Mix a bit of the oil with a dab of brown sugar and honey. Apply the mixture with a soft toothbrush and then use a circular motion to lightly exfoliate your lips. Let your lips enjoy the treatment for a few minutes, then rinse off.

Go Crazy for Cranberry

For a seasonal solution to chapped winter lips—and a great DIY gift idea for the holidays—try this cranberry lip balm! In a microwave-safe bowl, mix together 1 tablespoon avocado or almond oil, 10 fresh cranberries, 1 teaspoon honey, and 1 drop vitamin E oil (from a capsule). Microwave on high until the mixture begins to boil. Remove carefully as the bowl may be hot. Mash the berries with a fork and stir well to combine. After the mixture has cooled for 10 minutes, strain it into a small portable tin, making sure you remove all of the fruit pieces. Cool completely, and smile because you've made your own great-smelling lip balm!

Plump Up the Volume

Even those amazing plumping lipsticks can be made at home. For lips worthy of Angelina Jolie, try this plumping balm. Melt 3 tablespoons beeswax and 1 tablespoon vegetable oil in a double boiler. Using a rasp grater, grate 1 teaspoon of ginger onto a piece of cheesecloth. Squeeze the cheesecloth over the wax mixture to release some of the fragrant ginger juices, and stir to combine. Keep the balm in a small container (save used-up lip balm containers, or use a travel case for contacts), and spread a little on your lips anytime you want a little extra boost. The ginger will not only plump your lips but it will also smell wonderful!

The Perfect Color

To find your ideal lip color, purse your lips together tightly for 30 seconds, then release and take a look in the mirror. Look for a color that matches that slightly deepened shade. Like your lips, only better!

Get Every Bit of Gloss

Running low on lip gloss? Place the closed tube of gloss in a glass of warm water for 10 to 15 minutes. The heat will loosen those last little bits so you can use every drop.

Keep Lipstick Where It Belongs

To avoid getting lipstick on your teeth, after you apply, close your mouth over your finger and slowly pull it out. This will save you time and time again!

Cool as Ice

Keep your lipstick from smudging or setting with this simple trick: Just rub an ice cube over your lips after applying lipstick! It will last longer than ever before.

THE EYES HAVE IT

Cool Away Puffy Eyes

Here's a unique twist on the traditional cucumber-slices-on-eyes trick. Peel and chop half a cucumber and puree it in a blender with ½ cup cold water. Strain the mixture into a spray bottle. Spritz it onto round cosmetic pads to saturate, and place the pads on your eyes for 10 minutes. Do this anytime you have some extra redness or puffiness around the eyes for immediate relief!

Herbal Eye Treatment

Reduce puffy or swollen eyes with a green tea compress. Dip cotton wool into the green tea, drain off excess moisture, and dab gently around the eye area. This will help tighten the skin around the eyes.

Soothe with Spoons

If all else has failed in your efforts to de-puff your eyes, try frozen spoons. Put two spoons in the freezer for 5 minutes, then roll them slowly back and forth over your eyes until you feel them start to warm up. Make sure your skin is completely dry before you do this, or you'll be faced with an entirely new problem.

Ditch Dark Circles

Dark, saggy rings under your eyes? A handful of fresh parsley with its vitamins C and K can do the trick. In a bowl, crush and grind the leaves with a spoon to release the juices. Pour 1 tablespoon hot water over the parsley and stir. When cool, dab the liquid goodness onto the dark skin beneath your eyes with a cotton ball. Let it sit for about 15 minutes, and rinse.

Emergency Coverup

For emergency undereye concealer, use your foundation. A good trick is to dab from the little bit on the cap, which is thicker. You can use this on blemishes too.

Smooth Out Concealer

Partied a little too hard over the weekend? Don't make the mistake of covering the bags under your eyes so dramatically that you draw attention to the spot by making it too light. A little bronzer applied over the concealer should even things out.

Firm in the Freezer

If you have an eyeliner pencil that keeps crumbling when you try to use it, stick it in the freezer for 20 minutes to firm it up.

Get Fuller Lashes While You Sleep

Just as you can condition your hair, you can condition your eyelashes. The best all-natural conditioners are oils: almond, castor, or coconut oil. You can simply apply the oil of your choice with a cotton ball at the base of your lashes before bed. Or use a clean mascara wand to apply a mixture of 2 parts vitamin E oil, 1 part castor oil, and 1 part 100 percent pure aloe vera gel. Rinse off and reveal healthier lashes in the morning! Want full brows as well? The recipe works for them, too.

Give Mascara a Boost

Sneak two drops of lavender, rosemary, or tea tree oil into your mascara to boost its conditioning power. Rolling the tube and moving the mascara wand up and down will mix in the oil. So simple!

Out of Mascara?

Applying the finishing touches to your makeup and realize you're out of mascara? Here's a great tip to get that last bit out of the tube. Simply roll the tube quickly between your hands for 30 seconds. The heat generated by the friction is enough to soften the mascara stuck to the sides of the tube, so you'll have just enough to apply to your lashes before you run out the door.

WHO KNEW?
READERS' FAVORITE

Mascara Miracle

Mascara starting to dry out? Just add several drops of saline eye drops and shake. The eye drops will keep the mascara lasting much longer than you ever thought possible!

No More Mascara Mess

Tired of getting mascara on your skin when you apply it to your lower lashes? Next time, grab a plastic spoon and gently place it under the lower lashes, with the curved side facing out. When you apply the mascara, the excess will stick to the spoon, not your face.

Natural Makeup Remover

For a gentle way to remove mascara, eyeliner, and shadow, try coconut oil. It works just as well as eye makeup remover but is useful in so many other ways— so you get the most for your money. Plus, it's moisturizing! Dab a small amount on a tissue or cotton ball, rub over closed eyes, and rinse with water. Baby shampoo also works.

Keep That Magic Wand

When you toss an old tube of mascara, don't throw away the wand! It can become a valuable tool in your makeup arsenal. Clean it with warm soapy water, then use it to separate lashes stuck together with mascara. Or add a bit of petroleum jelly to the wand and apply as you would mascara to moisturize dry lashes.

BEST FACE FORWARD

Wake Up Your Face

In the morning, your face can look pale and puffy because of the natural nocturnal slowdown in the body. When putting on your moisturizer, take the opportunity to gently massage all the muscles in your face to waken up the lymphatic system and jump-start the circulation.

Discover a Natural Highlighter

Fancy highlighter kits can be pricey and complicated. (What goes where?!) A simple solution to get a dewy glow: coconut oil. Dab a bit along your cheekbones—it lightens just like a highlighter. No special brushes or YouTube tutorials required!

One Terrific Tube

Lipstick can serve double-duty as a cream blush. Just dab a little on your cheeks and blend. This is also a great tip for an evening out when you're carrying a tiny clutch that barely has enough room for your keys and cell phone.

BRUCE SAYS

Keep Brows in Line
If you can't convince your husband to trim his giant eyebrows, you at least might have some luck getting him to keep unruly hairs in line! Just use an old toothbrush, but make it extra effective by spraying it with hair spray first. Then comb over brows to tame any wild hairs and rinse the brush after using.

Never Buy Face Powder Again

Make your own loose face powder with cornstarch! After all, most commercial powders, whether drugstore brands or pricey makeup-counter options, use cornstarch as a base. To add color, sprinkle in a little cocoa powder until you get your desired shade. Store it in a pretty tin and use just as you would your usual loose powder.

Strong Foundations

Some of the most expensive makeup is foundation. Make it last longer by buying a shade darker than your natural one, then mixing it with moisturizer until it matches your normal color. You'll have more than twice as much, and you'll never be able to tell the difference!

Revisit the Moisturizer

How do some women get that otherworldly glow? You've tried all the bronzers and sun-kissed blush powders you can find, but can't seem to achieve radiant-looking skin. One trick that works: Apply a little bit of moisturizer after you put on your makeup.

Baby Your Brushes

You should wash makeup brushes and sponges regularly to rid them of dirt, oil, and bacteria—none of which you want to transfer onto your face. Lather them up with baby shampoo, massage gently, rinse in cool water, and let them air-dry.

DIY Brush Cleaner

If you're having trouble getting your makeup brushes and sponges clean, make a simple cleaning solvent. Combine ½ cup baking soda with 2 tablespoons water and mix together. Then add the resulting paste to 1 cup water and ½ cup fabric softener. Dip your brushes and sponges in the resulting solution, rinse clean, and reshape before allowing to air-dry.

Quick Makeup Removal

You should never leave makeup on overnight, as it can dry out your skin (and leave marks on your pillow!). One of the quickest ways to remove cosmetics is with a premoistened wipe, but skip the expensive makeup removal wipes and keep a stash of baby wipes near the sink instead. The next time you come home after a late night, rub one over your face before you hit the sack.

GROOMING TRICKS

Spend less time and money on grooming with better results! From whiter teeth to a smoother shave, these simple tips go a long way toward making you smile wide and feel fresh.

GET A CONFIDENT SMILE

Whiten Your Teeth Naturally

Don't buy expensive whiteners—you can make your own with a favorite fruit! Mash 4 or 5 strawberries with ½ teaspoon baking soda. Brush onto your teeth with a toothbrush and let sit for 10 to 15 minutes. Then rinse out and brush your teeth as usual, making sure no strawberry seeds got caught between your teeth. Repeat this process every night and you'll start to see results in 3 to 4 weeks.

Another Fruit Solution for Whitening

Before you spend a small fortune on teeth whitening procedures, try a banana instead. The inside of the peel contains both citric acid (a bleaching agent) and salicylic acid (an astringent that fights plaque). After brushing, rub one on your teeth for 2 minutes and it'll lighten stains naturally without harming your enamel.

Hard Cheese for Healthy Teeth

Serve hard cheeses like Romano and aged Cheddar as an after-dinner snack. They'll help scrub your teeth of acids found in other foods, and the calcium inside helps make teeth stronger.

Rinse Away Bacteria

Another benefit to add to the list for apple cider vinegar: antibacterial power! Use it as a mouth rinse to help prevent plaque buildup and yellowing. Swish with a solution of 1 part apple cider vinegar and 2 parts water each morning to keep your smile strong and beautiful.

Pull In Coconut Oil

Coconut oil is an antibacterial that can work in much the same way as apple cider vinegar to fight plague and whiten teeth. Use 1 tablespoon coconut oil like a mouthwash, a technique called oil pulling. Your teeth care routine just got tropical!

Stretch That Toothpaste

To get every bit of toothpaste out of the tube, soak the nearly empty tube in a cup of hot water for several minutes. It will loosen the remaining toothpaste from the sides of the tube, and you'll be able to brush a few more times before having to buy more. Every penny counts!

Go for Yogurt

The "good" bacteria in yogurt have been found to be effective in targeting the odor-causing bacteria in your mouth. Make sure you go for the plain kind, no sugar. Breath mints and sprays mask the odor but they don't help the underlying problem—eating yogurt does.

Beat Bad Breath on the Go

Certain herbs and spices are natural breath fresheners when you chew on them. Repurpose an old pill bottle to carry cloves, fennel, or aniseed with you.

Keep Mints Sugar Free

If you go the traditional route with mints or gum to freshen breath, make sure the label says "sugar free" or else you could be worsening the situation. Sugar feeds bacteria, which can contribute to bad breath.

Reach for a Cup of Tea

Whether you enjoy green or black, tea provides polyphenols, which prevent the growth of bacteria.

Denture Wash

Anyone with dentures knows how costly store-bought cleaners can be. Luckily, making your own denture cleaner is super-easy as well as cheap! Baking soda is the miracle disinfectant that will get your dentures bright white and completely deodorized. The tiny granules offer abrasive powers that'll get at all bits of food and dirt. Just sprinkle it onto your dental brush and get scrubbing! You can also soak them overnight in a solution of 1 part white vinegar and 1 part water.

Brush Away Germs

Get a head start on flu and cold season by giving your toothbrushes a thorough disinfecting on a regular basis. Soak the bristles in a small cup of hydrogen peroxide for 5 minutes once a week; rinse the brush thoroughly and let dry uncovered (covering the brush only retains moisture and promotes bacteria growth). If someone in your house is already sick, give all toothbrushes a peroxide bath after every time they're used.

Need to Relocate?

Store your toothbrush at least 6 feet away from your toilet to keep it safely away from any bacteria that can become airborne when you flush.

BRUCE SAYS

Surprising Use for a Coffee Bean
To freshen your breath, try sucking on a coffee bean. It's much cheaper than a breath mint, and tastes great to us coffee addicts!

SHAVING SENSE

Streamline Your Products

Instead of buying expensive shaving creams or foams, try shaving with hair conditioner. (Buy the cheapest kind.) The conditioner will soften the hair and provide a layer of protection between the blade and your skin. You'll even get a closer shave!

Natural Creams

If you're looking to go the natural route, both pure aloe and coconut oil make amazing shaving creams. They're both moisturizing and antibacterial—just in case of nicks. You can use them alone, or combine with a bit of castile or hand soap and water for a foamier result you can dispense from a clean soap pump. Shake before each use.

CALM MORE THAN HEARTBURN

For razor burn, try applying a liquid antacid. The active ingredient will calm redness and irritation. Rub some on the skin, leave for 5 minutes, then rinse.

Time It Right

Did you know that the time of day that you shave your legs matters? For the smoothest legs, shave in the morning. By evening, legs tend to be more swollen, making it harder for your razor to get as close to the skin.

Know Your Directions

Most women tend to shave from ankle to knee, but that's working against the direction of growth and can lead to ingrown hairs. Reverse your direction and go from knee to ankle for a smoother shave.

Ease Ingrown Hairs

Suffering from ingrown hairs? This all-natural solution will help the healing. Combine 1 cup sugar, the juice from half a lemon, 2 teaspoons apple cider vinegar, and ¼ cup honey. Blend together until smooth, then heat in the microwave until warm (15 to 20 seconds). Let it sit on the affected area for 20 minutes.

Soothe Razor Burn

Ouch! Your razor was a bit dull and now you have razor burn. Cure the redness and pain by applying a layer of plain yogurt. Let it sit for 5 minutes, then rinse off and pat dry. The lactic acid in the yogurt will calm your irritated skin.

Treat a Nick Quickly

Slipped and nicked yourself while shaving? Simple pressure usually works best. But if you're in a rush and can't keep up pressure until the bleeding stops, here's a little shortcut. Dab on a little astringent to staunch the flow, then follow with a rub of antiperspirant. You'll be set to head out!

WHO KNEW?
READERS' FAVORITE

Get Rid of That Ring

If your shaving cream can is leaving rusty rings on the side of your tub or sink, perform this trick right after you purchase a new container: Coat the rim around the bottom of the can with clear nail polish, then let it dry. The polish will keep out water so the can won't rust.

Razor Saver

The next time you open something that has one of those little silica gel packets in it, save it for your bathroom. Store your razor near these little wonders (like in the bottom of a cup) and they'll soak up any remaining moisture from the blades. It's minuscule rust that dulls the blades, so they'll last months longer.

Forget Facial Hair

To eliminate unwanted facial hair, try this unique trick. Mix together 1 tablespoon chickpea flour (if you can't find it, you can grind dry chickpeas) with 1 teaspoon turmeric. Add a little bit of water to make a paste and apply to any spots where you have facial hair. Allow the paste to dry completely, then rub it off. Rinse the area with cool water.

STAY FRESH AND CLEAN

Freshen Feet

Keep your feet smelling fresh by sprinkling a bit of cornstarch into your shoes once or twice a week. The cornstarch will absorb moisture and odors, and you won't be afraid to slip off those uncomfortable dress shoes under your desk.

Sage Advice

Go natural to get rid of stinky feet! Break up a few sage leaves and spread them around inside your shoes. They'll kill the bacteria that causes foot odor. To cut down on how much you perspire in the first place, try drinking sage tea. Herbalists say it will take several weeks, but you'll see results!

Treat with Peppermint Powder

Keep your feet fresh and dry with this powder. In a zip-top bag, place ¼ cup unscented body powder, 5 drops peppermint essential oil, and 5 drops tea tree oil; seal carefully. Massage the outside of the bag to get the oils to blend together evenly with the powder. To use, dust a little onto clean feet. The peppermint has a refreshing quality, and tea tree oil is a natural antifungal.

Pull Out Odors with a Potato

Did you know that we release toxins through the soles of our feet? To pull out those odor-causing toxins, place raw potato slices in your socks. Wait a few hours before removing. You'll be amazed at how the compounds in the potato work—the slices will likely be black to show the results!

TREAT YOUR FEET TO JELL-O!
Prepare Jell-O and pour it into a basin. Soak your feet until it sets; wash off with soap and water. What's the benefit? The gel blocks sweat glands. Many commercial deodorants rely on a similar effect.

Make Your Own Liquid Soap

Shower gel can get expensive, so make your own from the cheapest bar soap you can find. Use a cheese grater on two bars of soap, then add to 2½ cups warm water. Add a soothing oil of your choice (baby and almond oil work well), as well as rosewater or an essential oil like eucalyptus or marjoram. Refill an empty soap dispenser and shake. (You may need to shake each time you use it.)

Man Up to Odor

Did you know that on average, antiperspirants and deodorants made for men are $3 cheaper than their female counterparts—even when they have the same ingredients? If you're a woman who uses unscented deodorant, opt for the guys' stuff instead to save! You may also find a lightly scented variety you like.

Surprising Deodorants

If you've run out of deodorant, don't worry! You can still leave the house without fear of a stinky sweat smell: Apple cider vinegar and antiseptic mouthwash make great substitutions for deodorant in a pinch. Saturate a cloth with the vinegar or mouthwash and rub it under your arms.

Too Much Perfume?

Oops! You accidentally put on way too much perfume, and you're afraid the restaurant you're dining at will smell like someone just detonated a flower-scented bomb. To make your perfume less strong, dab a cotton ball dipped in rubbing alcohol wherever you applied the scent. Your friends will thank you.

Eliminate Excess Earwax

Although earwax is intended to protect your super-sensitive outer ear, too much wax can inhibit hearing, foster infection, and simply be uncomfortable. If you or your family members are prone to lots of earwax, try this easy cleaning solution. You'll need a medicine dropper or cotton balls, olive or almond oil, and hydrogen peroxide. With the head tilted so the ear faces upward, place two drops of oil into the ear canal and let sit for a minute or two. Repeat with a few drops of hydrogen peroxide, and leave for about 10 minutes. When time's up and the peroxide is no longer bubbling, tip the head to the reverse side so the solution can drip out. Wipe away any drips or excess solution with cotton balls or a towel.

JEANNE SAYS

Make Use of Soap Slivers

Don't throw out those last few slivers of soap! Instead, cut a slit in the side of a body sponge and slip them inside. Now lather up and rinse. You'll get so many soap suds, you probably won't need to repeat.

WARDROBE FIXES

Help your clothing, shoes, jewelry, and more look great and last longer with these simple solutions that save you money.

KEEP CLOTHING AT ITS BEST

Erase Armpit Stains

Is there anything more annoying than pulling on a black blouse before you head to work and realizing you have white deodorant marks on it? Remove them in a flash with a pair of pantyhose. Just rub the nylon material briskly over the stain and it will lift it right off.

No More Shoulder Bumps

Hanging is often the best space-saving strategy in your closet. But what can you do with sweaters? Hanging them the usual way leads to shoulder bumps—and we're way past the decade when big shoulders were fashionable. There is a sweater-safe technique! First, lay your sweater flat, then bring arm over to arm to fold in half. Now, grab your hanger and place the hook in the armpit, with the top pointing down. Fold the waist up and the sleeves diagonally over the hanger.

Sweater Stretched?

If the cuffs or necklines of woolen sweaters are stretched out of shape, dip them in hot water and dry with a blow dryer. They should shrink back to their original size.

Never Lose a Button

Dab a small drop of clear nail polish on the front of a button to keep the threads in place and never lose a button again.

Fix That Pilling

Sweaters pilling with those annoying fiber bits? You can buy a fabric shaver to solve the problem. Another (cost-saving) strategy: Check your household beauty supplies. First, call into action a razor with a sharp blade and no lotion strip. Glide the razor over any areas of clothing that have started to pill. It'll work gentle magic but leave a pile of pills. Your next tool: a Velcro roller/curler. Simply roll it over the pills to pick them up easily—and maybe even erase more pilling along the way.

Crease Prevention

Don't buy special pants hangers, but still avoid creases in suit pants with this clever tip: Cover the bottom of a hanger with a paper towel tube which you've cut lengthwise, and gently lay the pants over it. Hang them while they're still wet and you might not even have to iron them!

Quick Wrinkle Fix

No need to lug out the iron and board when you have a wrinkled shirt. A straightening iron can smooth out clothing creases as well as hair. It makes especially easy work of the space between buttons!

Spray Away Wrinkles

Why buy a wrinkle-releasing spray when you can make your own with ingredients you probably have on hand right now? In a spray bottle, add 2 cups water, 1 tablespoon vinegar, and 1 teaspoon hair conditioner; shake to combine. Spray clothing until damp, smooth with your hands, and let dry.

Kettle Steam Solution

Minor wrinkles in your clothing? Fill your teakettle with water and bring it to a full boil. Hold the clothing item 8 to 12 inches from the steaming spout for a wrinkle-battling blast.

Iron On Your Favorite Fragrance

This smart tip will make your clothes smell wonderful. Add a drop of perfume or cologne to the water in your steam iron. You'll enjoy your favorite fragrance wherever you go.

PRESS ON!
6 SMOOTH IRONING TRICKS

When it comes to chores, ironing probably ranks low on many of our lists. But you can do what you need to do for polished clothing in less time and with less struggle.

Make your own wrinkle spray. When ironing, vinegar can be your best friend for removing (or making) creases. In a spray bottle, mix 1 part white vinegar with 1 part water. Spray it on your garment and then run your iron over the spot to remove even ironed-in creases! A few spritzes of this vinegar-and-water solution can also help remove those shiny areas on fabric that are caused by hot irons.

Stop that stick. We've all been there: You're ironing a delicate item and the iron gets stuck, rippling or even snagging the fabric. Avoid a sticky iron with this simple tip. Sprinkle a little baby powder onto the ironing board or a cloth, and iron it on medium heat until it disappears. You'll create a smooth surface on the iron that will protect your garment!

Speed up the smoothing. Covering your ironing board with shiny-side-up foil before you iron your clothes will get them unwrinkled twice as fast, saving you time and energy!

Get neat pleats. Ironing pants with pleats? Use bobby pins to keep the pleats intact and you won't have to worry about ruining them with the iron.

Iron too hot? If you scorch a garment when ironing, cover the scorch mark with a vinegar-dampened cloth, then iron with a warm iron (not too hot). Presto! The burn is gone. For scorches on white cotton garments, you can also use hydrogen peroxide or lemon juice instead. Just dab onto the scorch and leave out in the sun, which will bleach away the stain.

Let starch rest. If you use spray starch while ironing, you may notice that it sometimes leaves a film on your iron. To remove this film and clean any other dirt on your iron, let the iron cool and then wipe the area with a cloth dampened with white vinegar. To keep the starch off in the first place, simply let it soak in for several seconds before ironing.

Revive Water-Resistant Items

Do you have a jacket, backpack, or tent that used to be water resistant but has lost its effectiveness over time? Set your hair dryer to its highest setting and blow air evenly over it. The warmth will reactivate the coating on the cloth that makes it repel water.

Drawstring Problem, Solved

Having the drawstring completely come out of a hoodie or yoga pants doesn't have to be a clothing calamity anymore! Just grab a straw, thread the string through it, then staple one end so they'll stay together. Use the straw as a giant needle to guide the drawstring back where it belongs.

Create a Garment Bag

Taking a lot of hangered items on vacation or to a new home? Keep them protected and gathered with a large kitchen trash bag. Simply slip the hanging items into the bag from the bottom up, then crisscross the bag's loop handles around the hangers to hold them together.

Swap Mothballs for Lavender Oil

When you store your off-season wardrobe, skip the toxic mothballs and choose lavender oil instead. Add several drops of lavender oil to cotton balls and tie them up in a sachet (you can use cheesecloth or even an old nylon). You'll repel any pests who might want to munch on your items, and when you take your clothes out again, they'll have a lovely lavender smell.

Smart Sweater Storage

When putting away your sweaters for the spring and summer months, wrap them in newspaper and tape the sides. The newspaper will keep away both moths and moisture.

THE ZIPPER FIX

Got a zipper that won't stay closed? Spray it lightly and carefully with hair spray after zipping up.

WHO KNEW?

READERS' FAVORITE

Eradicate Static in a Snap

Here's a quick fix for clothes plagued by annoying static cling: Squirt a couple drops of lotion onto your hands and then smooth it over the garments. You can also solve this annoyance by rubbing the positive end of a battery over your clothing. (If this happens to you a lot, keep a AAA battery in your purse!)

TIPS FOR SHOES AND ACCESSORIES

Tight Shoes? Give Them a Stretch

Rubbing alcohol can help you increase your shoes' size. Apply a thin coating on the insides of your shoes, then walk around in the shoes until the alcohol dries. You can repeat the process to further the stretch and work magic.

Stop the Pinch

Here's another way to stretch out pinchy shoes. Fill two quart-size plastic bags about one-fourth of the way with water, place one in each shoe, then put them in the freezer until it turns to ice. Let the ice thaw for around 20 minutes before trying to remove the bags so you don't accidentally damage your kicks.

Clean with a Tablet

To loosen dirt and get rid of odor, place non-leather sneakers in a basin with warm water and a couple of denture tablets. Use an old toothbrush to scrub stubborn stains. Rinse shoes and let them air-dry.

White Sneakers That Stay White

After purchasing new white canvas sneakers, treat them with spray starch to help them resist stains. The starch will repel grease and dirt, keeping them whiter!

Love Your Leather

Tackle dirt, residue, even salt on your leather shoes with two simple steps. First, in a spray bottle, mix equal parts vinegar and water. Spray on a clean cloth and wipe your shoes. To guard against drying from the vinegar, finish by applying leather polish or (even easier!) a small amount of hair conditioner. Buff with a clean cloth, and your shoes are back in business.

Shine Patent Leather

Patent leather shoes need a spruce-up? Believe it or not, the best cleaning solution is a glass cleaner like Windex. Spray onto a soft cloth and then use to buff patent leather shoes back to their old shine.

Lift Scuffs with Lemon

If you have black scuff marks on shoes, luggage, or other items, try wiping lemon juice on them. Rubbing alcohol also works well.

Chase Away Odor

Stinky shoes? Make your own odor solution! Mix ½ cup baking soda with 10 drops essential oil (choose your favorite scent). Cut the feet off a pair of hose or tights, then place half of the mixture in each foot and tie in a knot. Each little odor-fighting bundle will fit perfectly inside a shoe!

Sock It to Smelly Shoes

Here's another great tip for preventing smelly shoes. Take a couple of old socks without holes and fill them with scented cat litter. Then place them in the shoes when you're not wearing them. They'll suck up any moisture—and odor.

Save Your Soles

You just dug out last spring's heels from the back of your closet, but they look like they've been flattened by a truck! Reshape your shoes by stuffing bubble wrap, plastic grocery bags, or a combination of the two into them until they're back to their normal form. Leave inside your shoes for half an hour and they'll be permanently back to their old selves again!

Reboot Your Boots

Keep your boots looking their best by storing them with empty wine or soda bottles inside. They'll stay upright and maintain their shape.

SHOELACE TRICKS
Having trouble keeping your (or your kids') shoelaces tied? Shoelaces are more likely to stay tied if you dampen them with water first. You can also rub some lip balm onto the laces and they'll stay put.

A Spray Away from Love

Not happy with the color of a handbag or pair of fancy shoes? Instead of buying new accessories, turn that unbecoming chartreuse into an elegant black with a can of shoe color spray. You can pick up an inexpensive can of shoe color from a repair shop, then revamp those heels yourself instead of paying someone else to do it for you.

Prevent Pantyhose Runs

Weird but true: Freezing panty hose can keep them from running. Before wearing a pair of nylons for the first time, stick them in the freezer overnight. The cold strengthens the fibers, which will keep them from running.

Stop a Run in Its Tracks

If you notice a run in your pantyhose, don't despair. Just place a bit of clear nail polish at either end of the run and it will keep your hose from running any further.

DIY Jewelry Cleaner

Baking soda is safe and effective when it comes to cleaning gold and silver jewelry. For best results, use a paste of baking soda and hydrogen peroxide, and rub gently on your jewelry. It gets rid of dirt, grime, and body oils, and leaves your gold and silver sparkling.

Polish with a Banana Peel

The next time you eat a banana, don't throw away the peel! Get out your tarnished silver and put it to work—the inside of a banana peel can be used to polish silver jewelry! Just rub the peel against the piece and then buff with a dry cloth. The tarnish will come right off.

Get Sparkling Pearls

Because they're so fragile, pearls can't be cleaned with normal jewelry cleaners. Instead, use vegetable oil. Dab some vegetable oil on a soft cloth, then gently rub on each pearl. Let the oil dry overnight, then buff with a soft cloth to remove dust and oils that can make pearls look dull over time.

BRUCE SAYS

Just Don't Slip

Here's an unlikely tool for polishing your shoes: a banana. Just rub the banana peel over your shoes, moist side down. Then buff with a soft cloth.

Slide in Earrings

The secret to earrings that navigate holes with comfort and ease? Rub a small amount of petroleum jelly onto the earring stems.

Quick Bracelet Fastening

Having trouble getting that bracelet on? Make fastening easy by attaching the bracelet to your arm with a bit of tape. Then clasp, pull the tape off, and go!

Nifty Knot Remover

We've untangled the knottiest of knots with this surprising helper—cornstarch. Work small amounts of cornstarch into knotted chain jewelry, shoelaces, and string. Seriously, who knew?

Remove Water from Your Watch

If you've ever seen condensation under your watch face, you know how frustrating it can be! Luckily, there's a solution. Simply strap the watch to a light bulb and turn it on for a few minutes. The heat from the bulb is the perfect amount to make the water disappear.

Fix Broken Jewelry

If a stone has popped out of a piece of your jewelry and you were lucky enough to save it, you can easily put it back in place with a tiny dab of clear nail polish.

Save That Piece

Stray beads and pieces of broken jewelry can be salvaged even if you're not into making jewelry. All you need is a hot-glue gun to add a personal touch to a plain journal or daily planner.

DIY Collar Stays

If you're constantly losing collar stays (or if you're just looking for sturdier ones), try this clever tip. Cut old gift cards into the shape of collar stays, then file down any rough edges. Your new stays will be stronger than the ones that originally came with your shirt, and if you misplace them while doing the wash, you can always make more!

Quick Purse Cleanup

Even after you've cleaned out your purse, it still has crumbs, grime, and little pieces of who-knows-what at the bottom. Quickly clean it out with a lint roller. Just roll the inside and you're done!

Toothpaste Trick for Glasses

Most optometrists will try to sell you an expensive cleaner when you buy your glasses. Instead of buying theirs, simply use a tiny dab of white toothpaste (not a gel) on both sides of the lenses to polish them and keep them from fogging up.

Too Much Hair Spray?

If you've gotten hair spray on your eyeglasses, just wipe them down with rubbing alcohol and you'll be seeing clearly again.

WHO KNEW?

READERS' FAVORITE

Neat Way to Dry Gloves

You've just come in from outside, and your snowy gloves have quickly turned into sopping wet ones. To dry them out in time for your next excursion into the winter air, pull them over the bottom of a jar, then place the jar upside down on top of a radiator or heating vent. The warm air will fill the jar and dry out your gloves in no time!

9 SMART TRAVEL SOLUTIONS

Keeping your clothing, jewelry, and other essentials in good shape in the comfort of your home is one story. Taking your items on the road is another. But these hacks will help!

DIY necklace holders. Make sure your delicate necklaces don't get tangled while traveling—keep them safe with plastic straws. Cut a straw in half, thread your necklace through, and fasten the clasp. The straw will keep the chain straight and untangled.

Repurpose a cork. Don't throw away the cork when you finish a bottle of wine! Cork is a perfect material for storing and toting stud earrings. Cut the cork into thin slices, then poke the earrings through, put the backs back on, and toss them into your toiletry bag for safekeeping when traveling.

Bundle undies. Packing bras presents a challenge. The best technique to save space and protect their shape: Stack them inside each other, fold them in half, and tuck underwear in the space between the cups.

Cap shoe dirt. When you get plastic shower caps at hotels, save them for your suitcase. They make the perfect covers for dirty shoes!

Prevent packing creases. Save those empty paper towel rolls and use them while you're packing your suitcase for vacation! Roll your clothes around the paper towel rolls, and you'll help prevent creases. You'll also have a handy spot inside the roll for storing small items like socks and underwear.

Make kid travel easier. If you're traveling with young kids, make it easier to get ready each morning while you're away. When packing their clothes, pack full outfits, and place each one in a big zip-top bag.

Stop suitcase spills. When you're packing for a trip, keep some plastic wrap nearby. Before you pack shampoo, sunscreen, or other toiletries, take off the caps, place a layer of plastic wrap over the mouth of the container, and twist the cap back on. The plastic wrap will give you double the protection against suitcase spills.

Guard your razor. No cap for your razor? Cover the blades with a large binder clip to protect your fingers when digging around in your cosmetics bag.

Stash your camera. When packing a camera, place it in a plastic container for bar soap—usually the perfect size for your digital point-and-shoot.

Impromptu Glasses Cleaner

The next time you're digging through your pockets looking for a cloth you can clean your glasses with, try a dollar bill. Press hard and it will do the job of a glasses cloth in a pinch.

Screws That Stay

If the tiny screws of your glasses keep coming loose, add a dab of clear nail polish to the threads of the screws before screwing them back in. The polish will keep them from coming out again.

Patch Up Eyeglasses

Screw fall out of your eyeglasses? A stud earring is the perfect just-for-now replacement that will keep you from having to tape your glasses together for the trip to the optometrist. Just poke it through the hole and fasten its back.

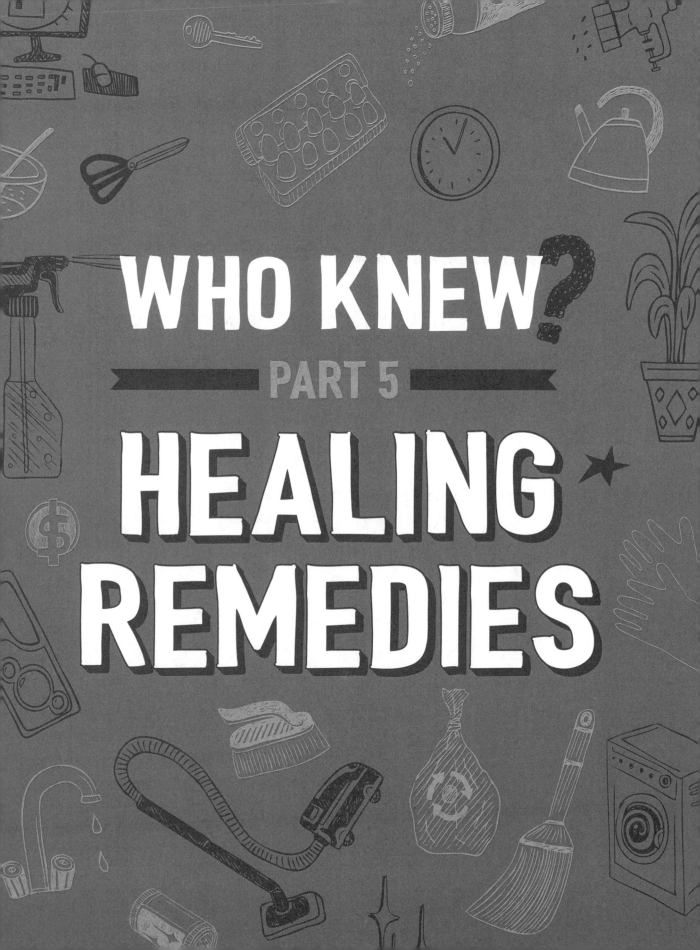

WHO KNEW?

PART 5

HEALING REMEDIES

COLD & ALLERGY FIGHTERS

Whether you're dealing with a sore throat, earache, congestion, cough, or all of it, get home remedies guaranteed to make you feel better fast!

SOOTHE YOUR THROAT

Ease an Itch Through Your Ear

If you've got an itch in your throat, scratch your ear. When the nerves in the ear get stimulated, they create a reflex in the throat that causes a muscle spasm, which cures the itch.

Salt Solution

Saltwater is a tried-and-true way to soothe throat irritation. But it does more than relieve pain—it may actually work to draw infections or irritants to the surface of your throat, where your body is better able to deal with them. Dissolve ½ to 1 teaspoon salt in 8 ounces warm water for an inflammation-taming gargle that you can use every hour or two. (Hint: Save those salt packets from restaurant takeout orders—each one is 1 teaspoon, making it easy to bring relief on the go.) For even more infection-fighting power, add a few dashes of turmeric.

Give Honey a Shot

Fill a shot glass with honey, then warm it in the microwave for about 10 seconds on high. Stir in ¼ teaspoon ground cinnamon, then drink. Repeat this delicious method for a few days and it will help your poor, aching throat.

Pain–Relieving Gargle

Aspirin does more than just relieve headaches! If you have a sore throat, dissolve two non-coated tablets in a glass of water and gargle. Just be sure to note that this only works with aspirin—don't try it with other pain relievers like ibuprofen.

Put Pain on Ice

Ice can numb pain all over your body, so don't just save it for sprains and strains. Fill your cup with an icy-cold drink and you'll enjoy relief from the swelling and irritation after you get past the first few uncomfortable sips. Staying hydrated can also help any infection move on out of your body more quickly.

Love Lemon

Relieve your sore throat with a time-tested home remedy. Slice off two-thirds of a lemon and place it on a shish kebab skewer or barbecue fork. Set your gas stove to high and roast the lemon over the open flame until the peel acquires a golden brown color. (This works on electric stoves, too, although not quite as well.) Let the lemon cool off for a moment, then squeeze the juice into a small cup. Add 1 teaspoon honey, mix well, and swallow. The heat really brings out the antibacterial power in the lemon and soothes your throat. No time to heat your lemon? Gargle with 1 part lemon juice and 1 part warm water.

Tea for Relief

Any warm beverage will feel great going down, but this tea contains honey and herbs that fight infection and reduce inflammation. Combine 1 clove, ¼ teaspoon powdered ginger, and ⅛ teaspoon ground cinnamon. Place the spice mixture in a tea infuser in 2 cups boiling water. Stir in 4 teaspoons honey, and sip your way to soothing relief!

Sage–Echinacea Throat Spray

Another infection-fighting herbal combo works great as a spray! Pour ¾ cup boiling water over 2 tablespoons each sage leaves and marshmallow or licorice root. Steep for 30 minutes, then strain. Add ¼ cup echinacea tincture and 1 tablespoon honey. Pour into a clean spray bottle, and shake before spraying twice for each use a few times a day. Keep in the fridge between uses for up to a week.

JEANNE SAYS

Baby Your Watery Eyes

If your eyes are itchy, try this quick fix to cut down on your misery: Rub a small amount of baby shampoo on your eyelids. It should reduce your symptoms dramatically.

Claim the Right to Remain Silent

Resting your throat and voice can go a long way toward making you feel better when they're sore and strained. But when you do need to answer the ever-ringing phone or referee the kids' latest battle, don't whisper—it can actually strain your throat more than simply speaking at a slightly lower volume.

Do Some Jell-O Shots!

Here's a tasty way to soothe a sore throat that you and the kids will love! Prepare Jell-O according to the package directions, but instead of sticking it in the refrigerator to set, put some in a mug and heat it in the microwave with a squirt of honey. When you drink the warm mixture, the gelatin will coat and soothe your throat, and the honey will help kill germs. Watch out with this one, though, or the kids will start playing sick just to get some liquid Jell-O!

Ancient Cold Relief

Ayurveda is a practice of natural medicine that's been used in India since around 1500 BC. Try this cold remedy that's been passed down through the ages: At the very first sign of a cold (often a scratchy throat), mix 1 teaspoon water with 1 teaspoon raw honey and ½ teaspoon turmeric. Consume every hour until symptoms disappear.

CLEAR YOUR NOSE

Press for Relief in 20 Seconds

Let's get right to the (pressure) point! You can clear your stuffy nose and pressure-filled head by pushing your tongue against the roof of your mouth while pressing a finger between your eyebrows. Hold for 20 seconds, and you'll start to feel draining—and freedom to breathe again! The science: Pressing these two points causes the vomer bone (running through the nasal passages to the mouth) to rock, which loosens your congestion and moves fluid.

DIY Saline Drops

You can buy saline nasal spray or drops to soothe dry nasal passages and sinuses, and clear out mucus, bacteria, and allergens. But it's simple to make your own nasal rinse that's just as effective. In ½ cup warm water, mix ¼ teaspoon sea salt and ⅛ teaspoon baking soda. Pair with a neti pot or small squirt bottle (available from a health food store or drugstore) to get it where it needs to go.

NOSE SORE FROM BLOWING?
Relieve the rawness and lubricate for that next blow with a dab of petroleum jelly. To minimize germ spreading, apply with a cotton ball or swab.

Scent Your Shower

Steam alone can help clear your head, but pairing it with the right essential oil makes it all the more powerful. Try putting a few drops of eucalyptus oil (a natural decongestant) on the floor of a hot, running shower just behind the stream of water—so it doesn't go down the drain or create a slippery situation. Then simply inhale the steam.

Breathe In Deep

You can also add a drop of eucalyptus oil to a glass bowl of steaming water. Drape a towel over your head to create a tent, close your eyes, and lean your head over the bowl to take deep breaths for about 10 minutes. Repeat several times throughout the day, as needed.

Cold Cure from the Fridge

Stuffy nose? Don't spend money on a decongestant—head to your fridge instead. Cut the "root" end of two scallions and carefully insert the white ends into your nose (being cautious not to shove them too high!). You may look silly, but your nose will start to clear in a couple of minutes.

On-the-Go Solution for Sniffles

You can clear up a stuffy nose without making a trip to the medicine aisle. Just pop a couple strong mints (like Altoids) in your mouth instead—the potent peppermint will help clear your sinuses and also soothe any irritation in your throat.

Kick Congestion Through Your Feet

If you have a cold that's been hanging around forever, try this remedy to rid yourself of congestion once and for all. Get a pair of cotton socks damp, but not dripping, with cold water. You can even put them in the freezer for a couple minutes to make them extra cold. Put them on, and then put a pair of dry wool socks on over them. Go to bed immediately. As you sleep, the heat from your upper body will be drawn down to your feet, allowing the inflammation to reduce. You'll also be stunned to find that your feet are warm and dry by morning!

BRUCE SAYS

Make a Tissue Trash Can
Have a sick kid on your hands? Keep your couch from getting covered in used tissues with this simple trick: Take an empty box of tissues and use a rubber band to attach it to a new box of tissues. That way, you'll have a mini "garbage can" and tissue box all in one!

5 EASY, EFFECTIVE WAYS TO AVOID ALLERGENS

The best way to attack allergy symptoms is to avoid the allergens that bring them on in the first place. Try these simple but powerful tactics.

Stop pollen at the door. If you have a pollen allergy, try to keep sneeze-inducing allergens out of your home. Take a shower immediately after doing any yard work to get rid of pollens you may have carried in on your hair and skin, and throw your clothes in the laundry basket. Animals can carry in pollen, too. After taking your dog for a walk or letting your cat out, wipe him or her down with a wet rag or baby wipe. Showering at night can also reduce pollen on your hair and skin and help you sleep better.

Choose the right plants. If you're prone to nasal allergies, be sure your houseplants aren't contributing to the problem. Many potted plants give off mold spores, thanks to damp soil, but you can reduce this risk by choosing varieties that don't need a lot of water. Cacti, jade plants, and dragon tree fit the bill.

Be a mold detective. Check your home for mold—it can be under the sink, in the bathroom, in the basement, or in any other damp, dark place in your house, like behind furniture that isn't moved very often. Disinfecting walls and furniture with Lysol is enough to kill minor mold infestations; putting a dehumidifier in the basement may also help.

Get your ducts in a row. If you find yourself getting headaches or sinus trouble more often than you used to, it might be that your home's ducts simply need a good cleaning. Whenever air conditioning or heating is on, tiny particles that have accumulated inside the ducts blow out, too, including mold, mouse droppings, and plain old dust. If you have severe allergies, a professional duct cleaning may be just what the doctor ordered.

Use a top allergen-fighting tool. It's simply your washing machine! Wash all bedding weekly in water that is at least 130°F, and dry everything in a dryer on the hottest setting to kill dust mites. And don't forget to throw in those stuffed animals from the kids' rooms!

RELIEVE A COUGH

Slippery Solution

Slippery elm lozenges are a natural way to stifle that wracking cough. You can also make a tea: In 2 cups hot water, add 1 teaspoon slippery elm powder or liquid, 1 tablespoon sugar, and a dash of ground cinnamon. Then drink it up! Save this treatment for kids five and older.

Homemade Vapors

VapoRub can be a lifesaver for late-night congestion. Here's a do-it-yourself version that has all of the benefits without any of the chemicals: Mix ¼ cup melted beeswax (available online, in health stores, or from honey purveyors) with 1 cup olive oil, 15 drops eucalyptus essential oil, and 10 drops peppermint essential oil. Pour into a small container to cool. (You may need to reheat when reusing.)

Healing Honey

Yep, warm liquids are perfect to settle that cough. But be sure to add honey—it soothes cough receptors in the throat. Or you can take honey straight up. For adults, try up to 3 teaspoons every 2 to 3 hours as needed (don't give to children younger than one year).

Go for Grapefruit

Here's an oldie but a goodie: Place a whole unpeeled grapefruit, sectioned into four pieces, in a pot and cover with water. Heat until just before boiling. Stir in 1 tablespoon honey, then drink the vitamin-filled, soothing liquid like a tea.

Enjoy the Best Cough Cure Ever

Chocolate—yes, chocolate! What's the secret? It has theobromine, which medical studies have found actually suppresses coughs better than codeine (a common ingredient in cough medicine). Next time a cough comes on, suck on a piece of dark chocolate.

SPICE UP CHICKEN SOUP
Add garlic to your soup to keep away more than vampires! Garlic is rich in compounds that help weaken cough-producing viruses in the respiratory tract.

WHO KNEW?

READERS' FAVORITE

Onion Ear Muffs

Oil found in raw onion is antimicrobial, which makes onion helpful for a minor earache. Slice an onion and microwave it on high for 1 minute. Wrap it in thin cloth and then hold it against the ailing ear for 20 to 30 minutes. See a doctor if the pain gets worse or continues for longer than 24 hours.

PAIN RELIEF

Painkillers aren't your only option. Try these simple rescues for everything from headaches and tooth pains to back problems and arthritis.

HEADACHES

Hit the Spot

That pain in your head might actually start in your neck. Use your thumbs, index, and middle fingers to squeeze just below the large muscle that runs from the high point of both shoulders and joins your neck. Or even better, have a partner do it for you. Hold for 30 to 45 seconds.

Tame Tension

If you're prone to tension headaches, you may be unconsciously clenching your jaw when you're stressed. Try paying closer attention to your body, and the next time you notice yourself clenching, gently place a pencil between your teeth and hold it. It will serve as a reminder not to bite down hard. With time, you may be able to train your jaw not to clench, thus avoiding those painful headaches. Try placing colorful notes or stickers around your desk, work area, or home to mentally remind yourself to check and see if you're stress clenching. (Then stop!)

Herbal Headache Relief

If you suffer from headaches but don't want to rely on pricey painkillers, try taking the herbal route. Feverfew, a relative of the sunflower, has been shown to help reduce inflammation that causes headaches. Look for it in capsule form in your health food store. Ginger can also reduce inflammation—try adding freshly crushed ginger root (about 1 inch) to boiling water to make a potent tea.

Aromatherapy Answer

Tension headache getting you down? Head to the health food store and purchase some peppermint oil. Rubbing a small amount into your hairline and temples will bring a tingly feeling and refreshing aroma that will encourage relaxation.

Get a Lift from Lime

An old-fashioned and effective way to treat headaches is to cut a lime in half and rub it on your forehead. In a few minutes, the throbbing should subside.

Grab a Green Apple

When you feel a headache coming on, crunch on a green apple. In research, the scent of green apple helped relieve pain for people suffering from a migraine. Other studies have found that the same smell can reduce anxiety, which could be connected to migraines. An apple a day may keep migraines away! Don't love the taste of green apples? Treat yourself to a scented candle.

Uncover a Hidden Cause

Many headaches are caused by dehydration. Before you reach for the pain reliever, try drinking two or three glasses of water or an energy drink like Gatorade. You may find you're back to normal in no time.

Watch the Timing

If you tend to get headaches in the late mornings, late afternoons, and after a long nap, they might be due to low blood sugar, also known as hypoglycemia. These headaches can be helped by eating foods that release sugar slowly, such as bananas, whole grains, and oats.

Help a Hangover Headache

Party too hard last night? Just spread a little honey on your favorite crackers. The honey provides your body with the essential sodium, potassium, and fructose it needs after a raucous night out!

Are Your Eyes Causing Headaches?

Less-than-perfect eyesight can trigger headaches because the muscles around the eyes squeeze in order to focus. If your headaches come on after reading or working at a computer, make sure you give your eyes a rest every 15 minutes by focusing on a distant object for at least a minute. You may also want to get your eyes examined to see if you need glasses.

Spice Up Your Cure

Dab a cream containing capsaicin, the active ingredient in hot peppers, inside the nostril on the side of your head where pain is concentrated. Studies show it can help block the pain of cluster and migraine headaches! See page 310 for a DIY recipe.

Migraine? Give Yourself a Brain Freeze

Okay, so it sounds crazy! But tons of migraine sufferers and even medical experts highly recommend this strategy. Here's how to bring on a brain freeze to stop a migraine in its tracks: Simply drink ice-cold water or slurp a slushy drink through a straw held against your upper palate. Eating ice cream or an ice pop can work, too—aim for the roof of your mouth.

Prevent a Brain Freeze

If your headaches aren't migraines but are actually brought on by that infamous ice-cream effect, turn the science around. You can prevent brain freeze by pressing your tongue flat against the roof of your mouth, covering as much surface area as possible. Brain freeze (also known as ice-cream headache) happens because the nerves in the roof of your mouth get extremely cold, so your brain thinks your whole body is cold. It compensates by overheating, which causes your head to hurt. By warming up the roof of your mouth, you'll chill your brain and feel better.

MUSCLE AND JOINT PAIN

End Desk Discomfort

If you find sitting at your desk is causing lower back pain, try slightly elevating your feet. An old phone book is perfect for the job.

WHO KNEW?
READERS' FAVORITE

Cure Everyday Aches and Pains

If you regularly suffer from sore muscles, cramps, headaches, and other pains, a magnesium deficiency could be to blame. (Be sure to check with your doctor first.) Fortunately, it's easy to boost your body's stores of magnesium by a third, just by soaking in Epsom salts a few times a week. The mineral is easily absorbed by the skin, and is great for fighting aches and pains, particularly after strenuous exercise. Just add ¼ to ½ cup to your bathwater before getting in the bath.

Know a Kitchen Cure

If you have chronic back pain—especially associated with arthritis—or other sore muscles, try adding yellow mustard to a hot bath. Add a few tablespoons for mild pain, and up to a whole 8-ounce bottle if the pain is severe. The bathwater may look strange, but your aching back will thank you.

Alleviate Neck Tension

Been leaning over your work too long? Try this to help a hurting neck. Inhale and raise your shoulders up to your ears, pulling them as high as they will go. Then let go with an "ahhh" and drop them slowly back down. Repeat several times to release muscle tension.

Hot Potato Help

Ease a sore neck with the help of a potato turned heating pad. First, pierce it in several places with a fork, then heat it in the microwave on high for 2 to 3 minutes, or until warm. Wrap it in a dish towel and place on aches and pains. The warmth will ease sore muscles, and will last for up to half an hour!

Ease with Arnica

Old-time remedies for muscle soreness often included arnica. Now it's easy to find this herbal healer in lotions available at health food stores. Rub on for relief!

Natural Recovery Drink

Tart cherry juice serves up anthocyanins, natural anti-inflammatory compounds that can reduce muscle pain and swelling. Just make sure you choose unsweetened juice to get the most benefit. Don't like cherries? Raspberries also contain anthocyanins to bring you relief from soreness.

Aid Arthritis with Oatmeal

Believe it or not, you can help relieve arthritis pain with oatmeal. Just mix 2 cups oatmeal with 1 cup water, warm the mixture in the microwave, and apply to the affected area.

> ### BRUCE SAYS
>
> **Back Pain? Check Your Wallet**
>
> If you're a man who suffers from back pain, your wallet may be to blame. Sitting on a bulky wallet can cause your spine to become misaligned and your muscles to compensate. Try carrying your wallet in a front pocket (where it's also safer from pickpockets), or make sure it's as thin as possible.

Ease the Aches of the Flu

If the flu's got you feeling sore and achy in your muscles, try using this concoction on your sore spots: Combine 1 cup olive oil with 1 tablespoon horseradish, and let sit for a half hour. Gently rub the oil mixture on your achy muscles.

Arthritis Relief Rub

Massage can feel great and help both your pain and your mood. Researchers in Korea found that bringing in aromatherapy has amazing benefits for people suffering with arthritis. Here's the blend they used.

1 ounce almond oil

1 ounce apricot oil

2 teaspoons jojoba oil

8 drops lavender essential oil

4 drops marjoram essential oil

8 drops eucalyptus essential oil

4 drops rosemary essential oil

4 drops peppermint essential oil

Simply combine and rub on any joints affected by arthritis.

DIY Capsaicin Cream

Capsaicin is a timeless remedy for arthritis pain relief. It works by reducing levels of a compound called substance P, which transmits pain signals to the brain. You can buy over-the-counter capsaicin creams for arthritis and back pain at any drugstore. But it's simple enough to make your own. All you need to do is mix a few dashes of ground cayenne with 2 or 3 teaspoons olive oil. Apply it to unbroken skin at the painful joints several times a day. You may feel a mild burning sensation at first, but that will fade with use. Wash your hands after application to avoid getting the salve in your eyes or mouth.

COMMON ACHES AND PAINS

Castor Oil for Cramps

You may be familiar with castor oil as a home remedy for constipation, but did you know that it can also help with menstrual cramps? When applied to the skin, the acids in the oil can reduce pain. Soak a rag or paper towel in castor oil and apply it to the abdomen, cover the towel with plastic wrap, then apply a heating pad. The pain should subside within 30 minutes.

Get Tooth Relief from Your Hand

You can relieve a toothache by rubbing the back of your hand between your thumb and index finger (the V zone where the bones of the two fingers meet) with an ice cube. Rubbing the hand on the side of the body where the toothache is located may reduce pain intensity by as much as half, according to the results of a small study. What's going on? Researchers believe this little trick can block pain impulses traveling to the brain. It can't hurt—and might take away the hurt.

Stay Comfortable with Clove

If you have an achy tooth or gum, clove oil can offer some temporary relief while you're waiting to get it looked at by a professional. Just dab on with a cotton swab; after a few minutes, it'll be good and numb.

Canker Cure

Hydrogen peroxide may help reduce and relieve canker sores. Simply mix 1 part peroxide with 1 part water, then dab on any affected areas several times a day or swish around in your mouth for as long as possible.

Sweet Relief from Sores

Cold sore or canker sore got you down? Dabbing unpasteurized honey on sores four times a day will help them disappear fast, thanks to the enzymes it contains.

Roll Away Achy Feet

Stretch, relax, and find relief by rolling your bare feet over a tennis ball, lacrosse ball, or soup can. For cooling relief, try a frozen water bottle.

Treat Feet to Tea

Steep four peppermint tea bags in 2 cups boiling water. In a basin, add that tea to 1 gallon comfortably hot water. Let your feet enjoy a soothing soak.

Make It a Head Game

There may be a method behind that madness of saying, "This will only hurt a bit." Research shows a procedure may hurt less if you tell yourself it's not a big deal. In a lab experiment, a group that was told the pain would be "mild to moderate" reported feeling 28 percent less pain than the group that was told it would be "moderate to severe." Their pain report was backed up by MRI scans of pain-processing areas in the brain. This is one case where it definitely pays to set your expectations low!

FOUR-LETTER RELIEF

Need to endure a procedure that comes with discomfort? People could keep their hands submerged 35 percent longer in a tub of ice-cold water when they repeated a swear word versus any old word.

STOMACH SOOTHERS

Digestive distress have you down for the count or taking note of the nearest restroom? Find the best and most natural ways to settle an upset tummy so you can get back to enjoying life!

SETTLE THE QUEASIES

Better with Bitters

If you've got an upset stomach due to indigestion or a hangover, try drinking a glass of club soda with a dash of bitters. It should help ease your pain.

Root Out Nausea

Your grandmother was on to something when she suggested you drink ginger ale when your tummy hurt. Ginger root works directly in the gastrointestinal tract by interfering with the feedback mechanisms that send sickness messages to the brain. Look for ginger root at your health food store in the form of powder, tea, or lozenges, and take some when you're feeling nauseated to help alleviate your symptoms. Pregnant women: This is also a great trick to ease morning sickness.

Pep Up with Peppermint

Peppermint contains menthol, which is a digestive aid. Try peppermint tea to ease nausea and vomiting. It's simple to make your own pure cup (no sugar or other artificial flavors!) by steeping 1 tablespoon peppermint leaves in 1 cup hot water and then straining.

BRUCE SAYS

Get 1-2-3 Relief!

Nothing's worse than a bad bout of nausea. A trick for relief: Drink a little ginger ale, then chew a handful of crushed ice, and finally sniff a piece of black-and-white newspaper. It may seem like an old wives' tale, but it works!

Rein It in with a Rub

Gently rubbing a point on your wrist has been proven to work as well as some drugs designed to fight nausea! To find the spot, turn your hand so that your palm is facing up. Measure three finger-widths down from your wrist. The spot is between the two tendons. Apply gentle downward pressure as you massage for 5 seconds.

Can the Nausea

You may be able to settle an upset stomach with canned pear juice. Honestly, there is no scientific reason that has been uncovered as to why this trick works, but tons of people swear by it! Some doctors suspect it's similar to the old-time remedy of cola syrup.

Stop Olive the Rumbling

Feel the pits due to motion sickness? Bring some olives along next time! Motion sickness causes you to make excess saliva, which can give you a gaggy feeling. But olives contain tannins, which dry out your mouth. Munching a few when you first start to feel the queasies may settle the nausea. Sucking on a lemon can produce the same effect.

Night Moves

If you're prone to motion sickness, try to travel as much as you can at night. You'll be less likely to feel sick when you can't see the motion as well as you would during the day.

RELIEVE GAS

Rub Your Belly Right

Feeling bloated? It could just be trapped gas. Encourage it to move by gently stroking from your right hip up toward your ribs, then across the bottom of your rib cage and down toward your left hip. Repeat several times.

Send Gas Away with Caraway

End your meal with a cup of tea to head off any after-dinner grumbling. Simply sip 1 cup hot water steeped with 1 teaspoon caraway seeds. Caraway can improve digestion and relieve intestinal spasms. For gas relief on the go, carry sugar-coated fennel seeds. In fact, many Indian restaurants serve sugar-coated fennel seeds instead of after-dinner mints.

The Power of Pineapple

Bloated? Try eating some pineapple. It's a diuretic that also contains helpful enzymes that speed digestion. To help a chronic problem, eat several slices (about 1 cup) each day. Or drink a daily glass of pineapple juice, which is delicious mixed with orange juice or in smoothies. Bloating and gassiness should subside within 72 hours.

STOP THE BATHROOM RUNS

A Tea to Stop Diarrhea Fast

To soothe a sudden bout of diarrhea, try drinking chamomile tea. The herb has an antispasmodic effect that stops contractions in the lower intestine.

Rice Water to the Rescue

Rice water may also be helpful. Boil ½ cup brown rice in 3 cups water, let simmer for 45 minutes, strain, and drink the rice water on its own. Eat the rice, too: a high-fiber diet helps combat diarrhea, and the B vitamins will help your digestive system heal.

Save Those Pomegranate Peels

From trash to a digestive treasure! Tea made from pomegranate peels can appease your belly and help healing start to happen. Next time you enjoy the fruit, grind the washed and dried peels in a blender or coffee grinder. The resulting powder will keep in the fridge for up to 6 months. Then when you need relief, steep a teaspoon of the powder in a cup of boiling water for 3 minutes, strain, add a bit of honey, and sip slowly.

WHO KNEW?
READERS' FAVORITE

Mix Up Some Pedialyte

When your little ones are recovering from a tummy bug, you can help them feel better sooner with this homemade (and natural!) version of Pedialyte. Mix together 1 quart water, ½ cup orange juice, 2 tablespoons sugar, ¾ teaspoon baking soda, and ¼ teaspoon salt. Serve once their vomiting has stopped for a few hours. Make sure to contact a doctor if any problems persist.

HELP HEARTBURN

Drink to Reflux Relief

Acid reflux results when your body makes too much or too little hydrochloric acid (HCl), the acid that breaks down food in your stomach. When you experience heartburn, do a little test by drinking a tablespoon of apple cider vinegar. If it alleviates the symptoms, this means your body isn't producing enough HCl, and you'll benefit from sipping pure apple cider vinegar mixed with water as you eat. If the test makes the symptoms worse, this means your body is producing too much HCl. Try drinking up to 3 teaspoons baking soda daily, mixed with water in increments of ¼ to ½ teaspoon per glass.

Grab Some Gum

Chewing gum boosts saliva production, and that saliva neutralizes acid and helps push digestive juices back down where they belong.

Adjust Your Sleeping Position

If you sleep on your right side, roll over! The esophagus enters the stomach on the right side. Sleeping on your left side prevents food in your stomach from pressing on the opening to the esophagus, a good bet to bring on reflux.

Soothe with Juice

Sure, aloe is soothing for your skin, but can it really help your digestive tract? Some people with acid reflux swear it relieves heartburn symptoms. Backing up the claims, a study found drinking about an ounce of aloe vera syrup could safely relieve reflux symptoms. Run the idea by your doctor to see if it could work for you.

SLEEP MIRACLES

Sleep is connected to energy and so much more—immunity, mood, even weight and risk for disease. So make sure you get your best night's rest with these natural remedies!

END THE INSOMNIA

Supplements to Help You Sleep

Gamma-aminobutyric acid, or GABA, is a neurotransmitter in the brain that is a crucial component of the body's ability to relax and fall asleep. When the body isn't producing enough GABA or the GABA it is producing breaks down too quickly, it can leave one feeling tense, with thoughts racing. Supplements that promote GABA in the brain include valerian root, theanine, and magnesium. You may also want to try melatonin supplements. Talk with your doctor about the right levels for you.

A LEGIT REASON FOR MORE BED PILLOWS
Sleeping with your head elevated prevents stomach acid from flowing into your esophagus.

Nod Off with Nuts

If you have a hard time winding down at the end of the day, try eating more nuts! Rich in sleep-promoting nutrients such as magnesium and selenium, nuts are a healthy, drug-free way to help you get that much-needed shut-eye. In research, peanuts and pistachios have been the biggest standouts for bringing on deeper sleep.

Take a Deep Breath

When you're having trouble sleeping, try taking a deep breath. Take five, as a matter of fact. Start in your belly—envision blowing up a balloon there—and move to your chest, filling your lungs to their capacity. Exhale slowly. This will signal your nervous system that it's time to relax, and help you nod off naturally.

Snooze with Seafood

Serve up more dinners from the sea! Cod, tuna, snapper, halibut, and shrimp contain levels of sleep-promoting tryptophan comparable to those found in turkey.

Blue Lights Out

Melatonin is a hormone the body produces to help you sleep. Research has shown that staring at a screen that gives off blue light (such as a TV, computer, or smartphone) will decrease the amount of melatonin your body is producing. If you're having trouble sleeping at night, be sure to set aside the TV, laptop, and video game after dinnertime. Or spend as little as $8 for a pair of blue light–blocking glasses.

Make Pink Your Favorite Color

You've probably heard of white noise—like the constant hum of a fan to cover up harsher background sounds that could stir you in your sleep. So what's pink noise? It has more variation, coming out louder and more powerful at the lower frequencies. Think of rain falling on pavement or waves crashing on the beach. And it's been shown to lead your brain waves into deep sleep. Try a color test to see whether white or pink works better for you—free apps such as Simply Noise offer both.

Skip the Nightcap

Alcohol can make you feel really sleepy . . . at first. But you'll pay for it at 3 a.m. when the alcohol is metabolized and that effect wears off and wakes you up. It's smart to limit alcohol within 3 hours of bedtime.

BRUCE SAYS

Make Your Bed

I now have a science-backed reason to nag the boys to make their beds: It helps you sleep better! The simple way it works, according to the study's researchers: It creates positive vibes around bedtime.

WHO KNEW?

READERS' FAVORITE

The Scents of Sleep

Mix a few drops of lavender, chamomile, and ylang-ylang essential oils and water in a spray bottle and give your pillowcase a spritz. These scents activate the alpha wave activity in the back of your brain, which leads to relaxation. You'll be ahh-sleep before you know it!

Invite Fido In

But not on your bed! Surprisingly, a recent study out of the Mayo Clinic found that people sleep better when their dogs are in the bedroom. So take advantage of the comfort and security but not your dog's rustling. Help him settle in a sweet spot on the floor or set up a dog bed nearby.

Use a Pillow Prop

Back pain keeping you up? Sleep on your back with a pillow under your knees. Or if you can only sleep on your side, slip a pillow between your knees. It helps support your lower spine and a good's night slumber.

Keep Your Socks On

You may think you want to go sockless to keep cool. But keeping your socks on will actually accomplish that for your whole body! Warming your feet widens the blood vessels there and helps regulate temperature more evenly across your body. The result: overall cooling, which is a ticket to better sleep.

NO MORE SNORING

Give a Snoring Partner the Brick

Hold the throws! Slip a couple of bricks under the legs at the head of your bed. This little adjustment will elevate your snoring culprit's upper torso to prop open airways and stop the snoring. An extra pillow can give some elevation as well, although it's not as effective as the brick trick.

Sing in the Shower

Go ahead, belt out those tunes! Amazing but true: In a research study, regular snorers who sang for 20 minutes a day snored significantly less once they started singing. It may work by firming up flabby muscle in the upper airways. However it works, it's worth a try to snag better sleep!

Accessorize with a Tennis Ball

Take a basic T-shirt and sew a pocket on its back. Place a tennis ball inside the pocket. Or you can try duct tape to attach the ball to the shirt. Wear the shirt to bed and the hard ball will keep you off your back—the prime sleep position for snoring. Over time, you probably won't need the shirt anymore—you'll train yourself to sleep in a better position.

HIT THE JUICE AISLE

Tart cherry juice is packed with melatonin! Try drinking 8 ounces an hour before bed to set yourself up for a good night's sleep.

FEELING FATIGUED?
6 EASY WAYS TO REV YOUR ENERGY

Feeling tired all the time? Even when you are getting the sleep you need, you can still feel like you're dragging through the day. Put down that energy drink! Here are some natural ways to give yourself a boost.

Grab gum. Chewing gum increases heart rate, which increases blood flow to the brain. Peppermint and cinnamon rise to the top when you're looking for flavors to boost energy. In research, just their scents can energize! But you get a double benefit when you sniff and chew.

Press your body's energy buttons. Putting pressure on certain points on your body has been proven to increase energy. A few spots to apply very firm pressure with your thumb or index and middle fingers:

▶ The base of the skull, one finger-width to the side of the spine
▶ The rim of the ear
▶ The pad between the joint of the thumb and index finger
▶ The outside of the leg bone, 3 inches down from the kneecap

Hold each press for 3 minutes, massaging in both directions.

Get herbal help. Check health food stores for rhodiola. One study found that people who took rhodiola reported less mental fatigue and more physical energy and coordination. A typical dose is 100 milligrams twice a day, but check with your doctor first.

Swap protein for sugar. A feeling of fatigue may be due to the food you're eating. If you feel tired in the middle of the day, sugar is actually one of the worst things you can eat. It messes with your blood sugar levels and gives you a sense of "false energy" that will only cause you to crash and burn. Instead, aim to eat 90 to 120 grams of protein per day, spread evenly among meals and small snacks. Consistent protein intake will also help stave off sugar cravings!

B energized. If you're always exhausted, vitamin B_{12} might be able to help. This nutrient is found naturally in meat, fish, eggs, and dairy, but you may want to consider taking it in pill form, such as in a B complex vitamin. Taken with breakfast or lunch, B_{12} helps keep your energy level high throughout the day.

Step into the light. Exposure to sunlight is a wakeup call to your brain. Feeling sluggish? Try to sneak outside for even a few minutes to capture a little natural light.

Help from a Humidifier

Many bedrooms are warm and dry, which can cause airways to dry out and bring on a rattle. Keeping your nasal passages moisturized may be a super-simple way to stop the snoring. Set up a humidifier in your bedroom to run as you sleep. Live, leafy plants also help raise humidity levels.

DIY Snore Relief Gel

You can add sleep-smart scents to a DIY gel air freshener. Boil 1 cup water, then mix in 1 packet unflavored gelatin, 1 tablespoon salt, 10 drops eucalyptus essential oil (to relieve nasal congestion), 10 drops lavender essential oil (to induce relaxation and sleep), and several drops food coloring (to look nice on your nightstand). Once the gelatin dissolves, pour it into a glass cup or jar to set. Cover with a lid once set and not in use. Uncover each night to release the scent (for a month or more!) and allow it to lull you into sleep. Keep away from kids and pets.

SOLUTIONS FOR RESTLESS SLEEPERS

Try a Tonic

Get a creepy-crawly feeling in your legs at night that keeps you or your bed partner awake? Drink a 6-ounce glass of tonic water before bed until symptoms go away. Tonic water contains quinine, which stops repeated muscle contractions.

Take Two

Experts can't say why it works, but taking two aspirins before bedtime can reduce symptoms of restless legs syndrome (RLS) in some people.

What You Knead

There's good evidence that massage eases the tingling, restlessness, and sleep interruption that come with RLS. Don't want to go to a pro? That's fine—just try a gentle rub yourself. Or treat your legs to a foam roller, a cool fitness tool that lets you place gentle pressure wherever you need it just by rolling over it.

The Stocking Solution

Wearing compression stockings (you can find them at any drugstore) for just an hour before bed can soothe those restless legs. In one study, a third of the people who tried it got complete (drug-free!) relief from their RLS symptoms, and the rest reported big-time improvement.

JEANNE SAYS

Keep Restless Sleepers in Place

Whether you have a child who falls out of bed or a spouse who likes to kick, you can limit their nighttime moves with a clever trick. Place a pool noodle under your fitted sheet just where you need it. It will stay tightly tucked as a barrier to limit the places they go.

STRESS BUSTERS

You can calm your mind and body quickly and naturally with surprisingly easy little strategies—from common scents to ice cream and chocolate cures!

APPEAL TO YOUR SENSES

An Orange a Day

Oranges offer vitamin C, which can lower levels of the stress hormone cortisol. But before you eat that orange, make sure you take a good whiff as well. The citrus scent has been shown to reduce anxiety, improve mood, and promote calmness. It's easy to take an orange on the go into potentially stressful situations. At home, you can add a few drops of citrus-scented oil to a room diffuser.

Homemade Heating Pad

Don't spend your money on an aromatherapy pillow! Instead, add uncooked long-grain rice to a sock and tie it shut. Whenever you need a little heat after a long day, stick it in the microwave on high for 1 to 2 minutes, and you'll have soothing warmth. To add a little scent to the pillow, mix a few drops of your favorite essential oil into the rice.

Affordable Massage Therapy

Feeling stressed out? Getting therapeutic massage can aid in stress reduction. Check to see if massage is covered under your health insurance plan—it may fall under chiropractic care or physical therapy. Another source for inexpensive massages are massage therapy schools, where students offer discounted sessions as part of their education.

Match Point Massage

If you can't afford a back massage (and haven't had any luck recruiting the unemployed minor that lives in your house), take matters into your own hands by using two tennis balls in a tube sock. Drop the balls in, tie it shut, take a hold of each end, and roll away. You can also use your body weight to get more pressure by lying on top of the balls.

Ease Stress with Essential Oils

The right essential oils can help relieve tension and stress. Try lavender, chamomile, geranium, spearmint, or peppermint. Add these delicious-smelling oils to your bathwater for a relaxing soak, or inhale them by placing a few drops on a cotton pad.

RUB YOUR EARS

They're covered in trigger points that can help release tension! Rub them gently to ease stress throughout your body. Start with the crease between the back of your ears and your skull.

Put On His Sweater

Ladies, if you have a special man in your life, reach for his laundry on the floor when you're feeling stressed. Women had lower stress levels—even after being put through research activities designed to make them more anxious—when they had smelled a shirt their male partners had worn for 24 hours without deodorant. The jury's still out on whether this trick works for men, whose sense of smell isn't as strong.

Enjoy the View

Just like we tend to hold tension in our necks, we can also lock tension around our eyes. Go to a place where you can gaze off to a distant, pleasant view. It doesn't need to be a tropical island; even green trees or children playing can work. It will help you relax your eyes, focus away from a tense moment or situation, and take in a fresh perspective.

Calm with Contrast Showers

You'll love the feeling of this simple routine that will help boost your immune and circulatory systems and relieve stress. Toward the end of your shower, turn it up as hot as you can stand it and allow it to warm your body for 3 minutes. Then turn it down so the water is cool, and let it run over your body for 30 to 60 seconds. Repeat as many times as you like, ending on cold. When you get out of the shower, rub yourself vigorously with a towel to encourage circulation. Do not continue the contrasting temperatures, however, if you feel dizzy, nauseated, or excessively chilled.

Sip Some Tea

Slowing down to drink any kind of tea can help you deal with stress. But the amino acid L-theanine in green tea has special calming effects. Take several green tea breaks instead of coffee breaks throughout your day. Worried about the caffeine jitters? Green tea is lower in caffeine than coffee and black tea. Or just go decaf—you'll still get the L-theanine!

SLOW DOWN

Go to Your Camera Roll

Whether it's a beach vacation or a favorite baby or fur baby, choose a soothing photo to focus on. Just like that, you can change your brain wave activity.

Go Belly Down

Suddenly feel out of control? You can put your hand on your belly and try to slow and deepen your breathing. If that seems impossible in the moment, try another trick: Lie down on your stomach, which will naturally slow your breathing.

Back-and-Forth Breathing

It may sound wacky, but it's a proven way to slow your heart rate and lower blood pressure. Block your right nostril and breathe only through your left, or alternate breathing through each nostril.

Fake a Smile

Even if you're just going through the motions, forming your face into a smile can lower your heart rate. Experts aren't sure why it works, but it does.

Hot Way to Chill Out

When we get anxious, our bodies automatically pull blood flow to our large muscles, preparing for what's called the fight-or-flight response. But when the stressful situation doesn't actually require a fight or flight (as is usually the case in our modern world), all that redirected flow does is amp up your stress levels. Here's an amazing trick: You can help bring your mind and body back into balance by warming your hands or even just imagining they're warm. It's a simple little tip you can use anywhere!

CALM HEAD TO TOE

Tense each muscle group for 5 seconds and then relax as you move down. Start with your eyes and work down through your neck, shoulders, back, belly, butt, thighs, calves, and feet.

5 BATH TREATS TO SOAK AWAY STRESS

We all know how good time in the tub can feel. And science backs it up: One study even found that soaking in warm water daily for 8 weeks is more effective at easing anxiety than a prescription drug. Here are a few special treats to try.

Milk and cookies bath. This calming and exfoliating oatmeal bath smells like warm cookies—without the extra calories! In a food processor, pulse together ½ cup oats with 3 tablespoons powdered milk, 3 tablespoons baking soda, and ¼ teaspoon ground cinnamon. Pour the powder into running bathwater and enjoy.

Citrus a–peel. Give yourself a luxurious bath treat without spending a cent. Just save the peels of citrus fruit like lemons, limes, and oranges in a container in your fridge. When it's time for a bath, throw them in the warm water. They'll not only release a lovely scent but also help slough off dead skin cells.

Honey-lavender bath. Good for soothing dry skin and relieving stress, this honey-lavender bath is quick and easy to make. Process 2 tablespoons dried lavender in a food processor until it becomes a powder, and transfer it to a small bowl. Whisk in 1 cup milk, ¼ cup honey, and 3 drops lavender essential oil until well combined. Pour the mixture into a hot bath and enjoy the relaxing benefits!

Soothing salt. Don't spend a bundle on bath salts. Instead, make your own by combining 2 cups Epsom salts and 2 drops essential oil. Epsom salts are made from the mineral magnesium sulfate, which draws toxins from the body, sedates the nervous system, and relaxes tired muscles.

Homemade bath pillow. To make your own bath pillow, reuse a household item no one seems to be able to get rid of: packing peanuts! Pour them into a large resealable freezer bag, then let out some of the air and seal. Use in the bath as a soft resting place for your head.

Sit on a Sponge
Before you head to the kitchen to look for a sponge, we should tell you that all this tip requires is your imagination! Simply imagine you're sitting on a giant sponge and breathe in. As you breathe out, imagine all your stress leaving you and getting absorbed into the sponge.

Relieve Stress with Yoga

Numerous studies have shown that yoga, a gentle exercise that is easily tailored to any skill level, is a fantastic tool for relieving stress. Look for yoga DVDs at your local library and engage in an invigorating yoga routine first thing in the morning or a relaxing yoga routine after dinnertime.

FEEL BETTER WITH FUN

Pet Therapy

Playing with or stroking your pet is known to reduce blood pressure, improve your mood, and reduce stress. It's been proven to work with all kinds of pets: dogs, cats, hamsters—every type but dust bunnies.

Break Out the Crayons

Colored pencils will do, too! You're never too old to color. In fact, adults who color patterns see a big drop in anxiety compared to adults who don't color or who draw on blank sheets of paper. Treat your racing mind to a coloring book today.

Dig in the Dirt

Did you know 30 minutes of gardening can reduce stress levels more than 30 minutes of reading can? The benefit could come from the physical activity, fresh air, certain good bacteria in the soil, or a combo of all.

Create an Ice Cream Menu

When you feel stress and anxiety rising, start mentally composing a list of your favorite ice cream flavors. Part of the power lies in the distraction—you're taking your mind off your worries. But ice cream works better than, say, state capitals because of associated happy memories. We all dream of ice cream . . . for stress relief!

WHO KNEW? READERS' FAVORITE

Reach for Sweet Stress Relief
Craving chocolate? Your body knows what it needs! A bit of dark chocolate (an ounce or two) can help reduce stress levels. Some research has even found that it can lower blood pressure nearly as well as drugs.

Let It Go

Don't worry if you look silly! Let your tongue go limp in your mouth, then open your mouth slightly. The result: You instantly relax your jaw, which sends a message to your brain that all is well and it can halt the stress hormones.

Do a Dance

In addition to providing great exercise, dancing lowers stress and improves your mood. In fact, one study found that people who tangoed for 20 minutes felt happier and had lower levels of stress hormones than people who sat on the sidelines watching. But any kind of dance will do—even a little rocking out in your living room!

FIRST-AID SOLUTIONS

Bandages, ointments, tweezers, and ice packs are smart, but sometimes they're not right at hand. Check out these other helpful healers that might work even better for your needs in certain situations.

HEALING CUTS, SCRAPES, AND BRUISES

Sanitize a Cut

You just got a nasty cut on your hand, but don't have anything to clean it out with before you put the bandage on. Luckily, there's something in your medicine cabinet that you may not have thought of—mouthwash. The alcohol-based formula for mouthwash was originally used as an antiseptic during surgeries, so it will definitely work for your cut, too.

Paper Cut Relief

Instantly ease the sting of a paper cut with a bit of white glue. Just dab a small amount onto the area. Once it dries, it creates a liquid-bandage barrier that will seal out germs and make it hurt less.

Easier Splinter Removal

Got a splinter you can't get out? Try soaking the area in vegetable oil for several minutes. It should soften your skin enough to allow you to ease the splinter out.

A Sweet Treatment

Honey has a long history of healing, dating back to at least Roman times. Modern-day medical experts agree that it's effective as an antibacterial ointment that also provides a moist, protective barrier—perfect conditions for skin healing. Just dab a little on!

Stick It to Splinters

The easiest way to remove a splinter? Just put a drop of white glue over the offending piece of wood in your finger, let it dry, and then peel off the dried glue. The splinter will stick to the glue and come right out.

Keep Finger Bandages Dry

You put a Band-Aid on your finger to cover up a scratch, but you still have to go through your day full of hand-washing, child-bathing, and dishes-doing. To keep the bandage dry while you work, cover it with an uninflated balloon—any color will do!

Make Ripping off Band-Aids Painless

Before removing a bandage from your child's skin, douse the area with baby oil. The baby oil will soak into the bandage and make it easy to remove without hurting her.

Ease Bruises with a Banana

Bananas to the rescue! A simple way to help bruises fade fast is with a banana peel. Just apply a piece of banana peel, flesh side down, to the bruise, cover with a bandage, and leave on overnight. By the morning, the bruise will have faded.

SPICY SOLUTION

Keep cayenne nearby! Just a little cayenne powder alone or mixed with hot water can help stop bleeding fast.

Instant Hand Sanitizer

To avoid spending money on expensive hand sanitizers, make your own at home with these ingredients: 2 cups aloe vera gel, 2 teaspoons rubbing alcohol, 4 teaspoons vegetable glycerin (available online and at health food stores), and 10 drops eucalyptus oil. Mix the ingredients well and use like you would the commercially made version.

Another Bruise Cure from the Kitchen

White vinegar will also help heal bruises. Soak a cotton ball in vinegar, then apply it to the bruise for an hour. It will reduce the blueness of the bruise and speed the healing process.

Apply Green Ice

Parsley is a superhero when it comes to reducing inflammation. Combine it with ice to help reduce the swelling of a bruise or a black eye. The recipe for the remedy: In a blender, puree 1 cup fresh parsley with 2 tablespoons water. Freeze the mixture in an ice-cube tray. When ready, wrap the cubes in a washcloth before holding them to a bruise for 15 to 20 minutes.

BEST BETS FOR BITES AND STINGS

Curry-ous Cure

To reduce the pain from insect bites, make a paste of curry powder and water. Apply it to the bite and let dry, then wash off. The spices in the curry powder will relieve discomfort and swelling.

Turn the Tide on Mosquito Bites

Rub liquid laundry detergent on the bite and let dry. The liquid soothes the skin, dries the bite to reduce irritation, and seals the area from outside irritants. Take some single-use packets on the go!

SOOTHE WITH OIL

Been stung by an insect? It's lavender oil to the rescue! Rub a bit directly onto the sting to alleviate the pain. You can use the healing oil on scrapes, burns, and bug bites as well.

First Steps When Bees Strike

When you're stung by a bee, carefully grasp the stinger and pull it out as fast as you can. The less venom that enters your body, the smaller and less painful the resulting welt will be. Ice the area immediately to reduce the swelling.

Kitchen Relief for Bee Stings

Nobody likes a bee sting, but sometimes they're inevitable. Bring down the pain and swelling by rubbing some raw onion on the sting. The sulfur in the onion will detoxify the area and give you relief.

Rub It to a Bee Sting

Ouch! Suffering from a bee or wasp sting? Soothe the pain with Vicks VapoRub. It contains menthol, which will provide a natural cooling, anesthetic effect.

Ease Wasp Stings

Stung by a wasp? Apply apple cider vinegar to the area with a cotton ball and the sting will subside.

SOOTHE BURNS

DIY Healing Gel

Give regular aloe vera gel a little boost with soothing peppermint. In a small bowl, combine ¼ cup aloe vera gel and 2 tablespoons filtered water. Microwave on low, stirring regularly, until they are well combined. Stir in 3 drops peppermint oil and allow to cool. Place the mixture in a cosmetics jar. Use this lotion on sunburned or dry skin. Massage into skin for a few minutes, and rinse if desired. The aloe will have a cooling effect, and the peppermint will provide a little relaxing tingle.

Cream on Relief

You had a great day at the beach, but now you're suffering from a terrible sunburn. Help ease the pain by rubbing shaving cream over any sunburned areas. The soothing ingredients will make your skin feel better, and the foam won't trap heat near your skin like heavier lotions will.

CALM WITH A SPRAY

In a spray bottle, mix equal parts cool water and apple cider vinegar. Mist over sunburned skin for natural soothing.

Care for Your Face

This face mask is perfect for sunburned or irritated skin. Combine ¼ cup full-fat yogurt with 2 tablespoons oatmeal. Mix vigorously for 1 minute, then apply to your face. Leave on for at least 10 minutes, then wash off with warm water.

Toothpaste for Burns

Soothe burns with an unlikely hero from your medicine cabinet: your toothpaste! If you've sustained a minor burn, cover it with white, non-gel toothpaste to ease the pain and help it heal. Simply dab a small amount onto affected areas and leave overnight.

Grab Some Ginger

If you sustain a minor burn in the kitchen, reach for some ginger. Cut off the end and press the exposed area against your burn. Many say ginger works even better than a piece of aloe plant for soothing burns. Other foods that can help soothe: the inside of a banana peel, honey, or a piece of raw potato.

BEAT BLISTERS AND BOILS

Blister Protection in a Ball

If you've ever used a Band-Aid to cover a blister, you know that it isn't quite enough protection when it gets touched or bumped. A better way to keep a blister safe is with a cotton ball. Just tape it on with a bit of medical tape.

Surprising Blister Banisher

Painful blister? Antiseptic mouthwash can dry out blisters (not to mention kill germs), helping to speed the healing process. Just dab some on three times a day and cover the area with petroleum jelly. You'll be back to your summer sandals in no time.

The Battle of the Boils

Boils, or skin abscesses, are pimple-like skin infections that can swell into large, pus-filled, sore-to-the-touch growths. To treat a boil before it gets too big and painful to handle without a doctor, try this easy home remedy that uses tomato paste. (Yep, tomato paste!) Apply a coat of tomato paste over the boil, and the veggie's acids will lessen the pain and encourage the boil to "come to a head"—meaning it'll soften and be ready for popping. Don't attempt to pop a boil until it's soft and you can see a small yellow dot of pus at the center.

MAKE YOUR OWN COMPRESSES

For a Cozy Cool

Here's a great DIY ice pack: Take a regular sponge (not the scrubbing variety), and soak it in a mixture of half water, half rubbing alcohol. Place it in a zip-top bag and freeze. Since alcohol doesn't freeze completely, the sponge will stay flexible and will easily and comfortably wrap around your achy spots much better than a hard ice pack would. If you want, you can even freeze multiple sponges so that when one gets warm, you can just get a replacement from the freezer.

JEANNE SAYS

Got Milk?

If you or your child bites into a piece of pizza that's too hot to eat, reach for a glass of milk. Drinking milk will soothe the roof of your mouth better than drinking cold water will, because the protein in milk will create a protective film over any burns.

Make a Simple Hot Pack

Transform a towel into a heating pad! Wet a dish towel until it's quite damp but not dripping. Heat it in the microwave for 20 to 30 seconds. Using tongs, carefully remove the towel and seal it in a zip-top bag. Wrap the bag in another towel and enjoy a little heat therapy.

A Different Kind of Ice Pack

If you're a vodka drinker, you're well aware that it doesn't solidify in the freezer. For this reason, it's also a great tool for making your own homemade gel ice pack to use on aches or injuries. Just pour 2 cups water, 1/3 cup vodka, and a few drops green or yellow food coloring (so everyone will know not to eat the contents) into a heavy-duty zip-top freezer bag. Put it in the freezer for a while, and you've got an instant ice pack. If you don't keep vodka around, you can simulate the same effect with liquid dishwasher detergent. Either way, make absolutely certain you label the bag so nobody ingests it.

Sea Salt Soothing

You know how quickly minor cuts, scrapes, rashes, and blisters heal at the beach! It's due to the healing power of saltwater. When you can't take a trip to the beach but need fast healing, make a sea salt compress at home. Combine 1/8 cup ice water with 1/4 cup sea salt—it's that simple. Then apply the mixture to the affected area with a damp washcloth; wrap around and hold for up to an hour.

WHO KNEW?

PART 6

FUN & FAMILY TIME

HOLIDAY HELPERS

Don't let financial and time burdens weigh you down when you should be simply enjoying the holidays! Here's how to boost the celebrations and ditch the stress.

TERRIFIC THANKSGIVING TIPS

Thanksgiving Activity for All Ages

Give hyper kids something to do *and* decorate your table at the same time this Thanksgiving by sending them out into the yard to find the last remaining yellow, red, and orange leaves. Make sure they're not visibly dirty, then arrange them along the middle of the table in lieu of a runner. This activity is good for kids of any age, and the older ones can help the younger ones.

Festive Fall Decoration

We love this festive-for-fall decoration: Cut a slice off the side of an apple so it lies flat on a saucer or candleholder. Then cut a hole out of the top, and you have an instant votive or tea-light holder! Coat the hole with some lemon juice to keep it from turning brown.

Post-Halloween Pumpkin Project

With this project, kids can enjoy pumpkin crafts all season long! Get a few small pumpkins—one for each child—and plan a leaf-collecting trip to the park or simply your backyard. Let the leaves dry completely, then use craft glue to paste them all over the pumpkins.

Reuse Corn Decor

Are your colorful corncobs missing lots of kernels already? Switch it up! Instead of hanging them on the wall, scrape off the rest of the kernels and pour them into a pretty candleholder, small vase, or mason jar.

Turkey Day Stains Be Gone!

Prepping for Thanksgiving dinner can be an enormously stressful task—and that's not even counting cleanup time. Here's a great preventative measure we've picked up over the years that helps with our post-meal cleaning: Spray-starch your tablecloth a day or two before T-Day, and let it dry for at least a full day. Drips and spills will be no match for your stain-guarded table!

Save a Soupy Stuffing

Without question one of the main attractions at many Thanksgiving tables, stuffing is hearty, creamy, and comforting—perfect for this family-centric holiday. However, stuffing mishaps happen; sometimes it's too goopy and wet to eat. To bring soupy stuffing back to life, first spread it onto a baking sheet. Layer cubes of stale bread or unseasoned croutons on top of the stuffing. Pop it back into the oven for about 15 minutes at 375F°; when finished, stir it all together and spoon into a serving dish. The bread will sop up excess liquid, leaving your stuffing in its intended scrumptious form.

Quick Turkey Fix

Did the star of your Thanksgiving dinner come out too dry? Don't panic! You can rehydrate your meat with an easy braise: Slice up the turkey and stick it in a baking dish. Fill the dish halfway with chicken stock, top with foil, and place it back in the oven for 10 minutes at 350°F. The turkey will be juicy and delicious.

WHO KNEW?
READERS' FAVORITE

Hold Off on Holiday Food Shopping

Sometimes saving at the store is all about knowing when to shop. Do your Thanksgiving food shopping on the Monday before the holiday, and you'll save a bundle. Stores will be evaluating their holiday stock and will offer discounts on items of which they have excess quantities.

Great Gravy

Add a tasty punch to your standard gravy with apple cider vinegar—its fruity-tangy flavor will give your turkey a bold, delicious boost. Just add a capful or two to your gravy right at the end of cooking.

CLEVER CHRISTMAS IDEAS

Christmas in the Books

Count down the days till Christmas with this fun family activity: Pull together all your holiday-themed books and wrap them as individual gifts. Let your children open one gift per night, and read the book together; save *The Night Before Christmas* for the 24th. The preholiday festivities might keep your kids satiated enough to lay off the present hunting until Christmas!

Advent Activity Calendar

For a new twist on the usual Advent countdown, make this year's calendar a family to-do list—full of fun activities for you and your kids. Print each day's item onto a small card or sheet of paper, then compile them all into a 25-day calendar. Activities can be anything you'll enjoy doing together: Watch a holiday movie, decorate the tree, make gingerbread cookies, go sledding, drink hot cocoa, or read a Christmas story.

Walnut Treats

For a holiday treat, carve the nuts out of walnut shells split in half and place fortunes or little prizes inside. Glue back together and decorate with sparkle paint. When the shells are dry, collect them in a basket for a unique centerpiece and fun activity. Pass around the table after dinner and let family members take turns reaching for a walnut and cracking it open to find out what's hidden inside. You can even turn the nuts into a countdown, marking a day of Advent on each.

Stretch That Ribbon!

Used wisely, a little holiday ribbon can go a long way. Wrap it around just about anything—a vase, throw pillow, lamp shade, curtain, pillar candle, and the list goes on—to create a festive atmosphere at little or no cost.

The Scent of the Holiday

This little gem of a recipe will give your home an instant cozy and home-for-holidays feel. Mix whole cloves, crushed cinnamon sticks, bay leaves, juniper berries, orange peels, nutmeg, and allspice. (You can store the mixture in a jar until you are ready to use it.) To get the smell to diffuse, boil water in a saucepan and pour in some of your homemade potpourri. Simmer gently and your house is guaranteed to start smelling like Christmas.

Two Wreaths for the Price of One

Making a wreath this Christmas with a foam form? Before you begin, slice the foam in half from top to bottom so that you have two foam circles, each with one rounded side and one flat side. Not only will your wreath hang flat against the door, but now you can make *two*—one wreath for outside and another for inside!

Outdoor Christmas Decorations

When pruning your trees and bushes in the spring or summer, be sure to save some branches for later use. Then spray paint them red, white, silver, or gold and you have an instant Christmas decoration! Place them in planters of flowers that are dead for the winter, and add lights or ornaments for extra flair.

Over-the-Door Hanger

Here's an easy way to hang a wreath on your door: Grab one self-adhesive wall hook—the 3M brand is perfect—and hang it upside down on the reverse side of your door. Loop the wreath's hanging ribbon around the hook on the opposite side of the door, then pull it over the top for an over-the-door setup. The wreath should hang securely on the front.

Long-Lasting Wreaths

We love the look of live pine wreaths and garlands, but hate it when needles get all over the floor. To keep the needles from falling, spritz your holiday greenery with hair spray right after you purchase it. The hair spray will keep the needles moist and where they belong.

First Feeding for the Tree

Just got your tree up? Great job! Next up: The first feeding. Water your tree with hot water—the temp should be around 80°F—then add 2 ounces antibacterial mouthwash. Heating the water helps the tree start absorbing efficiently, and the mouthwash keeps bacteria and mold at bay.

Keep Your Tree Luscious with LED Lights

Time for new tree lights this year? Choose mini LED lights over the traditional kind. Not only do they save energy (and cut the cost of electricity), but they're also not as hot, preventing your tree from drying out quickly.

Easy Christmas Decorating

Put those leftover holiday ornaments to good use in an inexpensive centerpiece. Simply pick your favorites and put them in a clear punch bowl, and add tinsel or pine sprigs around the base. It works great with those solid-colored orbs we always seem to have so many of!

Cleaner Pinecones

Pinecones are a family favorite during Christmastime, whether they're hanging on the tree or from a stocking, or simply radiating their delicious piney fragrance. But sometimes they're just too sticky to handle. To remove some of that sap, place the pinecones in the oven at 300°F for 10 minutes.

What to Do with Dusty Decor

Save your family from dust-inflicted sneezes by airing out your stored holiday decorations before you put them up. Place dusty stockings and ornaments in the freezer for a few hours to kill off even more allergens!

WHO KNEW?
READERS' FAVORITE

Safe Storage for Holiday Decorations

When it's time to bring down the tree and lights, take great care with the more delicate ornaments. Slip them into old socks or nylons for extra safety, then place them in disposable plastic cups before storing. Old egg cartons are another ultra-safe (and eco-friendly) way to store bulbs and glass trinkets.

Save on Your Tree Skirt

Don't waste your money on an expensive tree skirt this Christmas. Instead, look for a small round tablecloth. Cut a round opening in the center for the tree stand and a straight line to one edge. Place the opening in the back of the tree and you're done.

Make a Winter Wonderland

Got any spare cupcake liners on hand? Use them to make pretty paper snowflakes for your living room decorations: Set the liners on a flat surface and press to flatten them. Fold each liner in half, and fold in half again. Using scissors, cut shapes into the folds to create your snowflakes. String them all onto one piece of ribbon or yarn to form a garland, or hang them around the room individually for a beautiful snowy scene.

Easy-Peasy Pipe Cleaner Ornaments

Need last-minute (and cheap) Christmas tree ornaments? If you have holiday cookie cutters and pipe cleaners on hand, you'll be set in no time. Shape a pipe cleaner around the perimeter of a cookie cutter, making sure you get every corner and bend. When your pipe cleaner shape is complete, twist the ends together to close it up. If your wire is long enough, make a loop at the top for hanging; if not, attach a small loop with another piece of pipe cleaner. For a decorative touch, wrap the pipe cleaner ornament with a thin strip of festive fabric, winding the material around the piping to cover it completely and then knotting it once you've wrapped the entire shape.

BRUCE SAYS

Long Live Christmas

We've been known to keep our Christmas tree up until well into January, and with this little trick, you can enjoy the holidays a little longer too. Add a small amount of sugar or Pine-Sol to the water to extend the life of your tree.

Create a Sticker Mystery

Add a little more excitement and surprise to the holidays by labeling the kids' gifts with colorful stickers rather than gift tags. Color-code the stickers for each recipient, and don't reveal the code until gift-opening time on Christmas Day. It's a clever, fun, and inexpensive way to keep the kids guessing.

Make Your Own Poppers

Make these a new Christmas tradition in your house! Cut paper towel tubes into three pieces and load them up with candy, little toys, and tissue paper crowns. Then use wrapping paper to cover the tubes completely, leaving extra paper on each end to tie up with ribbon. Everyone gets a popper with his or her place setting for Christmas dinner. Yank from the sides to release the goodies inside!

5 FUN USES FOR OLD HOLIDAY CARDS

Reluctant to simply toss the cards you've received in the recycling bin? Here are some great ways to keep the memories around through a new use.

Craft kids' sewing cards. You may have seen "sewing cards" for toddlers available in toy stores. They help develop fine motor skills, but are basically just big picture cards with holes in them. You can easily make your own. One easy way is to start with the front half of a greeting card. Punch holes around all four sides and use a piece of yarn to lace through the holes, over and under. Twenty inches of yarn should be more than enough. Put a knot at one end of the yarn. If it doesn't go through easily, use a tiny piece of tape as you would for a frayed shoelace.

Transform into tags. Save pretty cards to use for next year's gift tags. Cut them down to size, then stash in a cookie tin with a Christmas design.

Make artwork. Looking for easy holiday decorations this year? All you'll need is matboard, sturdy adhesive, and festive cards for hanging! Design a collage on one large piece of matboard, or trim the board down into a series of frames that hold one card each. Simply glue the backs of your cards to the matboard using glue or rubber cement. Let dry, and decorate!

Create pretty place settings. Cut strips from patterns on the cards, then use a dab of craft glue to create napkin rings. To complete your place settings, purchase a bunch of small votive candleholders—one for each dinner guest. Write the name of each guest on a slip of paper, then glue it to parts of an old card as a backing. Attach the name tags to the holiday candleholders using clear or patterned washi tape.

Whip up a centerpiece. Cut the front from a card, then slide it inside a mason jar. Bend the card so it fits the curve of the jar. Place greenery or berry branches in the jar, and tie a fun ribbon around the neck. Put in a place where it looks stunning in your home, or give it as a gift.

Perfect Mulled Wine

A no-fail holiday party potable: a sweet-and-spicy mulled wine. Here's an easy trick that helps keep the cloves in the pot (and out of guests' mouths!): Press all cloves into the whole fruits in your recipe, such as oranges and lemons. They'll simmer and spice up the pot, and when you ladle the yummy wine into cups, the cloves will stay lodged in the fruit.

Extend Gift-Opening Fun

Frugal Christmas? If opening presents is going to take drastically less time than usual this year, fill the gap by starting some new Christmas traditions. Make a popcorn string for the tree, cut out sugar cookies with different-colored sugars for decoration, or try this game to make gift-opening take longer (it's a favorite at our gatherings): Find as many holiday present rejects as you have people playing— all those candles with scents you can't stand, weird gifts from office gift exchanges, or your silliest finds from the dollar bin at Target. Wrap each one and have each guest pick a gift. Go around the room clockwise, starting with the youngest person. Before opening their gift, guests can decide to trade with someone else (even if that person's gift has been unwrapped). After one round of gift opening, have one more round of trades, with players deciding if they want to keep their current gift or switch with someone else. You'll be surprised by which gifts people actually like, and get a laugh at the expense of the person left with the worst one.

HAPPY HANUKKAH

Luscious Latkes

Making latkes for a Hanukkah dinner? For the best consistency, stick to high-starch potatoes: Yukon gold is the best choice for a richer batch, but standard baking potatoes yield delicious latkes, too. However, you'll want to avoid the waxier red bliss variety, which tend to turn out sticky.

The Starchy Secret to Great Latkes

Want the magic ingredient for the tastiest latkes? Potato starch. Here's how: Shred your potatoes into a bowl of cold water, remove them to another bowl using a strainer, and keep the liquids that remain behind. Wait about 10 minutes for the liquids to separate—the water will rise to the top and leave the chalky-looking potato starch at the bottom. Pour out the water, taking care to save the starch at the bottom of the bowl. Scoop this starch back in with the potatoes.

Make-Ahead Potato Latkes

If you don't have time to prepare latkes on the day of your dinner, you can make them ahead of time and stick them in the freezer. When you're ready to serve, pop them in the oven for 10 minutes at 350°F.

SMART STRINGING

Making a popcorn garland for the holidays? Use dental floss! It's stronger than regular string, and less likely to break when you wrap it around the tree.

NEW APPROACHES TO NEW YEAR'S

Balloon-Popping Countdown

Shake up New Year's parties by incorporating some creative spirit into the mix. On separate slips of paper, write down one activity per hour of the party—for example "Dance, dance, dance!" or "Karaoke time!" Insert each note into a balloon, then blow it up. Write a time on the outside of each balloon, and when that hour arrives during the party, pop the balloon and begin the designated activity. The balloon-popping countdown to midnight and the spontaneity of the party will be super-fun for everyone.

Auld Lang Time

Here's an original idea for a cheap New Year's Eve decoration: gather all the devices you use to tell time—stopwatches, alarm clocks, calendars, pocket planners, even the little hourglasses from board games—and place them on a tray next to the champagne bowl. Tell all your guests to set their alarms for midnight and do the same with the items you've collected.

Bubble Wrap Bop Till You Drop

For a kick-butt kids' party, collect sheets of bubble wrap and lay them on the floor before the clock strikes midnight. Let the kids celebrate the countdown by jumping, dancing, and stomping on the bubbles for a poppin' good time!

Nifty Noisemakers

These noisemakers are a surefire party-starter. Clean and dry empty water bottles, then fill them with coins, marbles, or beads. Twist the caps back on (tightly!) or glue them shut. Decorate the bottles with glued-on streamers, glitter, or paint. Hand them out to guests when they arrive, and instruct them to shake!

WHO KNEW?

READERS' FAVORITE

Don't Fizzle Out Before Midnight

Champagne lost its fizz? Place a raisin in the glass and the last bits of carbon dioxide that remain will cling to the raisin, then be released again as bubbles. You can also try throwing a few raisins into the bottle before you make the final pour.

Best Bubbly Technique

Do you love champagne as much as we do? If so, you probably want to avoid overpouring and spilling the bubbly all over the place. To make sure it all ends up in your glass (and, ultimately, in your mouth), fill only one-third of the glass at a time and wait until the fizz settles before you pour more.

Jazz Up the Glass

For a snazzy party treat especially good for New Year's, add some color and sweetness to champagne. First color some granulated sugar by adding a few drops of food coloring to it. Then wet the rim of each champagne glass and press into the sugar to give it a sweet, colorful rim—perfect for guests who find champagne a little too dry.

VERY SPECIAL VALENTINES

Baking with Heart

Once Christmas is over, snag a bag of tiny candy canes that are on sale and use them for these heart-shaped cupcake toppers. Flip one cane over and place them together ("hooks" and bottom edges touching). Bake on a nonstick baking sheet at 325°F for 3 to 5 minutes. Pinch together to seal, then cool and remove with a spatula. They're perfect for decorating cupcakes on Valentine's Day!

Lunch Is for Lovers, Too!

For a little less formality on Valentine's Day, consider taking your sweetie out to a romantic lunch or brunch rather than dinner. Not only will you make it more special by sharing it with fewer people (everyone else will probably be making dinner reservations), but the lunch menu is often less expensive.

Heart-Shaped Cupcakes

You don't need a special tin to make charming cupcakes or muffins for Valentine's Day. Simply place cupcake liners inside a regular tin, then stick a marble or ball of foil between each liner and the tin. This will create a V-shape for the top of the heart. Pour enough batter to fill the liners only slightly more than halfway. (Don't pour too much, or the heart shapes won't come through!) Bake as directed, and decorate as you like.

MIX TAPE LOVE

Even if you haven't made someone a mix tape since high school, handpicked tunes are a great, free Valentine's treat. Make a custom romantic playlist to show your sweetie you care!

Flowers Perfect for Any Celebration

Flora-lovers don't need fancy arrangements to celebrate every holiday with style. Start your own tradition of dyeing white carnations whatever color is fitting for the occasion: various shades of red and pink for Valentine's Day, green for St. Patrick's Day, a combination of red, white, and blue for July Fourth, orange and black for Halloween, and so on. It's also fun to do favorite colors for birthdays. All you need to do is add a bit of food coloring to your flowers' vase with some warm water. Half the fun is watching the flower take on the new color as it sucks up the water, so make sure the kids don't miss out.

Candy Dots Valentine

Here's an adorable Valentine's Day treat for your child's classmates—and the kids can help make these, too! You'll need a few sheets of candy dots, colored construction paper, scissors, scalloped scissors (if you like), and glue. Cut heart shapes out of the candy sheets, then glue each heart to colored construction paper (if it matches the candy color, even better!). For a pretty decorative border, use scalloped scissors to cut a larger heart "frame" out of the construction paper.

Leave a Trail of Love Notes

This romantic gesture is perfect for Valentine's Day and the whole rest of the year! Who wouldn't enjoy finding hidden declarations of love all year round? Either purchase a pack of valentines or create your own using pretty paper; on each one, write down something you love about your partner. Then place the notes all over the house, even in unexpected places.

Couples Coupons

Most busy couples don't have time to treat themselves (and each other) to special activities, like massages, breakfasts in bed, and romantic fondue nights. Instead, give one another personalized coupons, or IOUs, as gifts. To do this, compile a stack of "coupons" for special activities or freebie chores—one month of laundry, three mowed lawns, one dinner-and-a-movie night—and gift it for Valentine's Day, a birthday, or any holiday. It's creative and fun, and lets your partner choose how he or she wants to be spoiled. Does it get any more romantic than that?

CELEBRATING ST. PATRICK'S DAY

Shamrock Pepper Stamp

Making St. Patty's Day decorations with the kids? To fashion a stamp in the shape of a shamrock, simply cut off the bottom of a bell pepper—*voilà!* Dip the clover shape in green paint and stamp away.

A Leprechaun for Your Doorstep

Here's another great holiday project for you and the kids: Turn a plain-old flowerpot into an adorable green leprechaun hat. In addition to a clay pot, get some green paint and a paintbrush, a large metal washer (for the buckle), sandpaper to sand down the washer, gold paint, thick black ribbon, and a hot glue gun. Paint the pot green and set it aside to dry. Sand the washer to make it smooth and ready for painting; paint it completely with gold paint. Once both the pot and washer are dry, use your hot glue gun to secure the black ribbon around the center of the pot. Glue the washer—or buckle—on top of the ribbon, and your leprechaun hat pot is ready to grow some shamrocks!

Luck Be a Rainbow Collage

There really *is* a pot of gold at the end of the rainbow! At the end of this rainbow, at least. You and the kids can make this simple rainbow collage in a snap—all you'll need are paper plates, scissors, paints in all six colors of a rainbow, cotton balls, white glue, and gold glitter or sparkly paint. Slice a paper plate in half with your scissors, then paint the arches of a rainbow onto one half-circle. Dab a few cotton balls in glue and paste them along the bottom of each arch to form clouds. For the gold treasure, mix the glitter with a bit of glue to make a glittery paste, then paint gold coins near one end of the rainbow.

Corned Beef Cook Test

For lip-smacking, perfectly tender corned beef this St. Patrick's Day (or any day), give your meat the fork-slip doneness test: Poke a carving fork into the roast and lift upward slowly and carefully. The fork should slip out of the meat cleanly if it's moist and tender.

EASY EASTER CELEBRATIONS

DIY Egg Dye

Never, ever pay for egg dye! Simply mix ½ cup boiling water with ½ teaspoon white vinegar, and add food coloring until you get a hue you like. For a striped egg even the Easter Bunny would be proud of, wrap tape around the egg before dipping. Once the egg dries, remove the tape, tape over the colored parts, and dip again in a different color. You can also use stickers in the shapes of hearts, stars, and letters.

Natural Coloring

It's easy to make natural Easter egg dyes. Just add colorful ingredients to the water while you boil your eggs. Use grass for green, onionskins for yellow and deep orange, and beets for pink. If you plan to eat the eggs, be sure to use plants that haven't been fertilized or treated with pesticides or other chemicals.

Tidy Turntable Tool

Egg decorating can turn into a sloppy affair, with various bowls of dye shuffling around your worktable. Make it more efficient by using a lazy Susan to hold your dyes. That way, you can keep everything in one easy-to-maneuver place and avoid messy mishaps.

Remove Dye Stains from Your Skin

Got Easter egg dye on your hands? Remove stains from your skin with this easy solution: Spoon 2 tablespoons salt into a small bowl and gradually mix in vinegar until you have a paste. Scrub your skin with the salt-vinegar paste and stains will disappear in no time!

WHO KNEW?
READERS' FAVORITE

Use Easter Eggs Year Round

Instead of packing away those plastic Easter eggs for once-a-year use (or tossing them out all together), keep using them throughout the year. Instead of putting snacks in plastic bags, put them inside the eggs and liven up your child's packed lunch. They can be filled with small candies, crackers, trail mix, and more.

Easter Egg Accessory

The perfect holder for Easter eggs? The upside-down tops to soda and water bottles! For a little extra flair, glue a piece of Easter ribbon around the outside of them.

No-Break Easter Eggs

Before you hard-boil eggs for decorating this year, prevent cracks by first poking a tiny hole in one end of the egg with a pin or needle (make sure it's clean!).

Magic Marbling Effect

These eggs are even cooler-looking than other marbled eggs. Rather than dyeing just the outer shell, our food coloring seeps into the shells' cracks to create neat spider-web effects. First, hard-boil your eggs as usual. Once they're cooled, tap each egg on a hard surface to make cracks in the shell—but don't peel! Using a spoon, drip food coloring all over the eggs, and let them dry. Rinse with water and peel off the shells. You'll have beautiful marbled eggs that are ready to eat!

Tattoo Your Eggs

Punch up your Easter eggs this year by applying temporary tattoos in addition to colorful dyes. Your kids will want to put the tats on themselves, too!

Egg Hunt Hint

If you're hosting an egg hunt for kids of various ages, try color-coding the eggs by age group. Yellow eggs might be hidden in easy-to-find places for the younger kids, and green eggs can be stowed in sneakier spots for the big kids.

Beat-the-Sweets Easter Treat

Mix up Easter snacks so the kids aren't eating *only* sugary sweets. This treat is a little more healthful than the usual candy, plus it's super-cute and Easter-colorful. Pour small, cheesy crackers into a clear plastic pastry bag and tie the opening closed with green ribbon. You've got a carrot! (At least in shape, if not nutritional value.)

JEANNE SAYS

Branch Out with Holiday Trees

Our kids love to hang eggshell ornaments and tie pastel ribbons on the dracena in our kitchen at Easter. And when they were younger, we used to arrange their stuffed bunnies, ducks, and lambs on a blanket spread out on the floor underneath the tree.

Festive Table Settings

Make Easter dinner even more fun for the kids (and big kids, too!) by putting together these adorable table settings that look like carrots. You'll need orange paper dinner napkins, green plastic utensils, and green pipe cleaners. Fold each napkin in half to form a rectangle. Set a plastic spoon, fork, and knife on a bottom corner of each napkin, then roll the utensils up in the napkin. Wrap a couple of pipe cleaners around the top of each rolled-up napkin, and your carrot table settings will be good enough to eat!

Berry Cool Easter Baskets

Here's a creative tip for putting together cute baskets for the kids: Reuse the colorful berry baskets you find at the grocery store! Attach pipe cleaners to each side of the basket to form a handle, and either tie or glue a small bow to the very top of the handle. Weave colored ribbon through the tiny openings in the basket and secure the ends with glue. Finally, fill it with all sorts of Easter goodies!

Make Your Own Chocolate Molds

If you thought nothing was more fun than chocolate, you haven't tried making chocolate in the shape of your child's favorite plastic toy or another object in your home! And it's easier than you'd think—the secret is brown sugar. In addition to plenty of brown sugar, you'll need a baking dish, ideally an 8-inch square pan. First, fill the pan with tightly packed brown sugar. Next, find a sturdy object you'd like to replicate in chocolate (your child's toy box is often a good place to find something—a plastic bunny would be a good choice at Easter, for example). Press the (clean!) item firmly into the brown sugar so that it leaves an impression and remove. The brown sugar will hold the shape of the object, and you can now use it as a chocolate mold! Simply pour melted chocolate into the mold you've just created, then refrigerate for about 30 minutes, or until hardened. You can then remove your chocolate creation and wow your family!

FANTASTIC FOURTH OF JULY

Make a Patriotic Masterpiece

For this year's July Fourth celebrations, create your own centerpiece with items that make you feel USA-proud. Combine symbols of patriotism with holiday-colorful edibles for an awesome spectacle. The possibilities are endless, from Coca-Cola bottles, miniature flags, and an Uncle Sam hat to an apple pie and a bright-colored fruit platter of strawberries, blueberries, and whipped cream for dipping.

O Say Can You–Be Careful with Those Sparklers?

It's Fourth of July and time to bust out the legal explosives. Kids love to hold sparklers, but make sure their hands are safe by sticking the sparkler in Play-Doh inside its container, which is the perfect size for the kids to wrap their patriotic hands around.

Independence Day Decorative Stars

For a little added flair at your Fourth of July shindig, set your table with colorful jars adorned with stars! You'll need a few jars; white sticky glue; red, white, and blue spray paint; and—the secret ingredient—Epsom salts! Using glue, trace a star onto the front of each jar. Dab the still-wet star into a dish of Epsom salts, and set it aside to dry. Spray paint each jar in a different patriotic color; let the paint dry. When you're ready to party, fill each starred jar with napkins, utensils, straws, and anything else your guests will need at the dinner table.

America the Beautiful—and Delicious!

Here's a festive way to incorporate some patriotism into your Independence Day snacks: American flag open sandwiches! Spread cream cheese onto two slices of bread, then smear some red jam on top. Line up banana slices to form the stripes, and add blueberries in the top left corner for the stars.

Land of the Free, Home of the Boozy

Do you have some patriotic tipplers joining you for the Fourth? Mix up this tasty summertime cocktail that is sure to whet their whistles: Combine 1 ounce vodka, 1 ounce strawberry schnapps, and 3 ounces club soda. Then top it off with fresh blueberries.

Fourth Decor

Celebrate in festive style by making some holiday-themed decorations! If you can find a "4" birthday candle or house number, display it inside a large glass vase. Then fill the vase with red, white, and blue candies, and slip miniature American flags inside.

Bedeck Your Deck

Bring a little patriotism to the outside of your home by making bunting for your porch railing. All you'll need is an appropriate yardage of USA-themed fabric and some colored yarn to tie it up. Tie one end of fabric to the end of your rail. Then, about every 2 feet, bunch the fabric and tie it to the railing with the yarn.

HALLOWEEN TRICKS AND TREATS

Creepy Halloween Drinks

Getting dry ice to put at the bottom of the punch bowl is a bit difficult, so to make your punch seem haunted quickly and easily, freeze grapes to use as ice cubes. Once they're frozen, peel off the skin and they'll look like creepy eyeballs.

Add Halloween Atmosphere

Adding stretchy cobwebs to the doorjambs and corners of your home is a great way to add Halloween flair to the entire house. Instead of buying the ones packaged as spider webs, though, simply go to a craft store and buy a bag of fiberfill. It's the exact same stuff, and a 16-ounce bag of fiberfill is less than half the cost. You can usually find bags of plastic spider rings for super-cheap at party supply or superstores—add them to the webs and on tables around your house for more atmosphere, and encourage your guests to take them home!

Halloween Pumpkin Preserver

Disappointed that pumpkins get soft and mushy so soon after they're carved? It turns out that this happens because air comes in contact with the inside flesh, allowing bacteria to grow. So to solve the problem of every jack-o-lantern looking like an old man, spray the inside of the hollowed-out pumpkin with an antiseptic spray, which slows down the bacterial growth and increases the time it takes for the pumpkin to deteriorate. Just make sure no one eats a pumpkin that has been sprayed! You can also try using WD-40 spray instead.

Bloody Good Gore-fest

Mix up your own fake blood this year by mixing cornstarch, red and blue food dye, and a little milk. Use a small paintbrush to work your bloody magic on faces, necks, limbs, and clothing.

PUMPKIN GOOP SCOOPER

When you're carving your pumpkin, rather than using a spoon or your bare hands to scoop out the goopy insides, try an ice cream scooper instead! Less labor, less sticky mess, and more time for the actual carving.

WHO KNEW?

READERS' FAVORITE

Safe Storage for Vinyl Decals

Vinyl stickies look great on windows, doors, and other surfaces around the house. But when you remove them, they tend to wrinkle and stick to themselves. Prevent damage to your decals by laying them flat on a sheet of aluminum foil, then top them with another sheet of foil and fold the edges over to protect them. Store the decals flat and they'll be in great shape for next year.

Make Way for House Ghosts

Need some creepy Halloween decorations on the cheap? Of course you do! Here's a super-easy tip for making floating ghosts for the outside of your home: Open a white plastic garbage bag and stuff balled-up newspaper into the very bottom. Tighten the bag around the ball and tie it closed with a rubber band—this is the ghost's head and neck. Use a black Sharpie to draw a ghoulish face, then hang it in your front yard or near the doorstep to scare trick-or-treating guests.

The Early Ghoul Catches the Worm

Just like Christmas, you'll find the best Halloween deals way before the day actually rolls around. But why not start even earlier? During the week after Halloween, most related merchandise is deeply discounted—often 75 percent off! Shopping for costumes and decorations almost a year in advance might sound silly, but you'll save lots of cash, time, and stress prepping for next year.

Pumpkin Pointer

Got cookie cutters on hand? Use them to make cool shapes in your jack-o'-lantern! Hold the cutter against the pumpkin's shell, and use a rubber mallet to hit it softly until it penetrates—the cutter should enter at least halfway through the shell. Pull out the cutter, then trace the shape with a small serrated knife to remove the image from the shell.

The Ever-Glowing Pumpkin

A candle looks eerily beautiful when burning inside a carved pumpkin, but electric lights last longer and burn even more brightly. To give your pumpkin a long-lasting glow, curl up a string of Christmas lights, stick them in a clear plastic bag, and place the bag inside the pumpkin. Carve a small hole in the back of your pumpkin to plug the lights into an electrical outlet.

Estimate Your Trick-or-Treater Turnout

If you've ever stood in the Halloween candy aisle asking yourself, "How many bags should I buy?" you'll love this tip. As you refill your candy bowl this Halloween, keep track of how many empty bags you've got at the end of the night. Record this number somewhere safe, such as on your computer or smartphone calendar. (You can even set a pop-up reminder for next year's Halloween.) That way, you'll know approximately how much candy to buy ahead of time!

BRUCE SAYS

Create Glowing Ghost Eyes

Scaring trick-or-treaters is a huge part of the fun at our house. This super-simple outdoor prop is a doozy! Trace two eyes onto a cardboard toilet paper tube and cut them out. Place glow sticks inside the tube, and set your ghostly eyes in a sneaky-but-visible spot near your doorstep—in a bush or potted plant beside the front door.

Scare Up Some Face Paint

Skip the store-bought face paint this year (along with those yucky chemicals) and make your own nontoxic paints! All you'll need are a few common household items and food coloring: Combine 5 tablespoons cornstarch, 2 tablespoons shortening, 1 tablespoon flour, and a drop of petroleum jelly. Split this mixture into several different containers and add the food dyes as you need them.

Peanut Allergy Prevention

Are there any peanut allergies in your house? They can really put a damper on a child's trick-or-treating fun. To prevent any mishaps and still let your kids enjoy their Halloween outing, have some safe, peanut-free candy at home waiting for them. When your witches and ghouls return from their neighborhood prowl, go through their hauls with them and swap the questionable candies with your nut-free stash.

Trick or Treasure

Instead of candy this year, hand out cool party favors to all your trick-or-treaters. They might not be as conventional as the usual sweet treats, but they're still really fun. Hit the dollar store and pick up packages of stickers, temporary tattoos, finger puppets, or other amusing little toys.

Frankenstein Fingers

These string-cheese Frankenstein fingers are healthy *and* totally creepy. Serve them at a Halloween party or sneak them inside your kids' lunches for a little scare. Cut slits in each strip of cheese where the knuckles should be. Cut small rectangles out of a green pepper and press them into the tips of the cheese strips to form the monster's fingernails. If needed, add a little cream cheese as an adhesive to keep the nails in place.

Gross-Out Halloween Drinks

Need more spooky treats? Mix up these colorful drinks for the kids. They might look toxic, but they're totally safe—though packed with sugar! Combine 1 part Mountain Dew and 1 part blue Kool-Aid to make a Blue Ghost Punch. Or mix a bit of green food coloring into lemonade for a Toxic Tart.

JEANNE SAYS

Make Spooky Skeleton Snacks

Here's a Halloween take on a favorite seasonal snack: Bake gingerbread cookies in the shape of humans or animals, then ice them as skeletons.

PARTY & GIFTING SMARTS

Celebrations to remember don't need to cost you a lot of time and money! Use these expert tips to plan, save, and add those little special touches with ease.

SIMPLE PREP AND CLEANUP

Card Table Trick

This simple trick offers peace of mind when several folding tables are placed together to form a bigger table. Use cleaned-out coffee cans as holders for adjoining legs from different tables and rest assured that your grandmother's hand-blown glass punch bowl is safe.

Keep the TV Going

Pop a movie into the DVD player and let it run on mute. Play a scary movie if it's a Halloween party, or a Christmas classic if it's a holiday party. Or play movies from your teenage years or favorites among your group of friends. And if it's your birthday, of course, it's your pick! Once you've picked your theme, pile the rest of your DVDs that fit it on top of the player and change the movie throughout the night.

Extra Garbage Space

Having a party and need an extra trash bin for your guests? Just repurpose your hamper for the occasion. (Your dirty clothes will be fine in a garbage bag in the closet until tomorrow.)

FUN FOOD AND DECORATING

Fancy Up Your Dip

Here's a great way to display dip on your table. Cut off the top of a bell pepper, then hollow it out and spoon your dip inside. You can also use a sturdy bread like pumpernickel as a hollowed-out dip container. Put spinach dip inside, then cut the bread you removed into large cubes and use for dipping.

Creative Fruit Display

For a fun display on your buffet table, hollow out a melon, orange, or grapefruit and fill it with cut-up fruit (and maybe even some miniature marshmallows). For a more attractive holder, you can scallop the edges or cut it in the shape of a basket.

Keep Food Fresh

To keep meat or cheese hors d'oeuvres moist, cover them with a damp paper towel, then cover loosely with plastic wrap. Many fillings (as well as bread) dry out very quickly, but with this tip, you can make these simple appetizers first and have them ready on the table when guests arrive.

Candy Cone Centerpiece

What do kids love more than candy? Answer: Not much. So this candy centerpiece is always a hit at birthday parties. You'll need a piece of florist foam in the shape of a cone, plus lots and lots of yummy candy—choose your kids' favorites and also grab a few bags of lollipops. Set the foam cone on top of a tray, plate, or bowl loaded with candy. Insert lollipop sticks into the foam to cover it completely. If you like, make a cardboard or paper number for the guest of honor's age; alternatively, you can use a fun photo. Glue or tape the number to a skewer, then stick it through the top of the cone.

PIECE OF CAKE!

Throwing a birthday party? Opt for cupcakes rather than a large cake. That way, you'll save on forks, plates, and clean up! (Just serve on napkins.)

WHO KNEW?

READERS' FAVORITE

Perfect Appetizer Calculator

Wondering how much food to make for your big soiree? Wonder no longer. At a cocktail party (no dinner served), 10 to 12 bite-sized portions per person is a good bet. If you're also serving a meal, figure on 4 to 5 bites per guest. For dip, figure 2 tablespoons per person (plus veggies or crackers for dipping), and for cheese, 4 ounces for each person.

Easy Balloon Garlands

Balloon garlands are an inexpensive way to add festive fun to a party. And believe it or not, the easiest way to make one is with a needle! Using fishing line (or thread), run the needle through the tied-off ends of the balloons as close to the knot as possible. Have fun with color combinations!

Birthday Photo Collage

Collect all the photographs you can find that celebrate your guest of honor—from babyhood, childhood, school yearbooks, vacations, and other memorable events. Then compile them into a large wall collage: Arrange the photos into giant numbers to mark the person's age or year of birth, spell out a name or meaningful word or phrase, or simply form a fun shape.

Tablecloth Substitution

Your daughter's party is about to start, and you just realized you don't have a plastic tablecloth on which to serve the cake. Don't worry, your dining room table isn't ruined yet. Just use the mat from your Twister game. It's covered with colorful dots, and food wipes right off.

The Perfect Candleholder

Life Savers are an excellent accent for your child's birthday cake. Not only do kids enjoy sucking on them, but they are perfect for holding candles! Use the regular size (not the jumbo kind that come individually wrapped in bags), put them on top of the cake, and then insert a candle in the middle of each. The candy will hold the candle straighter and is easily disposed of if wax drips on it.

Sundae Fun

Repurpose a plastic ice cube tray by making it into a killer sundae station. Use the various compartments for nuts, crushed cookies, candy, and other toppings, then serve with ice cream and let the kids make their own sundaes. (Don't be surprised if they dump *everything* on top!)

Hold Your Cake and Eat It Too

Little kids usually end up eating cake with their hands anyway, so try this fun dessert treat: Place flat-bottomed ice cream cones in a high-sided baking pan and fill them two-thirds full with cake batter. Bake them at 325°F for 30 minutes, and once they cool you can hold your cake and eat it, too!

BRUCE SAYS

Get Jiggle with It

We love making Jell-O Jigglers for kids' party snacks—they're easy, sweet, and fun to eat. The best part? Jell-O pieces can take so many different forms. For your next batch, use your child's Duplos or Mega Bloks as molds (just be sure to wash them first!). Kids will love their edible "toys"!

CREATIVE VENUES AND ACTIVITIES

For Bigger Birthday Bashes

Thinking about throwing your child's birthday party in a larger venue? Contact local toddler co-ops and daycare centers to see if you can rent out their space on the weekend—some organizations offer fantastic rates!

Bowling Party in the Backyard

If your kids love to bowl, this party will be a memorable hit! On flat ground, create a bowling lane with different-colored party streamers. For the pins, collect 10 plastic bottles filled with water, and drop a bit of food coloring in each. Arrange the pins in proper formation at the end of the bowling lane. Use a soccer ball or basketball as your bowling ball and get your kids ready to score!

Party Like It's Wednesday Night

If your children's birthday parties are putting a hurt on your budget, there's a simple solution—have the party during the week instead of on a weekend. Sure, everyone wants a weekend party, and that's why restaurants and other popular birthday locales charge a lot more for Saturday and Sunday events. They'll be only too happy to accommodate your request for a weekday party, and it might even be easier for you, too—just offer to pick up your child's playmates from school that afternoon and have them picked up from the party later. The kids will have just as much fun as they would at a weekend party, maybe even more, since it's a rare weekday treat.

Out-of-the-Park Party

A great, but rarely utilized, location for a summer party is your local minor league baseball park. Tickets are cheap, kids will love interacting with the mascot, and there's no need to stay the whole game—five innings or so should suffice. The team might even offer you discounted group tickets and flash your child's name on the scoreboard.

All's Fair in Love and Piñatas

When it comes to piñatas, the spoils go to the bullies, but not if you separate the candies and prizes into zip-top bags for each guest before stuffing them inside the paper-mâché animal. The kids will still get a rush of excitement when the piñata drops, but the game won't dissolve into an "Are we having fun yet?" moment when they start fighting over Tootsie Rolls and Milky Ways.

Pass the Present

Here's a cheap and easy game for a kids' party that might just become a birthday tradition your kids ask for every year. Before the party, gather up enough party favors for each child who will be playing, then add a "special" party favor for just one child. Put the favors in a box and wrap it with an old scrap of wrapping paper, newspaper, or construction paper. Then wrap it again. And again, and again, and again…. After you've wrapped the box 6 to 12 times (depending on how many guests you're expecting), you're ready to play. Sit the children in a circle and start up some music. While the music plays, the children pass the present around to their right. When the music stops, the kid holding the present gets to unwrap a layer of wrapping paper. The game continues until the last child unwraps the present and discovers the special prize for herself and the favors for everyone else.

Higher-Ed Hired Help

If you're hosting a party that requires you to hire someone like a clown, face painter, or bartender, head to your local college first. There, you'll find hundreds of young people who will do the job for a lot less than a pro. Put up an ad near the cafeteria, and stop by the careers office to see if they have an online "bulletin board."

GREAT GIFTS AND WRAPPING

One-of-a-Kind Gift for a Bride-to-Be

Here's a thoughtful and thrifty gift for a bridal shower: Buy a blank hardcover book, add dividers, and create a family cookbook. Just ask the bride and groom's families to provide their favorite treasured recipes.

Art-of-the-Month Club

Looking for an easy, heartfelt (but inexpensive) holiday gift the kids can help make? How about a personalized calendar of your children's artwork? Pick up free calendars distributed by local companies, then paste drawings or paintings from the past year on top of each month's image. Your kids will feel proud of their work, and their grandparent, uncle, or godparent will love the new calendar.

Housewarm with Houseplants

Clippings from a houseplant make great (and free!) housewarming presents. Cut your plant at the "knuckle" (or joint) section of the stem, then place the cutting in a cup of water until it grows roots. To present it, plant in a fun mug!

Handmade Gift Soaps

Soaps never seem to lose their appeal as gifts. They're useful and don't add clutter to people's houses. You can make your own by grating white, unscented soap it into a bowl with a little warm water. For color, add a few drops of food coloring appropriate for the holiday. Next, a drop or two of an essential oil (lavender and rose are lovely), then knead like pizza dough and make into little balls. As an alternative, use candy molds for fun shapes. Leave them to dry on wax paper for a day or so.

The Gift of Memory Lane

For the couple who has everything, why not show them how much they've already had? A tour of places they used to live (or go to school or work) is a personal and moving way to celebrate a special day. For an anniversary, find out where they met, where they had their first date, and where they got married. You can start out narrating, but be prepared for the recipients to take over. They'll likely enjoy telling stories as much as anything else you can give them.

JEANNE SAYS

Wrap Up Your Gift Wrap

We hate it when our perfectly adorable wrapping paper gets frayed, creased, or ripped at the edges while still on the roll. To prevent this, try this crafty trick: Cut a lengthwise slit in an empty wrapping paper tube and wrap it around the roll of paper you'd like to protect. You can leave the very end of the paper sticking out of the cardboard wrapper to create a dispenser.

Better Than Packing Peanuts

Frequently send gifts in the mail? Make sure you save those little bits of unusable wrapping paper. When you've collected a good amount of scraps, run them through a paper shredder for a colorful, inexpensive alternative to bubble wrap or packing peanuts.

Smooth Move

Quickest buzz kill when wrapping presents: trying to reuse tired-out, wrinkled tissue paper and hoping the recipient won't take it personally. Turns out you can iron used tissue paper on low to get it to look "like new"! Amazing.

Bring Bows Back to Life

Planning to package your gifts with bows and ribbons from last year? If they're smashed and wrinkled, don't toss them out! Instead, stick them in the dryer on low heat along with a dampened cloth and run it for 2 minutes. The heat plus the moisture from the cloth will pump them back to life.

Save Your Cash to Gift

Instead of doling out cash for fancy bows to decorate gifts, use your actual dollars to make the bows. Fold a dollar bill (or more, if you're a high roller) accordion-style and affix with a ribbon over a wrapped gift. As a variation, give a nod to Chinese New Year by putting two dollars inside a traditional red envelope and taping it to the top of a gift for good luck.

DIY Gift Basket

Baskets that strawberries and other berries come in are perfect for presents. Thread ribbon through a berry basket, line it with wrapping paper, and use it as a gift basket for your little one to bring a few muffins to a new neighbor or friend.

Perfect Box for Baked Goods

If you like to bake goodies as gifts, consider reusing empty aluminum-foil and plastic-wrap boxes as gift boxes. Cover the box in festive gift wrap, line the inside with tissue paper, and stick your treats inside. They're the perfect size for some cupcakes or muffins!

Dedicate a Song

Copied sheet music makes for unique and festive wrapping paper. At your local library it should be easy to enough to find books of whatever music suits your friend (classical, show tunes, rock music, etc.). Make a copy on colored paper if you can, and be sure the title of the piece shows when you fold it over the gift.

DON'T TOSS THAT PRETTY CALENDAR!

Use pages from the past year's calendar (photo-side up, obviously) to wrap smaller gifts—two taped together are great for books or DVD sets.

PARENTING SOLUTIONS

What parent couldn't use some tested hints to make everything from bathtime to school lunches just a little bit easier? Plus, find ways to have more fun without breaking your budget!

FOOD AND NUTRITION FIXES

A Calcium Kick

Sneak some calcium into your kids' food by adding powdered milk to their meals. It'll be inconspicuous to them in dishes such as mashed potatoes, meatballs, and peanut butter sandwiches (mixed in with the peanut butter).

Eat Those Veggies!

If your child never wants to eat his vegetables at dinnertime, try putting out a plate of raw veggies like carrots, celery, and broccoli right before dinner. Since he'll be hungry (and probably pestering you in the kitchen), it will be more likely that he'll succumb to this healthy snack.

Slightly Less Sugar

You can reduce your children's calorie and sugar intake by diluting their apple and orange juice with a bit of water. When you open a new bottle, empty a quarter of the juice into a pitcher, then fill the original juice bottle back to the brim with water. It'll still taste delicious, but the kids will get less of a sugar rush, and the juice will last longer to boot.

JEANNE SAYS

Freshen a Funky Lunchbox

Kid's lunchbox starting to smell funky? Freshen it up with bread and vinegar! Just moisten a slice of bread with white vinegar and let it sit in the closed lunchbox overnight. In the morning, any bad odors should be gone.

Frozen Juice Box

When packing a sack lunch for your child, place a juice box in the freezer the night before and add it to the lunch bag while still frozen the next morning. It'll help keep the lunch cool, and as an extra bonus, the juice will be nice and cold when your child finally gets around to drinking it at lunchtime.

Makeshift Icepacks

No one looks forward to lukewarm packed lunches. Keep your kids' food cold and fresh with homemade ice packs! Pick up sponges from a dollar store, then soak them in water and stick in the freezer overnight. When packing lunch, slip the frosty sponges into plastic storage bags and stash inside lunchboxes along with lunchmeat sandwiches and any other snacks that should be kept cold. The plastic bags will prevent any spills or leaks.

TIME TO CLEAN TEDDY

To clean stuffed animals, just place them in a cloth bag or pillowcase, add baking soda or cornmeal, and shake. The dirt will transfer to the powder.

BATHTIME HELPERS

Get Creative with Craft Foam

If you have any colorful craft foam left over from a recent project, use it as a quick and easy bath toy. Craft foam will stick to flat surfaces like tile when damp, so simply cut the foam into various shapes and sizes and you'll have bath toys ready to go. Your kids can affix the shapes to the shower wall simply by getting them wet.

DIY Bath Crayons

Make bath time a little bit more fun (and colorful!) with these homemade bath crayons. In a medium bowl, grate a bar of Ivory soap with a cheese grater until you have about ¼ cup. Add 5 to 7 drops of food coloring and a few drops of water. Mix thoroughly, then microwave in a microwave-safe container until warm, about 20 seconds. Shape into a crayon-shape, or push into an ice cube tray until the soap takes the form of an ice cube. Let harden overnight before letting your kids have at them!

Save Your Bottles

If you're looking for a cheap and practical toy for kids, thoroughly wash old ketchup, salad dressing, and shampoo bottles and let the kids use them to play in the swimming pool or bathtub. They're also a good way to wash shampoo out of hair at bathtime.

5 PARENTING DILEMMAS SOLVED

Kids will keep you on your toes! It's a good thing there's a secret club of parents who are more than happy to share what's worked for them.

Erase that crayon. If the kids have drawn with crayons all over their bedroom walls, remove it with a bit of WD-40 spray, which works like a charm. Afterward, you'll need something to remove the grease—we like a mixture of dishwashing detergent and white vinegar. If you don't have any WD-40, dip a damp rag into baking soda and rub the mark to remove it.

Cut the toy clutter. When the kids make their wish lists, they should also decide which old toys they'd like to give back to Santa for Christmastime recycling—Santa and his elves refurbish the old toys so he can give them to less fortunate children. If your kids are older, bring the toys to Goodwill or Salvation Army together. Not only does this help de-clutter the house, but it also inspires heartwarming Christmas spirit in little kids and big ones alike.

Numb the "ick" of taking medicine. It's often a battle to get a sick child to take medicine he can't stand the taste of. To make things a little easier, have him suck on an ice pop for a few minutes before taking the medicine. The ice pop will not only act as an incentive, but will numb his taste buds a bit, making the medicine easier to swallow.

Settle temper tantrums. You probably take hand sanitizer and baby wipes everywhere. But what about bubbles? If (and when) a tantrum hits, take out the bubbles and start blowing. This distracts kids enough so that they calm down and you can actually speak to them! Handing over the wand and letting them help not only rewards them for stopping the screaming, but allows them to take deep breaths and become even more relaxed.

Make your kid stand out. If you know you're going to a crowded place, be sure to dress your children in bright colors so you can easily spot them. To make them stick out even more, buy each kid a cheap helium balloon and tie it around his or her wrist. Kids love balloons, and so will you when you realize you can see them from a mile away at the mall.

Drip Dry

Hang a mesh potato bag from a hook on your shower organizer to store your child's bath toys. The air will get at them and you'll keep mildew at bay.

Frozen Bath Buddies

For more fun at bath time, take all those little plastic toys your kids have gotten from vending machines and goody bags, and place one or two in each hole of a muffin tin. Then fill the tin with water and freeze. When it's time for a bath, pop one out and throw it in the tub. Your toddler will love watching it melt in her hands and then having a toy to play with.

Rubber Ducky, You're the (Moldy) One

It's gross, but true: Your child's floating bath toys (the kind with a hole in the bottom) are likely filled with allergy-causing mold. Even if you squeeze out the toys after every bath, some moisture remains and can cause mold build-up. To avoid this problem in the first place, seal the hole of a brand-new toy with hot glue. That way, water will never be able to penetrate it in the first place. To clean older toys, soak them in a solution of 1 cup bleach mixed with 1 gallon warm water for an hour or two to release the mold. Then scrub, rinse, and allow to dry completely before sealing.

BRUCE SAYS

Turkey Baster Time
Go ahead, spend as much as you want on popular bath toys. Your small child will love none of them as much as your washed-out turkey baster!

EASY ENTERTAINMENT

The Library: More than Just Books

Obviously, libraries are full of books you can borrow for free. But did you know that many libraries also carry DVDs? If there is a particular movie or TV show you are looking for and it's not available at your local branch, ask a librarian to get it for you through interlibrary loan. Libraries are also a great place to get magazines. If you don't mind reading back issues, save on subscriptions by getting older copies at the library. This is especially great for kids' magazines (because kids won't know the difference!). You never know what items your library might have in circulation—many offer musical instruments, games, and more—so make sure to ask a librarian.

Toy Parachutes

Make an old action figure fun again by creating a mini-parachute. First, cut out a square from a plastic sandwich bag. Poke a hole in each corner, then thread a foot-long piece of dental floss through the hole, tying a knot at the end so the floss can't be pulled back through. Once you've threaded a piece of floss through each hole, tie the other ends around the arms or—dare we say it—the neck of the figurine. Now you're ready to launch.

Give Toy Cars Roads

You'll love this new use for old jeans: Cut off the legs and trim into strips about 2 inches wide and as long as the entire leg. Turn them over so the inner, grayish side is face-up. Then draw dotted yellow lines on them in paint, marker, or even crayon to make fabric streets! The kids will love driving toy cars on them.

Ramp Up

Use a poster mailing tube as a ramp for toy cars. Hold it level while your child slides a car in, then raise the end you're holding so the car whizzes down and out the other side. You can also use multiple cars and collect them at one end in a bucket or pan for a pleasing clacking sound as they zip out of the tube and join the heap. When they're all in a pile, dump them out and start again.

Paper Log Cabins

If you collect enough paper towel tubes, you can make your own jumbo Lincoln Logs. Separate half the tubes and cut out 1½-inch squares at either end. Take the uncut rolls and stack them perpendicularly by sliding the ends into the openings you cut.

Daydream House

Tissue boxes can be converted into a makeshift dollhouse. Cut off the tops and place three or four boxes together, cutting doorways between them once you've decided on the layout for your miniature home. Use real doll furniture if you have it, along with pictures from magazines of household furniture, which you glue to the "walls."

SUPER SPORTS AND OUTDOORS

Bike Fixer-Upper

When bicycle season rolls around, make sure your kids' vehicles of choice are in prime shape for smooth riding. Remember that after months of sitting in the garage, the bike chain will need a proper lube job: You can fix a squeaky chain with a light spritz of cooking spray. Clean up any remaining spray and let your kiddos hop on!

Make Your Swing Set Safer

You've just bought your kids a new swing set, and you're peering out the window just waiting for one of them to fall off. Fear no more! Place carpet remnants or free carpet samples from a local store underneath the swings. They'll kill the grass underneath, but your kids would have done that anyway.

Make Slides More Fun

If your kids have tired of that expensive playground set you bought them, make the slide even more fun by giving them each a large piece of wax paper. If they sit on the paper as they're going down the slide, they'll move much faster, and they'll never call it boring again (or at least not for a few weeks).

Best Bubbles Ever

Warm weather is bubble season for kids who want some outdoor fun. Here's an inexpensive homemade solution for bubble greatness: Mix 1 tablespoon glycerin with 2 tablespoons powdered laundry detergent in 1 cup warm water. (Glycerin, often called "vegetable glycerin," can be found online and at many health food and vitamin shops.) Any unpainted piece of metal wire (like a hanger) can be turned into a bubble wand: Just shape one end of the wire into a circle. Blowing into the mixture with a straw will make smaller bubbles float into the air. For colored bubbles, add food coloring.

Get the Bounce Back

Almost all soft rubber balls, including tennis balls, can be brought back to life by spending a night in the oven with only the pilot light on. The heat causes the air inside the ball to expand. Just be sure to remove the balls before you turn the oven on!

Fix Dents in Ping-Pong Balls

The sound of Ping-Pong balls being paddled all over the basement is worth every minute if it's keeping your kids busy! Unfortunately, when the kids finally emerge from downstairs, you notice that the balls are filled with dents. To get the balls round again, fill a jar to the brim with warm water, then place the balls inside and close the lid so that they're submerged. In 20 minutes or less, the water's pressure will make them pop back into place.

COST-SAVING ARTS AND CRAFTS

Arty Aluminum

Art project? Make mixing paint easy by using a piece of cardboard covered in aluminum foil as your artist's palette. Kids will especially love it if you cut the cardboard in the shape of a palette first.

Flip a Flip-Flop

Lost a flip-flop? Might as well put the remaining shoe to good use. Trace a fun shape in the foam flop, then cut it out with an X-Acto knife. Now your kid has a brand new stamp for dipping in paints and ink!

SAVE THAT LINER

When it's finally time to replace your shower curtain liner, keep the old one and use it for a drop cloth while painting or doing art projects.

New Creations with Old Crayons

If your child has lots of little crayon pieces left over, turn them into a fun craft project that will give you some more use out of them! First remove the paper, then place the pieces in a muffin tin. Heat at 250°F until the crayons are melted (about 10 to 20 minutes), then remove from the oven and let cool. Your child will love the new, enormous crayons with unpredictable colors!

Turn Markers into Watercolor Paints

If your kids are budding Picassos and Georgia O'Keeffes, you'll love this crafty tip for making your own paints on the cheap! Rather than shopping for store-bought paints, reuse old dried-up markers. Simply gather colored markers into batches by color, and tie them together with a rubber band. Pour water into small glass jars (baby food jars are perfect), and fill to just below their screw-top necks. Place the markers tip-end down in the jars so the inky points are soaking in the water. Leave the markers to soak overnight, and *voilà*—beautiful, vivid color paints!

Painting with Peanuts

Here's a creative way to use up some of those Styrofoam packing peanuts: as little paintbrushes for the kids' craft time! Poke a plastic fork into each peanut, creating one for every color. The kids can dip the foam in paint and make all kind of fun patterns. Plus, cleanup is a breeze; just toss the foam and fork brushes in the trash when they're done.

Make Your Own Moon Sand

If your kids like Moon Sand, that soft sand that can be molded into all kinds of shapes, here's an inexpensive version you can make yourself. Mix together 2 cups sand, 1 cup cornstarch, and ½ cup water. Kids can use their beach toys as molds, or you can provide them with cookie cutters, measuring cups, and other baking tools that they can fill to make their sand creations. (For a larger quantity, double or triple the recipe.)

From Recycling to Shrinky Dinks

Who doesn't love Shrinky Dinks? For the uninitiated, they're plastic sheets of animals and other designs that kids color and decorate. The pieces are then baked in the oven until the plastic shrinks down to a tiny size. We've discovered that you can use #6 plastic to make your own version! Usually you'll find #6 plastic used for take-out containers or for packaging pastries in clamshells at the supermarket. First cut the plastic into the shape that you want. Then, using sandpaper, sand down one side to make it somewhat rough. Allow your child to draw his or her desired picture or image on the rough side, and stick it in a 350°F oven for about 3 minutes or until it shrinks down. (Keep a close eye on it. After all, watching it is the fun part!) Remove and allow to cool.

Super-Simple Silly Putty

This incredibly easy version of Silly Putty requires only three ingredients and takes just a few minutes to make. You'll need ½ cup Elmer's glue, ¼ cup liquid laundry starch, and food coloring. Pour the glue into a bowl, then add the laundry starch. Next, mix together for about 5 to 10 minutes, until it starts to form a ball. (It may not look like much at first, but keep mixing until a putty-like consistency forms.) Add a few drops of food coloring and knead until the color is evenly distributed. Store in in a sealed container the refrigerator between uses.

WIPES DISPENSER CLEANS UP!

An old plastic, cylindrical dispenser for baby or disinfectant wipes is perfect for holding your child's chunky markers. (Cut to size if necessary.)

JEANNE SAYS

Extend a Crayon

Once crayons break, they can be hard for little fingers to grasp and use. To help make them last longer, slide broken or worn-down pieces into a plastic straw, leaving the tip exposed. The straw will make the crayon easier to hold onto, and your kids will have all of their favorite colors back.

Rolling in Dough

Don't spend money on store-bought Play-Doh; make your own at home instead with the following ingredients: 2 cups flour, 2 cups water, 1 cup salt, 2 tablespoons vegetable oil, 1 tablespoon cream of tartar, and the food coloring of your choice. Combine the ingredients in a large saucepan and stir continuously over medium heat until a solid ball forms. Remove it from the heat, knead it until all the lumps are out, and you should end up with a finished product nearly identical to the real thing. Make sure you store it in a completely airtight container; you might even want to dab a few drops of water on the underside of the lid before sealing it.

Play-Doh Fun

Make Play-Doh play more fun with a garlic press! You may hardly ever find yourself using the designer garlic press you got for your wedding, but your kids will love it to make Play-Doh "hair." When you're tired of playing hairdresser, use the press to revert to the usual Play-Doh noodles or worms.

Homemade Ceramics

It's easy to make a clay for creating ceramics at home! Thoroughly mix the following ingredients in a bowl: 4 cups flour, 1⅓ cups salt, ¾ cup white glue, 1⅓ teaspoons lemon juice, and 1⅓ cups water. When you've got it all mixed together, you should end up with a pliable clay that can be either sculpted into different shapes or sliced with cookie cutters. Let the creations sit overnight, allowing them to harden and air-dry. Then kids can apply paint and/or glaze.

Frugal Finger Paints

Keep your kids busy and encourage their creativity with homemade finger paints: Start by mixing 2 cups cold water with ¼ cup cornstarch, then boil until the liquid is as thick as, um, finger paints. Pour into small containers, swirl in some food coloring, and watch them create their masterpieces (just keep those colorful fingers away from walls!).

Easy Invisible Ink

Get creative with watercolors and candles—but perhaps not in the way you think. Give your child a white tapered candle and have her "draw" a picture on a piece of paper. She won't be able to see the drawing, of course, until she adds a little watercolor to the paper—and the picture comes to life. This is an especially good activity for two kids. Let them write "secret messages" to each other, then exchange the papers, apply some watercolors, and see what happens.

ALL ABOUT BABIES

Baby Bath Seat

Make your bathtub baby-size by using a laundry basket as a bath seat! Give the basket a thorough cleaning before using, then simply place it in the tub for baby's bath time. The basket will keep floating toys within tiny-arms' reach and also prevent head-bumps against the tub.

Perfect Bottle Holder

The perfect holder for extra bottles for the babysitter: an old six-pack container. If you don't think it's funny to have "Heineken" written on the side, cover with contact paper, wrapping paper, or stickers. Your baby won't know the difference, and you'll be sure to leave with as many bottles as you came with.

Baking Soda for Baby Mamas

Baking soda is a gift to anyone who is feeding an infant. Keep some on hand, and if (and when) your baby spits up, sprinkle baking soda on the spot to neutralize odors and absorb the spill before it sets.

Diapers Love Vinegar

If you use cloth diapers, soak them before you wash them in a mixture of 1 cup white vinegar for every 9 quarts water. It will balance out the pH, neutralizing urine and keeping the diapers from staining. Vinegar is also said to help prevent diaper rash.

Never Buy a Baby Wipe Again

If you have a baby, you know that one costly item it's impossible to use less of is baby wipes. But you can save hundreds per year by making your own diaper wipes! They are easy to make and can be kept in an old baby wipes container, a plastic storage bin with a lid, or a resealable plastic bag. Here's how to do it: combine 2 tablespoons each baby oil and baby shampoo (or baby wash) with 2 cups boiled and cooled water and 1 or 2 drops of your favorite essential oil for scent (optional). Remove the cardboard roll from a package of paper towels, then cut the entire roll in half (you can also tear off sheets by hand and stack them in a pile). Put some of the liquid mixture at the bottom of your container, then place the half-roll in the container. Pour the rest of the liquid over your paper towels and *voilà*—homemade baby wipes! Let the wipes sit for about an hour to absorb all the liquid, and your baby will never know the difference.

FRESHEN UP STINKY DIAPERS

If you get a nasty whiff every time you open the diaper pail, drop a few charcoal briquettes under the pail's liner. You'll be amazed at what you don't smell.

GREAT VACATIONS & MEMORIES

You can stretch your budget for fun and adventure and create amazing memories with these smart ideas.

FREE OR AFFORDABLE FUN

The Best Discounts in Town

If you are an educator, a member of the military, or a government employee, always ask if there is a discount available to you. You'll often find travel and admission discounts offered to these groups. If you're over 60, of course, never, ever buy anything without asking if there's a senior discount. Some discounts even apply to those 50 and over. Even if you don't look your age, you might as well take advantage of the savings available to you!

Free Summer Fun

For ideas on fun, free activities to do over the summer, try checking out your community center or park district. Most towns have tons of free summertime events, from sports clinics for kids to free concerts for adults. See if they have a website or pick up a calendar at your local branch.

See a Movie for Free

Many museums and colleges offer free screenings of films. Sure, they're not the latest big releases, but if you're in the mood for a classic or artsy flick, check and see if they are offered nearby. Many facilities even have full-sized screens in auditoriums. And they won't get angry if you sneak in your own candy!

TV: Live and In-Person!

If you live near a big city, especially Los Angeles or New York, one of the most fun free activities you can do is attend a TV taping. Talk shows, sitcoms, and game shows are always looking for studio audience members, and it's a blast not only to see a show live, but also to get a peek at what happens behind the scenes. To get tickets to shows, visit TVTickets.com for shows in LA, or NYCGo.com for events and shows in New York. If a show you like is being taped in your area, try looking it or its network up online or seeing if there is a phone number at the end of the show to call for audience tickets.

Visiting Museums for Free

Even if they normally have high admission prices, most museums offer opportunities for you to visit for free. If a museum gets money from the government, it's usually required to either offer free admission one day a week or to charge admission as a "suggested donation"—that is, you only have to pay what you want. Other museums have late hours that are free to visitors once a week or month. If you like looking at art, also check out galleries, where you can find cool local art displayed for free in the hopes that someone will buy it.

Because a Good Game Is a Good Game

If you love going to see sports, but don't love the price tag of taking your whole family to a professional game, consider amateur sports instead. Colleges as well as intramural leagues have games every weekend for free or a couple of dollars. It's great to support local teams, and younger kids won't even know the difference in skill between a pro player and a Division Three league anyway.

Let Your Friends Pay

Try starting a movie-lending circle with friends or neighbors who also watch a lot of movies. Each person has another person they give movies to, and someone they receive them from. When you get your own movie back, it's time to pick a new one! You may want to pick a timeframe to exchange the movie—for example, sometime before each weekend or at a weekly book club or school-related meeting. Movie-lending circles are a great way to discover movies you might not have picked out yourself, but really enjoy.

JEANNE SAYS

Find the Cheapest Coffeehouse in Town

If you're a coffee fiend, you know how costly those delicious coffee-shop lattes can be. If there's a college or university near your home, check out the campus coffee shop for your caffeine fix—it's less expensive and just as good as the local gourmet chain.

Go with a Group

Headed to a theme park or attraction? Go with a bigger group and you could get a discount. If you have at least 15 people in your party, you can usually get a good deal, depending on the time of year. Just call up the venue or visit its website to see if it offers group discounts.

Theme Park Savings

Nothing's more fun than taking the kids to an amusement park, especially when they've been begging you to do it for two summers now. Whether you're going to a local Six Flags type of park, or going all out for that Disney World vacation, a lot of organizations offer discount packages. Check with any organizations to which you belong to see if you can save, such as the AARP, AAA, wholesale clubs like Costco, or a branch of the military.

Eat Out for Less

At Restaurant.com, you can purchase gift certificates for local restaurants—for less than a third of the price! Enter your zip code or city, and you'll be taken to a list of restaurants in your area that are offering $25 gift cards for only $10. Most of the big chains are absent, but if you've been looking for an excuse to try out a local joint, this is a great one.

Where the Kids Eat Free

It's easier to eat out when you go to a restaurant where the kids eat free. To find a bunch in your area, visit KidsMealDeals.com. Enter your zip code, and you'll find deals from chain restaurants and local joints alike. Remember, a restaurant that offers deals for kids also usually offers frugal prices for adult entrees, so this site could potentially save you hundreds per year. Bon appetit!

GET AWAY FOR LESS

Keep Scrolling

When searching for travel deals online, make sure you scroll through a few pages of results before making your pick. Many sites have "sponsored results," which means that companies have paid to be featured at the top of search results.

Move That Summer Vacation

The best vacation you'll ever take might not be in the summer. As soon as Labor Day goes by, the rates go down drastically on hotels and airfare to most vacation destinations. Some of the most-discounted areas are the Caribbean, Hawaii, California, and anywhere else there's a beach. In a warm climate, it will still be as hot as ever on the sand. But the price will be much less, and you'll get the added benefit of having fewer crowds.

Let's Make a Deal

When digging for discounts on rental cars and hotels, always call the hotel or rental company directly for the best deals. If the only phone number you have is a national, toll-free one, look up the local number for that particular location and speak to them directly instead. The closer you get to your travel date, the better—in fact, don't be afraid to call the day before to confirm your reservation and ask for a better rate.

Make Your Points Go Farther

Do you have reward points accumulating on several different airlines? Check out Points.com, which lets you keep track of your airline miles and other reward points, all in one place. Better yet, you can swap points from one reward program to another! In addition to airlines, Amtrak and some hotels participate as well.

Time to Go Camping!

Waking up to the sights, sounds, and smells of the forest can be one of the most peaceful things you'll ever experience—not to mention, the most inexpensive vacation you'll take in years. If you've never gone camping, it's time to start! If you don't have any equipment, ask friends if you can borrow theirs in exchange for lending them something of yours. You and your kids will enjoy working together while roughing it (and don't worry, "roughing it" can involve bathrooms and showers, electricity hook-ups, and even wireless internet). Best of all, with all that hard work each day, plus all the room in the world to run around in, your kids will get exhausted fast! To find campsites across the United States and Canada, visit ReserveAmerica.com.

BRUCE SAYS

The Cheapest Days to Fly

Flight days flexible? Try searching for trips that begin and end on a Tuesday or Wednesday, when we've found that flights throughout the United States and Canada are cheaper.

SAVE YOUR MEMORIES

Make Your Own Memory Boxes

You could spend cash on elaborate store-bought boxes to hold old photos, letters, and other special mementos. But why do that when you can use an assortment of boxes you already have? Pretty gift boxes and colorful shoe, hat, and clothing boxes will all do the trick—for free! Label them according to date or special occasion, and stick them on a shelf or in a closet for safe storage.

Memories on a Roll

To store certificates, degrees, and other valuable paper items, roll them up and pop them into a cardboard tube, like a toilet paper or paper towel roll. It will protect them from tears and creases and make them easier to tuck away.

Newspaper Mementos

To preserve special newspaper clippings, dissolve a Milk of Magnesia tablet in a shallow pan with a quart of club soda. Soak the paper for an hour, then let it lie flat to dry. Afterward, it's best to keep the paper under plastic in a photo album.

Frozen Moments

If you discover a couple of photos stuck together, don't lose hope! They can be unstuck. Place them in the freezer for half an hour, then gently pry them apart with a butter knife. You can also slowly unstick them with a hair dryer set on low.

Picture Perfect

If a beloved book or photo album has gotten wet, it's not ruined yet. Try sprinkling baby or baking powder on each page, then placing it in a closed paper bag for up to a week. The powder should absorb the water while keeping your book safe.

WHO KNEW?
READERS' FAVORITE

Joy in a Jar

Have some beautiful clear jars, but don't know what to do with them? Try putting photos inside! Add marbles, rocks, colored sand, or other decoration at the bottom, then bend the photo ever-so-slightly so it fits the curve of the jar. This is a great idea for birthday or anniversary parties. Put pictures of the honorees in the jars and you have some unique centerpieces! Or select photos of vacation destinations for a stress-relieving office display.

Solution for Stuck Photos

If your photographs are stuck to each other or to a glass frame, the solution is steam. Use a steamer, a steam iron set on its highest setting, or a pan of boiling water to get steam as close as you can between the photo and whatever it's stuck to (being careful not to burn yourself). As the photo gets warmer and wetter, it should become easy to peel away. Lay out to dry, then flatten with a fat book if it has curled.

A Folder Full of Memories

Have an impossible time keeping your digital pics organized, not to mention, continually saved on a back-up drive? While you may not have time to organize and label every photo, here's a simple strategy you can use to at least cut through the chaos and get a handle on your photo collection. Every time you upload photos to your computer, pick a few of your absolute favorites from the event or trip and keep them all in the same folder on your computer. Now you only have to back up this folder to make sure your most precious moments are saved, and it makes organizing easier. Use separate folders for different children and other family members and friends. When it comes time to gather pictures for a special event like a wedding, you just need to refer to that folder to choose a few of the honoree. Better yet, when your children leave home, you can give them a copy of the folder (in whatever form exists in the future!) and they'll have photos from their entire childhood in one place.

Binder Clip Photo Displays

Got spare binder clips? Not only do they come in handy around the house, but they also add a cool minimalist touch to your home décor. Use them to show off your photos or display important notes on a table or mantel. With the clip closed and sitting upright on its plastic base, slip a photo between the two standing metal crooks. To keep the clip steady, secure it in place with a folded strip of clear tape or a small dab of sticky tack, if needed.

INDEX

marbled, 347
poaching, ring for, 178
storage, 222
substitute for, in baking, 8
yolk-free, 37
Egg cartons
as fire starters, 207
as storage containers, 338
Egg white, as blackhead remedy, 261
Egg yolk(s)
in cakes, 199
as hair conditioner, 38
olive oil as substitute for, 37
storage, 222
Eggshells
in cracked eggs, removal, 230
as slug/snail deterrent, 148
Elbow(s), skin scrub for, 244
Electrical cord(s). *See also* Cord(s)
fraying, prevention of, 66, 138
labels for, 140
Electronic gadgets, recycling, 142
Epsom salts
in bath soak, 249, 324
in exfoliant, 38
as grass fertilizer, 153
hair volumizer made with, 270
as magnesium source, 308
and window privacy solution, 50
Eraser, homemade, 67
Essential oils. *See also* specific oil
in air freshener, 43, 97, 99
in arthritis relief rub, 310
in baby wipes, 369
in bath fizzies, 250
in bath salts, 249, 324
in bath soak, 33
in body butter, 252
in bubble bath, 252
in bug spray, 158
in car air freshener, 171
in carpet cleaner, 97, 103, 105
in fabric refresher, 7
in foot powder, 16
in foot scrub, 58
in gift soap, 358
in hand cream, 254
homemade heating pad, 321
in homemade vapor, 305
in laundry detergent pods, 108
in liquid soap, 288
in microwave cleaner, 82
in poo-pourri, 99
in reed diffuser fluid, 99
in scalp massage oil, 273
in shampoo, 269
in shoe deodorizer, 294
in sleep aid, 317
in snore relief gel, 320
in spider repellent, 146
in spray cleaner, 73
in steam treatment, 303

and stress relief, 322
in wood floor cleaner, 102
in wood polish, 75
Eucalyptus oil
as decongestant, 303
as flea repellent, 164
Exercise(s), for stress relief, 323
Extension cords, storage, 135
Eye(s)
black
parsley for, 329
tea for, 48
dark circles under, treatment for, 279
and headaches, 307
itchy, remedy for, 301
puffy, treatment for, 33, 46, 279
shampoo in, prevention of, 57
tea bag refresher for, 257
tension-relief exercises, 322
undereye concealer, 279, 280
Eye drops, for acne, 262
Eye shadow, homemade, 58
Eyebrow(s), unruly, control of, 52, 57, 281
Eyeglasses
cleaning, 296, 298
defogger for, 296
hair spray on, removal, 296
nonslip trick for, 70
screws in
lost, replacement for, 298
securing, 298
Eyelash(es), conditioner for, 280
Eyelash curler, how to use, 258
Eyeliner pencil, firming up, 280

F

Fabric
odor removal from, 98
storage, 134
Fabric refresher, 7
Fabric softener. *See also* Dryer sheet(s)
baking soda as, 14
releaser for, 108
vinegar as, 7, 109
Face, wake-up massage for, 281
Face paint
homemade, 352
removal, 38, 259
Face powder, 257
homemade, 282
Face skin, spritz for, 46
Face wash, lemon and baking soda, 260
Facial exercise(s), wrinkle fighting, 256
Facial hair, unwanted, removal, 287
Facial mask(s), homemade, 45, 245–247, 251, 254, 262
for sunburn, 330
Facial scrub, nutmeg-milk, 262

Facial toner, homemade, 24
Fatigue, dietary fixes for, 319
Faucet
mineral deposits in, removal, 19
polish for, 94
squeaky, fix for, 55
Fennel
as breath freshener, 284
for intestinal gas, 313
Feverfew, for headache, 306
Figs, storage, 213
Filing cabinet, as storage container, 134
Finger(s), Band-Aid on, protection for, 328
Finger paints, homemade, 368
Fingernail(s)/toenail(s). *See also* Nail polish
broken, fix for, 265
cleaning, 265
cream for, 39
fungus, treatment, 9, 266
growth, promotion of, 39
hot oil treatment for, 265
lightener for, 25, 265
nail polish stains, removal, 265
protection from dirt and grease, 265
remedies for, 264–265
stain remover, 265
Fingerprints, on furniture, prevention, 75
Fire, putting out, 28
Fire extinguisher
baking soda as, 16
beer as, 51
Fish
antiaging effects of, 255
burned, fix for, 224
cooked but dry, fix for, 225
cooking time for, estimating, 182
fried, stick prevention, 32
frozen, milk added to, 202
grilling without sticking, 23, 209
marinade for, 22
and sleep, 317
thickness, for grilling, 209
Fishy odor, neutralizing, 15
Fleas
getting rid of, 31, 164
repellents for, 22, 164
testing for, 164
Flies
fans as deterrents for, 145
hair spray as repellent for, 144
orange peel repellent for, 145
at pool, repelling, 159
Flip-flops
recycling, 366
reuse as stamps, 366
storage for, 130

Floor
ceramic, cleaning, 6
laminated, cleaning, 106
tile, cleaning, 105
vinyl
cleaning, 6, 105
scuff marks, removal, 12, 106
shining, 106
wood. *See* Wood floor
Flour
bags of, storage, 239
freshness, testing, 190
as oven thermometer substitute, 191
Flower arrangements
artificial, holder for, 27
helpers for, 68
Flowerpot, leprechaun hat decoration, 345
Flowers
artificial
cleaning, 29
holder for, 27
for attracting hummingbirds, 153
dyeing, 344
scent from, preserving, 30
Flu, muscle aches of, treatment for, 310
Folder (paper), reinforced, 60
Folding tables, to make bigger table, 353
Food
cooked-on, removal, 42
frozen, separating, 183
oversalted, rescue for, 227
shopping for, at holiday time, 335
stored in opaque containers, marking level of, 236
Food dishes, lids on, securing, 66
Food processor, cleaning, 12
Food storage containers, matching lids to, 237
Foot
aches, relief for, 311
corns on, remedy for, 26, 38, 59
Foot moisturizer, 39
Foot odor, prevention, 9, 16, 24, 287
Foot scrub
homemade, 58
peppermint, 244
strawberry, 243
Foot soak
beer as, 53
deodorant, 287
lemon in, 25
peppermint tea, 311
tea in, 46
Forehead wrinkle(s)
concealing, 258
vertical, prevention, 255

CONNECT WITH THE AUTHORS

Bruce Lubin and Jeanne Bossolina-Lubin are the best-selling authors, bloggers, and podcasters behind the *Who Knew?* brand.

After years of finding simple ways to save time and money through everyday hints and tips, they started their own business in hopes of sharing their knowledge with others. They wrote their first *Who Knew?* book in 2006 and since then have written fifteen more books and sold more than five million copies in the series. Married since 1992, Bruce and Jeanne are the proud parents of three boys, who have taught them more about maintaining a chaotic household than any book could.

Now considered household experts and consumer advocates, Bruce and Jeanne answer hundreds of questions each month through their website, WhoKnewTips.com.

VISIT US ON THE WEB AT WhoKnewTips.com!

• Money-saving tips •

• Quick 'n' easy recipes •

• *Who Knew?* books and ebooks •

• And much more! •

Facebook.com/WhoKnewTips • Daily tips, giveaways, and more fun!

YouTube.com/WhoKnewTips • Watch demos of your favorite tips

Pinterest.com/WhoKnewTips • Hot tips from around the web!

Instagram.com/whoknewtips • Photos of tips you can use everyday

SHARE YOUR HINTS & TIPS WITH US
at whoknewtips@gmail.com or *Who Knew?* Hints and Tips, PO Box 1090, Hoboken, NJ 07030